Social History of Africa

GENDER, ETHNICITY, AND SOCIAL CHANGE ON THE UPPER SLAVE COAST

Social History of Africa
Series Editors: Allen Isaacman and Jean Hay

African Workers and Colonial Racism: *Mozambican Strategies and Struggles in Lourenço Marques, 1877–1962* JEANNE MARIE PENVENNE

Are We Not Also Men?: *The Samkange Family & African Politics in Zimbabwe 1920–1964* TERENCE RANGER

Burying SM: *The Politics of Knowledge and the Sociology of Power in Africa* DAVID WILLIAM COHEN AND E.S. ATIENO ODHIAMBO

Colonial Conscripts: *The* Tirailleurs Senegalais *in French West Africa, 1875–1960* MYRON ECHENBERG

Cotton, Colonialism, and Social History in Sub-Saharan Africa ALLEN ISAACMAN AND RICHARD ROBERTS (editors)

Cotton is the Mother of Poverty: *Peasants, Work, and Rural Struggle in Colonial Mozambique, 1938–1961* ALLEN ISAACMAN

Cutting Down Trees: *Gender, Nutrition, and Agricultural Change in the Northern Province of Zambia, 1890–1990* HENRIETTA L. MOORE AND MEGAN VAUGHAN

Feasts and Riot: *Revelry, Rebellion, and Popular Consciousness on the Swahili Coast, 1856–1888* JONATHON GLASSMAN

Gender, Ethnicity, and Social Change on the Upper Slave Coast: *A History of the Anlo-Ewe* SANDRA E. GREENE

Insiders and Outsiders: *The Indian Working Class of Durban, 1910–1990* BILL FREUND

Law in Colonial Africa KRISTIN MANN AND RICHARD ROBERTS (editors)

Money Matters: *Instability, Values, and Social Payments in the Modern History of West African Communities* JANE I. GUYER (editor)

The Moon is Dead! Give Us Our Money!: *The Cultural Origins of an African Work Ethic, Natal, South Africa, 1843–1900* KELETSO E. ATKINS

Peasants, Traders, and Wives: *Shona Women in the History of Zimbabwe, 1870–1939* ELIZABETH SCHMIDT

The Realm of the Word: *Language, Gender, and Christianity in a Southern African Kingdom* PAUL STUART LANDAU

"We Spend Our Years as a Tale That is Told": *Oral Historical Narrative in a South African Chiefdom* ISABEL HOFMEYR

Women of Phokeng: *Consciousness, Life Strategy, and Migrancy in South Africa, 1900–1983* BELINDA BOZZOLI (with the assistance of MMANTHO NKOTSOE)

Work, Culture, and Identity: *Migrant Laborers in Mozambique and South Africa, 1860–1910* PATRICK HARRIES

GENDER, ETHNICITY, AND SOCIAL CHANGE ON THE UPPER SLAVE COAST

A HISTORY OF THE ANLO-EWE

Sandra E. Greene

HEINEMANN
Portsmouth, NH

JAMES CURREY
London

Heinemann
A division of Reed Elsevier Inc.
361 Hanover Street
Portsmouth, NH 03801-3912
Offices and agents throughout the world

James Currey Ltd.
54b Thornhill Square
Islington
London N1 1BE

ISBN 0-435-08979-X (Heinemann cloth)
ISBN 0-435-08981-1 (Heinemann paper)
ISBN 0-85255-672-1 (James Currey cloth)
ISBN 0-85255-622-5 (James Currey paper)

Library of Congress Cataloging-in-Publication Data
Greene, Sandra E., 1952–
    Gender, ethnicity, and social change on the upper slave coast : a history of the Anlo-Ewe / Sandra E. Greene.
        p. cm. — (Social history of Africa)
    Includes bibliographical references and index.
    ISBN 0-435-08981-1 (pbk. : alk. paper). —ISBN 0-435-08979-X (cloth : alk. paper)
    1. Anlo (African people)--Social conditions. 2. Ewe (African people) — Social conditions. 3. Sex roles--Ghana. 4. Ethnic relations--Ghana. I. Title. II. Series.
DT510.43.A58G74   1995
305.3'09667--dc20   95-34120
                                                          CIP

British Library Cataloging-in-Publication Data
Greene, Sandra E.
    Gender, Ethnicity and Social Change on the Upper Slave Coast:History of the Anlo-Ewe. — (Social History of Africa Series)
    I. Title II. Series
    305.896334

ISBN 0-85255-622-5 (Paper)
ISBN 0-85255-672-1 (Cloth)

Cover design: Jenny Jensen Greenleaf
Cover photos: "Yewe priest" and "Yewe priestess," courtesy of the Staatsarchiv, Bremen, Germany

Printed in the United States of America on acid-free paper
99 98 97 96 DA 1 2 3 4 5 6 7 8 9

To
My parents, Sara and Robert Greene
and to
My husband, Kodjopa Attoh

CONTENTS

List of Maps and Figures viii

List of Photographs ix

Acknowledgments x

Introduction 1

1 Transformations 20

2 Gendered Responses: Ethnic Outsiders in
   Eighteenth- and Nineteenth-Century Anlo 48

3 Ethnicized Responses: Women in
   Eighteenth- and Nineteenth-Century Anlo 79

4 The Road Not Taken 108

5 Ethnicity in Colonial Anlo: The Gender Connection 136

6 Gender in Colonial and Post-Colonial Anlo:
   The Ethnic Connection 156

Conclusion 181

Sources 185

Index.. 200

LIST OF MAPS AND FIGURES

Map 1. The Location of the Anlo and the Ewe in Ghana xii

Map 2. Contemporary Anlo xiii

Map 3. The Gold Coast and Upper Slave Coast after the
1730–1733 Collapse of Akwamu 56

Map 4. Anlo Expansion: 1730-1770 60

Map 5. Anlo in 1784 84

Map 6. The Partitioning of the Ewe 146

Figure 1. Groups that Share in Common Clan Names 3

Figure 2. Groups that Share in Common Funeral Customs 3

Figure 3. Matrilateral Cross-cousin Marriage 23

Figure 4. Patrilateral Cross-cousin Marriage 23

Figure 5. Schematic Representation of the
Wards and Districts of Anloga 29

Figure 6. Matrilateral Cross-Cousin Marriage and the
Matrilateral Distribution of Labor and Acquired Property 43

Figure 7. Genealogy of the Anlo Clans 149

LIST OF PHOTOGRAPHS

1. The Keta Market in 1928 70

2. Yewe Women and Men in 1927–28 113

3. The Keta Fort in 1893 132

4. The Sugar Cane Market in Anloga at the Turn of the Century 163

5. Fishermen Using the *Yevudo* in the mid-1960s 166

6. Coconut Groves on the Keta Lagoon in the Early 1900s 168

7. The Shallot Market in Keta in the mid-1960s 175

ACKNOWLEDGMENTS

This book is the culmination of seventeen years of research on the history and culture of the Anlo-Ewe. As a result, I am indebted to the many, many people who encouraged and supported me throughout this period; not all of them, unfortunately, can be mentioned here. I began work on the Anlo as a graduate student in 1977 at Northwestern University where Ivor Wilks and George Fredrickson of the History Department introduced me to the interdisciplinary and comparative methods that are so evident in and important to this study. I am most grateful for the training they gave me and for their encouragement.

My most profound gratitude goes to the people of Anlo, and especially to the late T. S. A. Togobo, the late Boko Seke Axovi, and the late Afatsao Awadzi, who took me under their wings and shared with me their vast knowledge of Anlo history and culture. Of these three gentlemen, my mentors, I will always have particularly moving memories. The hours they spent guiding me, teaching me, and redirecting my efforts as I attempted to understand how the Anlo viewed their own history and culture were invaluable to this study. I would like to give special thanks to Sonia Patten, who provided both welcome and stimulating company during my first field research trip in 1977–1978. Special thanks also go to Togbui Adeladza II, who welcomed me into his home and made available the Minute Books of the Anlo Traditional Council; G. K. Nukunya, who supported and encouraged my work; and John Fiafor, Jasper Ackumey, and K. A. Mensah, who gave me important insights into Anlo and Ewe culture, scheduled interviews, and served as interpreters during my field research in 1977–1978 and 1987–1988. Many thanks are due to Kiran Cunningham, John Hansen, Richard Roberts, and Stillman Bradfield, who read various drafts of selected chapters and offered important editorial ideas that have significantly improved the final product. I am especially indebted to Claire Robertson, Jean Allman, Maria Grosz-Ngate, Jean Hay, and Allen Isaacman, who read the entire manuscript, sometimes more than once. Their advice, encouragement, and persistence in pushing me to "go that extra mile," to make those critical revisions, is appreciated more than I can express in words.

Research for this study was greatly facilitated by several archivists and librarians. I am particularly grateful to Dan Britz, Mette Shayne, and Hans Panofsky of the Melville J. Herskovits Memorial Library at Northwestern for their unswerving interest in and support of my research. I would also like to thank the archivists at the Rigsarchiv in Copenhagen, Denmark, the Staats Archiv in Bremen, Germany, Pastor Lenz at the Norddeutsche Mission also in Bremen, and the archivists at the

National Archives of Ghana, Accra; the Anlo Traditional Council Office in Anloga; the National Archives of Ghana, Ho; the District Grade II Library in Anloga; and the Institute of African Studies.

Funding to support my research has come from the Ford Foundation, Kalamazoo College, the Fulbright-Hays Program, Stanford University Humanities Center, the Lounsberry Foundation, and the Africana Studies and Research Center at Cornell University. To all of these institutions, agencies, and programs, I offer my sincere thanks. I am also grateful to Sara Pryor, Pat Dean, and Sheila Towner, all of whom helped me through many a computer word processing crisis, and to the many German students at Kalamazoo College and at Cornell University (especially Rudiger Bechstein and Don Stansberry) who helped me with the translation of the German documents used in this study. All Danish and French translations are my own.

Last, but certainly not least of all, I would like to thank my husband, Kodjopa Attoh, who supported with enthusiasm my efforts to complete this study.

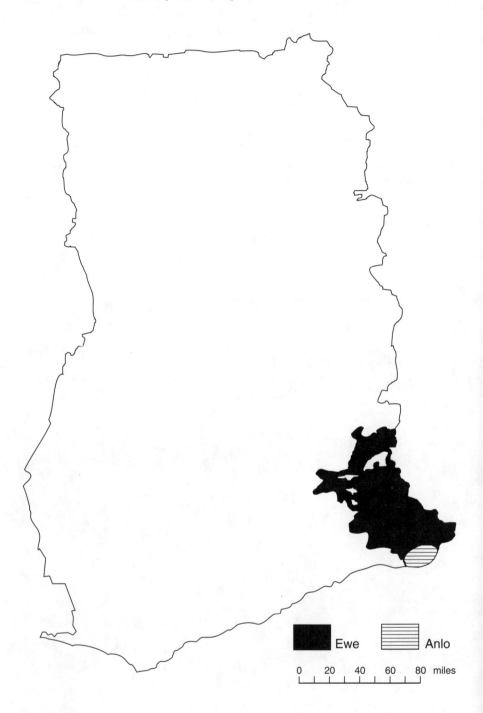

Ewe

Anlo

0   20   40   60   80 miles

MAP 1: The Location of the Anlo and the Ewe in Ghana

Ada	30
Afiadenyigba	23
Afife	28
Aflao	24
Agave	32
Agbosome	25
Alakple	16
Anloga	7
Anyako	22
Atiavi	19
Atiavi Glime	20
Atito	14
Atoko	4
Attiteti	1
Avenofeme	29
Bakpa	34
Batefe	3
Bator	37
Blekusu	13
Dzita	2
Dzodze	40
Exi	38
Fiaxo	17
Fenyi	39
Fenyiko	18
Kedzi	12
Keta	10
Kliko	26
Kodzi	15
Mepe	36
Malfi (Mlefi)	35
Noefe	41
Srogboe	5
Tegbi	9?
Tefle	31
Togbloku	21
Tsiame	11
Vodza	27
Weta	6
Whuti	8

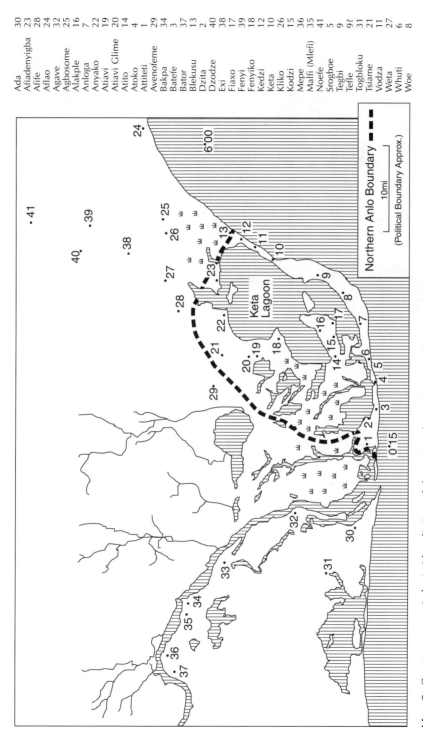

Map 2: Contemporary Anlo (with a listing of the pricipal towns and villages in the area)

Introduction:
Gender and Ethnicity
among the Anlo-Ewe

An Overview of Present and Past Social Relations

Gender and ethnic relations have been studied by historians of precolonial Africa for at least the past twenty years, most often in separate studies. In this book, I unite these two within a single work to emphasize the fact that the history of male-female relations and the changes that occurred in precolonial African ethnic relations were inextricably connected. Each directly and significantly influenced the other.

To illustrate these connections, I focus on the history of gender and ethnic relations in the polity of Anlo, an Ewe-speaking community which today is situated on the Atlantic littoral in the southeastern corner of the Republic of Ghana. Its location on what was then the upper Slave Coast during the seventeenth, eighteenth, and nineteenth centuries brought a steady stream of men and women into the community as traders, conquerors, slaves, and/or refugees. Some became incorporated individually into existing social groups; others coalesced into distinct entities that maintained their own identity into the twentieth century, so that today the current long-term resident population of Anlo, roughly 110,000 people, is organized into thirteen separate social groups known as *hlowo* or clans (sing. *hlo*).[1] Every Anlo male and female is said to belong to one of these clans because of their patrifiliation with a male ancestor. Each *hlo*, in turn, is identified as consisting of a number of patrilineages called *to-fome*. All clans are said to have played an important and complementary role in maintaining the political structures and military competence of the polity. This particular viewpoint is held by many of the elders I

---

[1] "Special Report on Localities by Local Authorities," *Population Census of Ghana—1984* (Accra: Eddy Williams, 1989), 22–24; for earlier estimates on the Anlo population dating from the late seventeenth century up through the 1970 census, see Sandra E. Greene, "The Anlo-Ewe: Their Economy, Society and External Relations in the Eighteenth Century" (Ph.D. dissertation, Northwestern University, 1981), 8–13.

interviewed in 1977–1978 and 1987–1988. It is also present in the scholarly works of G. K. Nukunya. In his 1969 study of Anlo kinship, Nukunya noted that:

> There are no aristocratic clans in Anlo. All are equal in status, but they perform different functions in the settlements and the tribe at large. For instance, the paramount stool belongs to the Adzovia and Bate clans, who alternately provide the King; the Lafe are the Kingmakers; and the Lafe together with the Amlade are the hereditary priests in each settlement and at the national level while the Dzevi provide the chief priest for the War God, the Nyigbla.[2]

The only distinction Anlo elders make among the various Anlo *hlowo* concerns the Blu clan. Unlike all others, this particular *hlo* is said to be composed of the descendants of strangers or outsiders who have been resident in Anlo for some time.

Many of the oral traditions I collected between 1977 and 1988 about each clan indicate that a very different understanding of Anlo society existed in the past. These traditions categorize the Anlo clans not just into one very large group of complementary units (from which only the Blu are distinguished as being of different origin), but rather they position the various Anlo *hlowo* on a hierarchical scale that defines certain clans as ethnic insiders and others as ethnic outsiders according to their geographical origins and time of arrival in Anlo. The oldest of these classification systems states, for example, that prior to the entrance of the present Ewe-speaking peoples into the Anlo area, there existed an indigenous population that later disappeared. The Anlo deified the last-known members of this population and then distinguished these gods, the *dzokpleanyiwo*, and the families that worshipped them from those gods and families that came later from Notsie, the Togo town from which the majority of the contemporary residents of Anlo are said to have come. A second and third more recent classification system categorizes the individual *hlowo*, to which all Anlo residents belong, not according to their affiliation with autochthonous or immigrant gods, but on the basis of shared names and funeral customs.[3] These are shown below.

According to Anlo elders, the sharing of both common names and funerary customs by various groups arose from the fact that each set of clans listed above traveled together, during which time they meshed their various cultural practices into a single form.[4] Thus, the *hlowo* listed under Group I in Figure 1 include a set of clans whose ancestors are known as the "first five." They are said to have emigrated from Notsie to Anlo together. Also included in Group I are those clans that developed as offshoots of the "first five." All are believed to have come to share the same naming and funerary practices (as members of the *nkeke-kpui-towo* group) because of their common experiences and genealogical connections to one another. Those clans in Groups II, III, and IV in Figure 1 (the *nkeke-legbe-towo* in Figure 2)

---

[2] G. K. Nukunya, *Kinship and Marriage among the Anlo-Ewe* (New York, 1969), 23–24.

[3] Drawn from Ibid., 198. The earliest written account about Anlo funeral customs can be found in A. B. Ellis, *The Ewe-Speaking Peoples of the Slave Coast of West Africa* (Chicago, 1890), 157–60; see also Gottlob Binetsch, "Beantwortung mehrerer Fragen über unser Ewe-volk und Seine Anchauungen," *Zeitschrift für Ethnologie* (Braunschweig, 1906), 38, 50. Binetsch, in particular, notes that each clan let elapse a certain number of days between the burial and the funeral, but he doesn't specify which clans were associated with how many days.

[4] Nukunya, *Kinship and Marriage*, 198.

FIGURE 1: Groups that Share in Common Clan Names

Clan Group I	Clan Group II	Clan Group III	Clan Group IV
Lafe, Amlade	Agave	Ame	Dzevi
Adzovia, Bate	Tsiame		Wifeme
Like, Bame			Blu
Tovi, Klevi			
Getsofe			

Male/Female	Male/Female	Male/Female	Male/Female
Fui/Kokui	Fui/Wi	Ame/Kui	Tete/Dede
Tsatsu/Abui	Tsatsu/Gbo	Adze/Akoe	Tete/Koko
Tsidi/Dzoe	Tsidi/Tolo	Tsidi/Tolo	Te/Mable
Akoli/Sa	Akoli/Sa	Akoli/Sa	Da/Mabui
De/Kuya	De/Kuya	De/Kuya	Date/Aladza
Lotsu/Awaye	Lotsu/Awaye	Lotsu/Awaye	
Letsa/Awala	Letsa/Awala	Letsa/Awala	
Dra/Wala	Dra/Wala	Dra/Wala	
Akolo/Walawala	Akolo/Walawala	Akolo/Walawala	
Akolotse/Walawui	Akolotse/Walawui	Akolotse/Walawui	
Tui/Gbato	Tui/Gbato	Tui/Gbato	

FIGURE 2: Groups that Share in Common Funeral Customs

Nkeke-kpui-towo	Nkeke-legbe-towo
Lafe, Amlade	Tsiame, Agave
Adzovia, Bate	Dzevi, Wifeme
Like, Bame	Getsofe, Blu
Tovi, Klevi, Ame	

The two groups identified, the *nkeke-kpui-towo* and the *nkeke-legbe-towo,* are said to differ from each other because the *nkeke-kpui-towo* require their members to let three or five days elapse between the day they bury their kin, and the time they perform a second ceremony designed to ensure that the spirit of the particular deceased joins their ancestors in the ancestral home. In contrast, the *nkeke-legbe-towo* require that six, seven, or eight days elapse. Nukunya, *Kinship and Marriage,* 200.

came later, from different places, at different times, and have therefore been categorized differently.[5]

The existence of these four different classificatory systems, some of which are of more ancient origin than others, suggests that the way in which the Anlo have defined the groups that collectively constitute their society has changed consider-

[5] The only discrepancy between Groups II, III, and IV in Figure 1 and the clans listed under the *nkeke-legbe-towo* in Figure 2 involves the Ame clan. This *hlo* is listed as a member of the *nkeke-kpui-towo,* but is included in Group III in Figure 1. This is probably the case because of the Ame clan's special position within Anlo society. Oral traditions indicate that members of the Ame clan are the descendants of war captives. As such, they became attached to the earlier immigrant groups in Anlo (those included in the *nkeke-kpui-towo*) but because they entered Anlo later than the earlier immigrants they are also considered late-arrivers and are thus included in Group III in Figure 1.

ably over time. During the precolonial period, the Anlo divided their resident population into two groups, distinguishing those associated with autochthonous gods from those associated with immigrant gods. A second and third system separated Anlo *hlowo* into two or four groups based on their naming and funeral customs. By the late twentieth century, these systems had also begun to give way to a fourth system that distinguished primarily one group, the Blu, as outsiders within Anlo society.

Close examination of these classificatory systems indicates that they have also been deeply influenced by subjective considerations. For example, in Figure 1 it is obvious that most of the names listed under the Groups I, II, and III are virtually the same except for a few discrepancies. Yet the Anlo have highlighted these differences to separate the second and third group from the first. Similarly, the groups in Figure 2 are distinguished from one another on the basis of whether they observe longer or shorter waiting periods between the burial and the second mortuary rite. Some observe a period of three or five days, others six, still others seven or eight.[6] Yet only those who follow the three- and five-day waiting custom are called the *nkeke-kpui-towo*; all others, including those that are different by only one day, are grouped into the *nkeke-legbe-towo* group. In the more contemporary classification, the Blu clan is the only *hlo* distinguished as a particularly late-arrival group, yet many of the ancestors of the Blu entered Anlo no later than others. Why the Anlo devised these particular categorization systems at different points in time will be addressed later in this study. Of greater significance here is the fact that we/they relations in the history of Anlo have undergone significant change over time.

Gender relations among the Anlo-Ewe have also undergone considerable change. Prior to the late seventeenth century, Anlo women inherited land from their mothers and fathers. They also had the right to bequeath this land to their children, despite the fact that the Anlo patrilineal system defined their children as members of a different patrilineage. Older women participated in the decision-making processes that concerned the community as a whole as well as their particular families. Younger women were involved in deciding to whom they would be betrothed. All women were also active members in the various production activities in which the Anlo were involved. Early travelers'accounts and oral traditions indicate that these production activities included the cultivation of millet and sorghum; women planted and harvested the crops with their husbands or male relatives on land allocated to them. Women took principal responsibility for weeding and then processing the grains after they had been harvested. They also received from their mothers and bequeathed to their daughters specific plots on which they harvested the wickers and reeds that they used to make baskets. Anlo's location on a narrow sandspit sandwiched between the Atlantic Ocean and a larger inland body of salt water known as the Keta Lagoon made fishing another major economic activity, although their technological expertise in boat building and the conditions off the Atlantic coast confined Anlo fishing to the lagoon between the late seventeenth and late eighteenth centuries. Oral traditions and studies of other

---

[6] Note that Nukunya, *Kinship and Marriage*, 200, describes the *nkeke-kpui-towo* group as observing five days; in his account of late nineteenth-century Anlo, however, Binetsch states that greater variation existed than this; some also observed three days. See Binetsch, "Beantwortung mehrerer," 50.

societies in the area indicate that women were involved in this industry in the same way in which they were active in agriculture. They were restricted to specific activities within the fishing industry; in this case, the collection of shellfish and the smoking, drying, and salting of the harvests of their husbands and their male relatives.[7]

Much had changed by the late nineteenth century. Older women continued to play active roles in the affairs of their particular clans and patrilineages, as well as in the larger society, but younger women had lost their ability to participate in the decisions that determined who they would marry. All women lost the right to harvest shellfish and were confined to the processing and selling of the catches of their male relatives and their husbands. Women lost access to the lands from which they had harvested reeds and wickers, lands that they had previously received from their mothers. The amount of agricultural land allocated to them as daughters and wives also decreased. Colonialism and the expansion of Christianity in the twentieth century brought additional changes. Young women gained the right to choose their own husbands, but they also found themselves completely eliminated from the landed inheritance system by their families. Husbands refused to allocate land to their wives; instead, wives were expected to work on their husbands' farms. At the same time, commercialization of the fishing industry meant that women no longer had either the automatic right or responsibility to process the catch of their husbands, fathers, or brothers, and then sell the same so as to garner at least some of the profits for themselves.

The changes that have taken place in gender and ethnic relations in Anlo society outlined above have occurred in many societies in Africa and elsewhere. More important for this study is the fact that these changes were closely related in precolonial Anlo society. In Chapter 1, for example, I note that when refugees and immigrants entered Anlo in substantial numbers beginning in 1679, competition over scarce resources arose between the prior inhabitants and the new arrivals. The way in which the earlier residents responded to this competition had a major impact on both gender and ethnic relations in Anlo. Fearing a loss of control over the lands in the area, the earlier residents of Anlo established a clan system. They grouped together the individuals and families who had been living in Anlo before 1679 into separate *hlowo* according to their supposed kinship ties to a common ancestor, the relative time at which that ancestor entered the early Anlo area, and the place from which that same ancestor had immigrated as manifested in his descendants' naming and funeral customs. These groups then claimed for themselves all lands in the Anlo area and defined others as ethnic outsiders.

Earlier resident families also began to place increasingly severe limits on the rights of women in their midst. Prior to 1679, women in Anlo could inherit family land and had the right to pass this property to their children. But as many of the immigrants and refugees began to integrate themselves into their new communities, the land rights that had been granted to women became a problem for

---

[7] Anlo women's historical involvement in the smoking, drying, and salting of fish has been well-established, but their role in the collection of shellfish is more speculative. Other Ewe-speaking women in the area continue to be involved in this activity. Their subsequent exclusion by the mid-nineteenth century was probably a result of the overfishing of the Keta Lagoon, and the successful effort by men to take over this activity as the demand for fish in the interior and the profits from such sales expanded with the opening of new trade routes.

many earlier resident lineages and clans. Such land could be lost to "outsiders" if daughters married young men from ethnic outsider families, since women could pass their landed property to their sons, who technically were outsiders since they were members of their father's and not their mother's patrilineage and/or clan. To counter this threat, the elders in the earlier resident families opted not to deny women access to land. Rather, they preferred to marry their daughters to a fellow clansman, and to deny their young women the right to object to the individuals chosen. The young women's objections were ignored, stifled, or discouraged by their family elders. The women's interests were marginalized, their rights abridged.

Gender relations changed again during the second half of the eighteenth century. After 1750, profits from involvement in the Atlantic slave trade expanded considerably. The gap between the wealthy and the not-so-wealthy also increased. This generated fierce competition among the various lineages in Anlo, as all attempted to demonstrate publicly their social and economic status. Family elders incurred enormous debt in order to stage elaborate funerals. Many also began to use their authority to gain access to the labor needed to produce the wealth required for such public displays. Those male elders who pursued this particular course began insisting that at least one of their daughters marry a sister's son. This also affected gender relations, since family elders became even less willing to hear their daughters' objections to arranged marriages.

In Chapter 2, I document the fact that many who were disadvantaged by the changes that occurred in ethnic relations after 1679 challenged their social definition as "other" throughout the eighteenth and nineteenth centuries. Some managed to alter their identities. Others were able to take advantage of the opportunities that came their way to become central members of the Anlo political and religious leadership. Their success meant that the norms that had previously governed ethnic relations were significantly expanded. In addition to the geographical origins of one's ancestors and their time of arrival in Anlo, wealth and service to the community became important bases for social prestige. I also argue, however, that this change had its own costs. In their struggle to establish themselves as integral members of Anlo society, ethnic outsiders frequently adopted a gendered approach to managing their affairs that was identical to that used by ethnic insiders. They formed themselves into clans and then adopted a preference for marrying their daughters to fellow clan members. Family elders placed increasingly severe limits on the ability of their young women to object to the decisions made about their marital affairs. As a result, all women found themselves increasingly disadvantaged by their own kin during the eighteenth and nineteenth centuries because of the changes that had occurred in ethnic relations.

In Chapter 3, I show that women who felt marginalized by the changes that had occurred in Anlo gender relations acted to counter their disadvantageous position during this period. Many did so by joining the religious orders formed by ethnic outsiders for the worship of their gods. This particular course of action appealed to young women because these orders freed them from the strictures imposed by their families. As the "wives" of a particular god, they gained the power to influence the decision as to whom they would be betrothed. They were also able to exercise greater influence within their husbands' households. Their example, in turn, encouraged other women in Anlo to find additional ways to achieve these same rights. As a result, by the late nineteenth century concubinage had become much more common, and family elders were forced to adjust to the fact that they could not control the women under their authority as they had in the past. The so-called "reckless" women of Anlo did more than alter the norms that governed gender relations, however. They also contributed to significant changes in ethnic relations, for it was the support these young women gave to the religious orders organized by ethnic outsiders that allowed the latter to propel themselves into the center of the Anlo political and religious hierarchy and to silence those who would ridicule them publicly as outsiders.

Despite all the changes in gender and ethnic relations between 1679 and the end of the nineteenth century, much also remained the same. In Chapter 4, I note that many in Anlo continued to be marginalized as ethnic outsiders. The majority of women still found themselves excluded from discussions about their own marital affairs. This was the case, I argue, because of the nature of the opportunities and choices available to them. Women who sought to challenge the ways in which their families handled their affairs had to obtain support for their decisions. In many instances, they received that support from their mothers and their maternal relations. Some women found support in the religious orders organized by ethnic outsiders. Most women in Anlo, however, accepted the need to sacrifice their own personal interests for the benefit of their lineage and clan. Many did so because they had been taught from an early age to support the decisions of their fathers, brothers, and husbands. Other women were aware that they could pursue a different course, but they were either prevented from doing so, or they opted not to, because of the perceived risks associated with aligning themselves with non-kin. The fact that so many women did not challenge the prevailing pattern of gender relations had a major impact on ethnic relations. By refusing or failing to challenge the gendered way in which their families handled their marital affairs, Anlo women reinforced, whether consciously or not, the notion that there was indeed something different, untrustworthy, and dangerous about the ethnic outsiders with whom their parents had discouraged them from associating.

Many of those defined as ethnic outsiders during the eighteenth and nineteenth centuries were either unable or unwilling to challenge the prevailing norms that governed ethnic relations. Some tried and failed. Others had no interest in pursuing such challenges. The resulting continuity in ethnic relations, where an ethnicized "we" continued to view itself as different from an ethnicized "they," had a signficant impact on gender relations. As long as there existed a feared "other" within Anlo society, elders could continue to exercise greater control over the women in their families. That they did, indeed, respond in this way is indicated by the fact that by the late nineteenth century, many in Anlo continued to be defined as outsiders, and the majority of women continued to find their voices ignored as family elders gave preference to fellow clan members and attempted to exclude others, especially ethnic outsiders, when arranging marriages.

Twentieth-century Anlo

The principal focus of this study is on the history of gender and ethnic relations in before 1900, but in Chapter 5 and 6 I extend this history into the twentieth century.

My purpose is to explore the extent to which gender and ethnic relations in Anlo continued to influence one another during the colonial and post-colonial periods while both also shifted and changed on their own.

The twentieth-century developments in ethnic relations examined here include the declining significance of clan identity as the means used by the Anlo to regulate we/they relations. As indicated, during the nineteenth century, the identity of one's clan as ethnic insider or outsider very much influenced one's social position in Anlo society and the kinds of influence men and women from particular clans could exercise within the polity. By the mid-twentieth century, however, the factors that had generated the permeable, yet still quite limiting, boundaries between "we" and "they" within eighteenth- and nineteenth-century Anlo society had changed to the point where only a few groups were still defined as "other" within this polity. The Anlo increasingly accepted as genuine fictive kinship ties between clan ancestors and recently invented connections to Notsie. They ignored or explained away the earlier emphasis on difference as manifested in naming and funeral customs. They also gave priority to the new, broader identity of being Ewe.

Similar changes occurred in gender relations. By the mid-twentieth century, young women exercised individual control over their own marriages. Divorce became much more common. Women continued to suffer disadvantages within both their marital and familial households, however. One area in which this was most apparent was in the landed inheritance system. During the eighteenth and nineteenth centuries, women received land from their fathers, mothers, and husbands on which to grow their own crops. By the mid-twentieth century, the quantity of land received had decreased considerably. By the late twentieth century, women received nothing at all.

These developments occurred because of specific changes in the Anlo political and economic system, but more important for the discussion here is the fact that they promoted continued intimate connections between gender and ethnic relations. During the early part of this century, the Anlo political elite shifted the way in which they managed threats to their authority. Instead of undermining potential challengers by defining them as outsiders, they began to embrace the majority of the ethnic outsiders in their midst, working with them to redefine their identities. This compromise was necessary to create the unity they felt was necessary for them to interact successfully with the colonial and post-colonial independent state into which they had been absorbed. But as outsider groups found it possible to recast their identities with the support of the influential in Anlo, the alliances they had developed with individual Anlo women of all ethnic identities collapsed. The religious orders previously used by these groups to bolster their own social status, and used by young women to increase control over their own lives, declined in popularity and power with the expansion of Christianity and the colonial government. More importantly, ethnic outsiders declined to replace these linkages by developing new alliances with interested young women. Instead, they focused their efforts on working with the political elite of Anlo to redefine their ethnic origins. As a result, women lost what few opportunities had been available to them in the past to exercise greater control over their own marital lives.

Women responded to these twentieth-century developments—the collapse of the opportunity to gain benefits through alignment with ethnic outsiders, and the loss of access to agricultural land—by altering the way in which they socialized their children. They also formed cooperatives and marketing networks that excluded men to benefit themselves. In so doing, they acted not only to reposition themselves and their children within their natal and familial households and within the larger society, but they also contributed to the changes that were occurring in ethnic relations in Anlo. They reinforced the increasing irrelevance of one's clan affiliation (which had previously been used to define individuals and groups as ethnic insiders or outsiders) by de-emphasizing that particular aspect of their social identity in the socialization of their children. In forming one of the most influential marketing organizations, Anlo women also emphasized the importance and value of the new Ewe ethnic identity by excluding non-Ewes.

The development of new ethnic identities and relations, and the changes that have occurred in gender relations during the twentieth century, should not obscure the fact that older relations and identities continue to exist. Some families in Anlo continue to be defined as ethnic outsiders. Many women continue to be disadvantaged because of their gender. What has occurred rather is a marked expansion in the total set of widely accepted norms that govern gender and ethnic relations in twentieth-century Anlo.

Considerations of Gender in Historiographical Context

While the principal goal of this study is to illustrate and analyze the intersection of gender and ethnic relations in precolonial Anlo, a second goal is to challenge the way in which historians of Africa have pursued the study of these two phenomena as separate fields of inquiry within the discipline of social history.

Historical studies of precolonial gender relations are rather few in number, but those that do examine this topic tend to focus on changes in one particular sector of a given society. Musisi and McCaskie, for example, both focus on the political. They discuss the jockeying for political power that occurred in the states of Buganda and Asante, respectively, and how the political elites of these two polities used marital practices to strengthen their status within their societies. These actions, in turn, are said to have resulted in women losing control over their sexuality.[8] Afonja, Alpers, Guyer, and Eldredge focus on the economy. They highlight the way in which expanding opportunities to accumulate wealth from trade impacted gender relations, to the detriment of women, within the societies they studied.[9]

---

[8] Nakanyike B. Musisi, "Women, 'Elite Polygyny' and Buganda State Formation," *Signs*, 16, 4 (1991); T. C. McCaskie, "State and Society, Marriage and Adultery: Some Considerations Towards a Social History of Pre-colonial Asante," *Journal of African History* [hereafter *JAH*], 22 (1981).

[9] Simi Afonja, "Changing Modes of Production and the Sexual Division of Labor Among the Yoruba," *Signs*, 7, 2 (1981), "Land Control: A Critical Factor in Yoruba Gender Stratification," in Claire Robertson and Iris Berger, eds., *Women and Class in Africa* (New York, 1986), and "Changing Patterns of Gender Stratification," in Irene Tinker, ed., *Persistent Inequalities: Women and World Development* (New York, 1990); Edward A. Alpers, "State, Merchant Capital and Gender Relations in Southern Mozambique to the End of the 19th Century: Some Tentative Hypotheses," *African Economic History*, 13 (1984), and "Ordinary Household Chores: Ritual and Power in a 19th Century Swahili Women's Spirit Possession Cult," *International Journal of African Historical Studies* [hereafter *IJAHS*], 17, 4 (1984); Jane Guyer, "Beti Widow Inheritance and Marriage Law: A Social History," in Betty Potash, ed., *Widows in African Societies: Choices and Constraints* (Stanford, 1986); Elizabeth Eldredge, "Women in Production: The Economic Role of Women in Nineteenth Century Lesotho," *Signs*, 16, 4 (1991).

One of the goals of this study is to expand discussion about the history of precolonial gender relations in Africa to include analysis of a much fuller set of institutional systems within a given society, and the ways these institutions interacted with, impacted, and were changed by the actions of men and women, individually and collectively. In Chapter 1, for example, I emphasize the connections that existed between the development of demographic pressures and the expansion of the Atlantic slave trade between the late seventeenth and mid-nineteenth centuries, and the particular social changes occurring in Anlo during this same period. I argue that one of the ways family elders responded to the difficulties and opportunities generated by these economic and population changes involved their exercising greater control over the marital affairs of their young women. I also note, in Chapter 3, that the same competitive conditions to which so many families responded provided young women the opportunity to circumvent the greater control their families were attempting to exercise over them. Those women who took advantage of these opportunities did so by joining a number of new religious orders. Their actions, in turn, profoundly influenced the political, religious, and social systems of the Anlo. Through their resistance, young women contributed to the emergence of new centers of political and religious power that challenged the authority of the political and religious elite. They contributed to changes in Anlo kinship, residency, and inheritance systems. They began to undermine the Anlo marital system well before it was challenged by the spread of Christianity and the expansion of European colonial rule. By analyzing the history of a wider range of institutional systems among the Anlo-Ewe during the precolonial period and then examining the way in which changes therein impacted and were impacted by the men and women of Anlo, I demonstrate that the history of gender relations and the history of political, economic, demographic, social, and religious change are intimately and inextricably linked. Reconstructing the history of one necessarily entails an historical reconstruction of the other.

A second goal is to offer a different conception of how gender relations operated within the African family during the precolonial period. Historians have defined the family in Africa in a variety of ways. Some focus on the household as a residential production unit; others define the lineage as the basic familial unit.[10] More important for this study is the fact that many who give specific attention to gender relations within the family emphasize the extent to which both the lineage and the marital household were major locations for the oppression of women. Guy, Schmidt, and Eldredge, for example, who have written about gender relations in patrilineal southern African societies, argue that when women created value through their reproductive and productive activities, it was men who appropriated this value as fa-

---

[10] The majority also tend to recognize the fact that both the lineage and the household were subject to change in the extent to which they emphasized matrilineal or patrilineal elements, and in their composition and size, as individuals attached and detached themselves under various circumstances. For a discussion of these issues, see the articles on the African family published in the *JAH*, 24 (1983). See also Robin Horton, "From Fishing Village to City-State: A Social History of New Calabar," in Mary Douglass and Phyllis Kaberry, eds., *Man in Africa* (London, 1969); Kajsa Ekholm, "External Exchange and the Transformation of Central African Social Systems," and I. Wilks, "Land, Labour, Capital and the Forest Kingdom of Asante: A Model of Early Change," both in J. Friedman and M. J. Rowlands, eds., *The Evolution of Social Systems* (Pittsburgh, 1977); Jane Guyer, "Household and Community in African Studies," *African Studies Review*, XXIV, 2/3 (1981); and Eldredge, "Women in Production."

thers and husbands. Accordingly, both the male-dominated marital household and the lineage constituted a major source of women's oppression.[11] In this study, I equate the family with the patrilineage (or *to-fome*, as it is known among the generally patrilineal Anlo) and I, too, document the fact that male-dominated patrilineages exercised increasing control over the productive and reproductive capacities of women in eighteenth- and nineteenth-century Anlo. But I avoid demonizing African men and the African family as managed by male and female elders by discussing the increasing pressures felt by families as a result of demographic changes and the competition for prestige that arose because of the expanding influence of the Atlantic slave trade. I include this analysis not to excuse or deny the negative impact that certain family decisions had on women, but rather to place those decisions in historical context. I also emphasize the fact that while the patrilineage constituted the principal group with which an individual affiliated as family, a person's matrilineage played an equally important role in the lives of many Anlo. We know, for example, that in the eighteenth century mothers could and did have a strong influence on their daughters in encouraging them to join particular religious orders. This encouragement from a maternal relative provided an important alternative source of support to young women who wished to defy the ways in which their patrilineages managed their lives. Thus, while one can speak of the Anlo family as essentially the patrilineage—and I do, indeed, use the term family in this particular way—it is also the case that matrilateral relatives often played an especially important role in the lives of individual women within the society, offering them alternatives so that they could counter the influence of their patrilineage if they so desired.[12]

A third goal of this study is to emphasize the fact that patrilateral and matrilateral relations were not the only social groups that influenced the lives of various individuals in precolonial Anlo. Non-kinship based relations were also important. In Chapter 2, I trace the popularity of a number of new religious orders to the fact that they provided for many individual women the kind of support they were unable to obtain from their families. In Chapter 6, I attribute the emergence of similar, non-kinship-based organizations in the twentieth century to these same factors. It was the existence of these non-kinship-based groups, and the fact that they provided support networks to the young women of Anlo in addition to or as an alternative to the older social units present in the society, that generated changes in the way in which men interacted with each other and with the women of Anlo.

A fourth and final goal of this study is to offer a different understanding of the history of marriage in Africa. The literature on this subject discusses a wide range of associated practices, including historical and anthropological analyses of polygyny; marital preferences; the role of the family and the individual in the contracting of marriages; the residence of the wife, husband, and their children; the relations between a spouse and his or her in-laws; bride payments and bride service; the legal,

---

[11] Jeff Guy, "Gender Oppression in Southern Africa's Precapitalist Societies," in Cherryl Walker, ed., *Women and Gender in Southern Africa to 1945* (London, 1990); Elizabeth Schmidt, *Peasants, Traders and Wives: Shona Women in the History of Zimbabwe, 1870–1939* (Portsmouth, NH, 1992); and Eldredge, "Women in Production."

[12] By the mid-nineteenth century, nephews lived and worked, during a portion of their youth, with their mother's brother or *nyrui*, often receiving from him training in the business of trade. Nephews also inherited the acquired wealth of their maternal uncles and could expect assistance from them in collecting the necessary material goods they needed for a bride payment.

economic, and political status and rights of a spouse; and the status and rights of widows, widowers, the childless spouse, and divorcees.[13] Most of the studies of African marriage discuss change only in the context of colonial rule and missionary influence.[14] As a consequence, one is often left with the impression that there were very few changes in this institution before 1900. I offer an alternative understanding of the history of African marital practices by focusing on the changes that occurred in this aspect of Anlo social relations prior to the twentieth century. In Chapter 1, for example, I document the factors that contributed during the eighteenth and nineteenth centuries to the increased tendency for families to suppress young women's attempts to object to marriage arrangements. I also discuss the shift in Anlo preferences for marriages between cross-cousins of any kind to a preference for unions that involved matrilateral cross-cousins. In Chapter 3, I note the way in which young women responded to these changes and the impact their response had on the institution of marriage by the late nineteenth century. I conclude in Chapter 6 with a discussion of the fact that in the twentieth century, the Anlo have moved toward greater individual choice in marriage and have begun to engage in divorce at a much greater rate than in the past, but I also argue that these trends originated long before colonial rule or missionary influence had begun to impact Anlo social relations, and that they do not represent such a sharp break with the past as one might have thought.

Analyses of Ethnicity in Precolonial Africa

Ethnicity is defined here as a system of social classification embraced by groups of individuals who identify themselves and are identified by others as distinct on the basis of their shared putative or real cultural, ancestral, regional, and/or linguistic origins and practices, and where the identities of the groups and individuals so classified are also subject to periodic reinvention. This is the second focus of analysis in this book. Few scholars have focused specifically on ethnicity in precolonial Africa, and the majority have either tended to examine the *lack* of change in ethnic identity, or to examine shifts in ethnic identity only as they apply to individuals. For example, Wilks, Falola, Arhin, and Launay discuss the ways in which different groups within the same society co-existed while maintaining their separate identities.[15] Mouser and Barnes focus on the circumstances that permitted individual

---

[13] See for example, A. R. Radcliffe-Brown and Daryll Forde, eds., *African Systems of Kinship and Marriage* (London, 1950); Lucy Mair, *African Marriage and Social Change* (, 1969); McCaskie, "State and Society"; Karen Sacks, *Sisters and Wives: The Past and Future of Sexual Equality* (Urbana, 1982); John Thornton, "Sexual Demography: The Impact of the Slave Trade on Family Structure," in Claire Robertson and Martin A. Klein, eds., *Women and Slavery in Africa* (Madison, 1983); Jane Fishbourne Collier, *Marriage and Inequality in Classless Societies* (Stanford, 1988); Guyer, "Beti Widow"; Betty Potash, "Gender Relations in Sub-Saharan Africa," in Sandra Morgan, ed., *Gender and Anthropology: Critical Reviews for Research and Teaching* (Washington, D.C., 1989); Guy, "Gender Oppression"; Afonja, "Changing Patterns"; and Musisi, "Women."

[14] Exceptions include Guyer, "Beti Widow"; Thornton, "Sexual Demography"; and Musisi, "Women."

[15] I. Wilks, *Wa and the Wala* (Cambridge, 1989); Robert Launay, *Traders without Trade* (Cambridge, 1982); Kwame Arhin, "Strangers and Hosts: A Study in the Political Organisation and History of Atebubu Town," *Transactions of the Historical Society of Ghana* [hereafter *THSG*], XII (1971); Toyin Falola, "From Hospitality to Hostility: Ibadan and Strangers, 1830–1904," *JAH*, 26 (1985). I have confined this discussion to studies of West African societies, but this is by no means an exhaustive list. Many other studies have been done on this subject by historians and anthropologists working in other parts of the continent.

strangers to submerge their former identities and become socially integrated into their host communities.[16] Yet very few scholars discuss the fact that in some precolonial African societies the identities of individuals and entire ethnic groups were altered so that they became more centrally positioned within the social hierarchy of the communities in which they lived.[17] Even fewer note that the individuals and groups involved in such identity change influenced not only the way in which they themselves were defined, but also the very nature of ethnic relations within the polity as a whole.[18]

Other historians who have examined the character and history of ethnicity in Africa more broadly—for example, Ranger, Vail, Lonsdale, and Samarin[19]—have produced illuminating studies on ethnicity as a general social phenomenon, but their particular approach has also generated a number of erroneous impressions about the nature of ethnicity in Africa throughout its history. For example, all the authors noted emphasize the notion that ethnicity was an invention of missionaries, colonial government officials, and members of an educated African elite in the twentieth century. Yet Anlo oral testimonies recorded by German missionaries in the mid-nineteenth century suggest that such identities existed among the Anlo well before the advent of colonialism. Many within the Anlo polity were already defined and/or had already defined themselves as culturally distinct, based on the fact that their ancestors immigrated to Anlo from very different places by at least the mid-nineteenth century. These same authors also ascribe a purely passive role to non-elite Africans in the construction of their new identities. Vail states, for example, that while European missionaries, African elites, and colonial government officials "carefully crafted their ethnic ideologies in order to define the cultural characteristics of members of various ethnic groups," ordinary Africans simply accepted these definitions.[20] The history of ethnicity among the Anlo suggests a very different picture. Far from being passive, both individuals and groups within this society were very much involved in the shaping of their new identities, as I note in Chapter 2. They generated fresh traditions about their origins, silenced those who attempted to propagate the older versions of their history, explained away those cultural practices that they and others had previously identi-

---

[16] Bruce L. Mouser, "Accommodation and Assimilation in the Landlord-Stranger Relationship," in B. K. Swartz, Jr., and Raymond E. Dumett, eds., *West African Cultural Dynamics: Archaeological and Historical Perspectives* (The Hague, 1980); and Sandra T. Barnes, "Ritual, Power and Outside Knowledge," *Journal of Religion in Africa*, XX, 3 (1990).

[17] Exceptions include David Newbury, *Kings and Clans: Ijwi Island and the Lake Kivu Rift, 1780–1840* (Madison, 1991), and Neal Sobania, "Fisherman Herders: Subsistence, Survival and Cultural Change in Northern Kenya," *JAH*, 29 (1988).

[18] See Fredrik Barth, *Ethnic Groups and Boundaries: The Social Organization of Culture Difference* (London, 1969), who discusses the role that all play in maintaining and changing the boundaries that separate different ethnic groups.

[19] Terence Ranger, *The Invention of Tribalism in Zimbabwe* (Gweru, Zimbabwe, 1985); Leroy Vail, ed., *The Creation of Tribalism in Southern Africa* (London, 1989); John Lonsdale, "When Did the Gusii (or Any Other Group) Become a 'Tribe,'" *Kenya Historical Review*, 5, 1 (1977), and "African Pasts in Africa's Future," *Canadian Journal of African Studies* [hereafter *CJAS*], 23 (1989); William J. Samarin, "Bondjo Ethnicity and Colonial Imagination," *CJAS*, 18, 12 (1984). See also the numerous works cited in Ronald Cohen, "Ethnicity: Problem and Focus in Anthropology," *Annual Review of Anthropology*, 7 (1978); M. Crawford Young, "Nationalism, Ethnicity and Class in Africa: A Retrospective," *Cahiers d'Etudes Africaines*, XXVI (1986); and David Newbury, *Kings and Clans*, 228–30.

[20] Leroy Vail, "Introduction: Ethnicity in Southern African History," in Vail, ed., *Creation of Tribalism*, 11.

fied as markers of their identity, and in so doing, significantly altered the boundaries that had defined them as distinct.

In their definition of ethnicity, Vail, Samarin, Lonsdale, and Ranger also fail to consider the fact that ethnicity as defined by average Africans was more than an identity based on invented cultural, linguistic, and/or regional groupings. It also included the concept of kinship and the relative settlement time of one's ancestors in a given area. This is most evident when one examines how the Anlo distinguished one individual or group from another. Every Anlo was said to belong to a *hlo*, a term that has been translated as clan, but the identity that individuals assumed because of their membership in a particular *hlo* involved more than the idea of descent from a common ancestor. Individuals and groups were also defined on the basis of their *hlo* as latecomers or early residents depending on when their clan's ancestor is said to have arrived in the early Anlo area, and as ethnically distinct on the basis of the area from which their ancestor immigrated to Anlo. All three of these factors—kinship, time of arrival, and former homeland—defined individuals and groups as distinct. Members of specific clans embraced and propagated that aspect of their identity which identified them and their ancestors with a particular place of origin. At the same time, they employed the kinship feature (through the transmission of histories and rituals) to enforce adherence to this identity. By narrowly defining ethnicity as an identity based on invented cultural, linguistic, and/or regional groupings, Vail, Samarin, Lonsdale, and Ranger accept as valid for Africa a European definition of this social phenomenon and ignore the definition used by average Africans in which kinship, time of settlement, and the homeland of one's ancestors were integral parts of the we/they construction of ethnic identity. This, in turn, prevents them from understanding how average Africans were actively involved in the definition and redefinition of their own identities and how they altered the social boundaries that distinguished one group from another.

A fourth and final concern about the study of ethnicity in Africa has to do with the relationship between ethnicity and gender. Lonsdale has argued that women in patrilineal societies were "outsiders in the patriclan," and that because of their social location, women provided the framework that enabled their children to move from viewing themselves as members of a localized political community to that of a "tribe" or member of an ethnic group. The difficulty with this formulation is that it is premised on the notion that "women have no tribe [or ethnic identity]."[21] I argue that Anlo women viewed themselves and were viewed as integral members of their lineages and clans. They identified fully with these groups and it was because of this fact that Anlo women were deeply involved—consciously and explicitly—in supporting both the existing boundaries that defined "we" and "they" in Anlo, and the changes that occurred therein from the late seventeenth century on. When missionaries, colonial officials, a newly emergent educated elite, and average Anlos began to generate a new and larger ethnic identity in the twentieth century, women were not simply victims of this process, as suggested by Vail and White, Marks, and Jewsiewicki.[22] Rather, they actively participated for their own

---

[21] Ibid., 15.

[22] Leroy Vail and Landeg White, "Tribalism in the Political History of Malawi"; Shula Marks, "Patriotism, Patriarchy and Purity: Natal and the Politics of Zulu Ethnic Consciousness"; and Bogumil Jewsiewicki, "The Formation of the Political Culture of Ethnicity in the Belgian Congo, 1920-1959," all in Vail, ed., *Creation of Tribalism*.

reasons in de-emphasizing the old boundaries and reinforcing the more contemporary identity constructs developed in Anlo.

In this study, I offer a very different conception of ethnicity in African history by emphasizing the fact that ethnic identities did, indeed, exist in precolonial Africa, that these identities were as subject to change during this period as in the colonial period, and that such changes necessarily involved not only the powerful but also the marginalized. The latter operated as subjects, shaping, propagating, and using all means at their disposal (including kinship ties, whether fictive or real) to recast their own ethnic identities as historical circumstances allowed. These efforts led not only to changes in their own positions within the social hierarchy of Anlo society, they also contributed to a redefinition of the boundaries that defined we/they ethnic relations within the polity of Anlo.

The Challenge to Social History

Social history has been defined as the history of "ordinary men and women who had heretofore no voice in the historical record,"[23] where emphasis is placed on "conveying the experiences of [ordinary] people . . . independent of (though not in opposition to) the activities of dominant institutions or the canons of high culture."[24] For others, social history is "history from the bottom up," where the focus of attention is on the notion that "production and power were contested, that ordinary people had feelings, values and leverage," and "where, within limits, ordinary people made their own history."[25] Still others describe it as history that "illuminates the complex interplay between large . . . changes of the past . . . and alterations in . . . population, social hierarchies and routine social life."[26] This study has been influenced by all these definitions, and elements of each can been found herein. Scattered throughout this study, for example, are descriptions of the ways the Anlo interacted with their environment to sustain themselves. In Chapter 6, I describe where and how the Anlo cultivated crops; I discuss the fishing industry as it existed in the Keta Lagoon and on the Atlantic littoral. I also detail in Chapter 1 the rituals that Anlo families performed for births and deaths. All of these are included, in part, to convey a sense of the daily activities in which average Anlo men and women were engaged during certain times of the year, at certain points in their lives, despite the press of external forces.

I also emphasize the extent to which average men and women were actively involved in shaping their own lives. Many not only succeeded in redefining their social positions, but also contributed to changes in the way the Anlo handled gender and ethnic relations more generally. Young women who decided to resist their families and influence their own marital affairs established the foundation for the

[23] Olivier Zunz, "The Synthesis of Social Change: Reflections on American Social History," in Olivier Zunz, ed., *Reliving the Past: The Worlds of Social History* (Chapel Hill, 1985), 53.

[24] Peter N. Stearns, "Toward a Wider Vision: Trends in Social History," in Michael Kammen, ed., *The Past Before Us: Contemporary Historical Writings in the United States* (Ithaca, 1980), 213.

[25] William B. Taylor, "Between Global Process and Local Knowledge: An Inquiry into Early Latin American Social History, 1500–1900," in Zunz, ed., *Reliving the Past*, 142; Charles Tilly, "Retrieving European Lives," in Zunz, ed., *Reliving the Past*, 19.

[26] Olivier Zunz, "Introduction," in Zunz, ed., *Reliving the Past*, 6.

eventual decline of parental control over marriage that occurred during the colonial period. Those who were successful in recasting their own ethnic identities also
helped redefine the boundary that structured ethnic relations in Anlo. In addition,
I establish a direct correlation between the majority of the changes in gender and
ethnic relations that occurred between the late seventeenth and late twentieth centuries and the large-scale forces that were impacting Anlo society during this same
period. Included among these forces are the imperial expansion of Akwamu, the
Atlantic slave trade, the entrance of European missionaries, and the rise of European colonialism. Each event is discussed not as a vast abstraction, but as part of
the daily reality of average men and women in Anlo. Similarly, in my portrayal of
both the powerful and the average in Anlo, I attempt to present them—as far as
the sources allow—not as faceless, nameless representatives of their social positions, but rather as real people whom we can know through their actions and/or
their own words, people who managed their lives as best they could under changing historical conditions.

By focusing on the history of both gender and ethnicity within a single work,
I define social history as more than the history of such discrete groups as women,
slaves, workers, or immigrants, and the way in which they interacted with the
forces influencing their lives. I expand the definition to include the decisions made
by both the powerful and the less powerful within society, as all grappled with
changing demographic, social, political, economic, and religious conditions; and
the way in which these decisions generated actions that, in turn, profoundly influenced the way men and women in Anlo defined and redefined the norms that
governed gender and ethnic relations in their society.

Sources and Methodologies

The reconstruction of precolonial African social history has often been regarded as
a particularly formidable task because of the limited documentary sources that
describe social relations in early African societies, and because most historians are
reluctant to rely exclusively on oral data.[27] I have attempted to overcome these
problems by collecting what limited data exist (both archival and oral), and then
using both traditional historical methodologies and those more commonly associated with other disciplines to reconstruct the history of gender and ethnic relations
in Anlo. In 1977–1978 and 1987–1988, for example, I collected data from a number
of archival holdings located in Europe and in Ghana. Documents found in the
Rigsarchiv and the Kongelig Bibliotek in Copenhagen, the Public Records Office in
Kew, England, and the Archives des Colonies in Paris proved useful in reconstructing the large regional changes that influenced the political, social, and economic
history of the Anlo area during the late seventeenth, eighteenth, and early nineteenth centuries. Late nineteenth- and early twentieth-century unpublished descriptions of Anlo culture and society recorded by missionaries associated with the North
German Missionary Society and housed at the Norddeutsche Mission and the

---

[27] See Margaret Jean Hay, "Queens, Prostitutes and Peasants: Historical Perspectives on African Women,
1971–1986," *CJAS*, 22, 3 (1988), 436–37, for example, who discusses this problem with regard to precolonial
women's history.

Bremen Stadt Archives in Bremen, Germany, were especially useful in reconstructing the changes in Anlo social relations since the mid-nineteenth century; they also formed the base from which I worked backward in time to reconstruct the character of social relations prior to the Society's arrival in 1854. The archival sources I consulted in Ghana included documents written by Dutch travelers to the Gold Coast and upper Slave Coast in the seventeenth and eighteenth centuries that are part of the Furley Collection housed at the Balme Library at the University of Ghana, Legon, and various colonial government records about the Anlo area on deposit at the National Archives of Ghana in Accra and at its Volta Region branch office in Ho. The data contained therein supplemented the information I had obtained about the lower Gold Coast, the upper Slave Coast, and the Anlo area from European archival sources. I also utilized oral traditions collected by E. Y. Aduamah and held at the Institute of African Studies at Legon, several University of Ghana master's and bachelor of arts honors theses (which contain a wealth of recorded oral information about the Anlo area) as well as the records of traditional court proceedings held by the Anlo Traditional Council Office and the Grade II District Court in Anloga, Ghana. It was from these particular sources that I was able to determine how the Anlo themselves viewed and managed the social relations that German missionaries had described from their own vantage point.

Much of the material about Anlo gender and ethnic relations as it involved young women and ethnically marginalized individuals and groups came from oral traditions. For example, it was in interviews conducted in 1977 and 1978 with herbalist and diviner (*boko*) Togbui Seke Axovi and Like clan elder Togbui Awadzi, where I was informed that the Anlo did not always have clans and the attendant preference for clan endogamy that so impacted the lives of young Anlo women. Both are said to have developed after the Anlo settled in their present location in response to concerns about land. Information about the different ethnic boundaries within Anlo society also came from oral traditions recited to me by officials from a number of different clans. More importantly, the very topics on which this study is focused—changes in gender and ethnic relations—were those identified by my Anlo informants as critical for an understanding of the area's social history. In a 1988 interview with Mama Dzagba, the oldest female chief (*nyonufia*) in Anlo, it was she who first noted that the position of free women in Anlo had been profoundly influenced by the fact that free polygynous men had married slave women in the past.[28] Both Mama Dzagba and another female chief, Mama Ketor (in interviews conducted in 1978) also emphasized that women developed and/or supported separate institutions within Anlo society in order to protect their collective interests.[29] Ethnic identities and changes therein were similarly identified by male clan elders as an area of particular concern. In 1978, for example, I interviewed Togbui Ago Agbota and Togbui Ezu Agbota, elders of the Blu clan. They gave me an unexpected introduction into the heated issues that surround the question of how the Anlo have constructed and altered the we/they boundary that transects their society. In response to a question about the origins of their clan name, Blu, they stated in no uncertain terms:

---

[28] Field Note [hereafter FN] 82: Interview with Mama Dzagba, 27 January 1988, Anloga.

[29] FN 2: Interview with Mama Ketor, 12 June 1978, and FN 4: Interview with Mama Dzagba, 12 June 1978, Anloga.

We object to this name. It is meaningless. When we met with Togbui Adeladza II [the paramount chief of Anlo] this came up and *they* wanted to tell *us* the meaning *[emphasis in original]*. . . we must get together and choose the appropriate name [ourselves]. Blu is the name applied to those of Akan stock. . . . I think we were called this because our people came from the other side of the [Volta] river. Those people thought of us as the same as the Akans, and thus we were called Bluawo. We have never been ashamed to let people know where we have come from . . . [but] can we still be strangers after 100 years? What they wrote [in a festival brochure] is wrong and they wrote it without consulting us. . . . The way we are called strangers is offensive to us. [In addition, the name has, in the past] applied to [both] the Dzevi and Wifeme . . . [but now] these two say they don't belong to the Blu clan. . . . We have to find out about this.[30]

These informants and many others continually pointed out the fact that issues of gender and ethnicity were of historic concern to them; it is these same issues on which I focus in this study.

The vast majority of the interviews that I conducted in 1978 took place in the town of Anloga, the political and religious center of the Anlo polity; copies of which are on deposit at Northwestern University's Melville J. Herskovits Memorial Library. At that time, I was able to organize fifty-one sessions with nineteen different individuals and groups, the vast majority of whom were elderly men. My primary interest then was to record polity histories and clan traditions as part of the reconstruction of early Anlo history. Four of these original interviewees were women, and it was in these sessions that I was first introduced to the division of knowledge that characterized gender relations in Anlo. Males were much more informed about political and economic history as well as clan traditions; women were particularly knowledgeable about lineage histories (although the social injunction against discussing the origins of certain individuals and groups within the society limited the extent to which women were prepared to share in full this knowledge with non-Anlos like myself and other, especially younger, members of their lineages). In 1988, I conducted an additional sixty-three interviews with forty separate individuals and groups (the texts of which are available from the author) that took me and/or my research assistant to seven other towns and villages in Anlo besides Anloga as well as to the cities of Tema and Accra. Again, the vast majority of the interviewees were male elders. The few women whom I interviewed, however, provided particularly important insights about slavery and the Anlo inheritance system as these pertained to women within the lineage. This information helped me interpret the more detailed diaries and family histories written by individual Anlo during the late nineteenth and early twentieth centuries that are held in the national archives in Accra. It was also in these interviews that I recorded Anlo views about the history of various religious orders and the contemporary conflicts that exist around the issues of gender and ethnicity.

Another methodological tool that I use in this reconstruction of late seventeenth-, eighteenth-, and nineteenth-century Anlo social history comes from historical linguistics, a field that is also faced with the task of reconstructing the past from limited data. Historical linguists who attempt to reconstruct proto-languages

---

[30] FN 36: Interview with Togbui Ago Agbota and Togbui Kofi Ezu Agbota, 9 October 1978, Anloga.

(the parental ancestors of a number of related languages) approach their task by assuming that despite the differences that may currently exist among the related languages still in use, they nevertheless continue to share many characteristics in common because they developed from a single ancestral language. Those common linguistic elements are then used as a basis for reconstructing the proto-language before it diverged into separate languages and/or dialects. I use this same methodology, but apply it to culture. For example, I analyze nineteenth century and more contemporary accounts about the social culture of the Anlo and other Ewe-speaking peoples who are similar to the Anlo, linguistically and culturally. These accounts indicate that all share in common many social characteristics. They categorize the peoples that together compose their communities according to the length of time they were associated with a given area. They all practice patrilineal descent, give preference for intra-ward marriages, and subordinate women to men in most of their societal institutions. I then assume that these particular characteristics existed as part of the larger cultural package that all Ewe-speaking peoples retained after they diverged into their own distinct political and linguistic groups. I also assume that many of the differences that currently exist among these peoples can be explained as the result of the way in which each community responded to the particular historical events they experienced after their separation from the larger body of Ewe-speaking peoples. I argue, for example, that while almost all Ewe-speaking communities by the late nineteenth century preferred cross-cousin marriage and placed the greatest pressure on their young women rather than their young men to marry a particular individual, the Anlo were unique in preferring matrilateral rather than patrilateral cross-cousin marriages. This suggests that at one time Anlo families opted to change the way in which they managed their social relations by restricting even further the choice of individuals to whom they were prepared to betroth their daughters. In using this particular methodology, I establish the fact that changes did indeed occur in the social organization of the Anlo. The task remaining is to determine why the Anlo chose to manage their gender and ethnic relations as they did. This I do in the chapters that follow.

1

Transformations

It all began in 1679. In that year, an undetermined number of refugees flooded westward out of the lower Gold Coast in an effort to escape the advancing armies of the Akwamu state. Many traveled as far as the region that later became known as northwest Togo. Others sought and received permission to settle in Anlo, an area situated like their own former homelands on the Atlantic littoral but located just east of the Volta River. In this location they were close enough to their own homes to return if circumstances allowed, but distant enough, they thought, from the Akwamu empire to remain outside its imperial ambitions. For twenty-three years, these refugees and many others who were to follow remained safely on the margins of the political upheavals that were engulfing the lower Gold Coast. In 1702, however, Akwamu—in its ambition to dominate the trade between the coastal polities of Accra and Anecho—conquered Anlo as well. Akwamu citizens entered the area as administrators; they forcefully established themselves in the Anlo capital, Anloga, and then assumed the right to maintain order and to muster troops for additional military campaigns. Eleven years later yet another development engulfed the Anlo area. European traders involved in the Atlantic slave trade began to expand their operations on the Anlo littoral, bringing with them more opportunities for the Anlo to acquire wealth.

For those who had been resident in Anlo well before any of these developments took place, the presence of large numbers of refugees, direct exposure to the culture of the matrilineal Akwamu, and the opportunity to gain access to the wealth associated with the slave trade required and invited a response. The earlier resident families grouped themselves together into new social units known as *hlowo*, and then developed alternate ways of defining themselves socially in order to protect their rights to the limited arable resources in the area. Young women who had previously been allowed to express and have heard their opinions about whom they should marry found themselves—unlike the young men within these families—increasingly denied this right by their lineage elders. Married women and their children began to spend more time away from their husbands and fathers by taking extended visits to the homes of their brothers and uncles. By responding in this way to the many changes that were taking place on the lower Gold Coast and upper Slave Coast, the earlier residents of Anlo embarked upon a process that would result in major changes in gender and ethnic relations by the end of the nineteenth century.

20

That such changes did indeed take place is apparent from a comparative analysis of documentary accounts and more recent studies about Anlo social relations. According to contemporary anthropological accounts, Ewe-speaking communities currently located in southern Ghana and Togo, including the Anlo-Ewe, share in common a number of kinship and marriage practices. All practice patrilineal descent, where sons and daughters are considered to be primarily members of their father's and not their mother's kin-group.[1] All demonstrate a preference for lineage exogamy, in the form of cross-cousin marriage, and for intra-ward marriages, where the betrothed are residents of the same district within a particular village. Historical descriptions of Anlo and other Ewe-speaking marriage preferences indicate that these same kinship patterns and marriage preferences existed in the late nineteenth and early twentieth centuries. Westermann noted, for example, that:

> Descent from the father is the most important . . . for all Ewe tribes. . . . The Ewe does not eat the mother's brother's things, which means he does not inherit from the brother of his mother. They do this in contrast to other peoples where they have the mother's succession, for example, the Twi Asante. . . . [Among the Genyi Ewe of Togo] marrying a woman from one's own *kome* [that ward where members of one's own *to-fome* or patrilineage reside] is regarded as a good custom and the young man is thought to be arrogant or disloyal if he goes far away in order to find a wife . . . [this] is valid for the other Ewe. . . . The members of one *kome* are obliged to give their daughters primarily to men from their own *kome*.[2]

These same reports indicate that in the past, when the practice of parents arranging the marriage of their children was virtually universal, it was women who felt most constrained by this system. In the early 1960s, anthropologist G. K. Nukunya was informed by elderly residents of the area that among the Anlo,

> first marriages were arranged by parents without consultation with the young people. The young men, however, certainly managed to know that marriage negotiations on their behalf were under way, and there is no evidence that any *man* was ever forced into marriage against his will, though in some cases his own choice might have been vetoed by his parents. Older *women*, however, claimed that they were given little chance of studying the character of the partners chosen for them. Some of them even maintained that they were compelled to marry against their will—in some instances they wished to marry young men of their own choice, in others they disliked the young men chosen for them or rebelled at the thought of being a second or third wife. Willy nilly they were married.[3]

---

[1] The Ewe employ a number of terms to refer to this kin group: the northern Ewe refer to the patrilineage as *dzotinu*; the Anlo use the term *afedo*, or *fome*, a general appellation meaning family, to which they add the prefix *no-* or *to-* to distinguish the mother's lineage (*no-fome*) from the father's (*to-fome*); the Abutia- and Tongu-Ewe, who are situated to the north of the Anlo, but south of the area described as northern Eweland, use the term *agbanu*. See Dzigbodi Kodzo Fiawoo, "Ewe Lineage and Kinship Sub-Ethnic Group Variation," in Christine Oppong, ed., *Legon Family Research Papers, No. 1: Domestic Rights and Duties in Southern Ghana* (Legon, 1974); Nukunya, *Kinship and Marriage* ; and Michel Verdon, *The Abutia Ewe of West Africa: A Chiefdom that Never Was* (Berlin, 1983).

[2] D. Westermann, "Die Glidyi-Ewe in Togo," *Mitteilungen des Seminars für Orientalische Sprachen*, XXXVIII (1935), 133, 138, 139, 141, 264.

[3] Nukunya, *Kinship and Marriage*, 77; emphasis in original.

In the late 1870s, when the anthropologist A. B. Ellis traveled through the Anlo area, he also noted that "the marriage is arranged without, as a rule, any reference being made to [a girl's] wishes."[4] The German missionary, J. Spieth, who published an account of Ewe customs in 1906, indicates a similar disadvantaging of the young women in the marriage arrangements. He noted that it was not unusual for families with a betrothed daughter to have the girl "undergo an intensive indoctrination for the acceptance of the man chosen for her."[5] This emphasis on the extent to which the system of arranged marriages was viewed by women as more disadvantageous than men does not deny the fact that men, too, were often strongly encouraged to accept women they would not have chosen for themselves. Nevertheless, the social and economic structures of Anlo and Ewe society during the late nineteenth and early twentieth centuries provided more options for men. Ellis and Binetsch recognized this in the late nineteenth and early twentieth centuries when they noted the prevalence of polygyny. Although only chiefs might have more than four or five wives, women were expected to remain with their one husband.[6]

This description of kinship patterns, marriage preferences, and the significance of those preferences for young men and women emphasizes the commonality among the various Ewe polities in the late nineteenth and early twentieth centuries, but differences did exist. While most Ewe groups based their kinship system on the patrilineage, the Anlo had an additional kin-group called the *hlo* or clan. This unit was quite distinct from anything that existed outside Anlo in that it consisted of a number of dispersed patrilineages that retained their identity as kin groups. *Hlo* members also practiced clan endogamy; that is, they preferred to betroth their daughters to members of their own clan. Most Ewe groups preferred to give their daughters in marriage to a patrilineage that lived in their own residential ward. The Anlo preferred instead to give their daughters in marriage to a patrilineage residing outside their community if, other things being equal, that patrilineage shared the same clan affiliation. A third difference involved marriage preferences among cross-cousins. While most Ewe groups exhibited a preference for marrying cross-cousins without distinction (a practice known as *tasivinyruivisro*), the Anlo were distinctive in preferring marriages with matrilateral cross-cousins by a four-to-one margin.[7]

---

[4] Ellis, *Ewe-Speaking Peoples*, 199.

[5] Nukunya, *Kinship and Marriage*, 77–78.

[6] For a discussion of those situations in which men were strongly encouraged to marry a particular woman chosen by their families, despite their wishes, see Nukunya, *Kinship and Marriage*, 75–76; Binetsch, "Beantwortung mehrerer," 47; Ellis, "Ewe-Speaking Peoples," 204–205; see also Sonia G. Patten, "The Avuncular Family, Gender Asymmetry, and Patriline: The Anlo Ewe of Southeastern Ghana" (Ph.D. dissertation, University of Minnesota, 1990), 138; and Nukunya, *Kinship and Marriage*, 157.

[7] Nukunya, *Kinship and Marriage*, 72 In these two charts I have defined "ego" as the male cousin. All of the literature on marriage among the Anlo does the same, although it is significant that if "ego" was defined as the female cousin, it would completely alter the kinship terminology used here. With the male cousin as "ego," the appropriate term for the marital pattern is matrilateral cross-cousin (that is, the young man is marrying his mother's brother's daughter). I chose to follow the standard practice of defining "ego" as the male cousin not only because it is customary, but also because the male cousin is more likely than the female cousin to know the person to whom he is being betrothed. In addition, it is the female cousin's father (another male) who is most involved in working with his sister to arrange the marriage between his daughter and his sister's son.

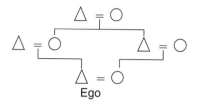

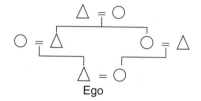

FIGURE 3: Matrilateral Cross-Cousin Marriage

FIGURE 4: Patrilateral Cross-Cousin Marriage

Since the Anlo share with other Ewe groups a common language, as well as many kinship and marriage practices, it is likely that all shared these common characteristics long before the late nineteenth century when they were first described by European observers. We may also assume that the development of the *hlo* as a distinct kinship group among the Anlo, and the development of different marriage preferences, represents a divergence from the pattern that once obtained among most Ewe groups. In this chapter, I argue that this divergence occurred during the eighteenth and nineteenth centuries, and that it represented a significant change in the way in which the Anlo handled gender and ethnic relations.

The chapter itself is divided into two sections. The first examines the historical origins of the Anlo clan system. I begin by discussing the political conditions on the lower Gold Coast and upper Slave Coast. Between 1679 and 1702, numerous refugees entered the Anlo area after fleeing war conditions that had enveloped their homelands to the west. I suggest that this influx of refugees placed considerable pressure on the arable resources in the area. In response to these events, the Anlo developed a clan system to distinguish the older residents (with their attendant political, economic, and social rights) as ethnic insiders and newer immigrant groups as ethnic outsiders. With the development of the clan system and its attendant alteration of ethnic relations also came changes in gender relations. After 1679, earlier resident families began to prefer marrying their children to fellow clan members. Most of the pressure to marry a particular individual, however, fell on the young women. This new system deprived women of the limited options that had been available to them through the lineage system to define the kin-group with whom they and their children would prefer to affiliate.

In the second section of this chapter, I document the emergence of additional changes in gender relations after 1750 which I associate with the cultural impact of the conquest of Anlo by the Akan state of Akwamu in 1702 and the increasing involvement of the Anlo in the Atlantic slave trade. Incorporation into this state system brought the patrilineal Anlo under the authority of the matrilineal Akwamu, exposing the Anlo to the matrilineal practice of sisters' sons working with and inheriting from their mothers' brothers. During this same period, the Anlo became increasingly involved in the Atlantic slave trade. As a result, social relations became much more competitive. Individual patrilineages sought to enhance their social position relative to others by retaining slaves (primarily female), incorporating them into their families, and then using them to generate the wealth needed for ostentatious social displays. Others, however, sought alternative ways of generating the wealth needed to enhance their own social standing. A popular alternative involved marrying the young women in one's family to their matrilateral cross-cousins. As a result, many young women found themselves strongly encouraged to marry one of their father's sister's sons. I conclude by noting that the emergence of clans and clan endogamy among the earlier resident families of Anlo after 1679 and the development of a preference for matrilateral cross-cousin marriage among all families resident in the polity after 1750 brought major changes in gender and ethnic relations in late eighteenth- and nineteenth-century Anlo. These developments occurred because of the competitive environment generated within the society by the influx of refugees between 1679 and 1702, by exposure to the Akwamu matrilineal system, and by the increase in wealth from the Atlantic slave trade. Those resident in Anlo responded as they did to these conditions because it was advantageous to their group interests, but in so doing they also created new categories that defined some groups as ethnic insiders and others as ethnic outsiders while also disadvantaging the young women in their patrilineages.

Clan Formation and Expansion in the Definition of We/They Relations

During the early seventeenth century, the major political and economic power in the lower Gold Coast and upper Slave Coast region was Accra, to the west. Included within its political boundaries was the immediate Accra area (the communities south of the Akuapem scarp, and the coastal towns of Senya Bereku and Ningo), the polity of Ladoku, the state of Akwamu in the Atewa Hills around the Pra, Birim, and Densu rivers and the Guan-speaking polity of Latebi in the Akuapem Hills.[8] Accra's economic power derived from its middleman position in the trade between the Europeans on the coast, who were offering manufactured goods for exchange, and the traders from the interior, who had gold, slaves, and ivory.[9] The success of this particular economic policy was greatly facilitated by the Akwamu, who were employed by the Accra to confine the inland traders to the Accra–Abonce market, located north of the state's capital, Great Accra. This limited the inland traders' access to the Europeans on the coast.[10] In the second decade of the seventeenth century, however, Akwamu began to undermine Accra's economic position

---

[8] For more information on the political history of the Ga state and its relationship to its dependent territories, see I. Quaye, "The Ga and Their Neighbors, 1600–1742" (Ph.D. dissertation, University of Ghana, Legon, 1972); a more complete description of Akwamu's location and early history can be found in I. Wilks, "The Rise of the Akwamu Empire, 1650–1710," *Transactions of the Historical Society of Ghana*, III, Pt. 2 (1957), and "Akwamu, 1650–1750: A Study of the Rise and Fall of West African Empire" (M.A. thesis, University of Wales, 1958); and R. A. Kea, "Trade, State Formation and Warfare on the Gold Coast, 1600–1826" (Ph.D. dissertation, University of London, 1974), 156–87. Note that Kea ("Trade," 170) and Wilks ("Rise of the Akwamu Empire," 101) associate Latebi with the present traditional area of Larteh; Barbot identified another polity east of Lay known as Soko—including the coastal communities of Angulan, Briberqu, Baya, and Aqualla—which was considered by some to be part of Ladoku. J. Barbot, *A Description of the Coasts of North and South Guinea* (London, 1732).

[9] Kea, "Trade," 171–72.

[10] Ibid., 168.

by assuming independent control over the flow of goods to the coast. They did so by requiring Accra to pay them to allow traders from the interior to pass through their territory in order to reach the Accra markets. In 1646, when Akwamu refused to open the roads between the interior polity of Latebi and Accra, and Accra responded by launching a military attack, the Akwamu retaliated by imposing a complete blockade on all paths to Accra they controlled. This turn of events is cited as the first period in Akwamu's expansion of its boundaries, as it effectively took control over the previously Accra-dominated interior polities of Latebi, Bunu, Equea, Akrade, and Kamana. By the 1670s, Akwamu had also brought into its sphere of influence the Agaves and Agonas, to the east and west of Accra, respectively. Seven years later, after having successfully retained control over former sections of the Accra state, Akwamu moved to extend its authority over all of Accra. In 1677, Akwamu successfully attacked and gained control of the Accra capital, Great Accra. In campaigns launched in 1678, 1679, 1682, 1688, and 1702, Akwamu consolidated its control in Ladoku by launching a series of retaliatory raids against the forces resistant to its domination of the district; they conquered the remaining Accra towns on the Atlantic coast, and then expanded the boundaries of their political authority even further by moving against and incorporating the Anlo in 1702.

The demographic impact of these expansionary wars was considerable. When the Ladoku province was attacked in 1679 and brought under Akwamu rule, many of the inhabitants in the subjugated area (which included the present traditional areas of Ada, Kpone, Osudoku, Ningo, Prampram or Gbugbla, and Shai) fled across the Volta and settled among the peoples on the upper Slave Coast and in the Krepi district.[11] The capital of the Anlo area, Anloga, is known to have received some of these Adangbe immigrants. From his knowledge of local traditions, the Ada lawyer, J. D. Amenyah noted in 1956 that in Anloga,

> [there] is a clan called Dzeviawo which is [a] branch of Adangmebiawe clan of Ada. They [the Dzevis] name their children [in] the same [manner] as the general Adangmes [in order to distinguish themselves] from the original Ewe element [with whom] they lived or settled. . . . *Dze* in Adangme means left or break-away, and *viawo* is an Ewe word which means children, but more correctly, peoples.[12]

Anlo traditions recorded in 1895 and 1911, and others collected between 1959 and 1978, confirm this. They note that Tay Tsrui, father of the founder of the Dzevi clan, Aduadui, came from Prampram, as did the clan god, Nyigbla, and the clan names.[13] In 1682 and again in 1688, when Akwamu initiated a second campaign

---

[11] Wilks, "Rise of the Akwamu Empire," 112.

[12] Amenyah Archives, Center for Research Libraries, Chicago, 31 June 1956, Letter from J. D. Amenyah to Ivor G. Wilks, Tamale.

[13] FN 21: Interview with Mr. T. S. A. Togobo, 31 August 1978, Anloga; J. Spieth, *Die Religion der Eweer in Süd Togo* (Leipzig, 1911), 50; and Carl Reindorf, *History of the Gold Coast and Asante* (Basel, 1895), 3. See also C. R. Gaba, "Sacrifice in Anlo Religion, Part 1," *Ghana Bulletin of Theology*, 3, 5 (1968), 18; Dzigbodi Kodzo Fiawoo, "The Influence of Contemporary Social Changes on the Magico-Religious Concepts and Organization of the Southern Ewe-speaking Peoples of Ghana," (Ph.D. dissertation, Edinburgh University, 1959), 56; Albert de Surgy, *La Pêche Traditionelle sur le Littoral Evhé et Mina* (Paris, 196– [sic]), 72n.2; C. R. Gaba, "Anlo Traditional Religion: A Study of the Anlo Traditional Believer's Conception of and Communion with the 'HOLY'" (Ph.D. dissertation, University of London, 1965), 83; and Nukunya, *Kinship and Marriage*, 198.

against Ladoku and Agave, many of the inhabitants who had opted to return home after the 1679 wars were forced to cross the Volta River again. Those who decided not to return to their original homeland probably joined the refugees who had settled in Anloga in 1681. A third Akwamu campaign against this same district occurred in 1702. This engagement, remembered among the Anlo as the Ako or Shai war, is associated with the events that brought the founder of the Wifeme clan, Amega Le, and his followers to Anloga.[14]

During this same period, the Anlo introduced the clan (*hlo*) as a new social organizational unit. Anlo traditions indicate that this grouping was formed by their founding ancestors after they settled in the early Anlo area. Elders interviewed in 1978 and 1988 indicated that they—who were old and infirm—were the ninth generation of those descended from the ancestors who had formed the clans, while the population between twenty-five and thirty years of age at that time was the tenth generation.[15] I interpret this to mean that there are at present ten generations separating those of childbearing age within the current population from the period when the clans were formed. Using a standard twenty-five to thirty years to represent one generation, this would place the period during which clan formation took place between the late 1670s and the early 1700s. These dates are consistent with other Anlo traditions, which place the beginning of clan formation after the first wave of refugees moved into the early Anlo area in 1679 (as documented by European accounts) but before the Ako war of 1702.

The events prompting the formation of this new social unit appear to have been closely connected to the demographic changes in the lower Volta area during the late seventeenth and early eighteenth centuries. The total land area of early Anlo was approximately ninety-four square miles; three-quarters of this consisted of swamps, creeks, and low-lying, salt-laden, clayey soils that could support little cultivation. The areas suitable for farming, less than twenty square miles, were placed under a system of shifting cultivation that yielded one crop per year. This method necessitated that each household have land in sufficient quantity to allow portions to be fallow, while the remainder provided the food requirements of the

---

[14] According to the Anlo traditions, Amega Le resided in many towns before coming to the Anlo capital with his followers, including Legon, Kpong, Kpone, and Lay (Lekponguno). After his arrival in Anloga, he and his followers established themselves in a section of the town which was later called Lashibi, because of his reputation as a wealthy person. This tradition indicates more specifically the origin of those associated with the Wifeme clan; for one can interpret the traditions as indicating the various communities from which they came: they included the Adangbe-speaking towns of Kpone, Lay, and Kpong, and the Ga-speaking town of Legon. The existence of a deserted settlement near Sakumo Fio lagoon, east of Teshi, known as Lashibi, suggests that the inhabitants of this town may have also been driven to Anloga in 1702 and that it was they who lent the name of their old town to their new residence. See Wilks, "Rise of the Akwamu Empire," 124–25; W. Bosman, *A New and Accurate Description of the Guinea Coast* (London, 1705), 330; R. A. Kea, "Ashanti–Danish Relations, 1780–1831" (M.A. thesis, University of Ghana, 1967), 18; Vestindiske-guineeske Kompagnie [hereafter VgK], Rigsarkiv, Copenhagen, 120, 3 February 1703, P. Werdrup, Whydah; VgK 121, 2 August 1705, Erich Lygaard, Knud Rost, Christiansborg; VgK 884, 25, 26, 28 February 1702, Christiansborg; VgK 884; 14, 25 March 1702, Christiansborg; VgK 884, 10 April 1702, Christiansborg. FN 8: Interview with Mr. T. S. A. Togobo, 3 August 1978, Anloga; FN 9: Interview with Mr. T. S. A. Togobo, 7 August 1978, Anloga; and FN 15: Interview with Togbui Le II, 15 August 1978, Anloga; see Anlo Traditional Council Minute Book, Anlo Traditional Council Archives, Anloga, No. 3, 119, 258, 287–88. R. G. S. Sprigge, "Eweland's Adangbe: An Enquiry into an Oral Tradition," *Transactions of the Historical Society of Ghana*, X (1969).

[15] FN 5: Interview with Mr. T. S. A. Togobo, 20 June 1978, Anloga.

household. In early Anlo, even these lands were subject to periodic flooding—a situation that often forced the Anlo to obtain food from the northern side of the lagoon. One such flood occurred in 1683, four years after the first wave of refugees moved into the area from the Ga and Adangbe districts of Accra and Ladoku. In addition, if one examines which clans are said to have received land as a right of prior residence in Anlo, and which ones acquired the same only in recognition of their having provided a service to the community, it is clear that land had become a coveted commodity at the time the clan system was developed. According to clan traditions, the ancestors of the Dzevi clan, who moved into the area after the 1679 Akwamu campaign against Ladoku, received land only for housing their god, Nyigbla, which subsequently became the national war god of the Anlo between 1769 and 1772. The land received consisted of a tract to the east of Anloga facing the Keta Lagoon, an area that could not support food crops given the cultivation methods of that time.[16] The ancestors of the Wifeme clan are said to have received lands from the Klevi, but were expected to share some of the proceeds of the harvest at a festival to which the members of the Klevi were especially invited.[17] Members of the Ame clan, who were captured between 1732 and 1740 in wars waged by the Anlo against the communities on the northern shore of the Keta Lagoon, were relocated from the Anyako area to lands in Anlo, but they were given those areas most subject to flooding because of their proximity to the Tale and Blolui ponds (situated in the depressions between the sandy ocean beach and the wider stretch of sand bordering the Keta Lagoon).[18] Because of the scarcity of arable land resources, the increase in population resulting from the undetermined number of refugees entering the area in three or four successive waves between 1679 and 1702, and the development of floods in 1683, the earlier residents of Anlo organized themselves into clans in order to guarantee for themselves and their future generations access to the land needed for their subsistence. That land was at the heart of the issue is indicated by the fact that the overwhelming concern of the clan system within Anlo by the late nineteenth century was the control and distribution of clan land for the benefit of clan members.

In creating the clan system, the earlier residents of Anlo not only developed a new social unit within their society, they also altered the community identity. Anlo oral traditions indicate that when the first Ewe-speaking immigrants entered Anlo, they encountered others already occupying the area. Numbering seven in all, this autochthonous population is said to have lived alongside the immigrants for some time. Later, however, they disappeared. In recognition that the autochthons had spiritual authority over the land on which the immigrants were now resident, several of the Ewe lineages deified the autochthons and took responsibility for their worship. As is often true with oral traditions, these accounts may or may not describe the events in precise historical detail. They are important, however, because they do indicate that the Anlo population at one time identified itself as a commu-

---

[16] FN 32: Interview with Togbui Sefoga, 30 September 1989, Anloga.

[17] FN 16: Interview with Togbui Le II, 16 August 1978, Anloga.

[18] D. A. Bates, "Geology," in J. B. Wills, ed., *Agriculture and Land Use in Ghana* (London, 1962), 76; FN 30: Interview with Mr. T. S. A. Togobo, 26 September 1978, Anloga; FN 45: Interview with Togbui Dzobi Adzinku, 8 November 1978, Anloga; and FN 53: Interview with Togbui Afatsao Awadzi, 16 December 1987, Anloga.

nity composed of two groups: one associated with a set of gods who had power
over the land, and another who had custody of those gods brought to Anlo by
immigrants from the town of Notsie in what is now southern Togo. The entrance
of additional immigrants into the area after 1679 challenged the prevailing conception of we/they relations in Anlo. Faced with the threat of having to compete for
the limited arable land resources in an area they had occupied for some time, the
earlier resident groups retained their identities as lineages affiliated with either
autochthonous or immigrant gods, but they elevated to much greater importance
the notion that they were nevertheless all descendants of the same set of related
ancestors and shared an association with a common ancestral home. As a group,
they stood as one, ethnically distinct from all others. Those who entered the area
after 1679 were denied access to land and socially stigmatized as "other." They
came late; they had different geograpical and genealogical origins; they were ethnic outsiders.

Clan Endogamy and the Women of Early Anlo

Clan formation also changed the ways in which earlier resident Anlo families managed the lives of their young. Studies of the lineage inheritance system employed
by the Anlo and other Ewe-speaking groups indicate that at one time all practiced
a form of patrilineal inheritance, where daughters received land from their mothers and fathers that they could pass to their own children, even though their children, by descent, were members of a different patrilineage. This is said to have
been the case in the 1960s and 1970s; it was also true in the early 1900s. Spieth
wrote of the Ewes in Ho that land could be inherited from both father and mother.[19]
In most cases, the brothers of a woman who received land from her patrilineage
would attempt to retrieve the land after her death or after the death of her children, so that the property was not lost to their patrilineage. Among the Anlo, however, the land given to a daughter would be left with her and her children to be
absorbed into the children's patrilineage. No mechanism existed within the Anlo
lineage system of inheritance to limit the transfer of property to a different
patrilineage, save through the diminution in the amount of land allocated to the
daughter.[20]

  This system of allowing land to pass out of the control of a particular lineage
would have been severely tested during the late seventeenth and early eighteenth
centuries, given the limited amount of arable land, the expansion in population
due to natural increase as well as the influx of refugees, and the marriages that
surely occurred between local women and some of the immigrants. With regard to
these latter unions, Anlo oral traditions indicate that when strangers first entered

---

[19] Cited in J. Dickson, "Martial Selection Among the Anlo Ewe of Ghana: From Parental to Individual
Choice" (Ph.D. dissertation, Duke University, 1982), 79–80.

[20] A. K. P. Kludze, "Family Property and Inheritance Among the Northern Ewe," 188-211; and T. Kumekpor,
"The Position of Maternal Relatives in the Kinship System of the Ewe," 213, both in Christine Oppong,
ed., *Legon Family Research Papers, No. 1: Domestic Rights and Duties in Southern Ghana* (Legon, 1974); Fiawoo,
"Ewe Lineage," 165; and G. Kwaku Nukunya, "Land Tenure, Inheritance and Social Structure Among the
Anlo," *Universitas*, 3, 1 (1973), 72, and *Kinship and Marriage*, 43–44, 46. Verdon (*The Abutia Ewe*, 125) and
Dickson ("Marital Selection," 81–82) note the existence of the separate system of homogeneous transmis-
sion as applied to personally acquired, less valuable property.

TAGBAMU or *KETA LAGOON*

Lashibi District		Agave District	
Aviame	Nyime	Nyaxoenu	Deti
Futu or Fudegbi	Atsite	Alagbati	

ATLANTIC OCEAN

FIGURE 5: Schematic Representation of the Districts and Wards of Anloga

the village of Anloga, the political and religious capital of the Anlo polity, they initially settled in the district called Lashibi, named after the numerous refugees from the Ladoku district who moved into the area after 1679. This ward was west of, but immediately adjacent to, the pre-existing districts of Deti, Alagbati, and Nyaxoenu. Over time, however, significant residential intermixing occurred; many strangers settled in the older areas, and the children of those who had established the earliest settled areas in the town moved into the more westerly districts of Lashibi as Anloga expanded in that direction.[21]

Reliable genealogical data about affinal ties between the various lineages of late seventeenth- and early eighteenth-century Anlo do not exist. Nevertheless, it is clear from family histories dating to the late eighteenth century and from traditions that discuss the particularly close relations that existed between specific stranger clans and earlier residents that it was not uncommon for relations between these two groups to be reinforced through marriage.[22] Their residential proximity to one another within the wards and the preference for intra-ward marriages facilitated such a development. The generation produced by these marriages would have been in a position to compete effectively for the limited resources in the area. The descendants of an immigrant male and a local woman, for example, would have had three avenues of access to land: they could inherit property from their fathers, who might have gained access to it because it was unclaimed land or because it had been given as a gift; they could inherit from their mothers; or like their fathers, they could claim land that had not been possessed by others. These were the same avenues open to the children of two local patrilineages.

Given the competitive pressures that must have been created by the geographical constraints of the area, and the nature of the inheritance system, which was not structured to maintain access to land within a particular patrilineage, the Anlo developed not only a clan system to protect their interests, but also a preference for clan endogamy as a means to deal with the competition over limited resources and the inadequacy of the lineage system in coping with the problem.

Unfortunately for young women in these earlier resident lineages, the development of the clan system and the preference for clan endogamy came at their expense. This is apparent if one contrasts the way the clan system governed social relations with the pattern that was probably typical within the early Anlo lineage system. As noted above, contemporary anthropologists who work among the Ewe

---

[21] FN 5: Interview with Mr. T. S. A. Togobo, 20 June 1978, Anloga.

[22] FN 16: Interview with Togbui Le II, 16 August 1978, Anloga; Special Collections [hereafter S.C.], Balme Library, University of Ghana, Legon, 14/2, pp. 125–27, 187; and S.C. 14/3, p. 272.

concur that all practice patrilineal descent where lineage affiliation is traced through the father. Sons and daughters of a man are considered to be members of their father's family, but only the children of a man's son are included within this same family. The daughter's children are associated with the lineage of their own father. Given this level of uniformity in the social organizational systems of the various Ewe groups, and the existence of many other common cultural features, it is likely that the Anlo and the other groups had a shared emphasis on patrilineal descent at a much earlier point in their histories. It is also likely that they handled residential affiliation in ways consistent with the pattern that obtained among other patrilineal societies. This residential affiliation system has been described by Goody and Goody, who note that

> patrilineal descent groups normally have a "simple" pattern of residence. Men usually live with their fathers (i.e., patrilocally) and women with their husbands (i.e., virilocally). The domestic unit thus contains a male core which persists over the generations, unless men go off to find new farm-lands in other parts. . . . [In such cases] women play primarily a wifely role, [although] they pay short visits to their natal kin. . . . husbands see themselves as having obtained the right to have their wives living with them (the right of bride removal) through the heavy bridewealth payments and farming services which they have rendered. They also see themselves as having acquired the same control over their children. . . .[23]

Contemporary descriptions of both the Anlo-Ewe and the Kouto-Ewe (Togo) suggest that these patrilineal societies adhere to the system described above. Nukunya notes that among the Anlo, marriage traditionally was virilocal and that even though a man might establish his own compound after his betrothal, he did so at a location chosen by his father. Most often this site was not far from the father's residence and the son was forbidden to begin building until the father had performed certain rituals. In addition, most sons began farming on land that had been part of their fathers' farms and the father retained the right to demand the son's labor for use on his own remaining lands at sowing, hoeing, and weeding times.[24] Kumekpor states that among the Kouto-Ewe of Togo, a woman and her children were welcome to return to and participate as members of their natal household, but only if the husband and the husband's family were unwilling or unable to care for them.[25]

Family histories that can be dated to the late 1700s and early 1800s indicate that a similar system operated among the Anlo during this period. Children were firmly associated by descent and residence with their father's family; only under specific conditions could children shift their affiliation to their maternal family. We see this most clearly in the case of Togbui Amenyah, chief (fia) of Atoko. According to C. Jacobson, a relative of Amenyah who began recording the family history in 1879, Amenyah's mother was from Anlo and his father was from the patrilineal Ada. When Amenyah's maternal family in the village of Atoko heard of the death of Amenyah's father, they requested that the boy return to their village. There,

[23] Esther N. Goody and Jack Goody, "The Circulation of Women and Children in Northern Ghana," in Esther N. Goody, ed., *Parenthood and Social Reproduction: Fostering and Occupational Roles in West Africa.* (London, 1982), 95–96.

[24] Nukunya, *Kinship and Marriage*, 39–40.

[25] T. Kumekpor, "Position of Maternal Relatives," 219–20, 224–25.

"Amenyah remained . . . till his full growth, [and] after the death of one of his uncles named Ashiagbor, he was established as captain or military leader [*awafia*] in place of the deceased." He retained this position as a maternal nephew until his death on 5 March 1878, even though many years earlier he had been eligible to assume the position of *matse* or military leader of Ada.[26] This suggests that the visits women made to their natal families served to reinforce their own ties to their families as well as those of their children, and that when difficulties arose, the children, though technically affiliated with their paternal family, could become full members of their maternal family.

The development of the clan system marked a significant departure from the pre-existing lineage structure in terms of the limited flexibility accorded women and their children after marriage. While the patrilineage system allowed mothers and their children to return to the mother's natal family if circumstances warranted, clan affiliation appears to have been more rigidly enforced. Children automatically became members of their father's clan and were taught by their mothers from an early age to take seriously the rights, responsibilities, and practices associated with clan membership. Failure to observe the food taboos and funerary customs of their particular *hlo*, for example, were said to bring illness and possibly death to the individual clan member. Individuals were also obligated to seek revenge for the death of a fellow clansperson by attacking the *hlo* of the murderer if that *hlo* refused to relinquish the perpetrator to the victim's clan. The requirements of clan solidarity enjoined one not to testify against another clan member in court unless the case involved manslaughter or murder. Clan members were also expected to handle their debts responsibly, because fellow clan members could be seized if such debts were not paid; if the clan member continued to act irresponsibly the clan could expel that person from the *hlo*. However, no one could become a member of one clan if he already belonged to another.[27]

These strict requirements governing intra- and inter-clan relations probably developed as a result of the conditions that gave rise to the clan system. The Anlo created the clan system to protect their landed rights; and at some point, they appear to have also developed a system of taboos, gods, and practices to reinforce member identification with the clan, so as to provide even better protection for the interests of this new social group. The emergence of clan endogamy served the same purpose. In order to minimize the loss of land to another clan, at an undetermined time after the 1670–1702 period of clan formation, the Anlo adopted the preference for marrying their daughters to men who shared the same clan affiliation as the woman's father. Thus, in his account of late nineteenth- and early twentieth-century Anlo society, Westermann noted that "marriage with a fellow *hlo* member . . . is regarded as particularly refined"; and more than a half-century later in the 1960s, anthropologist G. K. Nukunya observed that this same preference continued to exist.[28]

Although the early Anlo appear to have successfully used their clan system to defend their interests, this development brought with it a number of negative

---

[26] S.C. 14/1, p. 61; and S.C. 14/3, p. 337.

[27] Westermann, "Die Glidyi-Ewe," 142–45; FN 16: Interview with Togbui Le II, 16 August 1978, Anloga; Nukunya, *Kinship and Marriage*, 23.

[28] Westermann, "Die Glidyi-Ewe," 144; Nukunya, *Kinship and Marriage*, 74.

consequences. Westermann noted, for example, that if a clan refused to extradite a murderer to the clan of his victim, the obligation on the part of the murdered person's clan to seek revenge could result in decades of hostile relations, or *afewa*, home war, between the two clans. This was the case, according to Westermann, because at that time "the blood revenge [was] an inviolable right and duty."[29] Both women and men would have suffered in these circumstances, but women appear to have borne more of the burdens generated by this system. As noted, the Anlo defined clan membership solely and irrevocably on the basis of patrifiliation. This ensured those early lineages that had grouped themselves into a single clan gained access in perpetuity to certain lands claimed in the name of the clan. By eliminating the matrifilial option available in the lineage system, however, the Anlo clearly chose to protect the interests of the clan by limiting the role of women. As lineage members, women were able to take advantage of certain opportunities to encourage their children to affiliate with either their children's maternal or paternal relations. As clan members, they had no such power, and this power was assumed by the clan, who defined the children according to the clan of their father. In this way, a mother's clan affiliation was rendered irrelevant for her children; yet, in the context of marriage, her clan affiliation became far more important than that of her brothers. If a man was betrothed to a woman of a different clan, the land he inherited from his father would remain in the clan because those who could inherit from him included his own children and the children of his sister. But if a woman married a man of a different clan, her land could potentially be lost to the *hlo*, because her children belonged irrevocably to the clan of their father. Thus, the earlier resident families in Anlo chose to defend their rights to the arable resources in the area by increasing their control over the women in their families. In managing the marriages of their young women, families further restricted the group of men from which they would choose a daughter's husband by exercising a preference for clan endogamy.

By the middle of the eighteenth century, all Anlo women—whether affiliated with ethnic insider or outsider families—faced even greater restrictions on their marital affairs, as lineage elders shifted from a pattern of preference for cross-cousin marriages to one of preference for marriages to fathers' sisters' sons. The next section examines these developments by discussing the events that established the foundation for this change: the expansion of Akwamu cultural as well as political influence over the Anlo, and the expansion of the Atlantic slave trade to the upper Slave Coast.

Akwamu Domination, the Expansion of Trade Relations, and Changing Gender Relations in Eighteenth- and Nineteenth-Century Anlo

In 1702, the Akwamu launched a military campaign against the Ladoku district, but this time the Akwamu crossed the Volta River and extended their imperial control over Anlo. Anlo was then incorporated into Akwamu's Keta Province for

---

[29] Westermann, "Die Glidyi-Ewe," 144.

administrative purposes and remained a subordinate polity within the Akwamu empire until 1730. Very little information is available about the nature of Akwamu administration of the area beyond certain military and administrative matters. We know, for example, from traditions published by Westermann in 1935 and from those I collected in 1978, that the Akwamu mobilized troops from Anlo which they then used on occasion to assist their ally, Whydah, in its conflicts with Allada in 1705–1706. We also know that a number of Akan, perhaps Akwamu, settled in the area and were absorbed into existing lineages that subsequently gained a reputation for their military achievements.[30] Of concern here is the impact that the Akwamu as a matrilineal people had on the patrilineal Anlo. Given their role as administrators of the area, we can assume that the Akwamu also served as judicial mediators within the society. In such a position they would have had the opportunity to resolve disputes that could not be resolved by lineage elders and some of these disputes, no doubt, involved the issue of land inheritance.

As noted above, the Anlo and other Ewe groups recognized the inheritance claims of a maternal nephew, but only if that individual had worked, lived, and identified completely with his maternal uncle's family. During the period of Akwamu's occupation, inheritance claims by nephews considered specious by the Anlo because of their patrilineal orientation were probably taken far more seriously by the matrilineal Akwamu. That such an influence probably did occur is indicated by the existence of certain matrilineal features within the Anlo inheritance system. As Westermann noted of late nineteenth- and early twentieth-century Ewe societies:

> Some Ewe groups near the Volta River [specifically the Anlo] have adopted partly the inheritance by the son of the sister. . . . The law of succession of the sister's children includes that the testator in his lifetime has a right of supervision and disposal, that they work for him occasionally, that they have to take the blood revenge for him, and that they are responsible for his debts. [My Anlo informant testifies] that "when I die, my sister's children have to pay my debts in the first place, not my own children since they don't inherit my money. If I . . . get caught by a creditor, the children of my sister have to ransom me. I, too, am responsible for the debts of my sister and her children, and I, too, have to take blood revenge for them. On the other hand, I can, if I am in trouble, pawn or sell my sister's children, but not my own children since the clan of my wife would not agree with that."[31]

Barbara Ward sharpens this description by noting that only

> personal property (i.e., property acquired by a man's own efforts, such as land cleared by him from previously unclaimed bush as distinct from property rights acquired simply by virtue of his membership in a particular patrilineage) is transmitted through the maternal line, a man's heirs being his sister's sons.[32]

---

[30] Robin Law, *The Slave Coast of West Africa, 1550–1750* (New York, 1991), 250–51; Westermann, "Die Glidyi-Ewe," 148.

[31] Westermann, "Die Glidyi-Ewe," 264, 266.

[32] B. Ward, "An Example of 'Mixed' Systems of Descent and Inheritance," *Man*, 55, 2 (1955), 3. See also Binetsch, "Beantwortung mehrerer," 43.

Additional evidence to support the existence of matrilineal inheritance of acquired property exists in court cases from the early 1900s, and in Anlo oral traditions.[33]

According to Westermann, the practice of matrilineal inheritance of acquired (versus inherited) property and debts among the Anlo was due to the influence of the Akan (a group of which the Akwamu linguistically and culturally were a part). I would agree, given the fact that the matrilineal Akwamu exercised administrative control over Anlo between 1702 and 1730, and that as a dominating power they would have exposed the Anlo to their own culture. No other explanation can account for the existence of a system that so clearly departs from the pattern that obtained among the vast majority of other Ewe-speaking communities in Ghana and Togo during the late nineteenth and early twentieth centuries.

It is also likely that the Anlo maintained the matrilineal elements within their patrilineal system beyond the period of Akwamu domination because many within the population had come to benefit from them. This is apparent if one examines the way in which the patrilineal system of kinship and inheritance operated among the Anlo prior to their conquest by Akwamu in 1702. As noted above, the Anlo and other Ewe groups in the region practiced virilocal residence, in which women were expected to join their husbands after marriage. Visits by women to their natal kin took place, but were probably of limited duration, and the children came under the authority of their father, with whom they lived and from whom they inherited landed property. As a matrilineal society, the Akwamu system of residence and inheritance would have been substantially different. In such societies, women may have lived with their husbands (i.e., virilocally) or the men may have joined the woman's household (matrilocal residence), but in both cases, women were able to maintain much stronger relations with their families. For those women who continued to reside with their own families, this would have clearly been the case, but for those who lived virilocally, relations would have been maintained through culturally sanctioned, frequent visits to their natal households. Children of mothers who lived virilocally would also have spent considerable time with their maternal relations while infants, and would have eventually moved to reside and work with, and ultimately inherit from, their maternal relations. It is unclear whether the Akwamu in the late seventeenth century practiced virilocal or matrilocal residence, but in either case, the matrilineal character of their society would have provided women with the opportunity to sustain their roles as sisters, opportunities that were more limited for women in patrilineal Anlo society.

The adoption of certain aspects of the Akwamu matrilineal system would have had a significant impact on the position of women in their family. For example, if a man opted to claim the labor of his nephew, and, by so doing, he also agreed to have that nephew inherit the property he was able to acquire in his lifetime, his sister (the mother of his nephew) would have gained the opportunity to make more frequent visits with her children to her brother's household. That these hypothetical developments actually occurred among the Anlo is indicated by accounts writ-

---

[33] FN 61: Interview with Mr. Xovi Banini, 5 January 1988, Anloga; FN 70: Interview with Mr. Kwami Kpodo, 12 January 1988, Woe; Anlo Traditional Council Minute Book No. 3 (14/4/60–3/7/87), Chief Tsagli -v- Joachim Acolatse III, 122–23; Anlo Traditional Council Minute Book, 1931–1932, 877–927; and Anlo Traditional Council Minute Book, 1933–1935, 25–26, 86–87.

ten by Westermann and Binetsch. Westermann comments on the extent to which women spent time with their brothers:

> The mother's brother is called *nyrui* . . . the bond to the mother's family can be explained especially because the mother visits her relatives often and for long periods of time, so that sometimes the children spend just as much time living with the mother's brother as with the father. Therefore, the mother's brother is like a second father for the child.[34]

Binetsch notes that a young man's maternal uncle, whose acquired property the nephew would inherit, was as much involved in the life of that young man as was his father, from whom the son would inherit lineage and family property.

> [Among the Anlo, in particular] the uncle . . . wants his nephew . . . to work for him and support him. He [the boy] has to accompany his uncle on commercial trips and carry as much supplies and cowries for the road and merchandise as he can. In this way, he learns the trade himself. . . . The main thing is that the father *and the uncle* arrange for a bride. . . .[35]

Objections to these developments would have probably come most strenuously from the husband and his family, as they would have lost their predominant control over and access to the wife and children, a control that had been an integral part of the earlier system. That these objections did not prevent the Anlo from maintaining elements of the matrilineal Akwamu system after the collapse of Akwamu domination of the polity in 1730 had to do with the fact that the Anlo expanded and sustained their involvement in the regional trade in the area during this period and after.

According to mid-seventeenth-century travelers' accounts, the principal trade patterns on the lower Gold Coast and upper Slave Coast area included a north–south trade between the coast and the interior, as well as an east–west trade along the Atlantic littoral. It appears, however, that because of its geographical location Anlo was not in a position to participate in any substantial way in either of these exchange networks. At that time, the Anlo polity was limited to the southwestern margins of the Keta Lagoon. In this area, the inflow of fresh water from the Todzie River so diluted the saline content of the lagoon waters that it was virtually impossible to obtain sizable quantities of salt to be exchanged in the interior for the slaves and ivory in demand by the Europeans on the coast.[36] And although Anlo cattle are known to have been sold to Fante traders who then drove them westward to be sold in the Accra and Elmina areas, the major suppliers of livestock were the Adangbe living in the coastal savanna between Accra and the Volta River.[37] European establishments did not exist in the Anlo area at this time. Instead, ships would anchor off the coast to buy slaves and ivory, but because the supply was neither large nor regularly available, ship arrivals were infrequent at best.[38] Thus, because

---

[34] Westermann, "Die Glidyi-Ewe," 141.

[35] Binetsch, "Beantwortung mehrerer," 43; emphasis added.

[36] FN 61: Interview with Mr. Xovi Banini, 5 January 1988, Anloga.

[37] Barbot, *A Description*, 319, 223, 186; and Het Archieven van der Nedelandsche Bezittingen ter Kuste van Guinea, [hereafter ANBKG], Algemeen Rijkarchief, The Hague, 147: Accra Correspondence, J. van der Peuye to P. Woortman, 13 May 1778, Accra.

[38] Bosman, *New and Accurate Description*, 330, 331.

of the limited opportunities to produce salt, the small market for their cattle, and the lack of access to European traders from whom they could obtain manufactured goods, much of the north–south and east–west trade conducted by the Anlo during this period was primarily a use-value exchange involving the sale of locally produced surplus fish for those commodities not produced in Anlo society, such as yams and the red ochre used in religious ceremonies.[39]

This situation began to change during the second decade of the eighteenth century as a result of a number of conflicts that developed between the inland state of Asante and its southern neighbors. In 1712 and 1718, Asante came into conflict with Akyem. According to historian J. K. Fynn, these difficulties arose because

> the Akyem undertook certain actions which . . . [provoked] Asante. First, the Akyem decided to offer political asylum to the king of Denkyera [who had broken his ties of dependence to Asante]. . . . Secondly, the Akyem declared their support for and schemed to restore to his people, the chief of Twifo, Commomore [whose state lay to the south of Asante and west of Akyem, and] who had been deposed by the Asante. Thirdly, the Akyem promised to go to the aid of the peoples of Cabes Terra [located north of the Fante Kormantin coast] in whose country the Twifohene had sought refuge.[40]

The reasons behind Akyem's actions are unclear, but war with Asante ensued in 1717. Numerous difficulties had also arisen between Asante and Wassa, Aowin, and the Akanny peoples over Asante's political relationship with the latter polities and its access to the ports on the Fante coast. By 1729, Wassa, under the leadership of Ntsiful, formed an alliance with the coastal Fante and those polities that had come into conflict with Asante—i.e., Assin, Aowin, Twifo, and Akyem—to resist the expansion of Asante political and economic interests. To this end, they established an economic embargo from Cape Appollonia to the Volta River to prevent Asante traders from buying firearms and ammunition from the Europeans, or salt from the local manufacturers, the vast majority of whom were based in the Accra and Adangbe towns of Accra, Labadi, Teshie, Osu, and Nungwa. The alliance continued with intermittent breaks and realignments through the 1770s.[41]

These developments brought a number of changes to the Anlo area. First, that section of the coast on which Anlo was situated began to attract the attention of the Europeans, because the trade in slaves had begun to decline at their more established posts. The Dutch, who had expressed an initial interest in acquiring slaves from the lower Volta area in 1710, finally acted in 1713 (one year after the Asante–

---

[39] FN 35: Interview with Boko Seke Axovi, 4 October 1978, Anloga; FN 45: Interview with Togbui Dzobi Adzinku, 8 November 1978, Anloga; and FN 50: Interview with Boko Seke Axovi, 12 March 1979, Anloga. L. F. Rømer, *Tilforladelig Efterretning om Kysten Guinea* (Copenhagen, 1760), 286.

[40] J. K. Fynn, *Asante and Its Neighbors, 1700–1807* (London, 1971), 45.

[41] For more information on the political situation, see Fynn, *Asante*, 41–48, 61, 63–66; L. Yarak, "Political Consolidation and Fragmentation in a Southern Akan Polity: Wassa and the Origin of Wassa Amenfi and Fiase, 1700–1840," unpublished paper, 1976, 17–30; S. Tenkorang, "The Importance of Firearms in the Struggle Between Ashanti and the Coastal States, 1708–1807," *THSG*, IX (1968), 5–6, and R. A. Kea, "The Salt Industries of the Gold Coast, 1650–1800," unpublished paper (Institute of African Studies, University of Ghana, 1966), 5. For details, see Greene, "The Anlo-Ewe," 123–48.

Akyem conflict erupted) by sending the ship *Bosbeek* to Keta, "with merchandise to buy there as many slaves as possible." In the following year, the English did the same. In 1716, the Danes posted an assistant clerk and a constable at Kpone and Keta, respectively. Both were recalled in the same year because of the threats of war in the area, but in 1717, two men were again sent to these places. On 8 April 1717, the English began making plans to settle one of their men in Keta. In March 1718, the Danes—chronically short of personnel—nevertheless posted two of their men and several company slaves at Keta, primarily to impede Dutch initiatives. Three years later in 1721, the French proposed to do the same, and by 1727, both the Dutch and the English were established in Aflao, about twenty miles east of Keta. This trend continued throughout the rest of the century, during which time the various European groups not only sought to retain a presence in the area, but also engaged one another militarily in efforts to support their respective claims to trade exclusively in the area.[42] All this activity culminated in the establishment of a fort in Keta by the Danes in 1784.

A second change involved Anlo's trade relations with the interior. As noted above, Wassa, Akyem, and their allies imposed an embargo on Asante that included not only firearms and ammunition, but also salt. As Asante and others in the interior found it increasingly difficult to obtain this commodity from Accra, which had been the largest supplier of salt to the interior Gold Coast polities since at least the mid-1600s, they shifted their demand to the towns on the lower Gold Coast and upper Slave Coast. As indicated, the Anlo were unable to produce much salt from the Keta Lagoon because their location placed them too close to the fresh water rivers that emptied into that body of water, but their Keta neighbors who were located on the more saline sections of the Keta Lagoon responded to this new demand. The Anlo purchased much of this salt and then transported it into the interior along with their fish and European manufactures, which they then exchanged for slaves and ivory. Much of this traffic followed the established routes that had existed on the Volta River since at least the early 1600s, but by 1750 the Anlo had begun to develop more extensive contacts with the Krepi district. In that year, the Danes reported that the Agotime cabuseer (political leader), Keteku (or Kettecu)

> sent a message to Tette Cru [a prominent trader in Anloga] and Alovi [in Keta] that he [would] be coming in another month to have a palaver and also eat fetish with Angora [Anloga] and Quitta [Keta], so that the Agotime negroes [would] have free roads to bring their slaves to Quitta. . . . He will bring their slaves to Quitta. . . . He will bring more than 30 slaves

[42] A. Van Dantzig, *The Dutch and the Guinea Coast* (Accra, 1978), 173, Doc. No. 202: West Indian Company [hereafter WIC] 101, 7 November 1713; Treasury Papers, African Companies [hereafter T70/-], Public Records Office, Kew, 6, Abstracts from Africa, 10 May 1715, Cape Coast; 3 November 1714, Whydah, Messrs. Joseph Blaney and Martin Hardrett; 20 November 1716, Whydah; Furley Collection, Balme Library, University of Ghana, Legon, N40, 24 December 1716, Letter from Accra (Snork) received 1 January 1717. See also Van Dantzig, *The Dutch*, 187–88, Docs. No. 220, 228, 211, 234, 230, 237, and 238; Georg Nørregård, *Danish Settlements in West Africa, 1658-1850* (Boston, 1966), 95; Public Records Office, Phipps Papers c. 113/276), Outforts correspondence, 8 April 1717, William Baille, Whydah to James Phipps, Cape Coast. VgK 121, 15 June 1719, Knud Rost, Christiansborg; Nørregård, *Danish Settlements*, 95; D. K. Fage, "A New Check List of the Forts and Castles of Ghana . . .,"*THSG*, 1, 1 (1959), 65. Archives des Colonies, Archives National, Paris,: Series B, No. 44, Folio 48. VgK 122, 10 September 1727, A. Wellemsen, R. N. Kamp, N. Haugaard, Christiansborg. See Greene, "The Anlo-Ewe," Chapter 3, Section iii for a discussion of the Dutch–Danish war.

with him in addition to teeth [i.e., ivory]. . . . [Traders] from more than four to five negro towns are coming with him [as well].[43]

These routes and others established after Anlo gained its independence from Akwamu in 1730 and from Anexo in 1750 (after eight years of Anexo rule) remained open throughout the rest of the eighteenth century and much of the nineteenth century.[44]

It was during this period of expanded trade relations with the Europeans and the polities in the interior that Anlo not only increased its export of slaves to the Europeans, but also began to retain significant numbers of slaves within the community. Anlo traditions indicate, for example, that the Anlo tended to export their male and older female slaves, but that the younger women and children, particularly female children, were often retained.[45] This same pattern was discovered by Green-Pederson in his examination of Danish slave export records. According to these records, the male slaves, both adult and child, sold to the Danes and transported in Danish ships between 1778 and 1789, outnumbered female slaves by almost a two-to-one margin at a time when the Anlo town of Keta constituted the third largest exporter of slaves to the Danes on the Gold Coast and upper Slave Coast.[46]

The benefits that accrued to the Anlo from owning slave women were many. As laborers, they contributed to the production of the smoked, dried, and salted fish that was combined with European manufactures and sent into the interior to be exchanged for additional slaves and ivory. They served as carriers in such expeditions, and if they were married to male slaves, their offspring (known as *dzidome*, those who were born in-between) became the property of their master and could continue to contribute to this work as well, or they could be pawned or sold.[47] If a male owner chose to marry a slave woman, he benefited by gaining the kind of control over this particular wife and her children that was not available to him from his marriage to a free wife. Having no relations who could defend her interests, the husband and his family could do with his wife and children as they chose.[48] Women slave owners gained similar advantages, but these two groups were not the only ones to benefit from the Anlo incorporation of slaves, particularly female slaves, into their society. Wives benefited as well

---

[43] VgK 888, 30 November 1750, Ada, J. Sønne.

[44] See R. A. Kea, "Akwamu-Anlo Relations, c. 1750–1813," THSG, X (1969), 57–58.

[45] FN 70: Interview with Mr. Kwami Kpodo, 12 January 1988, Woe; and FN 76: Interview with Togbui Anthonio Gbodzo II and his councilors, 20 January 1988, Woe.

[46] Sv. E. Green-Pederson, "The Scope and Structure of the Danish Negro Slave Trade," *Scandinavian Economic History Review*, 19, 2 (1971), 186–87, 191.

[47] Westermann, "Die Glidyi-Ewe, "125.

[48] Scholars who have studied the impact of the slave trade on African societies indicate that one of the consequences for social relations within these societies was the growth of polygyny. As the number of women within African societies increased, it became more common for men to have more than one wife. See Claire C. Robertson and Martin A. Klein, "Introduction: Women's Importance in African Slave Systems," 6, Herbert S. Klein, "African Women in the Atlantic Slave Trade," and Carol MacCormack, "Slaves, Slave Owners, and Slave Dealers: Sherbro Coast and Hinterland," all in Claire C. Robertson and Martin A. Klein, eds., *Women and Slavery in Africa* (Madison, 1983). This appears to have been the case in Anlo as well, where many participated in a significant way in both the trade in slaves destined for the Americas as well as for domestic use, from 1716 to the early 1900s. In interviews conducted in 1978, many women over forty years of age recalled their grandmothers had been one of four, six, or even twelve wives. See Patten, "Avuncular Family," 137–38.

when their husbands took slave women as spouses. In Anlo, where a woman's position within the family after her marriage was defined most often as spouse, and where the husband claimed predominant rights to her labor and her children, the addition of a slave wife to the household served to loosen the grip of the husband and his family over the free wife. Slave wives contributed to the productive and reproductive interests of the family and, according to Anlo traditions, they often did so with greater enthusiasm than a free wife and her children because of the precarious situation in which they found themselves. Pleasing their master/husband/father constituted one of the limited means by which a slave wife and her children, bereft of the protective blanket of kin relations, could manipulate for their own benefit the social relations that existed between themselves and their owner.[49] In such a situation, it became less necessary for Anlo men to limit the number and duration of a free wife's visits to her natal kin. Free Anlo married women could begin to take advantage of the right to visit their brothers with their children for extended periods of time, a right that may have been introduced by the Akwamu between 1702 and 1730, but which the Anlo subsequently incorporated into their own kinship and inheritance structures. The Anlo maintained this quasi-matrilocal residential pattern and did so because women and their brothers supported this as a way to reinforce their own ties of support and responsibility to one another, while men in their roles as husbands were little affected because of the prevalence of polygyny involving slave women. Over time, however, the limited advantage that the incorporation of slave women as wives brought to free Anlo women eroded, as family elders used this newly adopted system to gain advantage in the inter-lineage competition for wealth and prestige that came with greater involvement in the Atlantic slave trade after 1750.

Intra-Family Relations and the Rise of Matrilateral Cross-Cousin Marriages

Scholars who have studied the impact of expanding trade relations on the social structure of precolonial African societies emphasize the extent to which involvement in this trade required considerable capital, yet access to capital was not available to all.[50] One of the consequences of this differential in access was that inequalities within such communities became accentuated. Certain households benefited economically more than others. These same households used their profits to accumulate wives, slaves, and other dependents, which put them in a position to dominate their communities numerically and economically. This, in turn, led the residents of such communities to place greater emphasis on social distinctions between the wealthy and the not-so-wealthy, between slave and free.[51] An examination of those Anlo towns most intimately involved in the trade after the second decade of the eighteenth century indicates that this was the case in those communities as

---

[49] An additional tactic used by slaves to gain some benefits for themselves was to join religious groups within the society, some of which were composed almost exclusively of slaves and slave descendants. See FN 54: Interview with Togbui Afatsao Awadzi, 16 December 1987, Anloga, and FN 55: Interview with Togbui Kosi Axovi, 17 December 1987, Anloga.

[50] See for example A. G. Hopkins, *An Economic History of West Africa* (London, 1973), 125–26, and Afonja, "Changing Patterns," 204.

[51] Hopkins, *Economic History*, 108.

well.[52] Very few studies, however, indicate the fact that this growing differentiation established a new social dynamic within precolonial Africa. As those with substantial means emphasized their status through various displays of wealth in people and material goods, those of lesser means also worked to achieve this same status through the more limited avenues available to them. This is, perhaps, most apparent among the Anlo in terms of how families handled the public aspects of those ceremonies associated with birth, marriage, and death.

In his account of the rites and ceremonies associated with the birth of a child, Binetsch noted that the first duty of a mother after giving birth was to consult with a priest to determine the identity of the child: was it one of those who dies and returns only to die again, or was it the reincarnation of an ancestor? If it were the latter, the child would probably live, but sacrifices had to be offered to insure that the ancestor's spirit would remain with the baby. It was also necessary to secure beads around the wrists and ankles of the infant; these served as protective charms but also as decoration. Only after these ceremonies had been performed would the father name the child, an event that took place during a general celebration of the child's birth. It was at this occasion that every effort was made by the family to emphasize their social standing within the community. They did so by providing as much food, drink, and entertainment for the guests as their means would allow. The beads used for decorating the child would also be the most beautiful and expensive that the maternal and paternal family had in their possession.[53]

A similar public display of wealth accompanied both marriages and funerals, but funerals appear to have generated the most competition among families, as all families attempted to use the occasion to demonstrate and enhance their social standing within the community. The earliest accounts about these ceremonies come from mid-nineteenth-century European reports, but it is probable that both the ceremonies and the difficulties suffered by those with lesser means became an integral part of Anlo social life as early as 1750, when Anlo trade relations expanded considerably and when the traditions indicate that Anlo saw its first wealthy families. This upsurge in trade brought considerable wealth to some, and it is likely that it was during this period that they began to use their wealth to stage elaborate funerals. Accounts indicate, for example, that when a wealthy man died, his family would mark the occasion by hosting two celebrations. The first would begin immediately after the burial, and would continue for the number of days that the clan of the deceased stipulated must elapse between the time of the burial and the date of the funeral. This celebration could last from three to eight days. The second celebration took place after the funeral during which final words were offered to the spirit of the deceased. At both occasions food and drink would have to be offered to the large number of guests who had come to mourn with the family, and a band would

---

[52] See FN 58: Interview with Mr. William Tiodo Anum Adzololo, 23 December 1987, Anloga; FN 70: Interview with Mr. Kwami Kpodo, 12 January 1988, Woe; FN 73: Interview with Mr. Johnnie Victor Kwame Adzololo, 14 January 1988, Keta; FN 76: Interview with Togbui Anthonio Gbodzo II and his councilors, 20 January 1988, Woe; FN 96: Interview with Togbui Amegashi Afeku IV, 24 February 1988, Woe; and FN 100: Interview with Togbui Awusu II, 29 March 1988, Atoko, in which the history of Woe and Atoko are discussed along with the families who dominated the trade in these two towns.

[53] Binetsch, "Beantwortung mehrerer," 42. See Maxine Kumekpor, "Some Sociological Aspects of Beads with Special Reference to Selected Beads Found in Eweland," *Ghana Journal of Sociology*, 6,2/7,1 (1970/71), for a discussion on the use of beads among the Ewe of Ghana and Togo.

be hired to entertain the guests for the entire period of the two celebrations. Those of lesser means are said to have confined their celebration to the day of the funeral because of their more limited resources,[54] but many were still prepared to go into debt in order to stage an elaborate ceremony. For example, in 1855 the German missionary F. Plessing noted that

> The funerals of the negroes are usually very expensive and often one or two members of the family have to give up their freedom [for a nice celebration]. . . .This kind of slavehood, called constraint, can be explained as follows: a rich man gives 30, 40 or 100 heads of cowries to the family depending on their desire for a splendid ceremony; in return, the family offers one, two, three and often even more children who are pledges [to the rich man in return for the money]. . . . The family . . . promises to redeem the debts, but that rarely or never happens. . . .[55]

It was this same kind of competitiveness, I would suggest, that led the Anlo to express a widespread preference for matrilateral cross-cousin marriage. In this case, however, the issue around which the competitiveness was focused did not involve material goods or monetary assets; rather it had to do with the practice of measuring one's wealth in people. Many Anlo engaged in polygyny when the opportunity presented itself because of the value placed on having a large household: slaves were retained by those involved in the slave trade so as to increase both the size and the productive capacity of their families. If an individual were successful in capturing prisoners during a war, he might sell some, but many, especially women and children, would be incorporated into his household. The opportunities to develop particularly large households were limited, however. Only those who were able to obtain the capital and then engage successfully in trade had the resources needed to acquire a large number of wives, retain significant numbers of slaves, and, during times of war, field a large number of males from the household who could then capture additional slaves to be sold or absorbed into the family. Those who had no such opportunities had to rely on the more limited resources available to them. Among those resources was the control that a family exercised over the marriage and residential affiliation of their young.

When the Anlo were conquered by the Akwamu, they practiced patrilineal descent; a married woman and her children resided primarily with her husband and his family, although they probably visited the mother's natal home on occasion for short periods of time. Akwamu conquest introduced into the Anlo inheritance system the matrilineally-derived practice of nephews inheriting the acquired property of their maternal uncle. The Anlo continued to transmit property according to this new pattern because the upsurge in trade relations with the Europeans, during the period of Akwamu domination and after, brought significant numbers of slave women into Anlo society. The presence of these women as wives in the household lessened the need for the husband to insist on having a free wife spend the vast majority of her time in his household; accordingly, free women began to spend considerable amounts of time with their natal kin, very often with a brother. The brother welcomed these visits because he gained access to the labor of his

---

[54] Binetsch, "Beantwortung mehrerer," 50.

[55] Friedrich Plessing, "Briefe aus Keta," *Monatsblatt der Norddeutschen Missionsgesellschaft*, 5/57 (1855), 248.

nephews, who could work for him and with his own slave children, which could provide him with the revenue to expand the size of his household even further. When certain families within the community began to accumulate more wealth in people than others, however, those with more limited resources may have been impelled to enhance their own position by taking better advantage of that which was available to them. One way they could accomplish this was by exercising greater control over their daughters. If, for example, a man betrothed his daughter to his sister's son, that man could not only demand access to his nephew's labor because he was obligated to bequeath to him his acquired property, this man (or his patrilineage) would have also had the right to claim the labor of those children produced by his daughter and his maternal nephew, since these grandchildren inherited the acquired property of their mother's brother. Again, this labor could be combined with that provided by the children of a slave wife to generate the surplus necessary to expand the household even further. (See Figure 6 below.) [56]

Evidence that this was precisely the way the Anlo preferred to manage their daughters' marriages comes from the statistical data recorded by Nukunya in 1969 on the marriage preferences of contemporary Anlo. These statistics indicate that unlike other Ewe groups in Ghana and Togo, the Anlo demonstrate a particularly strong preference for matrilateral cross-cousin marriage. At that time, 71 percent of all first marriages were *fomesro* (marriages within the matrilineage or patrilineage), 89 percent were cross-cousin marriages, and 80 percent of those were matrilateral cross-cousin marriages. That is, some 50 percent of all marriages involved matrilateral cross-cousins. This is considered to be a very high statistical average, comparable to that found in societies that have prescriptive systems supporting such marriage patterns. The fact that the Anlo have opted to pursue such marriages in the absence of such prescriptions, would suggest, as noted by C. Levi-Strauss and J. Dickson, that "far from being the outcome of unconscious processes, [it] appears to [be] . . . the legacy of an age-old wisdom . . . the cumulative result of numerous individual cases of marital selection."[57] To date no one has been able to explain adequately this Anlo preference for matrilateral cross-cousin marriage. I suggest here that this preference emerged after 1750 when trade relations expanded considerably in the area, and when Anlo traditions indicate that these developments led to the emergence of the first wealthy members in the society. In response to this growing socio-economic differentiation, individual families who had limited access to resources but wished to improve their position within the community began to expand upon the matrilateral relationships they had developed under the influence of the Akwamu. They did so by supplementing the existing preferences for endogamous ward and clan marriage, with the added preference for matrilateral rather than patrilateral cross-cousin marriage. This served both to reinforce the relations already established between one patrilineage and another; it also expanded the pool of labor available to the wife-giving patrilineage. In doing so, however, families also began to increase the pressure they placed on their young women to accept arranged marriages.

---

[56] Based on a chart found in Dickson, "Marital Selection," 124; among contemporary Anlos, first-cousin marriages are less common, as it is currently believed that intra-family marriages should take place between more distantly related relations. This was not the case in the past, however. Nukunya indicates that first-cousin marriages used to be quite common. See Nukunya, *Kinship and Marriage*, 73.

[57] Dickson, "Marital Selection," 116, 117–18, 121–22.

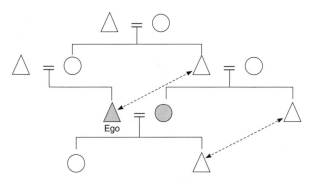

FIGURE 6: Matrilateral Cross-Cousin Marriage and Matrilateral Distribution of Labor and Acquired Property

In arguing that families began to exert greater pressure on their young women after 1750, I am suggesting that prior to this period, families were more open with their young, revealing to them at an early point the identity of the persons they were considering as potential spouses, and that parents were also more open to hearing a young woman's reaction to that choice. Evidence to support this comes from testimony from older Anlo women interviewed in 1962. Many objected strenuously, not to their parents arranging their marriages, but rather to the fact that they were denied participation in the proceedings. They also noted that some women "persisted in refusing to live with the husband chosen for them and succeeded in forcing their parents to relent."[58] I am arguing here that the ability of young women (whether as members of ethnic insider or outsider families) to engage their parents in a dialogue about their betrothal, where they could express opposition to a particular arrangement, was probably much more common when social pressures on the family were fewer.

A Note on the Role of Mothers, Aunts, and Sisters in the Anlo Marital System

Many studies on women in precolonial Africa emphasize the fact that females as a group did not constitute a homogeneous body within their own societies. Distinctions existed among women based on their status as free or slave, as individuals associated with royal or non-royal families, and as persons who were advantaged or disadvantaged based on their marital status, age, or specialized roles. These same studies also emphasize that those women who were in stronger economic, political, or religious positions often sustained their status by actively subordinating, for their own benefit, the interests of other women who were under their authority.[59]

---

[58] Nukunya, *Kinship and Marriage*, 77.

[59] See for example, the articles in Part IV: "Women as Slave Owners, Users and Traders," in Robertson and Klein, eds., *Women and Slavery in Africa*; Caroline Bledsoe, "The Political Use of Sande Ideology and Symbolism," *American Anthropologist*, 11 (1984); Eileen Jensen Krige, "Women-Marriage, with Special Reference to the Lovedu: Its Significance for the Definition of Marriage," *Africa*, 44 (1974); and Ifi Amadiume, *Male Daughters, Female Husbands: Gender and Sex in an African Society* (London, 1987).

This was true in precolonial Anlo. An examination of the roles played by older women within the family indicates their actions were governed not only by the desire for personal gain, however, but also by their responsiveness to the socially constructed emphasis on supporting the interests of their clan and patrilineage, and their personal desire to protect their own interests and the interests of their children. In discussing the development of clan patrifiliation and clan endogamy among the Anlo-Ewe, I noted, for example, that this process clearly favored the interests of the family at the expense of its female members. Evidence suggests that the male head of the household was not the only person involved in facilitating this process. Women supported this, in particular, by encouraging their children, especially their female children, to acquiesce to the limitations imposed on them by the various preferences that came to govern Anlo marital relations. In his discussion of mother-child relations among the late nineteenth- and early twentieth-century Anlo, Binetsch noted that "the education of a girl is mainly her mother's duty"; Spieth noted similarly:

> It is the mother who teaches . . . the first pagan songs and chants to her children and teaches them the first dancing steps. . . . it is the mother, as well, who introduces the child to the [clan] customs [of the father]. . . . it is the father who continues this kind of education from the seventh or eighth year onward as far as the sons are concerned, [but] the daughter stays with the mother and remains thus throughout her older years entirely under the influence of the mother.[60]

Included as part of this education was an emphasis on the desirability of marrying someone within one's own clan. Westermann noted, for example, that children whose mothers and fathers belonged to the same clan expressed great pride in that fact.[61]

A similar situation appears to have provided the foundation for the Anlo preference for matrilateral cross-cousin marriages. In this instance, if a family chose to give greater preference to these unions for a daughter in order to gain access to the labor of her children who would have technically been members of a different patrilineage, they could accomplish this only with the active intervention of the older married women in the family. Mothers and aunts were in a particularly strong position to influence marriages between their own sons and their paternal nieces. Again, we have no data from the eighteenth century that would indicate that in fact this was the role married women played in supporting the interests of their brothers and their common patrilineage, but more recent accounts suggest that this was probably the case given the relationships that existed between mothers and sons, aunts and paternal nieces and nephews, and between sisters and brothers. In 1889, for example, Spieth noted that

> both daughter and son have unlimited faith in the old mother. When the daughter leaves her parent's home in order to live with her husband, she will keep her beautiful clothes and jewelry not in the house of her hus-

[60] Binetsch, "Beantwortung mehrerer," 13; J. Spieth, "Von den Evhefrauen," *Quartalblatt der Norddeutschen Missionsgesellschaft*, VI (1889) 6.

[61] Westermann, "Die Glidyi-Ewe," 143.

band. . . . The house of the mother is site of her salvation. . . . A son's trust in the mother manifests itself differently. If he, for example, has had an accident or has fallen victim to a [mysterious] illness, his wife is not allowed to take care of him. If his mother is still alive, she has to be around him permanently. It is she who cooks for him and does other services for him. . . . his mother won't poison him; he can trust her completely.[62]

The relationship that is said to have existed between father's sister and brother's children has been described by Nukunya:

> [This] relationship is formalized in specific terms with deep mystical overtones. The father's sister's curse is believed to be most dreaded. In fact this is the only relationship in Anlo which is expressed in terms of cursing. It is also believed that when a man is not successful in life it is for his father's sister to offer special sacrifices on his behalf. Her carelessness too can sometimes affect the health of her brother's children, because of the belief that if, when she is preparing porridge, some of the flour falls into the fire, they will have swellings, *dzodzongui*, on their bodies. Another belief is that in the past, when Anlo disliked people growing abnormally tall, the father's sister was the person who could stop this by making an incision at the back of her brother's son's knee. These prerogatives of the father's sister make her a very important person in the life of every Anlo, and it is said that a person's one important life-long consideration is not to offend [the] father's sister.[63]

Particularly strong relations are also said to have existed between men and their sisters.[64] By having such close personal ties with her own children and her brothers, while also wielding significant ritual authority over his brother's children, a woman was clearly in the position to have considerable influence over her patrilineage's ability to have access to the labor of the children of her own sons. Again, the fact that women did indeed use their position to accomplish just this is suggested by the very high rate of matrilateral cross-cousin marriages among the Anlo today, a phenomenon that is said to have been even more preferred in the past.[65]

Older women's interests in supporting the Anlo preferences for clan endogamy and matrilateral cross-cousin marriages (preferences that further disadvantaged young women relative to men in marital relations) appear to have been due in part to the same factors that generated marriage patterns of social and economic competitiveness. As jockeying for position within the society increased, so the families involved emphasized an ideology that gave priority to the value of all family members, male and female, supporting their kin-group. This is apparent from the strong prescriptions that outlined the responsibilities each clan member had to the *hlo*, and the ritual ties that are said to have bound father's sister and brother's children as members of the same patrilineage. Older women's actions in supporting both clan endogamy and matrilateral cross-cousin marriage can thus be seen, in part, as

---

[62] Spieth, "Von den Evhefrauen," 7–8.

[63] Nukunya, *Kinship and Marriage*, 40–41.

[64] Ibid., 51–52; see also Polly Hill, "Notes on the Socio-economic Organisation of the Anloga Shallot Growing Industry," draft paper (Institute of African Studies, University of Ghana, Legon, 1965), 7.

[65] Nukunya, *Kinship and Marriage*, 73.

a result of their acceptance of the socially constructed emphasis on family members protecting the interests of their kin-group.

It is also likely that these older women encouraged such unions because they supported not only the interests of the family, but also their own long-term interests as women and mothers. In situations where two clans clashed—a frequent phenomenon in precolonial Anlo, according to Westermann—a woman no doubt found it comparatively easier to operate within the marriage if she and her husband belonged to the same clan, rather than to a *hlo* with which her own clan was in conflict. A somewhat different set of considerations appears to have encouraged married women to support the betrothal of their brothers' daughters to their own sons. In this instance, a woman's loyalty to her patrilineage had direct consequences for her own and her children's welfare. By effecting a marriage between her own son and her brother's daughter, she strengthened her image within her own patrilineage as someone who acted on behalf of the patrilineage. This in turn appears to have provided her with the leverage needed to retain her inheritance rights to family land, land she then could pass on to both her sons and daughters.

Evidence to support this supposition—that women translated their role of facilitating matrilateral cross-cousin marriage into leverage within the family inheritance system—comes from a number of sources. If one examines, for example, the comparative history and culture of the Glidzi-Ewe and the Anlo, a number of similarities emerge. During the 1702 expansion of Akwamu control over the coastal areas east of the Volta River, both came under the administrative rule of this matrilineal power. Both adopted elements of the matrilineal system, where nephews inherited the acquired property of their uncles. Only among the Anlo, however, did women work with their brothers to create a system where families preferred matrilateral rather than patrilateral cross-cousin marriage; and only among the Anlo did women retain the right to inherit and bequeath to their children land that they had inherited from their patrilineages.[66] The existence of both these similarities and differences suggests that Anlo women participated in the development of the system of matrilateral cross-cousin marital preferences that came to characterize Anlo society, and by so doing, they strengthened their ability to retain their right to inherit and retain for their children land from their own patrilineage. The cost of operating successfully within this familial system, however, meant that they had to exert great pressure on the young women in their patrilineage to accept marriage to the individuals selected for them.[67]

---

[66] See Westermann, "Die Glidyi-Ewe, "141, who notes that in the late nineteenth and early twentieth centuries Glidzi strongly favored *fome-sro*, or marriage within the lineage, but there existed no specific preference for matrilateral or patrilateral marriage; in addition, Glidzi women, by this date, had begun to lose access to land. Westermann noted that "Sons gets fields and houses . . . daughters do not inherit from their father, but he sometimes gives them presents. They inherit from their mother, and . . . from the father only if there is no male heir; the mother's sister . . . can give something to them like jewelry, clothes, valuables and things made from gold."

[67] The fact that this system clearly worked for the long-term advantage of young women did not deter some from rebelling against the system. In his 1906 report on Anlo customs, German missionary Gottlob Härtter suggests that in earlier times young women did enter concubinage, that is, establish a sexual relationship with the man of their choice without the approval of her parents, although this was apparently rare. Gottlob Härtter, "Sitten und Gebräuche der Anloer," *Zeitschrift für Ethnologie* (Braunschweig), 38/1–2 (1906), 46.

Conclusion

This chapter has documented changes in gender and ethnic relations in Anlo during the eighteenth and nineteenth centuries. Included among these changes was the development of clans by the earlier residents and a preference for clan endogamy. Both of these I associated with the social dynamic that developed within the various "family" groupings in Anlo when pressures for land, labor, and prestige generated a competitive climate. Under the pressure of an influx of refugees between 1679 and 1702, the earlier residents of Anlo organized a clan system that redefined we/they relations. The prior dichotomy that defined families on the basis of their worship of autochthonous or immigrant Ewe gods remained, but was superseded in importance by a definition of everyone within the society as either ethnic insider or outsider based on their time of arrival and their geographical and genealogical origins. Over time the earlier resident families of Anlo also embraced a preference for clan endogamy. After 1750, both ethnic insider and outsider families also began to prefer matrilateral cross-cousin marriage as all competed to produce the wealth necessary to demonstrate their high social status. These strategies proved to be an effective means of protecting family interests, but it was the later immigrants and the young women in both groups who suffered the consequences of this success. Those defined as ethnic outsiders found themselves deprived of ownership rights to land, socially stigmatized as "other," and unable to gain easy access to land in Anlo through marriage with earlier resident families because of the latter's preference for clan endogamy. Young women within the earlier resident families saw their significance to the clan rendered either irrelevant or elevated to such importance that their families found it necessary to limit potential marriage partners. The period after 1750 also saw a further expansion in the marginalization of the rights of all Anlo women because of the inter-lineage competition generated by the Atlantic slave trade. The majority of young women found themselves pressured to marry a father's sister's son. Those who implemented this particular change included not only the male heads of the Anlo patrilineages, but also older women within these groups. As mothers, sisters, and aunts, older women made it possible for families to effect marriages based on preferences for clan endogamy and unions between sisters' sons and brothers' daughters. They did so, however, not only because they accepted the socially-constructed notion that it was important for family members to support the interests of their own patrilineages and clans, but because they too were operating within a familial social dynamic where it was necessary to ignore the voices of young women in order to protect their own inheritance rights to lineage property. From this analysis, it is apparent that late seventeenth-century demographic changes on the upper Slave Coast had a major impact on ethnic relations in eighteenth- and nineteenth- century Anlo. Combined with greater involvement in the Atlantic slave trade, these changes had a profound influence on gender relations after 1750.

2

Gendered Responses: Ethnic Outsiders in Eighteenth- and Nineteenth- Century Anlo

During the eighteenth and nineteenth centuries, as the earlier residents of Anlo altered the ways in which they managed gender and ethnic relations, the very outsider groups that the Anlo had identified as posing the threats to which they were forced to respond (the refugees, immigrants, and traders who came from different polities in the region) continued to filter into Anlo. Some came and went, but others remained as permanent residents. They attached themselves as individuals to particular Anlo clans and their descendants later became known as *hlo dome hlo*, sub-clans under the authority of another clan.[1] Others organized themselves into groups based on common origins, cultural affinities, language, kinship, and/or occupational roles, and then defined themselves as independent *hlowo*, having their own totems, taboos, unifying genealogies, and group histories. Precisely when these sub-clans and independent *hlowo* came into existence is unclear. What we do know is that by the late nineteenth century many outsiders had adopted the clan system as a way to give themselves a social identity and the unity with which to interface effectively with the earlier residents. We also know that by this time the socially and politically powerful in Anlo had generated a new way of defining social relations. They no longer categorized groups in Anlo according to their association with immigrant or autochthonous gods alone. Added to this system and given priority was an emphasis on when one's ancestors arrived in Anlo and from which place within the region they came. With this new definition, the Anlo elite ranked all the independent *hlowo*

---

[1] See Westermann, "Die Glidyi Ewe," 148–49.

hierarchically according to their relative social prestige.[2] They distinguished those clans whose ancestors were said to have been the first immigrants from Notsie to settle in the Anlo area from all others. This group, known as the "first five" or "the original old clans,"[3] ranked themselves above those whose ancestors had also immigrated from Notsie, but who were "junior" to the ancestors of the "first five." These two groups defined all others within the society as ethnic outsiders whose ancestors came "late" and not from Notsie. They denied those outsiders permanent access to land and stigmatized them socially by refusing to betroth their daughters to them They defined the outsiders' naming and funeral customs as different and limited the extent to which they were allowed to obtain central positions within the Anlo political hierarchy.

Evidence from Anlo oral traditions indicates that many who were defined as ethnically distinct managed to become quite influential within Anlo social and political circles, despite their social identity. Perhaps the best-known instance of this involved the Dzevi clan. During the eighteenth century, the elders of this *hlo*—defined as ethnic outsiders because the founding ancestor of their clan immigrated to Anlo later than others and came from the Adangbe area to the west rather than from Notsie—made a remarkably successful bid for political power. In 1769, they obtained the politically influential position of spiritually supporting the Anlo military previously held by the Lafe clan (a member of the "first five"). By 1772, the priest of the Dzevi god, Nyigbla, had also managed to secure for himself and his clan a position that was politically and religiously on par with the *awoamefia*. The Dzevi were not alone in finding their way into the "inner circle" of Anlo society, however. Other ethnic outsiders accomplished the same during the eighteenth and nineteenth centuries.

These facts raise a number of questions about ethnic relations in precolonial Anlo. Perhaps the most obvious one has to do with how the Dzevi and others managed to overcome the stigma associated with their status as outsiders. Did the political and social elite of this polity reverse the policies of their predecessors and open their arms to include these outsiders? If so, why? If not, how did the latter circumvent the social boundaries erected by the earlier residents of Anlo to confine them to the social and political margins of the society? What did success mean for these outsiders? Did it require a redefinition of their ethnic identities? If so, who did the redefining? How did alterations in the boundaries that defined we/they relations affect the character of ethnic relations within the society as a whole? And

---

[2] The traditions to which I refer include those collected and published by D. Westermann in 1935. See Westermann, "Die Glidyi-Ewe," 145–49. See also Greene Field Notes, passim, in which the traditions contained therein simply elaborate on what Westermann collected; I assume all were in this basic form by the late nineteenth century. Traditions about clan complementarity were also collected by local scholars. These emphasize the notion that each *hlo* performed a complementary role in collectively constituting the Anlo polity. They highlight the fact that the Adzovia and Bate clans provide the *awoamefia*, the political and religious leader; the Dzevi have placed their war god, Nyigbla, at the service of the entire polity; the Agave provide the leader of the army; and the Ame take responsibility for being the first to test spiritually the strength of their enemies on the field of battle. See Nukunya, *Kinship and Marriage*, 23–24, and Charles M. K. Mamattah, *The Ewes of West Africa* (Accra, 1979), 166–95.

[3] Westermann, "Die Glidyi-Ewe," 145. See also Administration Papers [hereafter ADM], National Archives of Ghana, Accra, 11/1/1661, p. 97.

more importantly for this study, what impact did these changes have on gender
relations? Did the development of a more inclusive understanding of the socially
and politically prestigious "we" within Anlo society generate more or fewer opportunities within the society for women? Was there any impact on gender relations at all?

To answer these questions, I examine the history of two outsiders who achieved
considerable social and political status in Anlo during the eighteenth and nineteenth centuries, respectively: the Amlade *hlo*, and the well-known chief of Woe,
Togbui Gbodzo. According to late nineteenth-century documentary sources and
more recently collected oral traditions, the Amlade clan is, was, and always has
been a member of the "first five." The ancestor of the Amlade, like those of the
Lafe, Adzovia, Bate, and Like clans, is said to have been a hunter. All immigrated
from Notsie and claimed for themselves and their descendants the land that existed in the early Anlo area.[4] This gave these five clans control over access to land;
others in Anlo had to come to them in order to obtain land.[5] In 1978 and 1988,
however, when I made inquiries about the so-called "first five," I discovered a
number of inconsistencies in the definition of who was included therein. As noted
above, traditions about the Amlade indicate that this clan has always been a member of the "first five" group. Yet when I interviewed elders of this clan, they admit-
ted rather reluctantly that their *hlo* possessed no land in those districts that once
constituted early Anlo, or anywhere else in the region. They persisted nevertheless
in asserting that they were among those who arrived first in the area. Some of the
Amlade elders responded elusively to the question as to how they could have been
among the "first five" and yet have no land on the Anlo littoral. Others suggested
that their ancestors had been too preoccupied with hunting or some other activity
to claim any land (an answer I found unconvincing). Still others said they simply
did not know why this was the case.[6] If, in fact, the earliest immigrant settlers did
claim most of the land, it would appear that the Amlade were not among the first
to settle in the early Anlo area. Rather, they were latecomers, and only later were
they redefined as members of the "first five."

I argue here that a transformation did indeed occur in the social identity of
the Amlade and that their inclusion in the "first five" was the result of a number
of factors. Among these was the political upheaval that propelled the Dzevi priest
into a leadership position which the Anlo considered to be on par politically and
religiously with the most influential groups in the polity. Evidence suggests that
the Anlo leadership did not embrace the Dzevi priest. Rather, they accepted him
only because individuals and families in Anlo forced them to do so. The men

---

[4] The early Anlo area included the western littoral between Woe and Atoko, and the islands and marshlands immediately north of this area. These particular territorial limits were described in testimony before the Crowther Commission in 1912, and are consistent with Danish and Dutch accounts of early eighteenth century. See ADM 11/1/1661, p. 139–40, 119. See also Greene, "The Anlo-Ewe," 97–98.

[5] FN 6: Interview with Boko Seke Axovi, 1 August 1978, Anloga, and FN 16: Interview with Togbui Le II,
16 August 1978, Anloga. See also FN 9: Interview with Mr. T. S. A. Togobo, 7 August 1978, Anloga, FN 14:
Interview with Togbui Trygod Yao Zodanu, 11 August 1978, Anloga, and FN 32: Interview with Togbui
Sefoga, 30 September 1989, Anloga.

[6] See FN 14: Interview with Togbui Trygod Yao Zodanu, 11 August 1978, Anloga; FN 53: Interview with
Togbui Afatsao Awadzi, 16 December 1987, Anloga; FN 59: Interview with Togbui Amawota, 23 December 1987, Anloga; and FN 60: Interview with Togbui Tete Za Agbemako, 5 January 1988, Anloga.

and women of Anlo had come to believe that only the Dzevi priest and his god, Nyigbla, were capable of leading the Anlo successfully into battle at a time when considerable competition and conflict existed over the control of valuable economic resources and trade relations in the region. Evidence also suggests that while the Anlo leadership technically accepted the Nyigbla priest as a member of the polity's governing body, at the same time they initiated a number of efforts to counter the power and influence that both the Dzevi priest and his clan had managed to amass. They kept alive traditions about this particular *hlo* that identified it as a group of foreign origin, which in turn, prevented the Dzevi from fully translating their political prominence into social prestige. They also opened their ranks to the Amlade, a *hlo* also associated with particularly powerful spiritual forces. By not only including the Amlade within the governing body of the polity, but by also redefining them as members of the socially prestigious "first five," the political and social elite of Anlo expanded both the religious base and the number of groups within the "inner circle" of Anlo society who had a stake in maintaining as much as possible the status quo as it existed before the Dzevi were thrust upon them.

The inclusion of the Amlade did more than alter the boundaries that had previously defined "we" and "they" within this society, however. It also generated a major shift in gender relations among the Amlade. Evidence to support this change comes from the fact that the Amlade (like the other clans in Anlo) practiced clan endogamy. Their reasons for adopting this practice must have been different, however, from those who initially introduced this preference. The Amlade, unlike other members of the earlier resident clans, possessed no land. Therefore, they would have had no reason to adopt clan endogamy as a means to keep such property within their *hlo*. I contend that Amlade elders embraced this particular practice because it provided them with the means to control their own social identity. In Anlo, women had the principal responsibility of socializing their children to identify with and abide by the customs of their fathers' clans. If the Amlade were to be fully integrated into the "first five" group, not only did they have to work with the other clans within this set to reconstruct the identity of the Amlade as an earlier resident *hlo* that immigrated to Anlo from Notsie, they also had to control the way in which their own members were socialized to view themselves. The latter goal, in turn, required that the Amlade exercise considerable control over the women affiliated with their *hlo* since it was their responsibility to educate Amlade children about the history of the clan even if the child's *hlo* was different from their own. I argue that the way in which the Amlade controlled this socialization process so that it reinforced their own interests was to marry their daughters (whom they educated into this new identity) to their fellow clansmen so that they (rather than non-Amlade women, who might have been introduced to a different understanding of who the Amlade were) could pass on this new identity construct to the next generation of Amlade members.

An examination of the history of Togbui Gbodzo of Woe reinforces with data from the nineteenth century many of the same points made with respect to the eighteenth-century activities of the Amlade. Like the Amlade, Togbui Gbodzo of Woe was defined as an ethnic outsider because his father had immigrated to Anlo much later than the ancestors of others in the society and because he had no obvious connection to the Anlo ancestral home, Notsie. Gbodzo, nevertheless, managed to obtain the position of *dusifiaga,* right-wing commander of the Anlo army, and so effectively obscured his origins that those whom the Anlo identified in 1978 as the individuals most knowledgeable about the Anlo past were unable to define Gbodzo's ethnic identity correctly. As with the Amlade, I argue that Gbodzo's efforts to minimize public knowledge about his ethnic origins resulted in his and his descendants exercising greater control over the activities of the women in their patrilineage.

These two cases illustrate the fact that ethnic outsiders were deeply involved in shaping the character of ethnic relations in Anlo during the eighteenth and nineteenth centuries. They challenged the boundaries that had defined them as "other." They participated in the redefinition of their own identities, and managed to alter their social status. Those who succeeded most fully in crossing over the boundary into the political, religious, and social center of Anlo society were able to do so principally because their interests happened to coincide with those of the powerful in Anlo. Success and luck had its price, however. Inclusion of one ethnic outsider group frequently came at the expense of another. More importantly for this study, ethnic outsider groups that attempted to redefine their positions within the Anlo social hierarchy founded their efforts on the backs of the women within their groups. Like the women in ethnic insider families, those in outsider families stood at the very center of the process that defined and reinforced the identity of the groups of which they were members. This, in turn, meant that those family elders who sought to redefine the identity and social status of their groups began to exercise greater control over the young women in their midst, limiting their ability to undermine the group's interests. As a result, women found their voices increasingly ignored and/or silenced.

This chapter is divided into two sections. The first focuses on the history of the Amlade. I begin by discussing the bases of political influence in eighteenth-century Anlo so that one can understand why the Dzevi were able to challenge the Anlo leadership's exclusive hold on power in 1769. I then discuss this challenge and the reasons why the political and religious elite in Anlo opted to work with the Amlade to include them within the governing body of the society as well as in the group known as the "first five." The second section focuses on the history of Togbui Gbodzo of Woe. It begins with a discussion of the circumstances which brought Gbodzo's father to Woe, followed by an analysis of the way in which Gbodzo used his social and economic connections first to obtain the *dusifiaga* position, and then to de-emphasize (if not obliterate from public view) his identity as an ethnic outsider.

Religion, Politics, and the Competition for Influence: Nyigbla's Challenge, 1769

A central theme in the oral traditions of the Anlo-Ewe is the idea that religious authority—understood as the ability to associate with and manipulate spiritual forces for the benefit of oneself and others—was an integral part of the highest leadership positions within the polity. This is perhaps most apparent in the traditions about the origins of the Adzovia and Bate clans' right to provide (on an alternating basis) the *awoamefia*, the political leader of the Anlo polity. Anlo traditions about Adzovia rights to the position state, for example, that before the Anlo migrated to their present homeland, they resided for some time in Notsie, a town located presently in the Republic of Togo, where they were known as the Dogbo. During the reign of their leader, Fia Sri, a number of quarrels arose between the Dogbo and the people of Notsie which eventually prompted the Dogbo to leave and settle in their present area. Shortly after their arrival, Fia Sri discovered he had left the stool of office in Notsie. According to the traditions:

> [A meeting was called] and they decided to go to Notsie to bring the stool. They sent a delegation to convince Togbui Agokoli to give up the stool. . . . When they went there, Togbui Agokoli refused to give it to them unless they brought the head of Togbui Sri I. The [delegation] conferred and left quietly. When they returned to [Anlo] they reported the message. . . . There was no alternative. . . . Having looked around, they saw that Amega Le I [founder of the Wifeme clan] had a follower whose arm was spotted by yaws [as was the arm of Sri]. . . . They had a council with Le and he agreed to allow his servant, Foli, to carry their baggage and accompany them to Notsie without revealing to Foli [their agreement to kill the servant and deliver his arm to Agokoli in lieu of Sri's head]. Foli ignorantly went on the errand. . . . When near Notsie, Foli was killed by Amesimeku [Sri's nephew] who with the arm wrapped in leaves, went with it to Togbui Agokoli. . . . They told him "Togbui Sri is old and feeble; it was useless to kill him and bring the head so we cut his arm."[7]

Agokoli accepted the explanation and released the stool. Not trusting the Anlo completely, however, Agokoli sent several spies to Anlo to determine if indeed Sri had been killed. In order to continue the ruse, the residents of the town hid Sri and the recently acquired stool in a sacred place called *awoame*. It was from this point, claim Anlo traditions, that the political leader of Anlo was called the *awoamefia* (that is, the *fia* in the *awoame*), and the Nyaxoenu branch of the Adzovia clan, founded by Fia Sri, provided the candidates for this office.

Discussions about the significance of this particular oral tradition for the political history and culture of early Anlo exist elsewhere.[8] Of greater concern here is the fact that it illustrates the importance of religious authority for political leadership in early Anlo. In his testimony before the Crowther Commission in 1911, Chief James Ocloo of Anlo stated that the stool obtained by Adeladza from Notsie was not only a symbol of office, but was also used for religious purposes to obtain rain.[9] In 1971, C. Tay-Agbozo conducted field interviews in Anlo and recorded information that confirmed Ocloo's testimony. According to his informants, the actual name of the *awoame* stool was *tsikpe*, translated as "rain-stone."[10] The reputed ability to induce rain spiritually would have brought considerable influence, for climatological studies of the Anlo area indicate that

---

[7] FN 11: Interview with Mr. T. S. A. Togobo, 7 August 1978, Anloga; this tradition is quite well known and appears in many published and unpublished sources.

[8] See D. E. K. Amenumey, *The Ewe in Pre-Colonial Times* (Accra, 1986), Ch. 1.

[9] ADM 11/1661, p. 22.

[10] C. Tay-Agbozo, "The Background History of the Anlos (Including Origins, Immigration and Settlement) . . . " (B.A. honors thesis, Department of History, University of Ghana, Legon, 1971).

droughts occurred with great frequency, especially during the seventeenth century, when the Anlo are thought to have established themselves in their present
area.[11]

Anlo traditions indicate that religious considerations were also an important
basis for the Bate clan's access to the *awoamefia* position. According to these traditions, the Bate clan and all its activities are organized solely around the worship of
the *tro* or god, Mama Bate. As a *dzokpleanyi tro*, Mama Bate is among the most
prestigious gods in Anlo, in part, because of the belief that she and other *dzokpleanyi*
gods lived in human form as the original inhabitants of Anlo. They later disappeared mysteriously. The Bate clan's association with this group of gods is established in traditions which state that Togbui Adeladza, founder of the Bate clan,
discovered a *dzokpleanyi tro*, in the form of a woman, Mama Bate, in the vicinity of
Anloga on his way to the Volta River estuary during a hunting expedition. Mama
Bate showed Adeladza where she got her drinking water[12] and taught him about
the ceremonies and taboos associated with her worship.[13] Association with this *tro*
is said to have given Adeladza and all his descendants considerable spiritual power,
particularly the priest.

> [P]eople from this clan are very strong-willed and physically strong be-
> cause of the spirit of the god. It's the leopard spirit that is the ruling spirit
> of the god. . . . when [the *tronua*, priest] recites prayers over a calabash of
> water and pours it on the ground, one would see fish and shrimp jump-
> ing out of the water, no matter how small the pool. . . . They never wash
> their *bisi* [or priestly] cloth with water, but put it in an ordinary flat wooden
> tray or in a very large calabash. It would immediately begin to rain, and
> rain so much that [the water which had collected in the container] was
> sufficient to wash the cloth.[14]

A reputation for having the ability to produce rain—like that held by the
Nyaxoenu branch of the Adzovia clan—would obviously have been important in
placing the Bate in an influential position within the community. It is likely, however, that an even more important basis for the Bate clan's claim to the *awoamefia*
position was their association with the power of creation through their god, Mama
Bate. She and the other *dzokpleanyi trowo* that lived in the area are said to have
created the very land on which the Anlo established their new homes. They reportedly did so by commanding the sea to retreat from the littoral, thereby creating the
extensive set of depressions (located within the sand dunes that separate the Atlantic Ocean from the Keta Lagoon) in which the Anlo found the only soils suitable
for agricultural activity. It was presumably the Bate clan's association with those
deities that had the ability to produce rain and to create (and no doubt destroy) the

---

[11] Droughts occurred in 1661, mid-to-late 1682, mid-1683, 1739, 1748, 1774, 1780, 1809, 1824, and 1852.
Floods developed in 1758, 1893, 1917, 1929, 1934, 1943, and 1963 J. M. Dotse, "Agricultural Geography of
the Keta District" (M.A. thesis, University of Ghana, Legon, 1969), 9; Sharon Elaine Nicholson, "A Cli-
matic Chronology for Africa: Synthesis of Geological, Historical and Meteorological Information and Data"
(Ph.D. dissertation, University of Wisconsin, Madison, 1976), 272–74; and D. E. K. Amenumey, "The Ewe
People and the Coming of European Rule: 1850–1914" (M.A. thesis, University of London, 1964), 20.

[12] FN 10: Interview with Boko Seke Axovi, 6 August 1978, Anloga; FN 27: Interview with Togbui Dzobi
Adzinku, 15 September 1978, Anloga; and FN 35: Interview with Boko Seke Axovi, 3 October 1978, Anloga.

[13] FN 10: Interview with Boko Seke Axovi, 6 August 1978, Anloga.

[14] Ibid.

very area in which the Anlo lived, which gave them access to the highest position of political leadership in Anlo.[15]

A second recurring theme in Anlo oral traditions is the extent to which various religious groups competed with one another to attract followers. Success is said to have brought not only religious influence over large numbers of people, but also political influence within the polity. In more detailed accounts about the retrieval of the *awoamefia* stool, for example, the traditions indicate that when the Anlo emissaries returned with the *tsikpe* (rain-stone), a dispute arose between Fia Sri and his relative, Gli, who had recently acquired the god, Tomi. The dispute is said to have been over who controlled the town. Some preferred to associate with Sri; others preferred to affiliate with Gli and the god, Tomi. The arrival of the stool (or rain-stone) appears to have shifted the balance in favor of Sri, for shortly after its arrival, the population is said to have elevated him to the position of *awoamefia*. While it is difficult, if not impossible, to verify the extent to which this tradition reflects an actual historical event, it does reinforce the connection suggested above that political and religious influence were intimately connected within the office of *awoamefia*. It also suggests that competition for political power in precolonial Anlo was waged, in part, on a spiritual battlefield. Those who could attract others because of their reputed spiritual power could translate this into political influence. The history of the Nyigbla religious order demonstrates that this is precisely how the Anlo political culture operated.

The most commonly recited traditions about the god Nyigbla and its first priest, Aduadui, are those that attempt to explain how this god, despite its foreign origins, came to be designated as the war god of the entire Anlo polity, entrusted with the responsibility of protecting its citizens. A number of these traditions begin with a discussion of the extraordinary powers of Aduadui, but perhaps of greater historical significance are the circumstances which gave the priest the opportunity to transform the god into one of the most powerful and respected deities in Anlo. These circumstances, as discussed in the traditions of the Dzevi, the clan that had custody of Nyigbla, are said to have involved the following:

> [Aduadui] was supposed to have been a wonderful man. . . . When . . . he brought the [god] his father sacked him and said he didn't want it, for he thought this wonderful boy had brought something to harass the people. Not quite long [thereafter], a year or two later, an incident happened that was attributed to the *tro* which he brought. The Anlos were going to one of the wars and Aduadui, who was the priest of Nyigbla was consulted. They were very successful in the campaign. And after their return, they began to admire the boy, and the father asked him to come home. Fortunes began to arrive. Gifts came. He was able to make friends with the *awoamefia*. There was a time when the people tried to recognize the boy more than the *awoamefia* because of the good fortunes he brought to Anlo. He, the *awoamefia*, invited the [the Dzevi] people [to a council] and said he would sack the people and the fetish because it was usurping his power. There and then, the elders met and reconciled the priest and the *awoamefia*.

---

[15] Anlo elders emphasize a very different basis for Adzovia and Bate rights to provide the *awoamefia*. See Sandra E. Greene, "The Past and Present of an Anlo-Ewe Oral Tradition," *History in Africa*, 12 (1985).

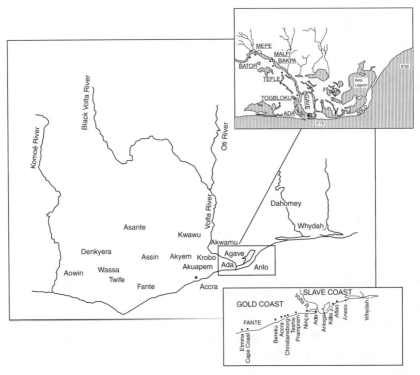

MAP 3: The Gold Coast and Upper Slave Coast after the 1730–1733 Collapse of Akwamu

> . . . that was the beginning of the chiefs and the priests walking hand-in-hand.[16]

The plausibility of this explanation—that the basis of Nyigbla's popularity lay in his supposed intervention on behalf of the Anlo during a time of war—is supported by a considerable body of data. Examination of the military history of Anlo reveals, for example, that this polity had been suffering from a long series of defeats throughout the first three-quarters of the eighteenth century. In 1702, they were conquered by the Akwamu and forcibly incorporated into their empire until 1730. In 1741, they were defeated again by Anexo and administered by them until 1750. During that period, they were also forced by Anexo to accept a Danish monopoly over trade in the area, which established a ceiling for the rates at which the Anlo were able to sell slaves to the Danes.[17] In 1750, after gaining their indepen-

---

[16] FN 5: Interview with Mr. T. S. A. Togobo, 20 June 1978, Anloga; and FN 32: Interview with Togbui Sefoga, 30 September 1989, Anloga.

[17] According to the provisions of this treaty, the Anlo were to demand no more than six ounces of gold for male slaves and four ounces for female slaves. They were also forced to agree to allow the Danes to build a fort in the area at a location of their own choosing. VgK 887, 7 September 1744, Quitta, L. F. Rømer, E. C. S. Quist, John Wilder, contained in a letter with same date, Fort Fredensborg, Christian Schmidt. See also VgK 887, 13 August 1744, Quitta, L. F. Rømer, Joost Platfues; VgK 885, 20 April 1744; and VgK 123, 21 July 1744, Christiansborg, J. Billsen, L. Klein, L. F. Rømer, Joost Platfues.

dence from Anexo, the Anlo engaged in a conflict known as the Nonobe war in which an initial victory over the Agave (then located immediately north of the Anlo littoral in the marshlands west of the Keta Lagoon) was reversed when the Agave and their Ada allies received assistance from the Danes in the form of fire-arms and the paid cooperation of the Krobo and a Larte contingent from Akuapem. With these additions to their forces, the Agaves and their allies were able to cross the Volta, rout the Anlo from their towns on the littoral, and capture at least sixty-four people whom they sold to the Danes.[18] This stream of defeats was finally in-terrupted with the defeat of the Ada in 1769. The success experienced by the Anlo in this conflict—their first major victory since the early 1700s—was so great that it completely altered the Anlo view of the Dzevi god, Nyigbla, to whom the victory was attributed.

The war began as a local conflict between the Anlo and the Ada on 14 Febru-ary 1769 but quickly escalated into a major confrontation between the various poli-ties in that area that were competing for access to and control over the trade on the lower Volta. Ada was assisted by forces from Agave, Malfi, Tefle, Mepe, Krobo, Anexo, Akuapem, and Akyem. Anlo received help from Akwamu. The battle be-gan with the movement of Anexo troops into Aflao to provide immediate protec-tion for its subject town Keta, threatened by Anlo shortly after their attack on Ada in February 1769.[19] In the meantime, the Ada cabuseers, Kwesi and Koranten, be-gan to regroup their scattered forces in Ada and prepared to cross the Volta. Seeing the possibility of war on two fronts—one with Ada on the west and another with Anexo on the east—Anlo attempted unsuccessfully to sue for peace with Anexo.[20] When the battle did take place in April 1769, however, it was the Ada who fared badly. Hasty preparations and poor communications were their undoing, as the following account indicates.

> King Obring Coran from Akim [Akyem] has hurriedly [sent] his mes-senger here and offered [the] Ada grandes his help if they could wait a little until he comes down to the coast. But the Ada grandes have dis-missed the messenger with this answer: "If Obring Coran will send us help, it must come to us in the field at Fitta [Weta] and Avens [Avenor]." The messenger left the [Ada] island on 19 April . . . shortly [before the Ada army crossed the Volta] Mathe Poppie from Offilihue [Aflao] sent a message to the Ada grandes in Malfi with [a message from] Cabuseer

---

[18] VgK 124, 17 December 1750, Christiansborg, Joost Platfues, C. Engman, M. Svane; the same is also in VgK 888. See also ADM 11/1661, p. 119; *Committee of Enquiry (Volta Region)* 78th Sitting,Thursday, 17 October 1974, 5; VgK 883, 25 May 1750, Christiansborg, J. Platfues, C. Engman, M. Svane; VgK 883, 30 December 1750, Ada, J. Sønne; VgK 889, 5 February 1751, Ada, J. Sønne, 7 February 1751, Ada, J. Sønne; VgK 188, 9 May 1751, Christiansborg, A. O. Tofte, "Enquiry about the former bookkeeper, Marcus Svane in Guinea, beginning 10 April 1752, ending 13 May ?1752/53" (The same is also in VgK 188, document no. 404, Marcus Svane); VgK 125, 7 May 1751, Christiansborg, M. Hacksen, C. Engman, M. Svane; and VgK 889, 7 May 1751, Christiansborg, M. Hacksen, C. Engman, M. Svane.

[19] Guineiske Kompaigne [hereafter GK], Rigsarkiv, Copenhagen, 15, 6 April 1769, Christiansborg, F. J. Kuhberg, J. F. Wrisberg, P. Bang, N. Aarestrup, J. L. Karrig, 26 December 1769, Christiansborg, E. Quist, J. Giønge, et al.; and GK 165, 16 January 1769, Quitta, E. Quist. See also FN 24: Interview with Boko Seke Axovi, 5 September 1978, Anloga; GK 165, 10 May 1769, Christiansborg, Kuhberg, J. Wrisberg, N. Aarestrup, J. Karrig; GK 15, 15 March 1769, Quitta, E. Quist; and GK 165, 18 February 1769, Ada, A. Dahl, 27 March 1769, Ada, Dahl, and 6 August 1769, Christiansborg.

[20] GK 165, 13 May 1769, Quitta, E. Quist.

Amoni of Popo . . . letting him know that they must hurry in coming, for the Popos were leaving to drive away Augna [Anloga] and Way [Woe]. In addition, it was reported that some of the Popo negroes were in Fita and Avens and some were in Offelihue [Aflao] and Aguja [Agudza], and really wanted the Ada grandes with their allies to hurry to take part with them in driving off Augna and Way. If they didn't come soon, Cabuseer Amonie had orders from his king in Poppo to attack Augna alone. . . .

Mr. Dahl [a Danish officer stationed in Ada] . . . advised the Adas to take their tour along the beach, to attack Way, but they told him they they themselves didn't know which way they would take. After this [information] was brought from Ada [to E. Quist in Keta, he] immediately despatched a message to Afraw [Aflao] where the Popos were situated and let them know that the Adas had broken up their camp . . . the Popos immediately sent another messege . . . to let the Adas know that if they were breaking camp, they should [instead] lay still until their important cabuseers [from Popo arrive] since they cannot and must not move before their arrival. [Despite this second message, the Danes reported that] on the 23rd and 24th, the Adas along with their allies, the River negroes, assembled in Malfie and today, the 25th, the men began to cross the river to get to Fita and Avens. . . . On the second of May . . . the Adas with their allies [were] ambushed by the Augnas and their allies at a town called Tjame [Tsiame]. The Adas fought furiously, forcing Augna and its allies to flee. With the help of those who were supposed to have come to their assistance, Ada [would have certainly] been the victors, if a town called Aveno had not been there to hinder [them]. The town had eaten fetish in loyalty to Augna and also with Ada, pledging to help them. The Avenor, whom the Adas thought were the Poppos who lay in Offelehue came and attacked the Adas from behind. As soon as this new attack by Aveno occurred, Malfie ran away as quickly as they could. According to reports . . . . from Graffie [Agave], the Malfie shot not once at Augna. They had also eaten fetish with [both] Ada and Augna, so the Adas with their other allies could not stand before this force, but had to flee [to Malfie and Agave].[21]

This victory was followed by other battles between June 1769 and May 1770. It was in the latter confrontation that the Anlo convincingly defeated the Ada, driving them completely out of the area to Togbloku, capturing at least five hundred prisoners-of-war, and gaining control of all the fish-laden streams and creeks in the marshlands west of the Keta Lagoon, and the fishing grounds on the lower Volta River, as well as the salt-water Songaw lagoon, from which the Ada extracted salt that was sold to the peoples in the interior.[22] As a result, the Anlo insisted, over the

---

[21] GK 165, 25 April 1769, Ada, Dahl, and 4 May 1769, Quitta, E. Quist. See also GK 166, 28 July 1769, Fredensborg, N. Scheven.

[22] GK 165, 16 May 1769, Ada, Dahl, and 22 September 1769, Quitta, E. Quist; another raid launched simultaneously against the Malfi who were in Agave to the west of the Volta was less successful. GK 167, 29 April 1770, Sinholdt, 8 May 1770, Quitta, G. H. Sinholdt, 14 May 1770, Fredensborg, J. Kiøge; GK 147, 15 May 1770, Christiansborg, G. Wrisberg; GK 167, 19 May 1770, Christiansborg, Wrisberg, Giønge, 29 May 1770, Christiansborg, Wrisberg, Froelich, Giønge; GK 12, 4 December 1769, Christiansborg, C. Jessen, F. J. Kuhberg, N. Aarestrup; GK 16, 23 October 1769, also in GK 155, 23 October 1769; GK 168, 29 May 1770, Christiansborg, Wrisberg, Froelich, Giønge; GK 16, 24 June 1770, Fredensborg, Joh. Westmann, 25 July 1770, Christiansborg, J. D. Froelich, G. F. Wrisberg, J. C. Giønge, 26 July 1770, Christiansborg, Simon

objections of their political and religious leaders, that those who brought them such an important victory, the god Nyigbla and its priest, be given a position on par with the *awoamefia*.

Another factor that contributed to the inclusion of the Dzevi priest and his god in the highest political and religious circles was Anlo's increasing involvement in the political and economic affairs of the region. We know, for example, that trade opportunities in the interior for the Anlo expanded significantly after the collapse of the Akwamu empire in 1730. The Anlo responded to this situation by conquering the northern shore of the Keta Lagoon. This success expanded their sources of fish for trade purposes and ensured them adequate agricultural land for their subsistence. Between 1741 and 1750, Anexo conquered Anlo. This briefly ended Anlo's economically motivated military activities, but after 1750, when they regained their independence, the Anlo again embarked upon expansionary activities, most of which were directed against the Ada, with whom they competed for control of the fishing areas around the mouth of the Volta. Their continual defeats at the hands of the Ada and their allies, no doubt, created a readiness for new approaches and tactics; for their ability to protect and expand interests depended largely on their military prowess. Accordingly, the Anlo established a formal alliance with Akwamu and turned to a new source of spiritual power, the Nyigbla priest and his god, which they insisted—after their defeat of Ada and its allies in 1769—should "walk hand in hand" with the *awoamefia*.

The inclusion of the Dzevi priest and his god as members of the Anlo political and religious elite expanded the size of this leadership group; it also altered the status of the Dzevi clan. No longer perceived as just another set of ethnic outsiders, Dzevi clan members were now seen as individuals associated with the most powerful god in Anlo. This transformation, however, also propelled the Anlo elite to keep alive the notion that members of this *hlo* were still ethnically distinct and not of the same social status as those clans whose ancestors had immigrated from Notsie before all others. The continued definition of the Dzevi as "other" within Anlo society is evident in testimony recorded by German missionaries in the late nineteenth century. Acording to these accounts, the Dzevi were defined as a group whose members descended from "a woman from the Ada area."[23] Efforts, presumably spearheaded by the Dzevi, did exist to minimize the significance of their foreign origins. These efforts—which focused *not* on denying the Dzevi's ethnic distinctiveness, but rather on emphasizing the notion that Nyigbla, the god they so closely identified with, "left his homeland, Gbugla near Accra, once and for all"[24] — had little effect on the social status of the Dzevi. Where the Dzevi failed, however, others achieved success. One such success involved the Amlade.

Tadtsen, 28 August 1770, Quitta, J. Kiøge; Kea, "Akwamu-Anlo Relations," 37–38; GK 156, 28 February 1774, Christiansborg, Aarestrup, Kiøge, Timmsen, Giønge, Rasmussen; GK 167, 15 February 1771, Christiansborg; GK 17, 7 March 1771, Quitta, J. F. Froelich; J. Kiøge; Board of Trade, Correspondence from the Committee, 1771–1788 [hereafter BT], Public Records Office, Kew, England, 6/1, 22 June 1772, Cape Coast Castle, David Mill to the Committee; GK 149, 17 November 1772, Quitta, J. Kiøge; the same appears in GK 169.

[23] Westermann, "Die Glidyi-Ewe," 147.

[24] Spieth, *Die Religion*, 145.

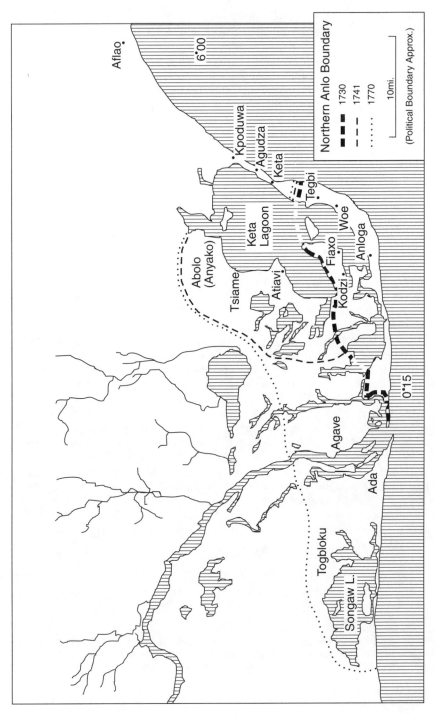

MAP 4: Anlo Expansion, 1730-1770

The Amlade Clan and the
Gendered Politics of Social Inclusion

Late nineteenth- and early twentieth-century accounts of the Amlade clan describe its members as primarily fishermen and businessmen, with whom almost everyone attempted to avoid annoying because of the power of their god, Togbui Egbe. As one account noted:

> If a dispute arose between you and the [worshippers of Togbui Egbe], they then go to curse your name in the presence of their *tro*. If you are on your way somewhere and are grazed by a sharp blade of grass, then a snake has bitten you. Thus everybody avoids becoming involved in a dispute with these people.[25]

These same accounts also note that members of this clan were considered the matrilineal descendants of the Lafe clan ancestor, Wenya, who was said to have been the very first person to explore and settle the Anlo littoral. It was because of these distinctions—possession of the god Togbui Egbe and their close genealogical connection to the Lafe clan—that the Anlo are said to have included the Amlade in the group that supposedly settled first in the Anlo area and accorded them, along with the Lafe clan, the right to offer prayers to their gods on important ceremonial occasions involving the entire polity. It was the Lafe and Amlade clans, for example, that took responsibility at that time for enstooling the *awoamefia*.[26]

In the introduction to this chapter, I noted that certain contradictions exist in the Anlo narratives about the Amlade clan. Perhaps the most important of these has to do with the issue of land. The Anlo claim that those who first settled on the Anlo littoral claimed all the lands therein for themselves and that those who came later or separated from the "first five" to form their own independent clans were able to acquire land only because the "first five" distributed the land as gifts or inheritable property. Examination of the land ownership patterns on the Anlo littoral indicates that most of the clans included in the "first five" group do, indeed, own substantial tracts on the littoral. Almost every other Anlo clan also owns land in this same area or on the northern side of the Keta Lagoon, but they also maintain traditions indicating from whom they obtained their property. The Amlade are alone among the "first five" in having no land anywhere in Anlo or elsewhere within the region. If we assume that this connection between early residence and land ownership is historically accurate, we can also assume that the Amlade did not, as they claim, enter the area earlier than many others, and that the traditions about their origins have been manipulated to support their inclusion in the group of earliest arrivals. Clues as to the identity of the Amlade ancestors can be found in the eighteenth-century relationship between Anlo and its neighbors, particularly Anexo, on the middle Slave Coast, and in the history of the Nyigbla order in Anlo.

In the late nineteenth century, Anlo elders noted that the ancestors of many clans came from areas outside the early Anlo territory or were members of communities quite separate from early Anlo. The Tsiame and Agave, as well as the ancestors of the Ame and Getsofe, are said to have been resident in their own polities on the north side of

---

[25] Ibid., 131.

[26] See Spieth, *Die Religion*, 131; Westermann, "Die Glidyi-Ewe," 147; and ADM 11/1/1661, p. 4, 43.

the lagoon before the Anlo ancestors settled on the Atlantic littoral; the Dzevi and Wifeme maintained traditions which state their ancestors entered Anlo from the Adangbe districts to the west of the Volta River, after the mid- to late-seventeenth-century expansion of the Akwamu state. Individuals are also known to have entered the area and to have been absorbed into existing lineages and clans within the society. One of the more interesting aspects of these accounts is the fact that none of the clans are associated with peoples who entered Anlo from the east, even though extensive ties existed between Anlo and the communities on the middle Slave Coast. In 1742, the polity of Anexo invaded and conquered Anlo, and then maintained control over the area until 1750. The *awoamefia* who reigned at that time, Togbui Anyage (also known as Kofi Fiayidziehe), is said to have lived for some time in Anexo, where his mother's relatives resided.[27] Danish records indicate that many of the traders who operated in Anloga during the mid-eighteenth century were of Anexo origin.[28] Yet nothing is mentioned about this connection in the Anlo narratives collected in the late nineteenth century or in those recorded more recently. When I asked Anlo elders about this lacuna in the oral traditions, most suggested that those who immigrated from the east integrated themselves into existing social groups; they simply blended into the earlier residential population. Further analysis of Amlade traditions suggests otherwise.

Early recorded accounts about the Amlade note, for example, that among the powers attributed to Togbui Egbe was the ability to enter snakes and use them to punish those who offended the god and its followers. Seventeenth-century European accounts about the middle Slave Coast indicate that Whydah and Dahomey were the first polities to use the snake as a symbol of a god's power. From there, use of this symbol spread west to Anexo, a community with which the Anlo had extensive economic, social, political, and cultural relations.[29] The name Amlade—distinct from those found among the Anlo—is also thought by some to be more characteristic of the names found in Anexo, where the Ge-dialect of Ewe is spoken.[30] Additional clues about the

---

[27] See Carl Spiess, "Könige der Anloer," in H. J. Helmot, ed., *Weltgeschichte 3: Westasien und Afrika* (Leipzig and Vienna, 1901), 574; R. S. Rattray, "History of the Ewe People," *Etudes Togolais*, 11, 1 (1967), 93; FN 30: Interview with Mr. T. S. A. Togobo, 26 September 1978, Anloga and FN 42: Interview with Boko Seke Axovi, 1 November 1978, Anloga. It was also Kofi Fiayidziehe (whom I identify as the same person as Anyage) who is said to have introduced into the area the Amlade god, Sui. See FN 35: Interview with Boko Seke Axovi, 4 October 1978, Anloga.

[28] GK 12, 4 December 1769, Christiansborg, C. Jessen, F. J. Kuhberg, N. Aarestrup; GK 16, 21 November 1769, Christiansborg, J. Giønge, E. Quist; and GK 17, 12 December 1771, Christiansborg, J. D. Froelich, N. Aarestrup, J. G. Giønge, J. Rasmussen.

[29] See Law, *Slave Coast*, 109–10, 332–33. See also Melville J. Herskovits, *Dahomey: An Ancient West African Kingdom*, II (Evanston, 1967), 248, who distinguishes the Dahomey Da from the Whydah god, Dangbe. Other groups in Anlo have gods associated with snakes, but all have traditions indicating an origin outside the Anlo area. The god Da (which means snake), for example, is worshipped in Anlo as part of the individually owned Yewe order and was introduced by Togbui Honi in the mid- to late eighteenth century from the Anexo area. The Dzevi clan's god, Nyigbla (which all in Anlo also identify as a foreign *tro*) forbids Anlos to kill the snake known as *anagbo*, and the god itself is said to appear as a snake stretched across the sky after it rains (that is, as a rainbow). According to Quarcoopome, the snake was the symbol for the Adangbe god, Aya. Whether this symbol was locally generated or came from the middle Slave Coast is unclear, however. See Nii Otukunor Quarcoopome, "Rituals and Regalia of Power: Art among the Dangme and Ewe, 1800 to Present" (Ph.D. dissertation, University of California, Los Angeles, 1993), 57.

[30] Conversation with K. Attoh, 2 September 1991; see also FN 61: Interview with Mr. Xovi Banini, 5 January 1988, Anloga.

identity of the ancestors of the Amlade come from the history of land ownership in Anlo. I noted above that the Amlade was the only "first five" clan in Anlo that had no land of any kind. If we examine the traditions of those who claim land elsewhere, the Agave stand alone in having no land in Anlo territory; they claim property in the Agave area, on the Volta River. Oral traditions indicate that the Agave came to Anlo in 1702 as intermediaries associated with the Akwamu administration of the area.[31] As such, their position was significantly different from other immigrants. The Agave came as conquerors; all other immigrants were in a dependent relationship to the "first five." The Dzevi and Wifeme, for example, are said to have come as refugees; they obtained land only after offering certain services to the polity or after establishing a subordinate relationship with a more established group.[32] The Ame and Getsofe were conquered and forcibly incorporated into the Anlo polity; they farmed on the lands they claimed as their own only after receiving permission to do so from their captors[33] The Tovi, Klevi, and Bame clans were described as more distant relatives or the descendants (and therefore the subordinates) of the "first five."[34] The Agave entered the area in a superordinate position and presumably failed to receive land because they were unprepared to subordinate themselves to another clan. I would suggest the Amlade entered Anlo in a similar fashion (as part of the Anexo state's conquest of Anlo in 1741) and that they, too, were unprepared to place themselves as a group under another clan in Anlo. They, like the Agave, never acquired land in Anlo that they could claim as clan property.

The Anlo inclusion of the Amlade clan appears to have developed as a result of the jockeying for power that accompanied the rise of the Nyigbla order. I noted above that after their highly successful war with the Ada in 1769, the Anlo began to honor Nyigbla in ways the *awoamefia* viewed as a threat to his position. The *awoamefia* and his advisors attempted to drive the Nyigbla priest and his god out of Anlo, but eventually they were forced to share power with the god's priest. The *awoamefia* was not the only one affected by the tremendous popularity of this new war god, however. According to Anlo traditions, at one time the Lafe clan had had the honor of praying to its gods for Anlo's protection and victory in battle. Belief in this god must have been

[31] FN 39: Interview with Togbui Christian Yao Gbotoza Fiadzo, 16 October 1978, Anloga; and Anlo State Council Minute Book, 1935: Chiefs Kata, Adaku, Avege, and Agblevo per Samuel Nutsuga for themselves and on behalf of Tsiame Tribe of Anloga, Atokor, Atiave and others -v-. Chiefs Zewu, Agbozo, Anakoo Attipoe and Zioklui, Davordji Banini and others for themselves and on behalf of Agave Tribe of Anloga, Djelukope, Anyako, et cetera, 372–73. See also Greene, "The Anlo-Ewe," 80, 112–13.

[32] See FN 8: Interview with Mr. T. S. A Togobo, 3 August 1978, Angola; FN 15: Interview with Togbui Le II, 15 August 1978, Angola; FN 32: Interview with Togbui Sefoga, 30 September 1989, Anloga; FN 53: Interview with Togbui Afatsao Awadzi, 16 December 1987, Anloga; FN 60: Interview with Togbui Tete Za Agbemako, 5 January 1988, Anloga; and FN 65: Interview with Togbui Dzobi Adinku, 6 January 1988, Anloga.

[33] E. Y. Aduamah, *Ewe Traditions* (Legon, 1965), No. 1, p. 23; Anlo State Council Minute Book, 1935, 374 75; FN 9: Interview with Mr. T. S. A. Togobo, 12 June 1978, Anloga; FN 18: Interview with Boko Seke Axovi, 29 August 1978, Anloga; FN 21: Interview with Mr. T. S. A. Togobo, 31 August 1978, Anloga; FN 32: Interview with Togbui Sefoga, 30 September 1989, Anloga; FN 35: Boko Seke Axovi, 4 October 1978, Anloga; FN 59: Interview with Togbui Amawota, 23 December 1987, Anloga; FN 60: Interview with Togbui Tete Za Agbemako, 5 January 1988, Anloga; FN 61: Interview with Mr. Xovi Banini, 5 January 1988, Anloga; FN 64: Interview with Mr. J. N. K. Dogbatse, 5 January 1988, Anloga; FN 65: Interview with Togbui Dzobi Adinku, 6 January 1988, Anloga; and ADM 11/1/1661, 97–98.

[34] FN 21: Interview with Mr. T. S. A. Togobo, 31 August 1978, Anloga; Patten, "Avuncular Family," 83–89; and Greene, "The Anlo-Ewe," 103.

sorely tested in the years of military defeat and subordination before the Anlo victory over the Ada in 1769. The Anlo attributed this success not to the Lafe god, Awadatsi, but to the Dzevi god, Nyigbla. Anlo traditions indicate that thereafter the Dzevi clan and its Nyigbla priest displaced the Lafe and assumed the responsibility of praying to their god on behalf of the entire polity for victory in war.[35] This loss in status does not appear to have affected the prominent position the Lafe clan's ancestors held in the traditional histories of the area. Wenya, their founding ancestor, was still said to have been the first to settle on the Anlo littoral, a status secured by the very fact that they were the largest owners of land in the area. It did, however, damage their reputation as a clan whose leaders were cunning enough to retain their position as the spiritual leaders of the Anlo in war. By the end of the nineteenth century, the Anlo were apparently still making the Lafe the butt of numerous jokes. The following was said to have been typical:

> If it was raining while the Lafeawo had just put their clothes outside to dry, they would say they had not taken off their clothes to get wet themselves. They would go into the bush (in the rain), to get a stick. Then they would go back into the house and use the stick to drag their clothes into the house. . . .[36]

The Lafe responded to this loss of status by aligning themselves with those in Anlo society who had custody of more prestigious gods, but who could, nevertheless, benefit from their association. That group was the Amlade.

As indicated, evidence suggests that the Amlade entered the area in the mid-eighteenth century as part of the expansionary efforts of the Anexo. Those who remained after 1750, when the Anlo regained their independence, apparently coalesced into their own clan and established themselves in the area, in part as a group associated with particularly powerful gods. The Amlade brought with them their god, Togbui Egbe, which had the ability to seriously incapacitate those with whom they argued; another god, Sui, acquired after their settlement in Anlo, proved powerful enough to demand from families who sought its services payment in the form of a *fiasidi*, a young woman who remained as a servant associated with the shrine for the rest of her life; if she died, the family had to replace her.[37] Lafe affiliation with the Amlade (a *hlo* that had one of the most powerful gods in Anlo, the *tro* Sui) would have greatly enhanced their reputation; the Amlade would have also benefited from an affiliation with the Lafe since they were still considered the oldest *hlo* in the polity, and thus were accorded the right to enstool the *awoamefia*.[38] That the Lafe and Amlade did, indeed, establish particularly strong bonds between themselves is suggested by the fact that the Lafe shared the responsibility of enstooling the *awoamefia* with the Amlade by the late nineteenth century, as the following account indicates.

> The [*awoame*]*fia* comes from two tribes, Bati [Bate] and Adjovia [Adzovia]. . . . the Amlade and Lape [Lafe] put him on the stool and the two persons

---

[35] ADM 11/1/1661, p. 54; and FN 6: Interview with Boko Seke Axovi, 1 August 1978, Anloga.

[36] Westermann, "Die Glidyi-Ewe," 147.

[37] FN 22: Interview with Togbui Yao Trygod Zodanu, 1 September 1978, Anloga; and FN 33: Interview with Boko Seke Axovi, 3 October 1978, Anloga.

[38] Recognition of this sort on the basis of prior residence is a very common phenomenon in Africa. See Igor Kopytoff, ed., *The African Frontier: The Reproduction of Traditional African Societies* (Bloomington, 1987).

carry him home. These are healthy young men of the tribe, not elders. There is no sword for the [*awoame*]*fia* . . . they simply pray to god and put him on the stool. . . . the elders of the Amlade and Lape tribe put him on the stool . . . [they] simply put up two arms to heaven and say "Long life to the Fia, may he have plenty of children, let rain fall so he has plenty to chop and let peace be among us." [The] brother [of a deceased *awoamefia*] looks after the stool when it is vacant until another person is chosen, then the brother gives it to the Amlade and Lape elders to take it to the [new] Fia.[39]

Equally important is the fact that the Anlo described the Amlade as the junior partners in this exercise, having the right to participate in the enstoolment of the *awoamefia* because their ancestor was the maternal nephew of Wenya, the Lafe clan's ancestor.[40] By positioning the Amlade within that group that administered the affairs of the entire polity, the Lafe no doubt enhanced their own reputation, but did so by maintaining their senior position within the polity and in their relationship with the Amlade.

The inclusion of the Amlade into the highest political and religious circles in Anlo was accompanied by a reordering of the traditions about the clan and its relationship with the Anlo area. Today, as I noted above, it is very difficult to find traditions that refer to the Amlade clan as anything other than a *hlo* whose ancestors were among those who first entered and settled the Anlo area from Notsie. I did record a number of traditions in 1978 and 1987, however, that give some indication of how the Lafe and Amlade clans may have reordered the traditions to emphasize the commonalities that existed between the Amlade and the earlier residents of Anlo without denying the Amlade's connections with Anexo, connections that would have been more widely known throughout the community in the second half of the eighteenth and in the nineteenth centuries. These traditions state that:

[The ancestor of the Lafe and Amlade clans was] Gemedra. [He] lived for a long time, accompanying the father [Togbui Egbe, in the Ewe's migration from the west] from Adza [in what is now known as Nigeria] to Notsie [in southern Togo]. Togbui Egbe . . . was noted to be a very powerful person in prayer. Whatever he set out to effect, the prayers came through. Of all the children that Togbui Egbe had, there was one who was as good in prayer as Egbe. That was Togbui Gemedra. Gemedra married and the first birth was twins: Atsu and Etse. These twins grew up to have the same facility in praying as their grandfather. Atsu gave birth to Wenya . . . who originated the Lafe clan. Etse gave birth to Adedzi Enyaki; he originated the Amlade clan.

Although the Amlade don't have land in Anloga . . . it doesn't mean they came late. . . . Those who came [from Adza] stopped at different places and some stayed a while before proceeding. . . . They [all] started

[39] ADM 11/1/1661, p. 4–5. See also FN 6: Interview with Boko Seke Axovi, 1 August 1978, Anloga; and FN 18: Interview with Boko Seke Axovi, 29 August 1978, Anloga.

[40] Westermann, "Die Glidyi-Ewe," 147. In more contemporary accounts, the Lafe and Amlade are described as the descendants of the twin brothers, Atsu and Etse. The ancestor of the Lafe, Atsu, is described as the senior of the twins. See FN 6: Interview with Boko Seke Axovi, 1 August 1978, Anloga; FN 14: Interview with Togbui Trygod Yao Zodanu, 11 August 1978, Anloga; FN 18: Interview with Boko Seke Axovi, 29 August 1978, Anloga; and FN 47: Interview with Mr. T. S. A. Togobo, 8 November 1978, Anloga.

from Adza to Dogbo to Notsie, from which they scattered. The Amlade
went to a number of places before coming to Alakple [and then Anloga].
Some of them went to Adaxo and settled there. The person there was called
Anexo; they [the Amlade] stayed there with the Ges. . . . this accounts for
the different arrival times.[41]

By asserting that the ancestors of the Amlade clan travelled together with the Anlo
to Notsie, and only then became separated, the Lafe and Amlade acknowledged
the Anlo's Anexo connection, but they also constructed a genealogical connection
with one another and a tie to the town of Notsie that was too ancient to be ques-
tioned and which could therefore be used to justify an alteration in the traditions
that served the interests of both the Lafe and Amlade clans. The Lafe enhanced
somewhat their religious reputation in Anlo by associating themselves with a group
that had particularly powerful and influential gods; the Amlade apparently took
advantage of the opportunity presented by the Lafe's interest in associating with
them to gain the right to participate in the administrative affairs of the Anlo polity.
We can assume that the Adzovia and Bate clans accepted this situation because
they were not directly threatened by the inclusion of the Amlade, while the latter
could serve as an important ally against further encroachments on their authority
by the Dzevi. It was under these circumstances, I would suggest, that the Anlo
political leadership opted to shift by the late nineteenth century the boundaries
that defined the Anlo clans socially and ethnically to include the Amlade among
the group that became known as the "first five."

    The redefinition of the Amlade as social and ethnic insiders rather than out-
siders must have involved more than the manipulation of popularly consumed
oral traditions in order to alter the way in which non-Amlades viewed the clan. We
must also assume that those among the Amlade—presumably the elders of the
clan—who decided to change the identity of the *hlo* had to convince others within
the clan to accept their decision and to act accordingly. How was this accomplished
and what were the implications of this change in the daily lives of the Amlade?
How did the clan enforce within their own ranks this change in social and ethnic
identity, and how did it affect their internal relations? Although evidence from the
nineteenth century when these changes were taking place is lacking, an analysis of
more contemporary data does suggest answers to these questions. At present there
exists one clan in Anlo, the Blu, whose members state that their ancestors, who
settled in Anlo later than others, had no prior connection to the town of Notsie. A
number of these Blu families not only acknowledge this fact, they also maintain
ritual connections to the homelands of their ancestors. In 1978, for example, when
I interviewed Blu elders Togbui Ago Agbota and Togbui Kofi Ezu Agbota, they
stated that:

    Our ancestors came from the Ga-Adangbes. Some came because of trade,
    some just for adventure. . . . The link between the original home and this
    place has been kept intact, though. For example, we come from Ningo,
    and we go there for the purification of the stool.[42]

---

[41] FN 14: Interview with Togbui Trygod Yao Zodanu, 11 August 1978; and FN 61: Interview with Mr. Xovi
Banini, 5 January 1988, Anloga.

[42] FN 6: Interview with Boko Seke Axovi, 1 August 1978, Anloga

The continued emphasis on maintaining ritual connections to one's homeland is rooted in the belief that ancestors continue to influence the lives of their descendants. Periodic visits to the area where an ancestor is actually buried must occur in order to restore the spiritual linkage that exists between the deceased relative and his stool, the object through which the ancestor's descendants communicate with their dead relative.

Belief in the importance of maintaining such spiritual linkages is also evident in the history of the Fofie religious order. According to oral traditions, this order developed in Anlo specifically to meet the spiritual needs of those enslaved men and women who had been removed from their communities and who were said to have become ill because their slave status had prevented them from communicating with and offering sacrifices to their ancestors in their own home areas. Although slaves were ritually stripped of their former identity and inducted into the clans of their masters, this ritual did not obviate the possibility that the slave's ancestors could still affect his or her life. The Fofie religious order—certainly in existence by the late nineteenth century—developed to provide the means through which slaves and their descendants in Anlo could communicate with the spiritual forces associated with their original homes.[43]

If Amlade clan members also accepted the belief that it was important to maintain communication between the living and deceased members of one's kin-group, any change in their identity from that of outsiders (whose ancestors immigrated late from Anexo) to insiders (whose ancestors came from Notsie and were among the "first five") would have also required them to modify their ritual activities. Instead of performing periodic visits to Anexo to maintain spiritual linkages to their ancestors, they would have had to find a way to modify or sever those linkages and develop others that reinforced their new identity as a clan whose ancestors came from Notsie. That this is precisely what happened is evident from the traditions about the Amlade ancestor, Togbui Egbe. Identified as the principal person linking the Amlade clan to the "first five," Togbui Egbe is said to have died in Tado (in east-central Togo) even before the Ewe-speaking peoples moved to Notsie. When they left Tado, however, his descendants disinterred his remains and reburied them on their arrival in Notsie. His remains were exhumed again when his descendants left Notsie to travel via Anexo to Anlo with the ancestors of the "first five." The remains were then reinterred in Anloga where they have continued to be the focus of worship by his descendants, who later formed the Amlade clan. By defining the shrine to Togbui Egbe as one that contained his actual remains, the Amlade elders shifted the spiritual orientation of the Amlade away from Anexo and instead emphasized their ritual connections to the remains themselves, which were now located in Anloga. If an individual Amlade member found it necessary to fortify an ancestral stool, he could do so by going to Togbui Egbe's shrine in Anloga. The connection to Anexo was rendered irrelevant for the spiritual well-being of the clan.

Another aspect of everyday life affected by this change in identity involved the socialization of children. In their descriptions of Anlo culture, Westermann and Spieth noted that the Anlo expected a wife to know a great deal about her

---

[43] FN 54: Interview with Togbui Tse Gbeku, 16 December 1987, Anloga; and FN 55: Interview with Togbui Kosi Axovi, 17 December 1987, Anloga..

husband's clan. It was her responsibility to introduce their children into the culture of the father's *hlo*. Failure to do so could lead to potentially harmful consequences for those children.[44] This educational imperative appears to have affected how Amlade families managed the marital affairs of their daughters. As noted in Chapter 1, the earliest residents developed the clan system and a preference for intraclan marriage during the late seventeenth and early eighteenth centuries in order to maintain their exclusive rights to the limited arable resources in the early Anlo area. This preference meant that young women were increasingly encouraged to marry fellow clan members so that the land they inherited from their parents, and which they had a right to bequeath to their children, would not pass out of the control of their clan.

Strongly urging daughters to marry within the *hlo* in order to retain land holdings could not have been the factor that motivated the Amlade to adopt this practice, however. They did not possess any land as a corporate unit, yet according to Nukunya, they did indeed favor marriages within the *hlo*. Several possibilities exist to account for this preference. Perhaps the various patrilineages that together formed the Amlade clan were few in number and therefore, to strengthen their numerical position within Anlo, they chose to betroth their daughters to men within the clan. A second possibility may have involved the imperative the Amlade must have felt to maintain control over the socialization of their children because of the change in identity they were attempting to effect during the nineteenth century. By giving their daughters in marriage to men within their own clan, Amlade parents could more safely assure that their own daughters would teach their children to view themselves as members of a *hlo* that traced its origins to Notsie, as did other members of the "first five." This also required that the young women sacrifice their own marriage plans for the sake of their patrilineages or the clan. That Amlade women did, indeed, willingly or unwillingly marry fellow clan members is evident from the fact that the *hlo* practiced clan endogamy at the same rate as others in Anlo. Thus, when the Amlade redefined themselves as ethnic insiders and members of "the first five," they also reordered gender relations within the *hlo* in order to reinforce their new ethnic identity.

Trade and Politics in Nineteenth-Century Anlo: The Historical Origins of the Gbodzo Family

In 1792 and 1807, Denmark and Britain, two of the major European powers operating on the lower Gold Coast and upper Slave Coast, officially abolished the slave trade and enacted laws forbidding their nationals to engage in that trade after 1803 and 1807, respectively. Neither of these powers, however, was able to influence significantly the trade in slaves from the lower Gold Coast and upper Slave Coast until the 1840s when they launched more aggressive measures.[45] In the intervening years (between 1803 when Denmark outlawed its citizens' participation in the trade, and 1841–1842, the time by which Britain had added more ships to the anti-slave squadron and all the major powers had signed treaties allowing the squadron to

---

[44] Westermann, "Die Glidyi-Ewe," 143; and Spieth, "Von den Evhefrauen," 6.

[45] W. E. F. Ward, *The Royal Navy and the Slavers* (New York, 1969), 39, 121, 162.

seize any vessel fitted with equipment to carry slaves), the buying and selling of human beings continued as independent local merchants—European, Afro-European, and African—filled the vacuum created by the departure of the European governments and trade companies. Carl Christian Reindorf describes one such independently operated business in Accra and its confrontations with the British who were attempting to suppress the trade:

> After [1815/16] . . . the country enjoyed peace, but then the slave-trade with the Portuguese became brisk. Chief Ankra was the general broker for the slave dealers. . . . As there was no commandant in the Dutch fort at that time, Dutch Town was made the depot. Slaves were sold during the night, and Ankra had the charge to keep them till a slaver arrived, and the poor people were shipped in the night, all to avoid detection by the English and Danish governments.[46]

As British opposition to the trade intensified in the Accra area, many traders shifted their businesses to the east, particularly to communities on the upper Slave Coast, where they had long-standing trade relations. Since the late seventeenth century, a small but lucrative trade in livestock had existed between the Anlo and the lower Gold Coast; and those who traveled along the coast throughout this same period to Anexo and Whydah to purchase the much-valued aggrey beads necessarily passed through the Anlo area and were therefore quite familiar with this particular route.[47] A second factor contributing to the increased movement of strangers into the Anlo area during the early nineteenth century had to do with the poor enforcement of the anti-slave trade laws by the European powers operating east of the Volta. For example, in the Anlo area, where the Danes claimed exclusive trading rights, Denmark virtually abandoned any active involvement after 1807.[48] The French and Portuguese refused to refrain from the slave trade at Whydah because this port had proven to be such a lucrative source of enslaved Africans. Accordingly, when Portugal agreed in its treaty of 1810 with England to abandon trade in areas outside its claimed dominions on the West African coast, Whydah was specifically reserved as a port at which they could continue to buy slaves. This "special reservation" ended in 1815, but independent Portuguese and Brazilian merchants continued to operate at the port through the 1860s. Similarly, France stipulated in its 1833 treaty with England that any French ship docked at Whydah would be immune from the provisions of this treaty.[49] Thus,

---

[46] Reindorf, *History of the Gold Coast*, 152. See also Susan B. Kaplow, "The Mudfish and the Crocodile: Underdevelopment of a West African Bourgeoisie," *Science and Society*, XLI, 3 (1977), who discusses a number of Afro-European traders, as well as Susan B. Kaplow, "Primitive Accumulation and Traditional Social Relations on the Nineteenth Century Gold Coast," *Canadian Journal of African Studies*, XII, 1 (1978), and Raymond E. Dumett, "African Merchants of the Gold Coast, 1860–1905: Dynamics of Indigenous Entrepreneurship," *Comparative Studies in Society and History*, 25, 4 (1983).

[47] J. E. J. M. van Landewijk, "What was the Original Aggrey Bead?" *Ghana Journal of Sociology*, 6, 2/ 7,1 (1970/71), 90–91. See Kea, "Akwamu–Anlo Relations," 50, who describes an alternate route to the eastern ports that passed north of the Keta Lagoon.

[48] The Napoleonic wars prevented any shipments of trade goods between that year and 1814; thereafter only a small garrison was posted in Keta, and this was further reduced in 1834 to a single soldier. Nørregård, *Danish Settlements*, 190–205.

[49] Ward, *Royal Navy*, 56, 78. See also Lawrence C. Jennings, "French Policy Toward Trading with African and Brazilian Slave Merchants, 1840–1853," *Journal of African History*, XVII, 4 (1976), for a discussion of French policies toward the independent slave traders on the coast.

Photo 1: The Keta Market in 1928

slave ships continued to dock at the ports on the upper and middle Slave Coast after such contacts to the west on the Gold Coast became more problematic. The movement of slaves from towns west of the Volta to the upper Slave Coast was still the case in 1845 when Governor Carstensen noted that

> what supposedly has been happening all the time is now clear: negroes are carried from [Accra] here and from all the towns [on the littoral as far west as] Cape Coast to the market in Vay [i.e., Woe in Anlo]. [For example, in] Dutch Accra . . . [are resident] several slave trade agents, especially immigrant Brasilian negroes who have correspondents in Vay and Popo [Anexo]. Three months ago, two negroes were thus caught in Ningo (Fredensborg). They were to have been brought to the lower coast escorted by a Brasilian negro. But if one is caught and liberated, hundreds get through without interference.[50]

---

[50] Edward Carstensen, *Guvenør Carstensen's Indberetninger fra Guinea, 1842–1850*, edited by Georg Nørregård (Copenhagen, 1964), 106–107, 141–42. This diversion of the trade in slaves to the upper Slave Coast was also facilitated by the fact that certain goods (particularly firearms and tobacco) that were in demand in the interior were easily available on the Anlo coast. The only reliable source of Portuguese tobacco on the lower Gold Coast and upper Slave Coast was along the Anlo littoral and at ports further east. Edward Reynolds, *Trade and Economic Change on the Gold Coast, 1807–1874* (Essex, 1974), 59–60; Kea, "Akwamu–Anlo Relations," 60; and T. E. Bowdich, *Mission from Cape Coast to Ashantee* (London, 1819), 337. Portuguese, specifically Bahian, tobacco was distinctive because of its "harsh" quality and because it was cured with molasses; see Joseph C. Miller, *Way of Death* (Madison, 1988), 462, and Reynolds, *Trade and Economic Change*, 38, 50.

These developments contributed to a large-scale immigration of African, Afro-European, and European traders into the Anlo area, who then established close relations with local political, religious, and economic leaders as a means of protecting their newly established businesses. Among these strangers was one Tettega, an Adangbe trader. During the late 1700s or early 1800s, he married into a wealthy family based in Woe. Around 1800, this marriage produced a son, later known as Togbui Gbodzo of Woe. Because of his father's non-Anlo origins, Gbodzo was technically defined as a stranger (or *blu*) and a member of the Blu clan. He nevertheless rose to become the *dusifiaga*, the right-wing commander of the Anlo army, a position that his descendants continued to hold despite the fact that they, like Gbodzo, were also technically defined as ethnic outsiders.[51] I argue here that his and his family's achievement was the result of two factors: Gbodzo's successful use of his maternal family's economic and religious connections to the cultural and political center of power in the Anlo polity; and his and his descendants' manipulation of gender relations within their own family to de-emphasize their identity as ethnic outsiders.

Gbodzo's Rise to Power:
The Politics and Economics of Political Advancement

The history of the Gbodzo family is one of wealth generating additional wealth, as members of the family successfully established ties to some of the most prestigious groups in Anlo society. We begin with Gbodzo's father, Tettega, who is said to have first entered Anlo as a trader from Ada, specializing in the buying and selling of beads. Involvement in this particular enterprise suggests that Tettega was fairly wealthy on his arrival, for this was a highly valued commodity, whose purchase and resale involved great expenditure and great profits. The most valued form of this jewelry was the aggrey bead, purchased from the upper Slave Coast towns of Anexo and Whydah, and marketed along the littoral to the west as well as in the interior. Extensive sales of these beads were noted by the Danes in 1810, during the period when Tettega is said to have participated in this trade.[52] Their great value was also noted by the German missionary, J. Bernhard Schlegel, in 1853, and in an English report written in 1883:

> What are known as Aggri beads usually met with among the tribes on the Gold Coast, are highly valued by them, and form part of the royal jewels of the Kings of Ashantee. . . . they have probably been given in barter for slaves, gold dust and nuggets; they fetch at the present day an equal weight in gold and the rarer sorts one-and-a-half to twice their weight in gold dust.[53]
>
> [They] are the most precious ones that the Negro knows; females, especially virgins generally hang or often load themselves with . . . the so-called "beads." The more one is able to do this, the more certain and firm she fastens the eyes of the males on herself. The complete clothing of a

---

[51] FN 5: Interview with Mr. T. S. A. Togobo, 20 June 1978, Anloga.

[52] For a discussion of the origins and manufacture of aggrey beads, see J. E. J. M. van Landewijk, "What was the Original Aggrey Bead?," 6, and Kea, "Akwamu–Anlo Relations," 29–63.

[53] Cited in Reynolds, *Trade and Economic Change*, 33.

real Ewe-virgin consists of a rich pearl decoration around her loins; the
more she can get, the more she puts on.[54]

Given the period in which Tettega operated along the upper Slave Coast and lower
Gold Coast (between the late 1700s and early 1800s), and the fact that his involvement in the trade in beads took him from the Ga-Adangbe area to Anexo and Whydah, one may assume that he was also deeply involved in the movement of slaves
within this same region. For, as noted above, beads were often exchanged for slaves,
and after the British abolished the slave trade and began to interdict the same in the
Accra area, many traders based in the Accra and Ada areas simply transported their
slaves across the Volta and sold them at ports on the Anlo coast or further east. It was
also at this same time that gold, used by the Asante to purchase the much-demanded
aggrey beads, began to appear in the towns on the upper Slave Coast.[55]

Tettega's principal base of operations in Anlo was the town of Woe.[56] His ability
to establish himself in this community can be attributed to his affiliation with Amegashi
Akofi of Woe, the son of an Alakple fisherman and member of the Ame clan who immigrated to Woe in the mid-1700s. Akofi, who is also said to have been "a rich man
indeed," gained his wealth by supplying slaves to the Europeans operating on the
Anlo coast. In such a position, he was able to attract wealthy traders like Tettega, whose
involvement in the slave trade complemented his own, and whose presence in the
community under his auspices served to strengthen his own prestige. That a close
association between Tettega and Amegashi Akofi did exist is indicated by the fact that
Tettega was married to Amegashi Akofi's daughter, Kpetsimine. This union, which
ultimately led to the birth of Gbodzo, appears to have served the interests of both
Tettega and Amegashi Akofi quite well. It strengthened Tettega's association with the
community of Woe, and with one of its more influential citizens; it secured for
Amegashi Akofi an additional buyer for his slaves; and it is likely that through his
wife Kpetsimine, a member of the Nyigbla religious order, Tettega obtained access to
the young women whom this order had begun to sell to the slave traders.[57]

Tettega and Amegashi Akofi, father and maternal grandfather of Gbodzo, were
not the only members of Gbodzo's family known for their wealth. Gbodzo's mother,
Kpetsimina, and his mother's brother, Kuwo Nunya, both had similar reputations.
Nunya acquired enough slaves to create for himself a *hozikpui* or wealth stool.[58]

[54] Bernhard J. Schlegel, Beitrag zur Geschichte, Welt- und Religionsanchauung des Westafrikaners,
namentlich des Eweer," *Monatsblatt der Norddeutschen Missionsgesellschaft*, 7/93 (1858), 397–400, 7/94 (1858),
406–408. See Kumekpor, "Some Sociological Aspects," for a more complete description of the uses of
beads among the Anlo-Ewe, as well as FN 96: Interview with Togbui Anthonio Gbodzo II and his councilors, 24 February 1988, Woe.

[55] Kea, "Akwamu–Anlo Relations," 60.

[56] FN 96: Interview with Togbui Anthonio Gbodzo II and his councilors, 24 February 1988, Woe.

[57] FN 53: Interview with Togbui Afatsao Awadzi, 16 December 1987, Anloga; FN 55: Interview with Togbui
Kosi Axovi, 17 December 1987, Anloga; and FN 65: Interview with Togbui Dzobi Adinku, 6 January 1988,
Anloga. See also Spieth, *Die Religion*, 146 and Carl Spiess, "Ein Erinnerungsblatt an die Tage des
Sklavenhandels in West Afrika," in *Globus* (Braunschweig) 92 (1907), 205–208.

[58] A *hozikpui* is a wealth stool, carved in the shape typical of those made by the Akan, and strung around
the base with cowries representing the number of slaves owned by the stool holder. Aduamah, *Ewe Traditions*, No. 14; FN 34: Interview with Togbui Alex Afatsao Awadzi, 3 October 1978, Anloga; and FN 70:
Interview with Mr. Kwami Kpodo, 12 January 1988, Woe.

Kpetsimina was also well-endowed financially. According to some oral narratives, her wealth came from marketing in the Anlo area the beads her husband purchased in the east, as well as from the wholesale buying of foodstuffs from communities on the northern side of the lagoon, which she then marketed to Anlo towns on the coast. It is likely, however, that she too was deeply involved in the Atlantic slave trade. She is known to have owned her own boats, capable of transporting her slaves and goods purchased from European merchants between the shore and the awaiting European vessels off the coast of Woe. These boats and the implied riches they conveyed are mentioned in the following praise poem about her, where she is referred to as Gbodzo's mother.

> Gbodzono fe de, menye nuka da ge woala o.
> Wutregodidi menye asiku o, Gbodzono fe wu le megbe gbona.
> Gbodzo's mother's oil palm, one does not know what it will cook.
> The first boat to arrive is not the right one; Gbodzo's mother's boat is on the way.[59]

The wealth generated by Gbodzo's paternal and maternal relatives provided Gbodzo with a particularly strong financial base upon which to establish his own business activities. As the son of Tettega, an Adangbe who like the Anlo practiced patrilineal descent, Gbodzo should have inherited much of this initial capital from his father. Tettega, however, did not remain permanently in Woe, but moved continually up and down the coast as did other traders during this period, staying for only limited periods of time at his various trade stations, while maintaining wives in each location to conduct his business on a more regular basis. Gbodzo, in contrast, remained in Woe, and through residency, affiliated not with his father's relatives but with his mother's. And although there is no record of the family from whom he inherited the bulk of his wealth, we can assume that Gbodzo probably obtained the majority of his training, the labor force, and the capital to engage in trading from his maternal relatives.[60] Like them, his reputation for great wealth, which he displayed through the creation of his own *hozikpui*, was based on his involvement in the slave trade.[61] It was Gbodzo who erected the holding cells near the Woe beach on the Atlantic Ocean from which the slaves were moved when the European ships anchored off the coast;[62] and it was these slaves who are said to have composed the following song while awaiting their transfer.

Avie mata na Gbodzo yee	I shall rub Gbodzo with tears
Avie mata na Gbodzo yee	I shall rub Gbodzo with tears

---

[59] FN 70: Interview with Mr. Kwami Kpodo, 12 January 1988, Woe. FN 96: Interview with Togbui Anthonio Gbodzo II and his councilors, 24 February 1988, Woe; note that this same saying is also used to praise Gbodzo; see Aduamah, Ewe Traditions, No. 13.

[60] The practice among the Anlo at that time of nephew's working for and inheriting the acquired wealth of the maternal uncle, and the practice of mother's bequeathing their wealth to both sons and daughters would have been the means by which Gbodzo could claim to be a rightful inheritor of his mother and uncle. See Chapter 1.

[61] FN 76: Interview with Togbui Anthonio Gbodzo II and his councilors, 20 January 1988, Woe.

[62] FN 76: Interview with Togbui Anthonio Gbodzo II and his councilors, 20 January 1988, Woe. Carstensen, *Indberetninger*, 141.

Fu nade gbe	The sea may roar
Ga nade gbe yee	The irons may clank
Nye wukula meva hade o	The rower has not yet arrived
Avie mata na Gbodzo yee	I shall rub Gbodzo with tears [63]

Residence with and inheritance from his maternal relations were only two of the many factors that contributed to Gbodzo's success in trade. Another factor involved his and his family's successful cultivation of close ties with Spanish, Portuguese, and Brazilian slave traders. Evidence of the closeness of these relations is found in the history of the Danish efforts to stop the export trade in slaves in the Anlo area. As noted previously, the Danish government did little to suppress the export in human beings in the early nineteenth century, and instead focused their attention on cutting their overhead by reducing the already small garrisons posted to their out-forts at Ningo, Ada, and Keta.[64] Only when these soldiers informed officials in Accra that the actions of the slave traders had become particularly blatant would the Danish governor dispatch local troops to the area to confront and drive out or arrest the offenders. Three such encounters occurred on the lower Volta between 1839 and 1845; all involved the Spaniard, Don Jose Mora. Reindorf describes the third such incident:

> Mr. Hesse [the commandant of Keta] one night saw old Don Jose Mora passing by the fort with a gang of slaves. . . . Joined by Mr. Walter Hansen and some young men from the town, he overtook the gang and ordered them to halt, upon which Don Jose pointed his pistol at Mr. Hesse, and three times attempted to fire, but without effect. He was then caught and the pistol taken from him. The slaves were brought to the fort, but the dealers were suffered to depart.[65]

In this and in a previous incident, Mora was actively assisted by the people of Woe, where he resided. In the 1844 incident, it was "the old men of the town," no doubt the advisors of Gbodzo, who by this time was chief of Woe, who urged him to relocate temporarily to towns east of Keta.[66] After Mora was captured and released in 1845, it was also probably Gbodzo who obtained support from the leadership in Anloga to defend the Spaniard's interests, by storming the Keta fort, taking custody of the slaves being held there, and returning them to their owner.[67] Gbodzo's willingness to engage in such action is indicative of the close economic relationship that had developed between himself and Mora, strengthened by the establishment of social bonds. Gbodzo's maternal cousin, Afedima, "was a wealthy woman . . . whom the European merchants used to entrust with money to buy slaves for them; she was [also] the first black woman [in Anlo] to befriend a white," and is remembered as the wife of Don Jose Mora.[68] Gbodzo himself chose to com-

---

[63] Aduamah, *Ewe Traditions*, No. 13-14.

[64] After its abolition of the slave trade, the Danish government concentrated its efforts on supporting the ventures of various Danes to develop plantations. See Nørregård, *Danish Settlements*, 205, Chs. 19–22.

[65] Reindorf, *History of the Gold Coast* , 155–56. See also 154–55, and the incidents described in Carstensen, *Indberetninger*, 87, and Nørregård, *Danish Settlements*, 209.

[66] Carstensen, *Indberetninger*, 87.

[67] The details of the retrieval and the involvement of the Anlo *awoamefia* are noted in Carstensen, *Indberetninger*, 149, and Reindorf, *History of the Gold Coast*, 156.

memorate the close relations he had established with another Iberian or Brazilian trader, remembered only as Antonio, by giving one of his sons this name.[69] Establishing such close relations with European slave traders allowed Gbodzo and his family to sustain their position as one of the wealthiest families in the area

The Gendered Price of Social Advancement

The opportunity for Gbodzo to obtain a position of power within the Anlo political hierarchy came with the 1831–1833 Peki War.[70] This conflict began as a local dispute in the interior, north of the Anlo littoral. Nyive had hired the polity of Agotime to assist it in a war against Atikpoe. In the battle that followed, Atikpoe was defeated, but only because Agotime continued to fight after the Nyive fled the field. In compensation for the heavy losses suffered by the Agotime because of their desertion, the Nyive chief gave his daughter in marriage to the brother of the Agotime chief. Several years later, when the daughter returned to Nyive with the children conceived from the marriage, and the Nyive chief refused to send her back, Nyive and Agotime went to war. Each sought allies. Nyive obtained the assistance of a number of Krepi towns including Shia, Tove, Agu, and Atigbe; Agotime received assistance from Accra, Akwamu, and the latter's subordinate ally, Peki. In the ensuing battles, Agotime and its allies defeated Nyive, but conflicts among the victors led to another series of disputes, the most serious of which involved Peki and Akwamu. The numerous differences that placed Peki and Akwamu in opposition to one another during this period have been discussed elsewhere;[71] more significant for our understanding of this event is the fact that their unwillingness to resolve these conflicts peacefully brought both to the battlefield in 1833, each again with its own allied forces. Peki gained support from Anum and Boso; Akwamu received troops from Anlo. Among the latter were Togbui Zewu, interim commander of the entire Anlo army, Adedze Gbekle of Woe, *dusifiaga* or right-wing commander, and Gbodzo, who was serving under the command of Gbekle.[72] Although their first encounters with the enemy were successful, subsequent battles took a heavy toll on Akwamu and its ally. Anlo suffered particularly large casualties.[73] As a consequence of the heavy loss

---

[68] FN 70: Interview with Mr. Kwami Kpodo, 12 January 1988, Woe; FN 76: Interview with Togbui Anthonio Gbodzo II and his councilors, 20 January 1988, Woe; FN 94: Interview with Mr. Klevor Abo, 20 February 1988, Accra-Legon; FN 96: Interview with Togbui Anthonio Gbodzo II and his councilors, 24 February 1988, Woe.

[69] See FN 5: Interview with Mr. T. S. A. Togobo, 20 June 1978, Anloga; FN 76: Interview with Togbui Anthonio Gbodzo II and his councilors, 20 January 1988, Woe.

[70] For detailed descriptions of this conflict, see Reindorf, *History of the Gold Coast*, 305–14; C. W. Welman, *The Native States of the Gold Coast, History and Constitution, Pt. 1, Peki* (London, 1969); Christian Hornberger, "Etwas aus der Geschichte der Anloer," *Quartalblatt der Norddeutschen Missionsgesellschaft* (1877), 460–61.

[71] See Welman, *Native States*; Reindorf, *History of the Gold Coast*, Ch. XXVI.

[72] L. P. Tosu, Anlo Traditional Council Documents: A Short History of the Awada-da Stool of Anlo, 5. On deposit at the Anlo Traditional Council Archives, Anloga, Ghana. FN 76: Interview with Togbui Anthonio Gbodzo II and his councilors, 20 January 1988, Woe.

[73] Reindorf, *History of the Gold Coast*, 313–14.

of life and the paltry reward in slaves acquired from the conflict, Adedze Gbekle resigned as *dusifiaga*. Gbodzo assumed the position thereafter.

Gbodzo's elevation to this post raises a number of questions. How did the Anlo leadership, who confirmed Gbodzo as *dusifiaga*, handle Gbodzo's identity as an ethnic outsider? How did Gbodzo himself manage this identity? We know that ethnic outsiders were viewed with suspicion, for many felt that association through kinship with another polity or culture compromised one's ability to support wholly the interests of Anlo. In 1750, for example, when Anlo successfully extricated itself from Anexo control, the *awoamefia*, Anyage (who had been born and raised in Anexo, his mother's home) resisted this move, and invited Anexo and Ada to attack Anlo. He subsequently fled into exile after a failed assassination attempt.[74] German missionaries recorded vivid accounts of this betrayal as late as the end of the nineteenth century. They recorded similar sentiments about foreign *trowo* or gods, as indicated in the following account.

> Apart from Nyigbla, . . . [*trowo* imported from areas other than Notsie] were . . . looked upon by their worshippers as foreigners and intruders, who, as they say, "were not one" on the side of the Ewes. In times of war, for instance, they were never on the side of the Ewes, and were, therefore, not taken with them to war. One could not trust them totally. Their nature was bad and they paid in general, no heed to the lives of men.[75]

The Anlo political and military leaders who elevated Gbodzo to *dusifiaga*, could have, of course, set aside these generally held negative sentiments about ethnic outsiders by emphasizing the following points: (1) Gbodzo was a maternal nephew to Amegashi Akofi, an Ame clan member, and as such was in a recognized position of kinship to an Anlo clan, the same relationship that by this period is said to have obtained between the Bate and Adzovia clans which provided the *awoamefia*; (2) Gbodzo had lived in Woe his entire life, and therefore was an Anlo both by matrilineal descent and by residence; (3) Gbodzo's military involvement in the Anlo war in Peki demonstrated his willingness to risk his own life and the lives of his slaves for the economic and political interests of Anlo; and (4) his support of the *awoamefia* by supplying munitions, and his continued ability to do so because of his close ties to the various Afro-European and European slave traders on the coast, were significant enough to warrant such recognition. That both the Anlo elders and Gbodzo may have used these very arguments to rationalize Gbodzo's identity as an ethnic outsider is suggested not only by the fact that the anti-stranger sentiments in existence in nineteenth-century Anlo would have required such action, but is also indicated by the ways in which Gbodzo's connection to the *dusifiaga* position is remembered in the oral traditions of Anlo.

When I made enquiries about Gbodzo in 1978 and 1988, it became very clear that his descendants were still quite sensitive about their stranger origins, and were unprepared to discuss these with other Anlo, who might use this fact against them. This self-imposed silence about their ancestor no doubt developed in response to

---

[74] FN 5: Interview with Mr. T. S. A. Togobo, 20 June 1978, Anloga; FN 30: Interview with Mr. T. S. A. Togobo, 26 September 1978, Anloga; FN 42: Interview with Boko Seke Axovi, 1 November 1978, Anloga; Spiess, *Könige der Anloer*; Rattray, "History of the Ewe People," 92–98. Anyage was also known as Kofi Adzanu and Fiayidziehe.

[75] Spieth, *Die Religion*, 145.

the fact that their own social and political status was directly linked to that of Gbodzo's image. As long as their ancestor is viewed primarily as a spiritually powerful, wealthy, and politically influential leader who served well his own community of Woe and the polity of Anlo as a whole, Gbodzo's descendants can continue to use this imagery to support their claim to occupy the *dusifiaga* position in the Anlo hierarchy and to provide the chief of Woe. Maintaining silence about Gbodzo's ethnic outsider origins did have negative consequences, however, which fell disproportionately on the women in Gbodzo's family. In his discussion of nineteenth-century Anlo culture, Spieth observed that both men and women took responsibility for the creation and dissemination of knowledge about Anlo society and culture. Women educated both boys and girls about the social life of their communities until they reached the age of seven or eight. Thereafter, women focused their attention on their daughters, while men continued with the boys, educating them to assume their roles as men.[76] Nukunya has emphasized this same division of knowledge and responsibility in contemporary Anlo.[77] Anlo oral traditions and nineteenth-century European accounts indicate, however, that certain activities were traditionally the preserve of men, knowledge about which women were structurally or intentionally excluded. For example, Härtter observed that women were not allowed to walk where fishnets were laid out to dry because of the belief that the nets would be unable to catch fish thereafter. Women were also forbidden to be present when men were actually catching the fish because their presence was said to cause premature rotting of the catch.[78] Women were excluded from the iron-smelting process.[79] Men were strongly enjoined to withhold hunting knowledge from women because to reveal such knowledge was believed to cause the hunter's death.[80] Sons were encouraged by fathers involved in the political affairs of their community to accompany them to gatherings where they could learn about the political and military history of their ancestors and the legal culture of the society. Young women rarely had such opportunities since they were encouraged to assist their mothers, who themselves were only irregular participants in the governing bodies of their lineages, clans, wards, and villages.

The decision by Gbodzo's descendants to de-emphasize his identity as a member of the Blu (an ethnically distinct clan) necessarily constrained the extent to which both male and female members of his family could use their intimate knowledge of Gbodzo's genealogical past as a means to boost their own social position. It is likely, however, that this constraint was felt more keenly by Gbodzo's female descendants, particularly those who were young, since their voices were already confined to a more restricted space within Anlo society. As women, they could not participate in the creation of re-enactments of Gbodzo's military victories, nor could they compose songs about his political acumen, since this would have required access to the kinds of detailed knowledge generally disseminated only to the male

---

[76] Spieth, "Von den Evhefrauen," 6.

[77] Nukunya, *Kinship and Marriage*, 148–49.

[78] Gottlob Härtter, "Der Fishfang im Ewelande," *Zeitschrift für Ethnologie* (Braunschweig) 38/1–2 (1906), 55.

[79] Madeline Manoukian, "The Ewe-Speaking People of Togoland and the Gold Coast," in Daryll Ford, ed., Ethnographic Survey of Africa (London: International African Institute, 1950), 18.

[80] FN 14: Interview with Togbui Yai Trygod Zodanu, 11 August 1978, Anloga.

members of the family. Thus, while all of Gbodzo's descendants benefited socially from their decision to de-emphasize their stranger identity, the decision had its costs for all, but especially for Gbodzo's female descendants.

Conclusion

Throughout the eighteenth and nineteenth centuries, refugees, traders, and others, individually and in groups, streamed into Anlo. Many opted to take up residence in their new location, but their decision to do so did not mean automatic acceptance by the existing residents. They found themselves stigmatized as ethnic outsiders, defined as "other" by the earlier residents, who sought to protect their economic and political interests by limiting the newcomers' access to land and to political office, while also placing greater restrictions on those to whom they were prepared to betroth their own daughters. This same period saw numerous efforts by ethnic outsiders to overcome these restrictions. The Dzevi managed to position their priest within the highest political and religious circles within the polity during the late eighteenth century. Political prestige, however, did not eliminate the stigma associated with their foreign origins. Social redefinition as ethnic insiders did occur for the Amlade. This clan took advantage of the continued hostility that the political and religious elite felt toward the Dzevi, the cultural significance that the Anlo accorded to association with powerful spiritual forces, and their own possession of one of the most respected gods in Anlo to alter its ethnic identity. By the nineteenth century, they were known as one of the most socially prestigious groups in Anlo, members of the "first five." Togbui Gbodzo and his descendants accomplished a similar feat in the nineteenth century by using their wealth and their connections to the Anlo war god, Nyigbla, and to the Afro-European traders operating in Anlo to obfuscate their identity as ethnic outsiders. To accomplish this alteration in their identities, both employed the same tactics used by ethnic insiders to protect their interests. They encouraged, cajoled, and/or required the young women over whom they had authority to sacrifice their interests for the sake of the social advancement of the group. Efforts on the part of ethnic outsiders to challenge the prevailing social relations defining them as "other" impacted gender relations in ways that saw the women within their groups lose many of their already limited opportunities to influence their own lives.

3

Ethnicized Responses: Women in Eighteenth- and Nineteenth-Century Anlo

By the end of the nineteenth century, Anlo women—whether members of ethnic insider or ethnic outsider families—found their voices increasingly silenced by the elders within their lineages and clans. Rivalry during the eighteenth century between earlier residents and those who entered Anlo after 1679 had prompted both to form themselves into separate sets of clans and to strongly urge their young women to marry fellow clan members. Rivalry between individual lineages for prestige and power during the nineteenth century induced the elders of many Anlo clans to prefer marriages between their daughters and their sisters' sons, and to ignore any objections the young women might have had. Nineteenth-century European accounts also indicate that by this period the young women in Anlo had begun to challenge successfully certain aspects of this system. In 1906, the German missionary G. Binetsch observed that during the fifty-year period in which the Norddeutsch Missionsgesellschaft (NDMG) had been working in Anlo, marital practices had changed significantly:

> concubinage has [begun] to replace the traditional [marriage custom] in recent times. . . . girls enter, behind their parents' backs, into concubinage with men of their choice. Even girls who have gotten presents from their intended husbands from the time they were infants, refuse to participate in [the traditional marital custom]. . . . love-matches happen more frequently [than in the past] among our Anlo.[1]

Scholars who have explored recent changes in African marital patterns such as the decline in arranged marriages and the rise of "love-matches" attribute these particular developments to colonialism. They argue that the spread of Western influence undermined Africans' beliefs in their religious systems and made largely irrelevant many of the knowledge systems that had informed the world view of

---

[1] Binetsch, "Beantwortung mehrerer," 46.

African men and women prior to the colonial period. These developments are said to have undermined parental authority in marital decisions as well. Love and individual choice became more acceptable as foundations for marriage under the influence of missionary-run schools.[2]

This explanation has some validity, no doubt, but it cannot fully explain the changes Binetsch observed in the late nineteenth century. Missionary education, introduced in 1853, had hardly begun to make inroads into the various villages and towns of Anlo by the end of the century. Schools existed in the towns of Keta, Anyako, Dzelukofe, Atoko, and Woe by 1902, but a number of these frequently lost some if not all their students. Most Anlos attended only to obtain the new skills needed to improve their families' businesses; many never converted to Christianity.[3] The British defeat of Anlo in 1874 certainly damaged the reputation of the gods which the Anlo had entrusted with their safety against foreign aggression, but did these events constitute the principal factors that introduced changes in the marital system of nineteenth-century Anlo?

Data from Anlo do not support this particular conclusion. Rather, the evidence suggests that the changes noted by Binetsch had their origins in the period between the late eighteenth- and the mid nineteenth-centuries. During this period, increasing numbers of young women took advantage of changes within the social, political, economic, and religious culture of the polity as a means to exercise greater control over their marital affairs. Among the more important of these eighteenth-century changes were those that involved the ethnic outsider Dzevi clan. In Chapter 2, I noted that in 1769 the Dzevi used their god Nyigbla to challenge the right of the Adzovia and Bate clans to preside exclusively over the political and religious affairs of Anlo. They achieved success because of the support they received from ethnic insiders and outsiders alike who believed that Nyigbla would bring them the military victories so vital to the Anlos' prosperity within the economically competitive environment of the lower Gold Coast and upper Slave Coast. The Amlade enjoyed even greater success. This clan not only used their gods to enhance their reputation as potentially powerful allies, they also managed to alter their identity as ethnic outsiders. The Dzevi success was particularly notable, however, because even though the Anlo still defined them as ethnically distinct, women seeking to defy the prevailing character of gender relations helped make possible the institutionalization of their position within the highest political and religious leadership circles in Anlo. I argue in the first section of this chapter that many women opted to support the Dzevi during the late eighteenth and early nineteenth centuries because the clan's religious order enabled them to strengthen their own or their daughters' positions in their husbands' households. For example, if a young woman wanted to make sure that her husband listened to her opinions and wishes, and/or if her mother wished to give her this opportunity, they could do so by having the young woman join the Nyigbla order. I argue that many Anlo women did indeed do this and that their support served as a foundation for the Dzevi to challenge their exclusion from power. In other words, the actions taken by late

---

[2] See Dickson, "Marital Selection," 297–330, for example, who discusses a plethora of studies on this subject.

[3] See Carl Osswald, *Fifty Years' Mission Work at Keta* (Bremen, 1903), for a description of the German missionary schools in the Anlo area. See also S.C. 14/2, 240.

eighteenth- and early nineteenth-century Anlo women in response to changes in gender relations directly affected ethnic relations in Anlo.

In the second part of this chapter, I discuss the way in which Anlo women expanded their efforts to defy familial decisions that impacted them negatively. I begin by documenting the rise of Yewe, a new religious order founded by an individual born and raised in Anlo but nevertheless defined as an ethnic outsider because of his membership in the Blu clan. I argue that Yewe provided women even greater freedom over their marital affairs. Those who joined this order obtained the right to select their own spouse. They were also able to interact on a more equal footing with their husbands. These advantages encouraged other women in Anlo unaffiliated with either Nyigbla or Yewe to become more active in influencing their own marital affairs. The ability of women to assert themselves was also related to developments in the Anlo economy, however. After the abolition of the slave trade, increased social competition and indebtedness became much more common. By the late nineteenth century this gave young men the opportunity to select their own spouses because of their parents' inability to help them obtain the increasingly substantial bridewealth payments. Women interested in having more control over their lives began to contract their own marriages, a right that had previously been open only to Yewe women. As a result of these two parallel developments—the emergence of competition between Yewe and Nyigbla, and of greater social competition among Anlo families resulting in increased indebtedness—by the late nineteenth century women were able to defy the efforts of their families to control their voices and bodies through participation in *dze hia*, concubinage (defined here as the establishment of sexual relations and co-residence without benefit of parental involvement or a marriage ceremony).

Women also had a major impact on ethnic relations. By joining the religious order founded by the ethnic outsider E. Quist in such great numbers, for example, they undermined the notion that genealogical and geographical connections to Notsie formed the principal bases for social prestige in Anlo. With the support of Yewe, they reinforced instead the emerging reality that wealth and service to the community were as important a basis for social status as ethnic origins.

Together, these two case studies illustrate the fact that gender relations had a direct impact on ethnic relations in eighteenth- and nineteenth-century Anlo. I begin this chapter with an analysis of the non-gender-based support that the Dzevi received in their bid to institutionalize their position within the political and religious center of Anlo society. I then document the important role that changes in gender relations played in encouraging women to support the Dzevi. I argue that ultimately women's support helped the Dzevi challenge the prevailing pattern of ethnic relations in Anlo society by expanding the permissible roles that ethnic outsiders could occupy.

Nyigbla and the Non-Gendered Politics of Institutionalization

Throughout the eighteenth and nineteenth centuries, political influence and religious authority were inextricably linked, as noted in Chapter 2. The more powerful one's reputation for being able to exert spiritual influence over worldly events, the more influential one became. This was most aptly demonstrated in 1769 when the ethnic outsider Dzevi clan rose to power after convincing others within Anlo that it was their god, Togbui Nyigbla, who had brought them victory in battle at a critical time. Even more significant is the fact that the Dzevi priest of the god Nyigbla and his supporters were able to institutionalize the charismatic character of his position. In 1772, only two years after the decisive victory that forced the *awoamefia* to share the religious and political leadership of the polity with the Nyigbla priest, the Danes reported that the person who received the tribute they paid to the Anlo for their right to trade in the area was "King Tecco." The name Teko is associated with the Dzevi clan and was probably the name of the individual from this *hlo* who was responsible for collecting rent from the Danes.[4] During the mid-nineteenth century, German missionaries reported that the Nyigbla order still received tribute from foreign traders.[5]

Several events appear to have been critical for this institutionalization. The Anlo suffered devastating military losses in 1784, and again in 1792, yet they chose, however, not to attribute these defeats to the failure of their recently installed "stranger" god. Instead, they focused on other causes, which only strengthened their belief in his power. In the first conflict, the 1784 Sagbadre War, a coalition of forces located to the east, west, and northwest of Anlo (including Ada, Akyem, Akuapem, Anexo, and several Ga, Adangbe, and Volta River Ewe-speaking towns, as well as the Danes) successfully launched a series of devastating attacks on Anlo. Anlo's undoing can easily be explained by the virtual encirclement of their army by the allied troops which, in moving from both the southwest and northeast, forced the Anlo either to retreat into the sea or to abandon their homeland by passing northward through a narrow corridor left open by their enemies.[6] Disunity among Anlo military ranks appears to have been an additional factor, however, and the Anlo appear to have focused on this for an explanation of their loss. The internal relations in question were those between Anlo and the Keta district.

Prior to 1774, Anlo and Keta had been separate polities, often in conflict. After both had been conquered by Anexo in 1741, for example, Keta failed to support the Anlo-led 1750 rebellion designed to secure their independence. Thereafter, Keta consistently supported Anexo and its ally, Ada, in their conflicts with Anlo.[7] Only after Anexo failed to support Keta and Ada in their 1769 conflict with Anlo—a failure which resulted in the massive defeat of Ada—did Keta alter its association with Anexo, breaking with them and shifting its political position to form an alliance with Anlo. Thus, in September 1772, a Danish officer stationed at Keta noted

---

[4] GK 149, 21 December 1772, Ada, J. Kiøge; see also GK 191, 31 December 1774, Quitta; 30 November 1773, Christiansborg; and FN 37: Interview with Boko Seke Axovi, 9 October 1978, Anloga. According to *Hogbeza, 1978* (Accra, 1978), 21, Teko is a female name. This suggests that the right to collect tribute from the Europeans in Keta was held by the female Dzevi medium through whom Nyigbla communicated.

[5] Schlegel, "Beitrag zur Geschichte," 399–400.

[6] Paul Erdmann Isert, *Voyages en Guinée et dans les îles Caraïbes en Amerique* (Paris, 1793), 27–93; Kea, "Akwamu–Anlo Relations," 40; Nørregård, *Danish Settlements*, 146–48; H. W. Debrunner, *A Church Between Colonial Powers: A Study of the Church in Togo* (London, 1965); Jean M. Grove and A. M. Johansen, "The Historical Geography of the Volta Delta, Ghana, During the Period of Danish Influence," *Bulletin de l'I.F.A.N.*, XXX, 4 (1968), 1392–94. See also Reindorf, *History of the Gold Coast*, 131–37.

[7] GK 166, 26 September 1769, Quitta, E. Quist.

that "the Quitta and Augona negroes . . . have eaten fetish. . . . to be united . . . [this] being in my [opinion], a new period in the Creepeiske system."[8] The benefits from this alliance for both parties were many. Keta's location on the eastern boundary of the expanded Anlo polity and the incorporation of the Keta troops (said to have been the largest military force on the littoral outside Anloga) into the military strengthened Anlo's defense capabilities at a time when military conflicts had become increasingly common. For Keta, incorporation provided an opportunity to associate on a equal footing with the polity that had direct control over the northern shore of the Keta Lagoon, through which much of the coastal–interior trade was carried. The 1784 war, known locally as the Sagbadre war, severely tested these relations.

When Ada, Anexo, Akyem, Akuapem, and their allies attacked Anlo in 1784, Danish officers J. Kioge and P. Isert (the latter of whom accompanied the forces that invaded Anlo territory) indicated that a number of men from Keta and its affiliated village of Agudza withdrew their support for Anlo when their towns were invaded. Some declared their neutrality; others accepted bribes and joined the campaign against Anlo.[9] The seriousness of the breach in relations between the Anlos and the Ketas is evident from the provisions of the treaty the Danes had all parties involved in the conflict endorse. These provisions included a stipulation that the Ketas allow the Danes to establish a fort in their town. The Danes also banned the Ketas from using their canoes to pursue off-shore trade with other European ships. These provisions were clearly detrimental to the economic interests of the Ketas, but they accepted them because they saw the Danish presence as a source of protection against possible Anlo retribution.[10] This suggests that the Anlo could have easily attributed their defeat to the betrayal of the Ketas and Agudzas, rather than to the failure of Nyigbla. That this was indeed the case is evident from the fact that less than a year later, in 1785, the Keta-affiliated towns of Agudza and Kpoduwa were attacked and destroyed by Anlo with Akwamu, Kwawu, and Agotime assistance. Keta itself was then threatened with the same fate.

---

[8] GK 149, 6 September 1772, Quitta, J. Kiøge. The extent to which Keta was incorporated into Anlo after the ceremony noted is difficult to discern because of the controversy that has surrounded the issue since at least the beginning of the twentieth century, a controversy that has politicized the traditions to such an extent that historical interpretation is quite difficult. Those whose ancestors are said to have lived in Keta at the time claim that the town was closely associated with the Anlo by marriage, but retained its political autonomy, and as such could only be considered a member of the allied group in southeastern Ghana known currently as Greater Anlo. Anlo traditions claim that Keta was an integral part of the Anlo polity, currently termed Anlo Akuaku, and constituted the entire right wing of their army. An additional source of information is a number of accounts of Anlo–Keta relations by the Danes who were in the area throughout much of the eighteenth century. These accounts are by no means uniform in their interpretation of the new relationship between Anlo and Keta. Nevertheless, one must conclude that Keta became part of Anlo Akuaku, for while the Danes note on the one hand that the two were different people and that Keta was politically independent, they also report on 14 January 1774 that "a Quitta negro" is to be installed as king or cabuseer in Anloga. No name was mentioned, nor was there subsequent information on the exact position this person was to occupy; however, it is significant that the ceremony was to take place in the ritual and political capital of Anlo Akuaku.

[9] Isert, *Voyages en Guinée*, 87–88, 65–66; Generaltoldkammerts Archiv [Gtk] Schimmelmanske Paper, 27 August 1788, Copenhagen, J. Kiøge.

[10] Isert, *Voyages en Guinée*, 87–88. Another provision in the treaty required Anlo to renew its relations with Keta and to live in peace with them.

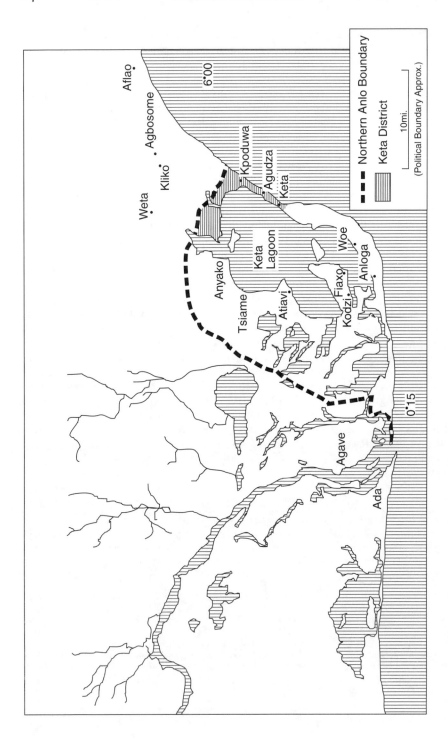

Map 5: Anlo in 1784, with the newly incorporated Keta District

A second military disaster, as devastating in its impact as the 1784 war, occurred in 1792, and it too does not seem to have challenged the Anlo belief in Nyigbla. In fact, this loss appears to have strengthened the Anlos' faith in their new god. Why this was the case is apparent from descriptions of the conflict. According to Danish accounts, on 21 June 1791, a Keta resident by the name of Degeni was killed in a skirmish with the Danish garrison stationed at the Keta fort. Degeni's relatives blamed his death on A. Biørn, the fort's governor. Shortly thereafter, they relocated to the village of Kpoduwa and from this location attacked any caravan associated with the Danes. In April 1788 and March 1790, they successfully captured two Danish officers, whom they held for ransom, and two Danish servants, whom they sold from the country. On 22 June 1790, Sape Agbo, Degeni's brother, attacked and killed Danish factor Thessen at Aflao. In an effort to end these attacks, Biørn sent a considerable sum of money to Ampofo of Akyem, requesting that he attack Keta, Agudza, and Kpoduwa, all of whom he held responsible for Thessen's death. Ampofo accepted the money but failed to follow through with the raid. Biørn then turned to Anlo, which accepted the offer in exchange for the payment of 1,672 rigsdalers' worth of commodities in powder, guns, and brandy.[11]

Immediately prior to the planned Anlo raid on Keta, the Anlos (who had reestablished good relations with their former enemy) informed Keta of their impending attack, for, as one Danish officer later observed, the Anlos viewed their agreement "as a splendid business transaction."[12] The inhabitants of Keta, Agudza, and Kpoduwa abandoned their towns with the assumption that their absence would prevent any further hostilities. The Anlos, however, were accompanied by a number of Danish officers, and felt compelled to continue with the ruse by burning all of the towns to the ground. The residents of these towns were angry, and Anlo's relations with Keta, Agudza, and Kpoduwa turned sour. A series of skirmishes broke out between the two districts, culminating in 1792 in the devastating defeat of Anlo in what became known as the Keta War.[13] This loss, however, appears to have even strengthened the position of Nyigbla in the religious and political hierarchy of the polity. Why this was the case is apparent from the following account of the battle.

On 22 February 1792, the Anlo army—reportedly two thousand strong, led by their military leaders, Awadada (military commander) Kwawuga, Dusifiaga (right-wing commander) Dacon, Miafiaga (left-wing commander) Ovan, and accompanied by Danish Factor Borgesen with an armed force of thirty men from the garrison of the Danish Fort Prindsensten in Keta—attacked the six-hundred man army of Keta, Agudza, and Kpoduwa, whose forces also included contingents from Kliko,

---

[11] Gtk, Schimmelmanske Paper, 21 June 1791, Christiansborg, J. P. Wrisberg; also in Gtk, Guineiske Sager og Akstykker, 1765-1802.

[12] Nørregård, *Danish Settlements*, 155.

[13] Danish disunity over how to deal with the Ketas also foiled the attack. See the accounts in H. C. Monrad, *Bidrag til en Skildring af Guinea-kysten og dens Indbyggere og til en Beskrivelse over de Danske Colonier paa denne Kyst* (Copenhagen, 1822), 70–71; Gtk, Schmimmelmanske Paper, 21 June 1791, Christiansborg, J. Wrisberg, also in Gtk, Guineiske Sager og Akstykker; Anlo Traditional Council Minute Book No. 3, Chief Tsagli of Kedzi, Plaintiff -v- Chief Joachim Acolatse III of Keta, Defendant; and Charles M. K. Mamattah, *The Ewes*, 636–39.

Weta, and Anexo.[14] The ensuing battle was brief and bloody. After a "fiery cannonade" the Ketas and their allies drove the right wing of the Anlo army out of its trenches and set fire to the paths on which they had begun to retreat. The fire then began to threaten all the other paths as well. Seeing this development, those in the left wing, followed by "all the remaining great caboseers and grandees," panicked, ignored the encouragement shouted by Awadada Kwawuga that they could overcome this situation, and then "threw down their weapons and overran their parents, leaving them to their fate." Dacon, surrounded by only the dead members of his division and the enemy, committed suicide by cutting "his stomach all the way to the heart." Awadada Kwawuga attempted to escape, but finding himself also surrounded, followed Dacon's example. Thirteen other military leaders—among whom were Ablera, Oklu, Ampam, Aboadzi, Koy Nantri, Kisseku, and Botsi—were captured and executed the next day, along with 111 others. As the Danes noted, one of the most amazing aspects of the battle was that it took only sixty Ketas to capture the 124 prisoners mentioned above. According to some, the outcome was due to the fact that the battle occurred immediately after the Anlos had completed a hot, dry march of approximately thirty-six miles to the field of battle which had left the troops exhausted. Others stated that a respected priest had predicted the Anlo defeat, and that the prediction was seen by the Anlos as an emerging reality when the left wing of the army was forced by fire to retreat.[15] If, in fact, this respected priest was the Nyigbla priest, the Anlo's defeat would have further enhanced his reputation and that of his god among the Anlo population. That this was precisely what happened is indicated by the institutionalized authority given to the Nyigbla order after this battle.

Danish records and Anlo traditions indicate that the Nyigbla order and the Dzevi clan were able to initiate a number of new structures in the early the nineteenth century that ultimately altered the relationship between the Anlo population and their political and religious leaders. By the early 1800s, for example, the Nyigbla priest had persuaded a number of clans to relocate to Anloga the shrines that had previously been scattered throughout the area in which each *hlo* had their clan land. A second innovation involved the way in which those who held the highest political and religious offices in Anlo reinforced their positions. Traditions about the Adzovia clan—which provided the Anlo *awoamefia*—indicate that it was common for this group to strengthen its authority by acquiring respected deities and priests from outside the area. They acquired, for example, the *tsikpe* or rain stone from the Notsie area, which they later used to support their right to provide

---

[14] Gtk, Guineiske Sager og Akstykker, 4 February 1789, contained in a letter dated 14 March 1789, Copenhagen; No. 37, 24 April 1793, Christiansborg, A. Biørn, F. Hager, J. E. Chuhtu, N. Lather. Anexo hoped to use the war as an opportunity to retaliate against the Danes for their support of an unsuccessful claimant to the Anexo throne.

[15] Gtk, Guineiske Sager og Akstykker, No. 37, 24 April 1792, Christiansborg, A. Biørn, F. Hager, J. E. Chuhtu, N. Lather. See also Mamattah, *The Ewes*, 636–39, who recounts Anlo traditions about the war. Note that while some of the events correspond with the discussion of the events in the Danish records, the traditions also include events that were clearly not associated with this war. See also Anlo Traditional Council Minute Book, No. 3, Chief Tsagli II of Kedzi, Plaintiff -v- Chief Joachim Acolatse III of Keta, Defendant, p. 107–108; and ADM 11/1091, Petition from Fia Adama II, Paramount Chief of Agbosome. Note that my interpretations of the relevant Danish documents on the last mentioned battle does not correspond with that of Nørregård, *Danish Settlements*, 156, but his interpretation is also not consistent with the events recorded by the Danes.

the *awoamefia*. They also united with a particularly powerful god and its priest from Avenor sometime after 1702 when the Akwamu conquest threatened their authority.[16] The Dzevi clan appears to have pursued this same approach in their efforts to enhance the status of their god, Nyigbla, within the society. However, they did so not by seeking outside assistance, but by expanding their base of support within the community as they formed a number of alliances with less powerful, but locally based deities and the families that had custody of them. This structure—which mirrored the military entourage of the *awoamefia*—was first described in the late nineteenth century. According to these accounts, the god Afu and its priest assumed the office of *agbotadua*, which was held by those who walked in battle ahead of Nyigbla; the god Dzotsiafe and its priest served as its linguist or spokesman (*tsiame*); the Lafe god, Awadatsi, and its priest became the first officer (*awadada*) in the army of gods which Nyigbla led in protecting the Anlo polity; the god Agbedzeme was the stool (*zikpui*) upon which Nyigbla sat; and the god Hanya served as Nyigbla's messenger (*atikploto*).[17] When the Nyigbla *tronua* or priest developed this structure is unclear, but since other aspects of Anlo life were being centralized under the the Nyigbla priest during the first years of the nineteenth century, it is likely this consolidation of religious orders occurred during this same period.

A third change initiated by the Nyigbla priest involved the relationship between the various *to-fomewo* or patrilineages of Anlo and the most influential religious orders in the polity. Families frequently consulted the most powerful gods when particularly serious disputes or difficulties arose; if the priest chose to do so, he or she could demand that the family dedicate one of their own to the service of the god, in payment for services rendered. Most often this person, known as a *fiasidi*, would be a young woman. Such cases were probably not particularly common, however, nor was a family obligated to patronize one god rather than another. This rather loose relationship between the most powerful Anlo gods and the population changed in the early 1800s when the Nyigbla priest initiated a new ritual known as *foasi*, which served as the vehicle for the Nyigbla order to induct two or more young women from each clan in Anlo once a year, every year. An elder whose family took part in this ritual recounted the following about this event:

> This ceremony was for these girls to become the temporary wives of Nyigbla. The parents did not elect to have their daughters do this: the *tro* Nyigbla chose them. They just disappeared. If they went out to fetch water, they might just disappear. Those who were chosen [previously as young women] gave [their own] daughters when they were of age. The young girls, virgins, were taken to the forest where Togbui Nyigbla was supposed to live. The custom was that the mothers sent food to the girls regu-

---

[16] See FN 9: Interview with Mr. T. S. A. Togobo, 7 August 1978, Anloga, which indicate that when the god Tomi came from the Avenor area, it initially competed with the deity of the Nyaxoenu branch of the Adzovia clan for followers. Subsequently, when clan formation took place, these two united along with another group to form the Adzovia clan. I would suggest here that this unification occurred in response to the Akwamu threat to their prestige, given the fact that clan formation took place during the period of Akwamu expansion, and the fact that reckonings by Adzovia elders indicate that this unification occurred some nine generations ago, a date that would place unification within the period in which Akwamu controlled Anlo.

[17] Spieth, *Die Religion*, 52, 56, 68, 110; FN 43: Interview with Mr. T. S. A. Togobo, 31 October 1978, Anloga.

larly. The food was left with the overseer of the forest at the entrance and was taken to them. They would stay there from six to twelve months. Afterwards, they were released to lead a normal life. The women would marry and have children, but when the *tro* was outdoored, they [were recalled into Anloga, where they] sang, et cetera.[18]

Many advantages accrued to the Nyigbla priest and his clan from the implementation of these innovations. By encouraging the relocation of clan shrines to Anloga, the Nyigbla priest brought each Anlo family into direct and regular communication with the political and religious leadership of Anlo, for every family was expected to bathe their children in the *agba metsi*, the clan's ritual waters, as part of the clan induction ceremony. It was also at the clan shrine that children had applied the facial marks that distinguished them as Anlos, and where family members were expected to perform burial rituals for deceased family members.[19] Development of the military entourage of deities expanded the size of the community associated with the Dzevi and their deity, and facilitated its propagation throughout Anlo. The *foasi* ceremony served the same purpose and became an important vehicle for insuring the continued recruitment of members into the order: all Nyigbla initiates, known as *zizidzelawo*, were expected to dedicate at least one of their future children to the worship of Nyigbla.

The Nyigbla priest, the Dzevi clan, and their religious order were not the only ones to benefit from these innovations, however. All appear to have been implemented with the consent of the Anlo people, in part because they too gained a number of advantages. If, for example, one reviews the details of the late eighteenth-century wars in which the Anlo were so severely defeated, it becomes apparent that a major contributor to the Anlo losses involved their lack of unity. In 1784, a number of Anlos shifted their allegiance to the enemy; in 1792, miscommunication created a breach of trust among the villages that composed the Anlo polity, a breach that eventually led to civil war. In both instances, those who broke with the Anlo forces came from the recently incorporated villages of Keta, Agudza, and Kpoduwa. This would suggest that these villages did not sufficiently identify their own interests with those of Anlo by the time this union was tested. Yet it was also the case that a significant portion of the people in these villages were of Anlo origin. They were members of Anlo clans; they were connected to Anlo families through marriage, and all associated with Anloga as the ritual and political center of the area. Clearly, however, these shared institutions were not enough to overcome the tendency for many Anlos to identify more with their villages than with the Anlo polity as a whole. That this local orientation was not specific to the Ketas, Agudzas, and Kpoduwas, but was a more general phenomenon is indicated by the fact that the only regular interaction said to have existed between Anloga and the villages that had comprised the Anlo polity involved occasional court cases, infrequent consultation of the Bate and Adzovia shrines when natural disasters occurred, and the enstoolment of chiefs. The limitations of such a loose confederation must have become obvious as a consequence of the 1784 and 1792 wars, while the need to address the problem was reinforced by the fact that after the 1792 Keta War the

---

[18] FN 20: Interview with Togbui Alex Afatsao Awadzi, 30 August 1978, Anloga; and FN 34: Interview with Togbui Alex Afatsao Awadzi, 3 October 1978, Anloga.

[19] T. E. Bowdich, *Mission*, 221.

Ketas and their allies, with British financing, continued to press for the complete conquest of Anlo.[20] I would argue that it was in this context that the Anlo agreed to the innovations proposed by the Nyigbla priest.

By relocating their clan shrines to Anloga, the Anlo leaders responded to the obvious need to enhance unity by having every Anlo family make regular and frequent visits to the capital.[21] Anlo acceptance of the entourage of gods for Nyigbla and the *foasi* ceremony reflects a similar overlap in interests. This is indicated by the relations that existed between the more powerful and less powerful gods worshiped in Anlo before and after the acceptance of these two innovations. As indicated above, the prestige of the most influential gods rested, in part, on their ability to attract those who sought their services. This was the basis upon which reputations were built, and those deities that were less influential had little status outside the families, clans, or villages with which they were associated. Relations between the less influential and the more influential were often competitive. Opportunities for cooperation no doubt existed, but they were also probably limited to those times when the entire polity was threatened by war or disease. The introduction of the entourage for Nyigbla altered this situation. The development of this spiritual support network meant that less influential families could enhance their reputations by establishing formal ties of association with the Dzevi clan and its god, Nyigbla.

A similar change occurred in the relations between politically influential families in Anlo and others. As noted above, the most politically powerful gods were in the custody of particular families, patrilineages, or clans, and relations with others revolved around the provision of certain services and the acceptance of *fiasidi*, boys and especially girls given to the religious order as compensation for services rendered. This provision of *fiasidiwo* to a particular god could be seen as a loss for the family, since they had to share control over the sexuality of their family members with the priest. If, for example, a young woman was impregnated by a man before she was betrothed, the fine for such a violation was claimed not by her family, but by the priest; and if the young woman was betrothed without incident, the priest still collected a fee for the "removal of the *go*" (loincloth), necessary before the husband could engage in sexual relations with his new wife.[22] This loss to the family was often compensated, however, by the fact that it was frequently a male member of the priest's family who married the young *fiasidi*. When this occurred, the union gave the families of these women

---

[20] Gtk, Guineiske Sager og Akstykker, No. 38, 24 January 1793, Christiansborg, A. Biørn, C. Hager et al. The British decided to finance the Anexos in hopes of receiving control of the Keta fort if the Anexo campaign was successful.

[21] In order to strengthen their military capacity, the Anlos also sought assistance from Asante and Akwamu. See T70/1565: 3 May 1792, James Fort, Accra, William Roberts; 10 April 1792, Christiansborg, A. Biørn to William Roberts; Part II, 6 May 1792, Christiansborg Castle, A. R. Biørn to Archibald Dazel; Part II, 12 October 1792, Cape Coast Castle, Archibald Dazel to the Committee of Merchants; 29 December 1792, Cape Coast Castle, A. Dazel, John Gordon, James Bannerman; and Part I, 3 May 17 1792, Cape Coast Castle, Archibald Dazel, William Roberts. See also Gtk, Guineiske Sager og Akstykker, No. 38, 24 January 1793, A Biørn, C. Hager, et al.; Gtk, Guineiske Journalen, No. 3, 14 March 1793; T70/33 "Copy of a Letter from A. Dalzel," Cape Coast Castle, 7 February 1793; Nørregård, *Danish Settlements*, 157; and Kea, "Akwamu–Anlo Relations," 46–47.

[22] FN 33: Interview with Boko Seke Axovi, 3 October 1978, Anloga.

the opportunity to establish even closer ties to the political and religious elite. In other words, the young women served as one of the few vehicles through which families could benefit from an association with the most powerful families in Anlo.

As indicated, limited opportunities existed for a priest (*tronua*) to expand his or her group of worshippers through the acquisition of *fiasidiwo* and for families interested in having their young women serve as bridges to the families of the political elite. The introduction of the *foasi* ceremony gave a family expanded opportunities to establish and benefit from close association with the most influential families in Anlo by allowing the Nyigbla order to incorporate the young women in the family.

That families did, indeed, have the power to allow their young women to be inducted as initiates, or *zizidzelawo*, is evident from the fact that during the mid-nineteenth century, when support for Nyigbla dropped temporarily, a number of mothers forbade their daughters to enter the order. This ban did not end with the re-emergence of Nyigbla as a powerful god within the community. If their husbands or their descendants violated the injunction, it was believed that they jeopardized the sanity of the young initiated women.[23] Thus, it is apparent that the Nyigbla order gained support from the Anlo community not only because all priests were feared and respected, but because many families believed it, brought benefits to the community as a whole and to their own families.

Nyigbla, Women, and the Gendered Politics of Ethnic Change

Anlo women also contributed significantly to the institutionalization of the Nyigbla order. To understand why this was the case, we must review the changes occurring in gender relations during the eighteenth century. In Chapter 1 I indicated that after 1750, a number of Anlo men were able to take advantage of the increasing numbers of slaves captured to retain female slaves as wives. This, in turn, created a situation in which husbands needed no longer exercise great control over their free wives because the contribution made by these wives to their husbands' households could now be replaced by slave wives. Free wives, with the support of their natal families, took advantage of this system to spend more time with their brothers. I also noted that at the same time, younger women were under increasing pressure to accept a more limited pool of possible husbands, including primarily their fathers' sisters' sons. Under such conditions divorce also must have become more problematic, since this type of marriage could enhance the family's social and economic position within their community. Divorce had the potential of souring relations between the families concerned. Accordingly, married women may have been allowed to spend more time with their natal families, but their influence in their own marriages was increasingly sublimated to the interests of their families. Divorce became more difficult as the social stakes associated with maintaining the marriage increased. The pressure to keep the union intact would have given husbands the opportunity to ignore many of their wives' complaints. We know, for

---

[23] FN 53: Interview with Togbui Afatsao Awadzi, 16 December 1987, Anloga.

example, that in late nineteenth century Anlo, husbands had the right to beat their wives if they felt this was necessary; and it is likely that the woman's family was unable or unwilling to raise serious objections, unless the abuse became excessive.[24]

This situation changed for many women with the emergence of the *foasi* ceremony. This early nineteenth-century ritual involved the recruitment into the Nyigbla order of at least two women from every Anlo clan each year; there were probably at least nine clans at the time. The secrecy that has surrounded the order since at least the mid-nineteenth century has prevented outsiders from obtaining a clear idea of how the Nyigbla order handled its recruits, but indirect evidence indicates that many of these women—unlike the *fiasidiwo*—entered the order of their own volition or with the strong support and encouragement of their mothers. This is suggested by recently gathered oral accounts and late nineteenth-century written descriptions of the recruitment into and association of initiates with similar orders in the area. According to these accounts, every effort was made to maintain the impression that people who joined a particular order were called by the god itself. In many instances, however, members of the order would encourage others to join, and then the priest would instruct the recruits how to behave. In the case of Nyigbla, this involved the young person, a woman in most instances, learning to behave as if she were slightly off-balance mentally. As one elder noted, "they were not normal anymore, but not so abnormal that people thought they were totally crazy. . . . They would roam about . . . so parents were not totally surprised by the possibility [that they had been caught by the god]."[25] Every year women responded to this recruitment effort, and every year these new members, *zizidzelawo*, recruited others. Young women who joined this order, no doubt, had many reasons for doing so: they gained prestige from their affiliation with one of the most powerful gods in Anlo; membership may have provided them with an expanded set of contacts that could be of potential social and economic benefit; and others may have joined at the urging of their mothers.

Of particular significance for our discussion here are the benefits that came to wives. Married women affiliated with this order gained considerable freedom of action within their husbands' households. Evidence to support the latter supposition can be obtained by comparing the limited mid-twentieth-century information available on the Nyigbla order with the more abundant late nineteenth-century data about the religious groups that operated in the culturally related Fon-speaking areas to the east. We know, for example, that the Nyigbla order at one time defined the women associated with the worship of this god according to the nature of their affiliation. Female priests or priestesses were called *trosiwo*. Those young women whose families permitted them to be initiated into the worship constituted a second group known as *zizidzelawo*. Children whose birth or continued existence their parents attributed to the actions of Nyigbla constituted another category of worshippers known as *troklu*. Descriptions of the late nineteenth-century religious practices of the Ewe-speaking peoples of Whydah and Dahomey indicate that this same categorization system existed in these so-

---

[24] Nukunya, *Kinship and Marriage*, 108. I am assuming that Nukunya's account, though recorded in the 1960s was also true in late nineteenth century Anlo.

[25] See H. Seidel, "Der Yew'e Dienst in Togolande," *Zeitschrift für afrikanische und oceanische Sprachen*, 3 (1897), 166–67, and FN 65: Interview with Togbui Dzobi Adinku, 6 January 1988, Anloga.

cieties.[26] Other similarities include the fact that in Anlo all Nyigbla *zizidzelawo* underwent an initiation ceremony that lasted at least six months. The same was also true for the ceremonies held by religious orders among the Fon. In both areas, initiates learned the songs, dances, and the secret languages associated with the worship of their gods during this period of seclusion. After their initiation, they adopted new names and returned to their homes, but continued to be associated with the worship of that god. In both systems, male initiates (who usually came from the family that had custody of that god) were trained by male priests, while the female initiates were trained by female priests.[27]

Given this level of similarity in organizational patterns, it is also likely that the marital status of the initiates (known as *kosio*) among the Fon was similar to that found among the Nyigbla *zizidzelawo* of Anlo. According to Ellis's 1872 account, the *kosio* (the prepubescent initiates) and the *vodu-viwo* (the children who had been dedicated to the god) either did not marry or their marriages contained the potential for great instability, as "the husband . . . [could] not punish her or reprove her for any excesses, sexual or other[wise]."[28] Barbot reported the same to be true in eighteenth-century Whydah. This also appears to have been the situation among adjacent groups on the Gold Coast. Studies on Akan priestesses in the Fanti area indicate that "the husband of a priestess [had] to be extremely cautious not to 'abuse' her, lest he offend her deity and then have to appease it by a series of costly gifts."[29]

From these accounts, it is clear that women closely associated with gods, including the Nyigbla *zizidzelawo*, gained considerable leverage within their marriages. This leverage, along with developments after 1750 in the Anlo marital system, encouraged some women to join Nyigbla. By joining Nyigbla or encouraging their daughters to do so, many Anlo women took advantage of the opportunity to better protect their own interests in a climate where their natal and marital families were less prepared to do so after 1750. In pursuing this course, Anlo women challenged those changes in gender relations that had begun to deny them a voice in discussions of their marital affairs.

The support these women gave to Nyigbla also helped institutionalize the Nyigbla priest's position within the Anlo political and religious hierarchy. This, in turn, significantly influenced ethnic relations, for the inclusion of the Dzevi as ethnic outsiders in the ranks of the most influential political and religious groups in the early 1800s brought the first expansion in the definition of people deemed so-

---

[26] A. B. Ellis noted that in these two areas, "those who actually minister to the service of the temple . . . are called *vodusio* [or *vodusiwo*; *trosivo* in Anlo] and may be regarded as priestesses proper. . . . Girls dedicated to a god . . . are . . . termed *kosio* [rather than *zizidzelawo* as in Anlo] *Vodu-sio* and female *kosio* must not be confounded with *vodu-vio* (*vodu*, and *vi*, a child), the latter [known among the Anlo as *troklu*] being children who are claimed by a god and who only wear the priestly raiment on ceremonial occasions." Ellis, *Ewe-Speaking Peoples*, 141, 142. See also FN 33: Interview with Boko Seke Axovi, 3 October 1978, Anloga.

[27] For information on the eastern Ewe communities, see Ellis, *Ewe-Speaking Peoples*, 142–44.

[28] Ellis indicates that fines imposed for adulterous sexual relations with these *fiasidiwo* or *kosio*, an act that Ellis misinterprets as prostitution, were collected by the priests; the same was true of the Nyigbla *fiasidiwo* of Anlo. Ellis, *Ewe-Speaking Peoples*, 140–42.

[29] Law, *The Slave Coast*, 114, and James Boyd Christensen, "The Adaptive Functions of Fanti Priesthood," in W. R. Bascom and M. J. Herskovits, eds., *Continuity and Change in African Cultures* (Chicago, 1959), 268.

cially eligible to hold high political and religious office within the Anlo polity. Those who had previously held such prestigious positions included only those who claimed to have immigrated from Notsie and to have been among the first settlers in Anlo. After the Dzevi's elevation in status, ethnic origins continued to be important, but service to the Anlo polity became an equally important marker of status. This expansion in the criteria used by the Anlo to determine one's political and religious, if not social, prestige, in turn, opened the door for other outsiders like Gbodzo, who became right-wing commander of the Anlo army in the 1830s.

The actions of those women who associated themselves with Nyigbla because of the freedom it gave them as wives also provided a foundation for women to further challenge both gender and ethnic relations in the second half of the nineteenth century.[30] And it is to this period that we turn in this next section. I begin by reviewing the impact of the slave trade on Anlo society. I document the rise of the Yewe religious order, which emerged in its contemporary form in large part because of the European effort to abolish the Atlantic slave trade. I argue that many Anlo women joined Yewe to challenge the prevailing norms governing gender relations; in so doing, they also undermined the prevailing pattern of ethnic relations, a pattern their counterparts in the Nyigbla order had begun to attack in the late eighteenth and early nineteenth centuries.

The Afro-Europeans of Anlo and the Export Trade in Slaves

The European effort to abolish the Atlantic slave trade was one of the most influential events affecting social relations in Anlo during the nineteenth century. Although the volume of slaves passing through Anlo during much of the eighteenth century had never been so great as in other coastal areas to the east and west,[31] this situation changed dramatically after the various European powers on the lower Gold Coast and upper Slave Coast began to interdict the trade from Africa. Denmark and Britain actually abolished the slave trade in 1791 and 1807, respectively; the Netherlands followed suit in 1814,[32] but only in the 1840s did these countries, especially Britain, begin to pursue more aggressive measures.[33] As British opposition to the trade intensified in the Accra area, many traders shifted their businesses to the east, particularly to communities on the upper Slave Coast, to which they brought their slaves for sale.

---

[30] It is important to note that this repositioning of the Dzevi within the inner circle of Anlo's governing council did not alter this clan's social identity as ethnic outsiders, but the institutionalization of the Dzevi priest's position established the foundation upon which this *hlo* (with the help of others) gradually redefined itself by the late twentieth century as an ethnic group whose founding ancestor may have come late to the Anlo area, but who came nevertheless from Notsie as did virtually all other clans. Without the intimate and institutionalized connection supported by Anlo women in particular, this redefinition (the details of which are discussed in Chapter 5) would not have been possible.

[31] See Ward, *Royal Navy* , 63; Reynolds, *Trade and Economic Change* , 40–41.

[32] For a discussion of the Dutch role in the Atlantic slave trade and its abolition, see Johannes Postma, *The Dutch in the Atlantic Slave Trade, 1600–1815* (Cambridge, 1990). Danish activities are described in Nørregård, *Danish Settlements,* and Carstensen, *Indberetninger.* See Ward, *Royal Navy,* for a detailed discussion of British efforts.

[33] Ward, *Royal Navy* , 39, 121, and 162.

This development contributed to a number of changes in the Anlo area. Included among these was the large-scale immigration of Afro-European traders, who began to challenge the prestige of the *awoamefia* and the Nyigbla religious order. Evidence of this challenge can be found in the oral traditions about this order, and by dating these accounts using eighteenth- and nineteenth-century European documentary sources about the area. Anlo clan elders state, for example, that the Nyigbla order took responsibility for enacting and enforcing a number of laws that all in Anlo were enjoined to obey. Among these were a ban on wearing sewn clothing and gold, and the use of horses in the Anlo capital.[34] German missionaries F. Plessing and B. Schlegel confirm that the latter two laws did indeed exist and were in place by the 1850s:

> On February 20 [1854], four o'clock in the morning, I [F. Plessing] mounted my horse to ride to Aungla [Anloga] which is five to six hours away. Only my boy, John, my groom and a "cowrie carrier" accompanied me. After three and a quarter hours, I reached Aungla, but I had to wait for the boys for quite a long time. In the meantime, I led my horse to a meadow. Finally, the boys arrived and we hurried towards the city. The boys led on foot and I followed on horseback. I rode through a few streets where the inhabitants started a terrible clamor. . . . John approached me and told me to get off my horse, Then I remembered that I had heard earlier, nobody may ride a horse in Aungla, not even the king, for the fetish would kill him.[35]
>
> [The priest of Nyigbla] . . . wears white clothes like the white people, and he cannot tolerate a black or half-white [person] entering the town, Aungla, in European clothes [although] the whites may appear in his clothes. . . .[36]

The fact that the Nyigbla order banned the wearing of sewn clothing specifically for Africans and Afro-Europeans suggests that these two groups of traders were perceived as posing the greatest threat to the prestige of the Nyigbla priest. Only in the early nineteenth century did large numbers of Afro-Europeans, whether Brazilians or Cubans, enter the Anlo area. It was these individuals (and many of the local African traders with whom they worked) who interacted on a more intimate level with their hosts than earlier Europeans, and yet who also distinguished themselves from the local population by adopting European forms of dress, wearing gold jewelry which had previously been worn in the area on a very limited scale, constructing rectangular, multi-story buildings rather than the traditional circular and single-story dwellings found among the Anlo, and using horses for transportation.[37] Their behavior and their financial involvement in the area attracted con-

---

[34] For a discussion of the Nyigbla ban on gold, see FN 35: Interview with Boko Seke Axovi, 4 October 1978, Anloga.

[35] Friedrich Plessing, "Station Quitta in West-Afrika," *Monatsblatt der Norddeutsche Missionsgesellschaft*, 4/42 (1854), 176.

[36] Schlegel, "Beitrag zur Geschichte," 400.

[37] See Robin Law, *The Horse in West African History* (New York, 1980), on the history of horses in West Africa, and J. Goody, *Technology, Tradition and the State* (Oxford, 1971), Ch. 4, where he discusses the conditions under which various groups ritually banned the use of horses. See also J. Michael Turner, "Les Bresiliens: The Impact of Former Brazilian Slaves Upon Dahomey," (Ph.D. dissertation, Boston University, 1975) on the Afro-Brazilians in the Anexo area. See also John Duncan, *Travels in Western African in 1845 and 1846* (London, 1847), 136, who establishes the linkage between the Portuguese and the Spaniards, and horses in the early to mid-nineteenth century on the upper Slave Coast.

siderable interest and support from the Anlo populace; it also won them the hostility of the political and religious leaders of the area, who viewed them as a major threat to their authority. Of particular interest here is the fact that the challenge to the Anlo leadership by outsiders was not confined to the economic realm, but extended into religious affairs, as is evident from the history of the Yewe religious order.

The Rise of Yewe

Anlo traditions indicate that Yewe (a religious order that consisted of three separate but related deities from the middle Slave Coast: Hebieso or So, Agbui or Avleketi, and Voduda or Da) became a force in the Anlo area immediately after the 1847 Danish bombardment of Keta. Prior to this event, it was just one among many of the *voduwo* or personally acquired gods brought into the area by individual Anlos. The earliest known Yewe shrine was established in the late 1700s by the Keta elder Togbui Honi and his wife Boe. Oral traditions indicate that Togbui Honi's wife suffered from barrenness; she and her husband traveled to a town called Xoda on the middle Slave Coast where she was cured by one of the Yewe gods. After their return to Keta, they established a shrine to this god and then offered its services to other residents. Others acquired Yewe by purchasing its power and hiring a priest to oversee its rituals. This was true for Togbui Gbodzo of Woe, *dusifiaga* or right-wing commander of the Anlo army, who established a shrine in the early 1800s to assist him in times of war. The reputation of this stranger deity to alleviate barrenness and to provide protection in war firmly established it in late eighteenth- and early nineteenth-century Anlo.[38] Its tremendous popularity by the late nineteenth century, however, had more to do with the fact that those who became shrine owners (*hubonowo*) during this period began to use it for economic gain and social prestige as well as a means to exert spiritual influence over the daily lives of their followers. Perhaps the most important person associated with this change was Elias Quist, an individual who, because of his descent from a Danish officer, was considered an ethnic outsider and a member of the Blu clan, a *hlo* that consisted of the most recent immigrants in Anlo.

Born in the early 1800s of an Anlo mother and an Afro-European father, Quist was particularly well-positioned to transform the worship of Yewe into one of the most influential and financially prosperous orders in Anlo. His father, Isaac Quist, was an Afro-Danish officer who had been posted to Keta in the early years of the nineteenth century. Because of the Napoleonic wars, Denmark was unable to ship goods regularly to its African forts during that period. Therefore, Danish officers and servants posted at outforts such as Keta were often forced to sustain themselves as best they could by engaging in private trade. One may presume that Isaac was among those who conducted trade on his own behalf, and that his son, Elias, acquired at least some

---

[38] For information on the shrine established by Honi and his wife, see Fiawoo, "Influence of Contemporary Social Changes," 68; Richard Tetteh Torgby, "The Origin and Organisation of the Yewe Cult" (B.A. long essay, Department for the Study of Religion, University of Ghana, 1977), ii–iii; and FN 24: Interview with Boko Seke Axovi, 5 September 1978, Anloga. See FN 76: Interview with Togbui Anthonio Gbodzo II and his councilors, 20 January 1988, Woe, on Gbodzo and Yewe. See Seidel, "Der Yewe's Dienst," 176, who discusses how one purchased Yewe.

of his father's skills and contacts. These he used to establish his first major businesses in Keta and Anexo, businesses that probably involved the sale of slaves to Brazilian and Spanish traders during the first half of the nineteenth century.[39]

Elias was also quite well-connected to religious circles in the area. His mother, Mama We, was the daughter of Togbui Lagbo of Anloga, a politically prominent and wealthy priest associated with the Nyigbla order;[40] at least one of Quist's wives was connected to the Yewe order as a patrilineal descendant of Togbui Honi, who, with his wife, Boe, first introduced Yewe into Keta[41]. Most notable about Quist, however, was the fact that he accepted a personal involvement with Yewe and used his entrepreneurial skills to transform the Yewe order into what some have described as its modern form.[42] Quist was apparently motivated to do this by a close encounter with death and the opportunity to respond to the changing economic climate in the area.

Histories of the Quist family indicate that shortly after 1847, Elias was traveling from Anexo to Accra by boat when the vessel on which he was a passenger sank. A *boko* (diviner) whom he is said to have consulted after this accident, attributed his near-drowning to the Yewe gods, who were calling him to their service. These events are said to have set the stage for his involvement with the Yewe religious order. Heeding this call, he established a Yewe shrine and became its *hubono* or owner.[43] In such a position he was required to support financially the activities of the members of the cult, to adjudicate disputes between members and non-members, and to manage many

---

[39] Speculation that Quist was deeply involved in the slave trade is based on the fact that this was the most lucrative business at the time and virtually every other known trader operating in the area participated in this trade.

[40] See FN 92: Interview with Togbui Amegashi Afeku IV, 18 February 1988, Tema; Hornberger, "Etwas," 458; and Osswald, *Fifty Years' Mission Work*, 2.

[41] See Judicial Council Minute Book, 1921: R. G. Tay for Kata and Ladje's Family, Plaintiff v. Quist Brothers, per J. J. Quist, Defendant, p. 302; Fiawoo, "Influence of Contemporary Social Changes," 67–69.

[42] See Christian Aliwodsi, "Der Schlangendienst," *Monatsblatt der Norddeutschen Missionsgesellschaft*, 2/5 (1880), 27; and FN 92: Interview with Togbui Amegashi Afeku IV, 18 February 1988, Accra-Nima. Note that it was quite common for religious orders to "call" wealthy traders to become members because they could enhance the reputation of the order and financially support its activities. See Seidel, "Der Yew'e Dienst," 174–76. For information on the Yewe order, see Stefano H. Kwadzo Afelevo, "Ein Bericht über den Yehwekultus der Ewe. Herausgegeben mit deutscher Übersetzung und Anmerkungen von D. Westermann" [1894], in *Mitteilungen des Seminarsfür Orientalische Sprachen*, 33/3 (1930) Torgby, "Origin and Organisation"; Seidel, "Der Yew'e Dienst"; Spieth, *Die Religion*, Chapter 3; FN 53: Interview with Togbui Afatsao Awadzi, 16 December 1987, Anloga; FN 54: Interview with Togbui Tse Gbeku, 16 December 1987, Anloga; FN 70: Interview with Mr. Kwami Kpodo, 12 January 1988, Woe; FN 72: Interview with Mr Christian Nani Tamaklo and Mr. Stephen Kodzo Quist, 13 January 1988, Keta; FN 74: Interview with Mr. A. W. Kuetuade-Tamaklo, 19 Janurary 1988, Tegbi; FN 77: Interview with Mr. Kwami Kpodo, 20 January 1988, Woe; FN 102: Interview with Togbui Midawo Alowu Attipoe, 6 April 1988, Anyako; FN 105: Interview with Mr. Kwami Kopodo, 20 April 1988, Woe; ADM 4/1/28: G. P. S., District Commissioner, Kwitta to the Honorable Colonial Secretary, 6 January 1900; Anlo Traditional Council Minute Book No. 3: 4/4/60 – 23/7/87): Fia Duklui Attipoe III, et al. -v- A. P. Attipoe, et al., p. 370; Judicial Council Minute Book, 1921: R. G. Tay for Kata and Ladje's family -v- Quist Brothers, p. 273–336; and Aliwodsi, "Der Schlangendienst," 27–28.

[43] See FN 70: Interview with Mr. Kwami Kpodo, 12 January 1988, Woe; and FN 92: Interview with Togbui Amegashi Afeku IV, 18 February 1988, Tema. He located the shrine in an uninhabited section of Dzelukofe, where many of the Keta residents had fled after their town had been destroyed in 1847; this district later became known as Nukpesekofe, Nukpese being another name by which Elias Quist was known. See S.C. 14/1, p. 208; and Anlo Traditional Council Minute Book No. 3: 14/4/6 –32/7/87, p. 14–37.

of the ritual affairs in which its members were involved.[44] No doubt, he also—as required of *hubonowo*—continued to provide assistance to and gain adherents from others the god had helped, but Quist did more than simply assume the expected role of a Yewe owner. He reorganized the way in which the order interacted with the community so that he could use the same to respond to the changing business climate in the area, changes involving the European abolition of the slave trade.

During the mid-nineteenth century, a number of European powers began to make significant efforts to abolish the slave trade in Anlo. The first to do so were the Danes, who had claimed the area as their exclusive trading zone since the late eighteenth century. They began in 1839 by launching periodic military expeditions against the slave traders operating in the area; and they continued these expeditions until they ceded their rights to the area to the British in 1850. The British then embarked on their own efforts to stamp out the slave trade. Anlo response to these developments resembled that of other communities in West Africa. Many of the wealthier Anlo traders who had profited handsomely from the slave trade attempted to continue their businesses by clandestinely moving their slaves from the Anlo area to the less-patrolled towns east of Keta. Quist accomplished this by using his Yewe order to shield his activities. We know, for example, that as part of the induction ceremony, all initiates were required to perform a series of secret oaths known as the *nukpekpe* ritual. Stefano Kwadzo Afelevo, who documented his experiences as a Yewe member after he left the order and converted to Christianity, described those oaths as they existed in the late nineteenth century.

> If a person wishes to enter Yewe or to become a Yewe servant, he must enter the Yewe compound. When you go into the Yewe compound, they will first say to you: "What are you going to do for Yewe." When they ask you that, you are to reply that you will repair his fence and will bring him everything you receive and that you will also [capture] people for him.
>
> During (the following night), [at the *nukpekpe* ritual] they teach you all these things: first they sprinkle water onto your face from a small pot. Then they bring the other implements and add them to it (the water). These things are: a folded white cloth, a two-edged ax, which they call "So ax" [*Sofia*] (So is the god of lightning), a ram's horn tied to a stick, a bent piece of iron called *ebi*, a roundish pierced stone called the So-stone [*Sokpe*], and an oval stone called Yewe's own ax. These are all the things which they lay down before the person.
>
> When they have brought all these things they lay them one by one in the water and they say about them: "Say nothing of anything you see in the Yewe compound to any man, unless he be a Yewe priest or one who frequents the Yewe compound. If you say anything to an ordinary man, this is what Yewe will do to you." Having said this, they take the So-ax and (with it) draw a line along your back from your loins to your head and they say to you: "if you betray . . . Yewe and Yewe matters to another who is no servant of Yewe, then you will be split like this." They then take the pierced stone and put it into the water and address you in the same way. They then take the ram's horn, which is tied to a stick, put it into the water as well and say to you: "If you betray Yewe, when you are coming from some place a thunderstorm will break and you will see a ram appear: it will butt you

---

[44] Torgby, "Origin and Organisation," 24, 31.

with its horns, so that you fall down and die." They then take a stone shaped like a man's tongue, put it into the water and address you again thus: "If you betray Yewe, when it rains it will thunder upon you and your tongue will come out and you will die." They next take the bent piece of iron, called *ebi*, draw a line with it and say: "If you mention Yewe affairs in any place, when rain falls, it will form a round sand dune, which will encircle you and it will thunder upon you and you will die."

When they have done all this, they will take a little gunpowder and pour it out in front of you. When they have poured it out in front of you, they will bind your eyes with the white cloth and then they will pour water into a small calabash and hand it to you to drink. After that they will set fire to the powder so that it burns round you and they will say to you: "If you dare to speak anywhere of Yewe affairs, you will be shot like this."

When they [have] finished all these things, then they will tell you everything about Yewe and all the prescriptions connected with it.[45]

Quist appears to have used these oaths to enjoin Yewe members to maintain absolute confidentiality about his use of the Yewe compound as a way-station for slaves. Evidence to support this comes from the following account by Anlo elder Togbui Awadzi, about the way in which Yewe shrines operated in the 1850s and 1860s.

In those days, slave traders formed large groups. . . . they surrounded people, caught them and sold them. My own grandfather was almost caught. My mother's mother was caught and hidden in the [Yewe] cult house at Woe. It belonged to her brother. When this man saw my mother's mother, Mable, he asked her why she was there. She said she had been caught by slave traders. Her brother, Nudali, approached the capturers and she was released. Only she and another woman were released. If you hide something with them, they don't release it and they sell them to the Europeans. They kept them in the Yewe shrine because no one had a right to go there. If you entered, they would force you to join them. After the sale, the shrines were paid a commission.[46]

Quist's efforts brought him economic prosperity and social prestige (despite his ethnic outsider status), which in turn greatly enhanced the reputation of Yewe. In 1858, German missionary B. Schlegel noted that "crowds stream to him."[47] By the late nineteenth century, many other wealthy members of Anlo society had established shrines of their own and it had become the most influential religious order in Anlo.

The Bases of Yewe's Popularity

Yewe's success among the Anlo population reflected its ability to make available to a large cross-section opportunities that benefited people individually but which did

---

[45] Afelevo, "Ein Bericht," 9–11; the translations of Afelevo's text used here can be found in D. Westermann, *The Study of the Ewe Language* (Oxford, 1930), 214–15. See also Torgby, "Origin and Organisation," 6; note that this more contemporary description is consistent with that of Afelevo's.

[46] FN 53: Interview with Togbui Afatsao Awadzi, 16 December 1987, Anloga.

[47] Schlegel, "Beitrag zur Geschichte," 406.

not directly threaten the social structure of the society. I noted above, for example, that many of the wealthy in Anlo either accepted a call from Yewe to become a *hubono*, or they purchased the god themselves in order to establish their own shrine. They did so because they found in Yewe a very useful means of obtaining labor, especially after the mid-1860s when the European demand for tropical oils encouraged many to cultivate and process coconuts into copra. For example, we know that in the late 1800s, Yewe members in Dzelukofe were deeply involved in the production and pro-cessing of copra for their shrine owners and their particular religious orders; others assisted their shrine owners by selling produce in the local markets.[48] Some also ben-efited financially from their ownership of Yewe by making the services of their Yewe members available to lenders who were having difficulty collecting their money. As one late nineteenth-century account indicated, "Yewe servants . . . having received a case of brandy [which the Yewe owner receives] . . . lay in ambush to arrest a family member of the debtor. If they are successful, the debtor has to redeem his captured relative. The cost includes the debt, the cost of the brandy, and a reward for the Yewe-servants who kidnapped the debtor's relative."[49]

Local chiefs also benefited from the presence of a Yewe order in their town. Mi-nor disputes between members of the community which would have normally been settled by the disputants themselves or some other intermediary were always handled by the *hubono*, if a Yewe member was involved. In such circumstances, the priest would go to the village chief during the night and seek his advice. Having received the chief's opinion, the *hubono* would then render judgment accordingly. Whatever fine was imposed would then be shared with the chief, who never would have had access to the payment without the involvement of the Yewe member in the dispute.[50]

Many average women and men joined Yewe because it supported their individual interests. Late nineteenth-century accounts indicate, for example, that some who be-came members did so in order to benefit from the Yewe practice which forbade any-one from addressing a member by their former, non-Yewe name. This appealed to individuals whose parents had given them a very unpleasant name as a means of of-fending a child that was believed to be continually returning to be reborn, only to die after a short period of time. Others—accused thieves, for example—hoped to allevi-ate the stigma that accompanied their former anti-social actions. If they joined Yewe, anyone who referred in their presence to them as a thief could expect to pay a fine to the person's *hubono* for offending them, and by affiliation, their Yewe god. Still others were apparently attracted to Yewe because it was associated with innovative musical and dance styles, and esoteric knowledge about herbal medicinal practices.[51]

---

[48] See Judicial Council Minute Book, 1921: R. G. Tay for Kata and Ladje's Family, Plaintiff -v- Quist Brothers per J. J. Quist, Defendant; and FN 75: Interview with Mr. Kwami Kpodo, 19 January 1988, Woe. Note that much of this labor could be described as "family" business activities since Yewe mem-bers—many of whom were purchased as slaves—were considered to be the relatives of their owners and *hubonowo*. See FN 70: Interview with Mr. Kwami Kpodo, 12 January 1988, Woe, and FN 72: Inter-view with Mr. Christian Nani Tamaklo and Mr. Stephen Kodzo Quist, 13 January 1988, Keta; as well as D. Westermann, "Ein Bericht über den Yehwekultus der Ewe," *Mitteilungen des Seminars für Orientalische Sprachen* (Berlin) 33/3 (1930), 1, on the "familial" connection between Yewe owners and Yewe members who had been enslaved.

[49] Spieth, *Die Religion*, 189.

[50] Ibid., 188.

[51] Afelevo, "Ein Bericht," 179–80; Torgby, "Origin and Organisation," 1

Yewe, Ethnicity, and the Women of Anlo

Women constituted yet another important group of supporters, particularly those who sought through their membership in Yewe to strengthen their ability to influence the decisions made by their family elders about their own lives. In Chapter 1, I documented the fact that families began to place increasing emphasis on managing the marriages of their daughters after 1679. Preference was initially given to males who lived in the same residential ward as a young woman's family, who were cross-cousins, and also members of the woman's own clan. After 1750, the majority of Anlo parents had added to these three considerations the additional preference for males who were matrilateral cross-cousins. The weight given to these factors gradually eliminated the voice young women may have previously had within the family to influence the choice of marriage partner, and significantly curtailed their ability to divorce. During the late eighteenth and early nineteenth centuries, Anlo women responded to this situation, in part, by joining or encouraging their daughters to join the Nyigbla order. Affiliation with this god gave women the support they needed to be more active participants in their natal families and in their husband's households. Nyigbla's stature in Anlo declined precipitously in the early 1800s for reasons that are discussed in Chapter 4, but it continued to play a prominent role within the political and religious cultures of Anlo between the early 1840s, when it was invited to lead the Anlo in battle after a short hiatus from this role, and 1874, when Anlo's defeat at the hands of the Europeans marked the beginning of its final decline as the Anlo war god. During this period, Yewe actively competed with Nyigbla for the support of women by offering wives as well as young unmarried girls the kind of support that was unavailable to them even in the Nyigbla order. For example, Nyigbla provided no recourse for young women who would have liked to refuse the man chosen for them by their elders. Their options had been limited to the following: they could simply resist the begging, pleading, threats of supernatural sanction, or the use of physical restraints by their elders;[52] or they could initiate sexual relations with their chosen lovers in order to disrupt their parents' marital negotiations.[53] It is likely that relatively few pursued these options. Most would have found it difficult to resist the pressure; and defiance could threaten the otherwise protective role their families played in their lives. Some joined Nyigbla, but this gave women control over their marital affairs only after they were betrothed. Yewe offered more.

Accounts about this nineteenth-century religious order indicate that it gave women the opportunity to choose their own spouse, which in turn forced the parents to acquiesce to their daughter's decision.[54] As one author noted, "[so-called] reckless girls . . . insist on joining Yewe in order to be able to do everything they like. There are those . . . who are promised to a man by their parents; if they do not like this man, they join Yewe, refuse to take the man to whom their parents have

---

[52] Dickson, "Marital Selection," 128–29.

[53] Schlegel, "Beitrag zur Geschichte," 399; he mistakenly suggests that this practice existed only among the Ewes in the Krepi district.

[54] Seidel, "Der Yew'e Dienst," 165. German missionary reports indicate that parental acquiescence to what was called concubinage became more common in Anlo society only toward the end of the nineteenth century; Binetsch, "Beantwortung mehrerer," 44–48.

promised them and marry a man whom they like on the Yewe farm. . . ."[55] Yewe also offered to a married woman a means to check the behavior of her husband if he proved abusive and if her own family was unwilling or unable to assist her. In both cases, female Yewe members obtained advantages in such situations because of the belief that an offense given to a Yewe member was an offense to her god. Evidence that the god was indeed offended took the form of the Yewe woman behaving in an obviously possessed state. For example, if a husband quarreled with his Yewe wife, beat her, or insulted her, she could declare herself *alaga*, that is, someone who has gone wild, a right all Yewe members had as members of this particular religious order. The same option was available to young unmarried female members who, according to former Yewe member Stefano Kwadzo Afelevo, were instructed to "go wild if [their] mother or father said something offensive to [them]."[56] The behavior of the offended party has been described by a number of late nineteenth-century observers and former Yewe members.

> The person who goes wild, be it man or woman, runs at once into the offender's house, destroys the thatch of their roof, tears down the fence and cracks their pots. . . . and no one dares get in the way of an *alaga* to defend themselves against her. . . . There are three kinds of Alaga or ones who have gone wild: Solaga, Agbuilaga and Amlimadodo. A Solaga wanders about at night and howls like a leopard. . . . an Agbuilaga, on the other hand, appears during the day and lurks around the roads, throws stones at passers-by and gets food and drink from people who are coming from the market. . . . [The person] who goes wild as an Amlimadodo does not go into the bush, but stays in the town, wallows in mud and dirt and runs about steadily shouting the name of the person [who has offended him or her and that person's god].[57]

The only way the parents or the husband of a female *alaga* could rectify the offense was to pay a fine to the Yewe priest, or *hubono*. According to a number of accounts from the late nineteenth century, these fines were often so large that the offender was forced to borrow the sum or place a relative in pawn.

No doubt this action did much to strengthen a woman's voice in her natal and her husband's household,[58] but it had other consequences as well. By the end of the nineteenth century, Elias Quist had become a major economic power and respected figure in Anlo. This was the case in large part because of the support his order received from women who sought to challenge the way in which their families handled their marital affairs. This change in Quist's status—from that of simply an ethnic outsider to one of the most prominent figures in Anlo—undermined

---

[55] Afelewo, "Ein Bericht," 27.

[56] Cited in Seidel, "Der Yew'e Dienst," 170.

[57] See Seidel, "Der Yew'e Dienst," 171–74 for a detailed account of several *alaga* incidents.

[58] Yewe also provided far more opportunities for women in mid-late nineteenth century Anlo to become spiritually and politically influential than did the Nyigbla order. The latter structured its priestly office so as to have both male and female leaders. The female chief priest of Nyigbla, however, was always subordinate to the male priest and came only from the Dzevi family that had introduced the Nyigbla worship into the polity. Yewe, as an individually-owned god, offered more to a much wider range of women. As noted, the *hubono* as the cult owner could be either a man or a woman. Some owners, *hubonowo*, combined this position with the office of chief priest (called the *mida* if the person was male, or *mina* if a woman); others simply bought Yewe and brought a chief priest to manage the same. Afelevo, "Ein Bericht," 39.

the prevailing norms that defined social status on the basis of ethnic identity. Added irretrievably to the emphasis on time of arrival, the origins of one's ancestors (both of which could be reinvented if necessary), and the contribution that an individual or group made to the welfare of the polity was the notion that wealth alone (along with a shorter period of residency) could define a person as an integral and central member of Anlo society.

The fact that many of the women who joined Yewe did so to defy the norms governing gender relations also contributed to the tendency for young men and women to establish their own unions (concubinage) without the benefit of direct parental involvement, a formal marriage ceremony, or association with the Yewe order. In the late nineteenth and early twentieth centuries, Binetsch observed that increasing numbers of women "enter behind their parents' backs into concubinage with men of their choice." The women so identified probably included some Yewe members, but other young women completely unaffiliated with Yewe also agreed to enter into concubinage. In so doing they joined the Yewe women in challenging the norms that governed gender relations, challenges that also had significant consequences for ethnic relations in Anlo. The only difference was that while the Yewe initiates took advantage of the competition for influence that developed between Nyigbla and Yewe in the early nineteenth century, those who entered concubinage on their own without the support of Yewe did so by taking advantage of the economic changes that were occurring in the area because of the abolition of the Atlantic slave trade. What those changes were and the way in which they generated a response among women in late nineteenth century Anlo is the subject of the next section.

Indebtedness, Concubinage, and the Gendered Challenge to Anlo Ethnic Relations

One of the well-known consequences of the European abolition of the Atlantic slave trade was the shift in West Africa away from the export of human beings to that of agricultural products. This, in turn, was accompanied by a concomitant rise in the number of individuals involved in the trade with Europe. As A.G. Hopkins has documented, those who had formerly engaged in the slave trade began to emphasize the production and sale of palm oil, beeswax, cotton, and rubber, but they were not the only ones to take advantage of the new demand for African agricultural products. Others entered this new agricultural trade as they found their access to family land and labor and a limited amount of capital sufficient to give them, for the first time, an opportunity to benefit from the lucrative trade with Europe.[59]

This was indeed the situation in Anlo after the European abolition of the slave trade. Wealthy slave traders shifted to the export of palm oil. Other less-affluent Anlos did the same. Most small-scale traders purchased their oil from the Krepi and Kwawu districts by buying European manufactured goods on credit, combining these with their locally produced salt and fish, and then conveying all into the interior and then exchanging them for palm oil. The price that local traders received for palm oil from

---

[59] Hopkins, *Economic History*, 125–26.

exporters fluctuated tremendously, however,[60] and as a consequence it was not uncommon for Anlos to return to the coast with their oil only to find that the European
purchase price had dropped so low that the money received from its sale did not cover
the debts they had incurred when they purchased the European manufactured goods.
In such instances, creditors would take custody of a relative of the debtor as a pawn,
woba, and hold that person until someone repaid the loan. Families were rarely able
to redeem pawned relatives, but this does not seem to have deterred others lured by
the prospects of quick profits.

By 1853 indebtedness had become such a problem that the *awoamefia* of Anlo,
Fia Letsa Gbagba, issued a decree forbidding all coastal merchants based in the
littoral towns from offering goods in advance to local Anlos. His action had little
effect, however, and so the families of those in debt began to resort to other means
to protect themselves and their relatives from creditors. Some, like the *awoamefia*—
who discovered in early January of 1857 that his son had incurred debts amount-
ing to forty heads of cowries that neither he nor his son could repay—requested
that the German missionaries pay the sum and then accept his son into their service.[61] Others took more drastic action. In 1858, German missionary B. Schlegel
reported that in the month of May alone, five families delivered errant relatives to
Anloga to be put to death because their heavy debts threatened the well-being of
their families.[62] Still others attempted to absolve themselves of responsibility for
their relatives' debts by publicly disowning them when they died. German missionary Plessing described one such incident in 1855.

> About a quarter of an hour away from Anloga, we saw a strange means of
> burying the dead. At the side of the road . . . stood a platform. . . . On this
> platform, lay the corpse of a man which was wrapped in a garment tight-
> ened by ropes. . . . At our request, we were told that this was the way the
> Anlo buried bad debtors if no one from the family would or was able to
> pay the debt. . . . The deceased had been a merchant who had carried on
> trade as far as Donko [the area in what is now northern Ghana] and who
> had become very rich. On his way back, he had been robbed in Peki by a
> man whom I know and who now owns 40 to 50 armed slaves. . . . All of
> the merchant's riches had been taken including his box in which he kept
> his nuggets, gold dust and dollars. So he returned completely bereft of all
> his wealth to Anloga. His story had evoked so little pity that his creditors
> sent him to Keta to languish in the [English government's] debtors' prison.
> Finally, as none of his relatives interceded for him, he was released and
> died soon after in greatest poverty. If anyone [including his family] had
> buried the debtor . . . he would have had to assume [the deceased's] debts.[63]

Those families uncertain of what debts their relatives might have incurred during
their lifetime took yet another approach to protecting their assets. They would rinse
the mouth of their relative with water after he or she died. If an unknown creditor

---

[60] For a more complete description of this trade see, Freda Wolfson, "A Price Agreement on the Gold
Coast—The Krobo Oil Boycott, 1858–1866," *Economic History Bulletin,* VI, 1 (Series 2) (1953). See also K. B.
Dickson, *A Historical Geography of Ghana* (Cambridge, 1969), who offers a different view about the prices
for oil from eastern Ghana.

[61] Bremen Stadt Archives, Letters: 23 January 1857, B. Schlegel, Keta to N. D. M. G., Bremen.

[62] Schlegel, "Beitrag zur Geschichte," 398.

[63] Plessing, "Briefe aus Keta," 246–48.

appeared, they would ask that person to drink some of the water, saying "If it is true that our father or our mother was your debtor, you may well get your money and stay alive, but if you lie, his spirit will kill you."[64]

The reluctance of most families to assume responsibility for the unsolicited debts of their relatives was due in part to the fact that many were already burdened with financial obligations. If, for example, a family wished to honor a deceased relative, it was socially important to do so by sponsoring a large, expensive funeral celebration. Similar expectations surrounded marriage ceremonies.[65] Binetsch noted that in late nineteenth- and early twentieth-century Anlo, the family of a pre-pubescent woman preferred to betroth their daughter to a young man who was economically prosperous, as evident in his ability to offer a substantial sum of goods to the young woman's family and take care of their daughter. Data about earlier marriage payments do not exist, but it is likely that the amount demanded by the parents steadily increased as wealth became more accessible to larger numbers of people and as economic status became an important basis for measuring one's social and political position. By the mid-nineteenth century, wealth stools had become an increasingly common basis for political influence; by the end of the century, young men who lived on the Anlo littoral—the most prosperous area in Anlo—were often expected to provide their bride's family with a substantial sum of goods that could include twelve bottles of brandy, six yards of cloth, two locally woven kente cloths, and twelve head scarves. The groom and his paternal family also had to finance the seclusion of the new wife in her husband's household for several weeks or months; during this period, the bride was to engage in only light work such as weaving baskets and spinning cotton, and anyone who came to inquire about her well-being was to be welcomed, if possible, with an abundant offering of brandy and palm wine.[66]

Descriptions of Anlo society in the mid- to late nineteenth century indicate that many Anlo families were unable to support all the activities of their members. Not only were some forced to request that the political authorities in Anloga execute relatives who had accumulated vast debt, by the end of the century many young men were required to raise the bulk of the marriage payments by themselves.[67] Their fathers or uncles on whom they would normally have relied for assistance had other obligations that took precedence.[68] One of the conse-

---

[64] Binetsch, "Beantwortung mehrerer," 50.

[65] Plessing, "Briefe aus Keta," 248; Binetsch, "Beantwortung mehrerer," 50.

[66] Binetsch, "Beantwortung mehrerer," 44. See also Judicial Council Minute Book, 1913, 2, 91, 92, 139–40, and 205 for descriptions of marriage payments in 1913, which were not substantially different from those described by Binetsch. See Nukunya, *Kinship and Marriage*, 85–96 for a description of the more contemporary ceremony and typical bridewealth requirements. Note that Nukunya's account departs very little from late nineteenth-century descriptions of Anlo marriage ceremonies.

[67] Binetsch, "Beantwortung mehrerer," 43, 44. It is unclear who contributed the bulk of the bridewealth prior to the nineteenth century, but it is likely that the amount of bridewealth required for marriage was far lower, that acquisition of bridewealth by the young man was not necessarily interpreted as an indication of that person's ability to support a wife, and that far greater emphasis was placed on the involvement of both families rather than on the goods exchanged between the two. Evidence to support this comes from Ellis's account that "amongst the poorest people, the sum paid may be merely nominal; but something, even if it be only a bottle of rum, must be paid as head money, in order to give a union the dignity of marriage." Ellis, *Ewe-Speaking Peoples*, 199.

[68] Binetsch, "Beantwortung mehrerer," 46.

quences was that the parents of many young women began to show a preference for wealthy suitors. The latter could afford to offer a more substantial bridewealth; their financial situation insured their ability to provide their wives with adequate shelter and money for trade. Unions of this nature also provided the bride's family with access to a potential source of financial assistance that the family could use to betroth their own sons, to engage in trade, or to settle debts.[69] That such unions were indeed common in the late nineteenth century was noted by Binetsch:

> Even before a girl has grown out of childhood . . . parents have already chosen a husband for her. He may sometimes be a boy or youth, but very often it is a man who is already married with several women and not seldom a total grey-head.[70]

Binetsch also observed that it was from these particular unions that most young women attempted to escape, and that such efforts were occurring with increasing frequency.

In the introduction to this chapter I noted that the expansion of Western colonial influence—the usual scholarly explanation—cannnot adequately account for these changes in marital practice in Anlo. Western influence was simply not that pervasive before the beginning of the twentieth century. I would argue instead that the young women who began to establish relations with men of their own choice as a means of escaping their betrothal to much older men, resorted to this action because others in the society were doing the same. As indicated, a number of women affiliated with Yewe had begun to use their association with this order during the second half of the nineteenth century to circumvent undesirable marriages. They joined Yewe and married someone they chose from among the Yewe members, or they used their right as Yewe members to "go wild" to force their parents to at least consider their own wishes. Young women, unaffiliated with Yewe, who had not been betrothed by their parents while they were still infants, also began to establish marital relations with men of their own choice during this period. Most who pursued this course did so with young men who lacked such means as the young woman's parents considered appropriate. As Binetsch noted, "not all young men [have the finances or] uncles and fathers who [can] provide for a bride." In the absence of such resources, these young men began to encourage their women friends to join them in concubinage.[71] We can assume that the young women who responded positively to these invitations did so because it gave them the opportunity to establish relations with the men of their choice

One of the consequences of these developments was that women successfully challenged the gendered manner in which Anlo families managed their

---

[69] Court cases concerning events that occurred in the 1860s confirm that brothers did, on occasion, receive trade goods from their sisters on credit. See Judicial Council Minute Book: 1919, p. 6–7.

[70] Binetsch, "Beantwortung mehrerer," 44.

[71] Note that this decision was sometimes made easier if the young woman they wished to marry was a cross-cousin or lived in the same ward. In such instances, a woman's parents were prepared to ignore custom and allow the two to live together, with the expectation that bridewealth would be forthcoming. It was probably these circumstances Binetsch described when he indicated that some entered concubinage with the tacit approval of the parents. Binetsch, "Beantwortung mehrerer," 46.

affairs. Elders were forced to accept women's participation in managing their own lives. A second consequence was that this response by Anlo women directly affected ethnic relations. By opting to engage in unsanctioned unions, women made it possible to defy not only parental control over marriage, but also the entire value system that governed the definition of acceptable bridegrooms. German missionary accounts indicate that marriage to individuals who were members of one's clan, one's ward, and/or a father's sister's son remained the preference in the late nineteenth century, but it is obvious that this emphasis had also begun to change. More contemporary anthropological studies indicate that by the mid-twentieth century, men and women in Anlo no longer favored so strongly marriage to ethnic insiders. This decline was caused in large part by the increasing social importance of wealth and service to one's community; it was reinforced, however, by the actions of many Anlo women, who in challenging the prevailing norms that governed gender relations, also challenged the values that defined marriage preferences along ethnic lines.

Conclusion

In this chapter we have seen that many women successfully challenged the gendered manner in which Anlo families responded to the competitive pressures generated throughout the late seventeenth, eighteenth, and nineteenth centuries from immigration and economic change. The challenge began in the late eighteenth century when women joined the Nyigbla religious order to defy their natal and marital families' efforts to silence them as women who need not have any voice in their own marital affairs. The challenge continued into the nineteenth century as Anlo women also joined the Yewe order and took advantage of the high levels of indebtedness to exercise greater control over their lives. As a result, gender relations changed significantly. Concubinage increased. Family elders were forced to accept the fact that at least some women were going to participate in managing their own lives. A second consequence was that the response by Anlo women to the changed character of gender relations directly impacted ethnic relations. The support they gave to the Dzevi's Nyigbla religious order prompted the Anlo to incorporate the Dzevi clan and its Nyigbla god as part and parcel of Anlo society As a result, service to the Anlo polity became an important criterion on which social prestige was based in addition to the origins of one's ancestors and the time of their arrival in the early Anlo area. This action, in turn, opened the door for others like Togbui Gbodzo, an ethnic outsider, who as we saw in Chapter 2 became in the 1830s the right-wing commander of the Anlo army. Gbodzo's acceptance further expanded the criteria upon which the Anlo judged one's social standing to include not only one's genealogical and geographical origins, time of arrival of one's ancestors, and service to the community, but also wealth. By the end of the nineteenth century, the stature of Elias Quist—elevated in part by the support of women—expanded even further the bases upon which a person or group could become established as an integral and respected member of Anlo's social hierarchy. Wealth became entrenched as an additional foundation upon which the Anlo judged the social status of the

individuals and groups. Equally signficant is the fact that the changes that occurred in Anlo ethnic relations as a result of changes in gender relations established a foundation upon which others in twentieth-century Anlo based their
efforts to introduce even more sweeping changes in Anlo ethnic relations. This
development is the subject of Chapters 5 and 6. But before moving on to the
twentieth century, it is important to note that while important changes had occurred in precolonial Anlo gender and ethnic relations, there was also continuity
in the way men and women, earlier residents and later residents, had interacted
with one another since 1679. Why this was case is the subject of the next chapter.

4

The Road Not Taken

Throughout the late seventeenth, eighteenth, and nineteenth centuries, dramatic changes were occurring in the way in which men and women, individuals and families interacted with one another in Anlo. The we/they divide within this society shifted from one that emphasized social identities based on either one's association with autocthonous gods or immigrants gods, to a definition that focused on the origins of one's ancestors and time of arrival. As soon as this latter definition became dominant, it too faced continuous challenge as ethnic outsiders successfully redefined their own identities or worked with others in Anlo to recognize wealth and service to the community as additional bases for social prestige. The ethnic outsider Amlade *hlo* became a member of the "first five." Togbui Gbodzo of Woe—despite his technical status as a *blu*, a stranger—obtained the position of *dusifiaga* (right-wing commander) of the Anlo army. The Dzevi clan and Elias Quist, founders of the Nyigbla and the reorganized Yewe religious orders respectively, achieved considerable social status even though they could not claim to have originated from the Anlo ancestral home of Notsie or to have been descendants of the earlier residents of the area.

Gender relations also changed significantly during this period. Prior to 1679, young women had at least been given by their families the opportunity to veto the individuals selected as their future husbands. After 1679, families increasingly silenced their young women and selected their daughters' spouses by focusing exclusively on what marital arrangements were best for the landed and labor interests of their *to-fomewo* and *hlowo*. Families also increased the pressure on their young women to remain married to the individuals chosen for them. These changes generated yet another shift in gender relations by the late nineteenth century. In defiance of their parents, young women increasingly opted for concubinage (*dze ahia*). This forced many family elders to accept the fact that they could not force the young women under their authority to sacrifice their own individual interests for the sake of their *to-fomewo* or *hlowo*. My analysis of these changes has indicated that one significantly influenced the other. Ethnic outsiders successfully challenged the boundaries that defined them as "other" by taking advantage of the prevailing gender relations to gain support for their inclusion within the social center of Anlo society or for their ethnic redefinition. Women responded to their marginalization by joining the religious orders of ethnic outsider groups. They then used these orders as an effective means to defy their families efforts to control their marital lives.

Much in late nineteenth-century Anlo remained the same, however. Social boundaries continued to stigmatize a significant portion of the long-term residential population of Anlo as ethnic outsiders. Parental control over marriage remained the norm. In this chapter, I argue that continuity existed in the midst of change for very specific reasons. Many in eighteenth- and nineteenth-century Anlo who found themselves in socially disadvantageous situations because of their gender and/or ethnic identities were either unwilling or unable, for example, to use the vehicles available to alter their positions. To illustrate this point, I focus first on those who were disadvantaged because of their gender, but who were either unwilling or unable to alter their status. Among the unwilling were many women who could have joined the Nyigbla or Yewe religious orders but who did not do so because of their socialization. Taught to honor and respect their elders, socialized to value marriage to a fellow kinsperson (whether that person was a fictive or real relative), and to place the interests of their kin-group over their own individual interests, the majority of Anlo women supported the interests of their families by accepting whomever their elders had selected for them to marry. Others were deterred by the risks that came with membership in the Nyigbla and Yewe religious orders. Yet another set of women were actively prevented from taking action by their families who resorted to spiritual injunctions.

I argue here that this situation reinforced the post-1679 character of gender relations, which saw families sacrifice the interests of their young women for the sake of the family, but more important for this study is the fact that this situation also reinforced the post-1679 character of ethnic relations. By accepting the prevailing notion that it was better to marry within one's own *to-fome* and *hlo*, many young women reinforced the notion that there did indeed exist a we/they division in Anlo society. By opting to remain under the authority of their fathers and husbands rather than joining Nyigbla and Yewe because of their fears of the latter, some women reinforced the notion that the owners of these religious orders as ethnic outsiders were, indeed, different, untrustworthy, and potentially dangerous. By being bound by the spiritual injunctions imposed by their own families even after the abuses for which the Nyigbla order was accused ended, the women of the Madzezilawo branch of the Like clan were forced to participate in the social stigmatizing of a group because, in part, of its ethnic outsider origins.

In the second part of this chapter I document the fact that the actions of those identified as ethnic outsiders also contributed to significant continuity in Anlo gender and ethnic relations. Many such individuals and groups in the eighteenth and nineteenth century (like so many women in Anlo during this period) were also either unwilling or unable to alter their social status. One such example involves the Tsiame and Agave clans. In analyzing the relationship that developed between these two *hlowo* and the Anlo polity, I note that these two groups entered Anlo during the early eighteenth century as immigrants from the politically independent areas of Agave and Tsiame to the northwest and north of Anlo, respectively. The Agave came as administrators associated with the Akwamu empire after it conquered Anlo in 1702. The Tsiame came at the invitation of the Anlo *awoamefia*, Togbui Akpotsui, who sought to use the Tsiame's reputation for spiritual power to boost his own status and the position of the Anlo polity vis-à-vis the Akwamu empire. In both cases, these two groups—defined throughout this period as ethnic outsiders—gained access to the position of *awadada*, military leader of the entire Anlo army, and adopted many Anlo social customs. Neither, however, was able to translate this achievement into the kind of social prestige achieved by the Amlade or the Dzevi, whose experiences were discussed above. I argue that the Tsiame and Agave clan elders were unable to counter the actions of the political and religious leaders in Anlo, who felt threatened by the spiritual power associated with these clans. In response to their failure, the Tsiame maintained connections with their former homelands. This provided them with a social anchor denied them in Anlo, but it also strengthened the prevailing norms that governed gender and ethnic relations. It reinforced the definition of outsiders as somewhat untrustworthy because their continued attachment to their home areas could compromise their loyalty to the Anlo. This, in turn, affected gender relations since distrust of others constituted one of the principal reasons ethnic insiders preferred not to betroth their daughters to members of a different clan and particularly not to outsiders.

Evidence from the nineteenth century also suggests that in some instances the Anlo allowed ethnic outsiders to alter their identity, but many who gained this opportunity chose not to follow this course and decided instead to leave unaltered their status on the social margins of Anlo society. One such individual was Geraldo de Lima of Vodza. I argue here that he very consciously calculated the benefits and drawbacks of changing his identity, and found that it was economically more beneficial to operate not so much on the margins but rather within the interstices that separated and connected Anlo society to the European world economy. Geraldo became a member of the Adzovia clan, one of the most powerful groups in Anlo, but he also maintained his European name and a Europeanized way of life to facilitate his business interests. In so doing, he identified himself as an outsider. Geraldo was not unique; others did the same. This approach—while financially and politically beneficial for Geraldo—also contributed to a significant degree of continuity in Anlo ethnic as well as gender relations since Geraldo focused his energies not on challenging the existing social order, but rather on making it work for his own personal interests.

Together these case studies illustrate the complex ways in which gender and ethnic relations generated a set of responses among the men and women of Anlo that supported continuity in the midst of change during the eighteenth and nineteenth century.

Gender Relations as a Foundation for Continuity in Anlo Ethnic Relations

Socialization and Customary Law in the Eighteenth and Nineteenth Century

Information about the socialization of Anlo children in the eighteenth century is virtually non-existent, but if we assume that nineteenth-century accounts are true for the earlier period, it becomes apparent why the majority of Anlo women opted not to take advantage of the changes in gender relations generated by a minority of women and ethnic outsiders. The socialization of boys and girls—as observed by German missionaries and confirmed by them in conversations with Anlo men and women—emphasized the value of group cohesion over individual interests. The following are excerpts from Binetsch and Westermann concerning these issues:

On the value of sublimating one's individual interests for the family and heeding the advice of one's family elders:
[A]ccording to the Negro's time-honored patriarchal point of view . . . , individual members of the family are of secondary importance in comparison with the family as a whole and the head who represents them. . . . [1]
. . . the ancestors . . . are believed to be omnipresent. . . . This [belief] makes some who would want to protest [against a particular decision] give in. When a father says to his son [or daughter], "If you do not act [according to my wishes], after my death, I will be after you as a ghost, just like a chicken after the hen, like a puppy after its master," this is no joke. No one can afford to make the ancestors unhappy with them. This could mean their death.[2]

On the socialization and social pressure to marry an individual approved by one's family:
Marrying a woman from one's own *kome* (ward) is regarded as a good custom and a young man is thought to be arrogant or disloyal if he goes far away in order to find a wife.
If a girl marries someone from another *fome* (lineage) or *kome* (ward), she must leave one of her daughters to her "brothers," which means to the members of her own *fome* or *kome* for marriage.
Marriage with a fellow *hlo* is . . . regarded as particularly refined.[3]

The socialization of young women to respect and obey their elders, to serve their fathers and husbands, was also reinforced by customary law. This is perhaps most apparent in those laws that dealt with adultery. First and foremost, women were expected to behave in a way that did not disrupt the social relations of the male-headed households with which they were associated. As Binetsch noted:

If . . . a wife breaks the marital faith, it may have serious results for her and her whole family . . . [for] if the wife abandons the husband, she or her parents have to reimburse the whole amount that the husband gave to her or her parents. This usually amounts to 200–240 marks. In addition to this, the husband gets 24 bottles of brandy.
Frequently, a heathen is not sorry if his wife betrays him once in a while, for he can profit from his wife's unfaithfulness. It is different, of course, if a woman becomes a regular adulteress, trapping many men in her yarn. Because such men have to pay the fine for adultery to her husband, they become the husband's enemies. It is because of this that the husband may feel compelled to dismiss his wife.[4]

These accounts attest to the notion that eighteenth- and nineteenth-century Anlo families consciously and deliberately socialized their daughters to accept the no-

---

[1] Binetsch, "Beantwortung mehrerer," 46.

[2] Westermann, "Die Glidyi-Ewe," 263.

[3] Ibid., 141, 144.

[4] Binetsch, "Beantwortung mehrerer," 47.

tion that they should adhere to the decisions made on their behalf by their family elders, that their proper role was to support their families, and that they must not do anything that would create difficulties for their lineage, their clan, or their husbands. That the majority of women viewed their own role in similar terms is suggested by the fact that most women in late nineteenth-century Anlo did, indeed, agree to marry the individual chosen by their elders. Even those who opted for concubinage appear to have been unable to depart completely from their socialization since the majority married cross-cousins, the very individuals whom their parents preferred as their husbands.[5] Accordingly, it should come as no surprise that the majority of young women in eighteenth- and nineteenth-century Anlo lent their support to continuity in Anlo gender relations. This also made them unwitting supporters of the prevailing pattern in ethnic relations, for their agreement to marry within their own *to-fome* and *hlo* reinforced the notion that there did indeed exist a we/they divide in Anlo society, a divide that required them to support the "we" against the "they."

Nyigbla and Yewe in Nineteenth-century Anlo

Women's socialization was not the only factor preventing them from challenging their *to-fomewo* and *hlowo*. Many were also deterred by the difficulties they knew others faced when they joined the Nyigbla and Yewe orders. In Chapter 3, I discussed the increased presence of wealthy Afro-European traders in the Anlo area during the nineteenth century. The presence of these wealthy traders in Anlo undermined the prestige of the *awoamefia* and the Nyigbla priest, who lacked the means to compete with their ostentatious displays. I also noted that the political and religious authorities in Anlo responded by banning the wearing of sewn clothing and gold jewelry, as well as the use of horses. This was not their only response, however. The Nyigbla priest also began to use the *zizi fo asi* ritual—in which young women were inducted into the order—in ways designed to enhance its economic position within Anlo. During this annual ritual, certain young women would allow themselves to be ritually captured (i.e., possessed) by the god. They would begin to act abnormally, in ways that would suggestion such possession. Such young women would then be ushered into the Nyigbla forest, where as *zizidzelawo*, Nyigbla initiates, they would be inducted into the order. This induction process lasted from six to twelve months, after which the young women were to be released to their families. It was not unusual, however, for some of these women to die before they emerged from the forest. In the early 1800s, the Nyigbla order appears to have taken advantage of this fact and its preeminent position within the Anlo political and religious hierarchy to sell some of the young women entrusted to them into the slave trade.

According to a number of Anlo elders, this action was detected when a dispute arose among the *awoamefia*, his advisors, and the Nyigbla order as to how they would share the profits. Others claim that a number of Anlo traders uncovered the Nyigbla order's abuse of authority when they saw a number of the *zizidzelawo* whom the Nyigbla order had declared dead about to be sold to slave traders in Whydah. Of greater significance is the fact that the discovery of the ac-

---

[5] See Dickson, "Marital Selection," Ch. 5.

PHOTO 2: Yewe women and men in 1927–28

tions of the *awoamefia* and the Nyigbla priest brought a number of changes. The *awoamefia* was executed and his name erased from Anlo oral records. The Nyigbla priest was forced into exile at Adina, a town located on the eastern boundary of Anlo. Fathers no longer acquiesced easily to their daughters being inducted into the order. Mothers no longer encouraged their daughters to view the opportunity to join Nyigbla as a desirable way to gain greater influence within their marital households.

In an effort to find for themselves an alternative to Nyigbla, some young women joined Yewe. But many associated this well-known order with difficulties so great that they preferred to maintain their current status rather than challenge the prevailing norms governing relations between men and women, parents and children. Perhaps the best-known and best-publicized problems faced by Yewe members had to do with their inability to leave the order. In 1881, Stefano Kwadzo Afelevo, from the town of Woe, decided to leave Yewe and become a Christian. His battle to sever his ties without cost to himself became widely known. Afelevo brought his case to the Anlo traditional courts as well as to the local colonial courts. His German missionary mentors also publicized his situation by writing about it and by sponsoring the publication of "A Yewe Servant's Story," his account of the incident. I present this here (even though it contains only Afelevo's own interpretation of the events in question) to illustrate the image of Yewe to which many Anlo women were exposed when deciding whether to join this order.

The Yewe service maintains a strong connection among its members. . . . Yewe people stick together in all instances and never do anything alone. . . . Some feel sorry about having joined Yewe, but because of the strong sense of community amongst them, they cannot detach themselves from it.

If a member has bent one of their rules only a little, he is punished heavily. They are authorized to tie him up and to beat him thoroughly. They take his money and they expel him from the community. This means they take Yewe out of his head.

In order to take the Yewe out of a person's head . . . all Vodu people fall into obsession when listening to the sound of the drums. While the drum is being hit, someone grabs the guilty person and leads him to the place where it is being drummed. With a knife, called the proper knife of Yewe, they shave the head while the people are watching. Afterwards, all the Vodu people start addressing him by his old name. That means that from now on he is not a Vodu member anymore. The Yewe people then take their head- and hip-cloths and hit him heavily with them. That is what they call taking the Yewe out of the head.

I have already written earlier . . . that my father was an important Yewe servant. . . . I was taught everything well . . . but I was not at all pleased with all their activities. . . . I explained to them that if it was like this, I could not stay with them. On the other hand, they were not satisfied with me or with my behavior and they hated me. I had been with them and given them assistance and because of this they had explained everything to me, and now I turn against them?

After that, I slowly started to move away from them and did not visit as often the Yewe cloister with them. But for exactly two and a half years, I was one of them. . . .

Just about this time, someone from Woe named Kristian Kwami returned home from the coastal region of Denu. . . . I explained my situation to him and asked him for advice. He told me that he wanted to found a school which I should attend and he was going to tell me the story of Jesus Christ. I was happy about it and totally agreed. We eagerly started school. My connection to Mr. Kwami made the Yewe people hate me even more than before. I did not hold it against them, but I steadily stuck to my school visits.

After our baptism, our brothers became even more angry because we had become Christian people. The Yewe priest, the *hunde* [?the female Yewe servants], the *husunu* [the male Yewe members] and all Yewe people rose against me, in particular. They agreed to kill me by all means, because they said that I was going to betray them. . . .

[One day Yewe members attacked some of the boys associated with the mission.] By that time, all the Vodu people, the *husunu* and *hunde*, had surrounded the mission farm and they started to beat us. They were more numerous than us. They numbered more than 200. We were completely beaten. In fact, they intended to kill me and cut off my head, but they did not succeed. The same day, we went to Keta and accused them at the European court. The officer, named Kirkham, had us tell our story and found them guilty. The trial . . . was in December . . . 1881. Three Vodu people received a week in prison each.

Because of this, the Yewe priest, the *husunu* and all the Yewe people were extremely angry with us. The very day the matter was debated in Keta, all the Vodu people from Anlo, Woe, Tegbui, Dzelukofe, Keta, Vodza, and Kedzi assembled to help them. Altogether they probably numbered 500 to 800 people.

During those days when the struggle between us was taking place, I did not feel very well. That made many of the Yewe people believe that their Yewe was killing me. In their praises, they mentioned my name constantly hoping that the Yewe would then kill me. They said repeatedly that one would now see if the Yewe was really impotent. If I bathed on my farm, some of them always stretched their necks over the fence, looked at me and then talked to their Yewe priests and to the Vodu people. In the evening in their cloisters, they prayed about me, begging Yewe to kill me. . . . They made all this effort for me and my brother David Besa so that we would die. Everything proved ineffectual. Nothing happened to us and it became their great shame, but still they did not leave us alone.

After all this, the Yewe priests decided to harm me in another way. They wanted to take away my land which my father had given to me before his death. The priest actually took the field and explained to me that I was not allowed to cultivate it anymore. It did not belong to me anymore. I had someone ask them why. I myself was not there at that time. He answered me that because I had refused to go on serving the Yewe, the land would not belong to me anymore because the money [my father's money] that had bought the Yewe, was the same money that had also bought the land.

One day, Missionary Daeuble came to Woe. He asked the priest to come to the house of Chief Antonio to discuss this matter. The priest promised to leave us the field. He had not only taken my field, but also one that belonged to another Christian named Timoteo Tete, and his brother.

He still did not give the land back to us; he had only said that he would. He kept the field and stubbornly refused to give them to us. That is why we brought the case to a European civil servant . . . on May 13, 1893. But the civil servant transferred the case to Chief Antonio and the elders of Woe. They debated the matter on May 16th and then we got the field back.

Now I am no longer in my hometown of Woe. At the end of 1892, our missionaries sent me to Wute in Aveno. It was in Wute that I wrote this book.[6]

This account links the difficulties experienced by recalcitrant Yewe members with their violation of Yewe rules or with a member's conversion to Christianity, but these were not the only circumstances under which individuals sought to leave the order. Some simply did not fully understand the extent to which they had committed themselves, as indicated in the following lament by an Anlo woman.

> Yewe is hard work
> They have caught me for it.
> I lacked the head to refuse,
> Now the misery has overtaken me.
> I am totally worthless in the world
> And not able to refuse anymore.
> That is the fruit of Yewe.
> Yes, hard and heavy is Yewe.[7]

---

[6] Afelevo, "Ein Bericht," 33–35, 45–51.

[7] Spieth, *Die Religion*, 183.

Many of the women who heard this song and/or Afelevo's account must have surely had second thoughts about joining Yewe and/or Nyigbla as a means to achieve greater influence over their own lives. In choosing to accept the decisions made by their elders, however, they not only lent considerable stability to the norms that had governed gender relations in Anlo since 1679, they also gave credence to the notion that these stranger gods (Yewe and Nyigbla) and their owners as ethnic outsiders were different and potentially dangerous.

The Madzezilawo in Nineteenth-Century Anlo

While some women considered and then rejected this form of defiance, others were denied the opportunity to even attempt such a change. Among this group were a number of women from the Like clan. Anlo oral traditions indicate that the elders from this *hlo* denied the women under their authority the opportunity to join either the Nyigbla or Yewe religious orders. The circumstances leading to this development had to do with the early nineteenth-century discovery by the Anlo that the Nyigbla religious order had been selling a number of its initiates into the Atlantic slave trade. I noted above that the Anlo then expelled the Nyigbla priest and his god from the area and executed the *awoamefia*, but this was not their only response. According to Alex Afatsao Awadzi, an elder of the Like clan, this incident generated a response by one of the Like clanswomen that changed profoundly the way in which his clan was organized.

> The ancestor of the [Like] clan was originally called Amesimeku, later changed to Atogolo. [Atogolo's] first wife was Notsiesi, whose son was Alewo. The second wife, Dede had Duadzie and others. . . .
> There was a split in the clan into two groups: one included the children of Dede and the other included the children of Notsiesi. Madzedziawo is the name associated with Dede's children and Dzeziziawo is associated with the group formed by Notseisi's children.
> The division was caused by a ceremony which is called *zizidzelawo* at which young girls, virgins, were taken to the forest where Togbui Nyigbla was supposed to live. This ceremony was for those girls to become the temporary wives of Nyigbla. The ceremony was called *foasi*. Two girls of Dede and two or more of Notsiesi's girls were taken with the others. The custom is that the mothers send food to the girls regularly. The food is left with the overseer of the forest at the entrance and it is then taken into them. They could stay there from six to twelve months. Afterwards, they were released to lead a normal life again. Dede's daughters never returned, however. . . . [They] put *kakla*, an herb, on [her] roof which means [her children were] dead. But these people were not actually dead, they were sold. [All the parents believed their children were dead, however so they] did not look for them again.
> [When this happened], there was an uproar. Dede vowed that all her descendants would never go through this ceremony again. The way in which she made this vow, by beating the ground, meant that the earth was her witness and that the oath should never be violated. Anyone who did violate it would become mad.
> These two groups can both be found in Anyako, Whuti, Tegbi, and all over Anlo. If you claim to be a Like, you will be asked if you belong to Madzeziawo or Dzeziziawo.

Because of this incident, [Dede's] offspring also do not get involved with Yewe. If a descendant joins . . . he or she will go insane. These are the only two they couldn't join.[8]

By spiritually barring her descendants from joining Nyigbla, the Like clanswoman, Dede, sought first and foremost to protect others in her family from the fate that her own daughters suffered. Inability to join Nyigbla prevented them from coming under the authority of outsiders during the long period of seclusion. Extension of the ban to include Yewe protected her descendants from the only other group in the area that was also shrouded in secrecy. By the late 1840s, the general opposition to Nyigbla within Anlo faded as the polity suffered one military defeat after another. In time, the political and religious leaders invited the Nyigbla priest to return so that his god could lead the Anlo into battle. As a result, by the end of the century Nyigbla had recovered much of its lost status.[9] For some, however, the breach in trust could not be so easily closed. Women who had sought affiliation with Nyigbla because of the advantages it had given them in their marital households turned instead to Yewe. This was not an option available to the women of the Madzeziawo branch of the Like clan, however. Their "grandmother's" spiritual prohibition against joining either Nyigbla or Yewe meant that they were forced to remain under the authority of their fathers and their husbands, whether they liked it or not. This, in turn, supported the continued existence in Anlo of the norms that had governed gender and ethnic relations since 1679. Madzezilawo women had to accept the authority of their elders or risk spiritual harm; they were also forced to uphold the prevailing ethnic boundaries that defined the Nyigbla and Yewe orders as different and dangerous.

Ethnic Relations as a Foundation for Continuity in Gender Relations

Tsiame and Agave in the Eighteenth Century

Not all who found themselves silenced or socially defined as "other" within Anlo society chose or were forced to remain within their defined positions. Many like the Amlade, the Dzevi, Togbui Gbodzo of Woe, and the women who joined Nyigbla and Yewe successfully challenged their marginal status, but many also failed. Two such groups operating in Anlo during the eighteenth century were the Tsiame and Agave. Oral traditions about the ancestors of these two *hlowo* indicate that both groups lived outside the early Anlo area prior to the period when the ancestors of the Anlo settled on the Atlantic littoral. The Agave traditions locate their earliest settlements at Agavedzi on the coast to the east of the contemporary town of Keta. They are said to have subsequently moved to the lower Volta where their presence was first noted by European travelers in the late seventeenth century.[10] The loca-

---

[8] FN 20: Interview with Togbui Alex Afatsao Awadzi, 30 August, 1978; FN 53: Interview with Togbui Alex Afatsao Awadzi, 16 December 1987.

[9] Schlegel, "Beitrag zur Geschichte," 399–400.

[10] Wilks, "Rise of the Akwamu Empire," 106, 113; see also Barbot, *A Description*, 319, who refers to them as the "Negroes of the Volta." See also FN 17: Interview with Mr. T. S. A. Togobo, 28 August 1978, An-

tion of their settlements on both sides of the lower Volta River gave them access to the particularly rich fishing grounds that existed both in the river and in the bordering marshlands and creeks. It also placed them in direct contact, through trade, with a variety of groups on the upper reaches of the river as well as with those political groups in the region (the Accras and the Akwamus) who fought to exercise control over this trade route. Agave traditions and European documentary sources indicate, for example, that when the Akwamu state began to expand, it attacked and brought the Agaves under its political authority as early as the mid-1670s. In 1677 Akwamu then commandeered a number of Agave troops which it added to its own forces and attacked the state of Accra, the polity that had dominated the political scene on the lower Gold Coast up to that point. The Agaves appear to have continued their involvement with the Akwamu state throughout the rest of the century. Ewe-speakers are known to have acted as intermediaries for the Akwamu state in its conquered territories; there they collected taxes, adjudicated disputes, and led armed contingents from the conquered areas in Akwamu military campaigns. Agave traditions indicate that this was the very role they played in the Anlo area after Akwamu conquered the district in 1702. According to these accounts, court cases of all kinds were brought to the Agave at Agowowonu in Anloga, a place they had specifically designated for such activities.[11] Late nineteenth-century accounts indicate that it was also the Agaves who "taught the Anlos how to fight"—that is, with the Akan-type three-wing formation, which they had become intimately familiar with during their participation in Akwamu military campaigns.[12] Akwamu control over Anlo came to an end in 1730 after this state was defeated by a coalition of forces. Many of the Agaves who had settled in the Anlo area remained, however, and formed the core of what was later to become known as the Agave clan.

Traditions about the Tsiame indicate that this group first occupied the area on which the present town of Tsiame is located, immediately north of Anloga on the northern side of the Keta Lagoon. There the Tsiame established their own polity, which is said to have gained considerable influence in the area by the beginning of the eighteenth century because of the reputation of their gods, Tsali and Tesi. The narratives about these gods—first recorded in the late nineteenth century—have, no doubt, been modified for a variety of social and political purposes since the early eighteenth century. I nevertheless reproduce here a number of these stories to

---

loga; FN 21: Interview with Mr. T. S. A. Togobo, 31 August 1978, Anloga. FN 34: Interview with Togbui Alex Afatsao Awadzi, 3 October 1978, Anloga; FN 41: Interview with Boko Seke Axovi, 31 October 1978, Anloga; *Committee of Enquiry (Volta Region)*, 78th Sitting, pp. 4–5; Aduamah, Ewe Traditions, No. 1, 1–2; ADM 11/1/1662, 9; M. E. Kropp Dakubu, "Linguistic Pre-History and Historical Reconstruction: The Ga–Adangbe Migration," *THSG* XIII (1972), 99–100; and Reindorf, *History of the Gold Coast*, 42. According to Fia Sri II, who testified before a commission of enquiry in 1912, the Agaves lived in the present Ada area before the latter moved into the area. The Agaves gave land to the Adas and subsequently constituted the Kudjeragbe clan in the Ada polity. ADM 11/1/1661, 202.

[11] FN 39: Interview with Togbui Christian Yao Gbotoza Fiadzo, 16 October 1978, Anloga; Anlo State Council Minute Book, 1935: Chiefs Kata, Adaku, Avege, and Agblevo per Samuel Nutsuga for themselves and on behalf of Tsiame Tribe of Anloga, Atokor, Atiavie and others -v- Chiefs Zewu, Agbozo, Anakoo Attipoe, and Zioklui, Davordji Banini and others for themselves and on behalf of Agave Tribe of Anloga, Djelukope, Anyako, and others, 372–73.

[12] See Greene, "The Anlo-Ewe," 80, 112–13.

illustrate the kind of powers to which the Anlo, believed the Tsiame priests and the Tsiame people had access.

Tsali and his father [Akplomeda were] miracle-workers. . . . the latter had sorcery [as did] his son. . . . Sometimes father and son competed in their sorcery. . . . One day Togbui Akplomeda took out his intestines, washed them, and then laid them on the ground to dry in the sun. Tsali turned himself into a hawk and snatched the intestines so his father ordered all the trees to lie flat on the ground. He then changed himself into the only silk cotton tree standing. The hawk couldn't land on any other tree. When he did land on the only one he saw [which was actually Akplomeda], the father grabbed his intestines from Tsali and said that Tsali could snatch intestines but he couldn't change himself into a silk cotton tree. . . . The Anlos watched them do these things and they said "These men are in reality *trowo.*"

. . . . [At one time] the whole of Tongu met and decided to drown Tsali. Tsali before his arrest had gathered all his personal effects into a haversack and slung it over his shoulder. At the meeting, he was tied hands and feet . . . with a great weight of granite rocks hung over his neck and fastened to his back. Looking like a monster, Tsali was drowned in the . . . Volta [River]. The villagers saw him sink, but on the third day, Tsali was seen by fishermen as he moved on the waters floating on the back of a crocodile he had commanded to come to his rescue. Floating adrift on the crocodile's back, Tsali held aloft all the granite rocks in his hands and was shouting "Vinowo, mikpo vida: parents behold your child." There was great consternation in the village: the fishermen abandoned their canoes and ran for dear life. The women yelled and screamed, calling on the whole village to come and see. Tsali [then] decided to leave Tongu for good.[13]

[After Tsali] grew old . . . he became so tired of life that he went to the underworld. The dwellers of the underworld drove him back, however, and told him he must die before he could come to them. After his return to [Tsiame] . . . he gathered all the inhabitants of the town together and told them he was going to die. He then took [out] his own jawbone and hung it on a tree. Hereupon, he sent a message to a crocodile telling it that it should come to him. When it had come, he sat upon its back and ordered it to carry him to the underworld. . . . After Tsali's death, the jawbone he left behind was made into a *tro*. Tsali [the *tro*] gives the people life and protects them. . . . Before the outbreak of war, the chiefs hold the council of war in Tsali's shrine. Only from there do they move to war.

Tesi is the wife of Tsali; [she] possessed many charms. After her death, she was made into a *tro*. She had seven white hens and a child. To this day, all are still alive. If some disaster is imminent, she goes out and gives emergency signals by clapping her hand to her mouth and calling "There comes disaster." . . . Her descendants are among the inhabitants of Tsiame. They are the beheaders in war for Tesi herself placed the sword into their hands for this purpose.[14]

---

[13] This account comes from Mamattah, *The Ewes*, 3-19-320, but is consistent with accounts recorded by Spieth in the late nineteenth century and by Tsiame linguist, Kwami Kwagbala in 1935. See Spieth, *Die Religion*, 135–136 and Anlo Traditional Council Minute Book, 1933–1935: Chiefs Kata, Adaku, Avege, and Agblevo per Samuel Nutsuga . . . -v- Chiefs Zewu, Agbozo, Anakoo Attipoe, . . . and others, 420–24.

[14] FN 40: Interview with Togbui Atsu Klogo and Togbui Avege II, 17 October 1978, Anloga; and Spieth, *Die Religion*, 135–36.

Anlo oral traditions state that it was the Tsiame's reputation for possessing such powerful gods that prompted the Anlo to seek closer political ties with their northern neighbor. The *awoamefia* said to have initiated these efforts was Akpotsui, who probably served as the political and religious leader of this polity during the 1702–1730 period when Akwamu dominated both the Tsiame and Anlo areas.[15] Although the alliance appears to have developed as part of both polities' efforts to counter Akwamu control,[16] it continued after 1730 when the two launched joint military expeditions to gain control over those areas on the Keta Lagoon inhabited by the Tefle, the Agave, and the Abolo.[17] By 1750, a number of Tsiames had immigrated to the Anlo area and were encouraged—presumably on the basis of their leadership abilities and their association with their gods Tsali and Tesi—to provide the commander of the Anlo military.[18] The most notable of these Tsiame military leaders was Adagla, who is remembered in Anlo oral traditions as having lead the Anlo in war against the Adas in the 1751 Abalenu war.[19] Their defeat is said to

---

[15] FN 38: Interview with Boko Seke Axovi, 16 October 1978, Anolga; ADM 11/1/1113 (n.d., not signed); Rattray, "History of the Ewe People," 92–93; ADM 11/1/1246, p. 1; and Mamattah, *The Ewes*, 199–200.

[16] In 1727, a Danish trader noted that Amega, an Akwamu royal and administrator of the Ladoku province attacked the coastal towns on the east side of the Volta, as far as Anexo. This particular action—unlike a previously threatened expedition—was directed against all the communities in the area, which suggests that all were also involved in challenging Akwamu authority. See Isert, *Voyages en Guinée*, 35. See also Kea, "Akwamu–Anlo Relations," 33.

[17] These wars were known as the Tefle–Agave and the Abolo wars. The Kovenor war with the Avenors occurred during this same period. See FN 9: Interview with Mr. T. S. A. Togobo, 7 August 1978, Anloga; FN 18: Interview with Boko Seke Axovi, 29 August 1978, Anloga; FN 21: Interview with Mr. T. S. A. Togobo, 31 August 1978, Anloga; FN 33: Interview with Boko Seke Axovi, 3 October 1978, Anloga; FN 44: Interview with Togbui Dzobi Adzinku, 6 November 1978, Anloga; FN 45: Interview with Togbui Dzobi Adzinku, 8 November 1978, Anloga; FN 47: Interview with Mr. T. S. A. Togobo, 8 November 1978, Anloga; ADM 11/1/1661, p. 19, 27–28; Anlo Traditional Council Minute Book No. 3: Acting Chief Gbadago III of Atiavi, Plaintiff -v- Chief Adri III of Atiavi, Defendant, passim; Tay-Agbozo, "Background History"; Anlo Traditional Council Questionnaire: Kwashie Misewo Akorli, Stool name: Dufia Akamu Adela Akpa, III, 3 April 1950; Aduamah, Ewe Traditions, No 1, p. 23, and No. 3, p. 13; Westermann, "Die Glidyi-Ewe," 148. Contemporary Dutch reports about conditions in the area report that not only were there considerable disturbances in the area in 1732 and 1736, but that the Adas—located west of the Volta River—also felt threatened by the actions of Anlo and Tsiame. See Van Dantzig, *The Dutch*, Doc. No. 384.

[18] Anlo elders indicate that the Anlo military leader was not an inherited position in the early history of the polity, nor was it known at that time by the title *awadada*. As one elder noted, "it wasn't a lineage position . . . [instead] they looked for someone who had courage and who had [the spiritual] power to back this courage . . . the one who was chosen to lead at that time was just called the leader of the three wings. They just recently started to call it *awadada*." FN 20: Interview with Togbui Alex Afatsao Awadzi, 30 August 1978, Anloga; FN 38: Interview with Boko Seke Axovi, 16 October 1978, Anloga; FN 39: Interview with Togbui Christian Yao Gbotoza Fiadzo, 16 October 1978, Anloga; and FN 41: Interview with Boko Seke Axovi, 31 October 1978, Anloga.

[19] The Abalenu war of 1751 occurred immediately after the 1750 Nonobe war with the Agaves. Traditional accounts of the Abalenu war indicate that the Ada invaded the Anlo littoral and defeated them. This certainly occurred in the war in 1751 and was not repeated until the Sagbadre war of 1784. Accordingly, I associate the Abalenu war with the conflict which occurred in 1751. See FN 39: Interview with Togbui Christian Yao Gbotoza Fiadzo, 16 October 1978, Anloga; FN 40: Interview with Togbui Atsu Klogo and Togbui Avege II, 17 October 1978, Anloga; FN 41: Interview with Boko Seke Axovi, 31 October 1978, Anloga; FN 108: Interview with Togbui Dzovi Adzinku, ? June 1988, Anloga; and VgK 125, 7 May 1751, Christiansborg, A. O. Tofte, "Enquiry about the former bookkeeper Marcus Svane in Guinea, beginning 10 April 1752, ending 13 May ?1752/53." The same is also in VgK 188, Doc. no. 404, Marcus Svane.

have prompted Adagla to commit suicide. Thereafter the Agaves provided the leader of the Anlo army.

As I noted above, members of the Agave community resident in Anlo had already served as military leaders among the Anlo, but they did so when this polity was under the authority of the Akwamu. Their ability to regain access to this office, despite their previous connections with the Anlo's conquerors, appears to have been the result of a number of factors, including the altered nature of the relationship between the Anlo and the Akwamu. In 1730, Akwamu lost control of its empire when a number of polities, including Akuapem, Akyem, Accra, and Anexo escalated their military involvement in a succession dispute to destroy the power of the state and thereby dismantle the empire. After their defeat, the Akwamus, being few in number and incapable at that time of reasserting their control over all their former territories, attempted to establish a new home by first reconquering the Krepi district. Their initial military efforts launched from their temporary home on the Volta River islands faced difficulties, but by early 1735 they had established enough of a foothold in Krepi in order to repulse an Akyem attack.[20]

During this same period, numerous difficulties had arisen between Asante, located to the northwest of the old Akwamu homeland, and the Wassa, Aowin, and the Akanny peoples, due to Asante's interest in expanding its political control to the south and obtaining direct access to the ports on the Gold Coast. By 1729, Wassa had formed an alliance with the coastal Fante and a number of other polities in order to contain Asante's efforts. Akyem, then in control of the western sections of the former Akwamu empire, was among those who joined the Wassa. To weaken their opponent, Akyem, Wassa, and a number of the Fante states established an economic embargo from Cape Appolonia to the Volta River to prevent Asante traders from buying firearms and ammunition from the Europeans, and salt from the local producers, the majority of whom were on the coast. The alliance continued with intermittent breaks and realignments up to 1742.[21] The economic effect of the embargo as it was realized in 1731—two years after the blockade was first established, and a year after the collapse of Akwamu—was described by the Danes: "This decision [to erect an embargo] causes us [here at Accra] to have no trade at all at this time from Acheny; what we should say [however] is that there is no trade on the entire Gold Coast."[22]

In order to break through the eastern section of the trade embargo that was being enforced most actively by the states of Akyem Abuakwa and Akyem Kotoku, Asante attacked the two on numerous occasions.[23] Ultimately, however, they failed to secure safe roads for their traders. Asante then sought assistance from Akwamu. In 1748, the two joined together to launch attacks against the

---

[20] See Rømer, *Tilforladelig*, 103 and 134, who states that the Akwamu numbered five hundred families, among whom there were no more than one hundred soldiers.

[21] For more information on this matter, see Fynn, *Asante*, 41–48, 61, 63–66; Yarak, "Political Consolidation," 17–30; and Tenkorang, "Importance of Firearms," 5–6.

[22] VgK 122, 25 March 1731, Christiansborg, H. Sparre, R. N. Kamp, Warberg; the same appears in VgK 886.

[23] For more information on Asante during this period, see I. Wilks, *Asante in the Nineteenth Century* (Cambridge, 1975), 18–25.

Akyem states; they also opened a road from Kumase, via Kwawu, Akwamu, and the Volta to the lower Gold Coast and upper Slave Coast communities. By November of that year, the Danes in Ningo reported having received three parties of Asantes—who presumably had used the new road—without their previously needed Akwamu escort.[24] This cooperative effort marked the beginning of an alliance that included not only Asante and Akwamu, but Anlo as well. Anlo aligned itself with Akwamu and Asante in the mid-1750s and 1760s after the Akyem states and their allies in Krobo, Akuapem, Tefle, Agave, Malfi, and Ada renewed their efforts to prevent the Akwamu (and by association, the Asante) from using the Volta River to reach the Anlo coast which, by this date, was the only area on the lower Gold Coast and upper Slave Coast where they could purchase firearms, ammunition, and salt.[25] Thus, Anlo came to share common economic interests with Asante and its former enemy, Akwamu; interests that each eventually expanded to include military support for one another.

The first tangible evidence of the alliance between Anlo and Akwamu comes from the war that developed between Anlo and Ada in 1769. On 14 February of that year, Danish officers posted in the area reported that:

> The Augna [Anlo] and Way [Woe] negroes who are between Ada and Quitta [Keta] have attacked the Ada negroes . . . ruined all the houses in Ada, removed all the slaves, women, girls and boys they could get [including a particularly prominent Ada elder by the name of Patta], but none of the men who were able to use guns. . . . [T]he reason for this attack was that the present broker in Ada, Aikei [or Kwesi] has killed the negro who should be cabuseer in Augna [Fia Xemelodzo of Atsito] over which the Augnas have become irreconcilable enemies of the Adas.[26]

The allies sought and secured by Ada and Anlo after this battle followed the pattern that had emerged after the 1730 collapse of Akwamu. In 1766 and 1767, Ada had joined with Akuapem, Krobo, and the riverine Ewes (the Malfis, Tefles, and Agaves) to assist Akyem in their efforts to block Asante and Akwamu access to the trade routes leading to the coast. On 18 February 1769, four days after the Anlos stormed Ada Island, the Adas requested and received assistance from these

---

[24] VgK 124, 23 May 1748, Christiansborg, Joost Platfues, L. F. Rømer, H. F. Hackenburg, and 7 November 1748, Christiansborg, Joost Platfues, L. F. Rømer. Note that Wilks, *Asante*, 25, has indicated that the new road through Kwawu, Akwamu, and down the Volta was opened only in 1749; however the citations noted above contradict this notion. For a short period of time, in 1749, the Akwamu attempted to maintain their middleman position between the coast and Asante by refusing to allow Asante traders to pass through their territory. This policy is said to have been abandoned in September of that year. See Kea, "Akwamu–Anlo Relations," 57.

[25] The actions taken by Akyem, Krobo, and Akuapem against the Akwamu and Asante were motivated by their desire to prevent the latter from obtaining the materials needed to wage war against them. Ada and the riverine Ewes—the Malfi, Agave, and Tefle—joined with Akyem, Krobo, and Akuapem in hopes of maintaining their middleman position in the coastal-interior trade by preventing Asante and Akwamu traders from reaching the coast. See Greene, "The Anlo-Ewe," 136–42, for a more detailed discussion of these efforts.

[26] GK 15, 6 April 1769, Christiansborg, F. J. Kuhberg, J. F. Wrisberg, P. Bang, N. Aarestrup, J. L. Karrig. See also 26 December 1789, Christiansborg, E. Quist, J. Giønge, et al; GK 165, 16 January 1769, Quitta, E. Quist; GK 165, 10 May 1769, Christiansborg, Kuhberg, J. Wrisberg, N. Aarestrup, J. Karrig; and GK 15, 15 March 1769, Quitta, E. Quist. For Anlo traditions about the incident which precipitated the war, see FN 24: Interview with Boko Seke Axovi, 5 September 1978, Anloga, and FN 108: Interview with Togbui Dzobi Adzinku, ? June 1988 Anloga.

same polities.[27] Anlo obtained support from Akwamu and Asante, again, because they had come to share common economic interests. The actual battle between these two forces took place in April 1769, but because they engaged the enemy before they had an opportunity to consolidate their forces, Ada and its allies were soundly defeated by Anlo without the military support of Akwamu.[28] The fact that Akwamu was prepared to assign troops to the field because of its support for Anlo, however, is indicative of the change in relations that had occurred. Anlo no longer viewed Akwamu as an enemy, but rather as a trusted ally with common interests. This change undoubtedly contributed to the willingness of the Anlo people by the 1760s, to ask the Agave clan to provide their military leader. They did so despite, or perhaps even because of, the Agave's past connection to the Akwamu.[29]

A second factor that facilitated the Anlo's encouragement of the Agave to provide their military leader had to do with the fact that the earlier residents of Anlo were often unprepared to assume the position themselves. A local authority on Anlo traditions, T. S. A. Togobo, informed me in 1978 that the Anlo found it difficult to get anyone to lead the army to war: "people used to run away because of the wars and the problems associated with them."[30] The accuracy of this observation is apparent from the history of those who assumed such posts. After suffering heavy casualties in the 1751 Abalenu war against the Danes, the Adas, and their allies, Adagla, the *awadada* or military commander of the Anlo military, preferred to delegate his office to another and drown himself in a river rather than return home after such a terrible defeat. In 1792, when Awadada Kwawuga found himself completely surrounded by his Keta enemies and then saw his forces fleeing the field in disorder, he also chose to commit suicide. In 1833, Adedzi Gbekle gave up the position of *dusifiaga* after the disastrous Peki campaign. In 1860 and in 1866, when the Anlo participated in wars in Anexo after being invited to do so by one of the political factions therein, their defeat in both years led Awadada Axolu to remain in self-imposed exile for approximately ten years,

---

[27] GK 165, 18 February 1769, Ada, A. Dahl, and 27 March 1769, Ada, Dahl. Anexo's antipathy toward Akwamu appears to have had its origins in the fact that the two were fighting one another over control of the trade routes that linked the eastern Krepi district with the middle Slave Coast. See Furley Collection N49 (A–F), p. 62–63; Kea, "Akwamu–Anlo Relations," 37; A. R. Biørn, "Biørn's Beretning 1788 om de Danske Forter og Negrier," *Nogle Bidrag til Kundskab om den Danske Straekning paa Guinea Kysten* (Copenhagen, 1788), 223; Kea, "Akwamu–Anlo Relations," 43–45; and GK 165, 6 August 1769, Christiansborg.

[28] GK 165, 25 April 1769, Ada, Dahl, and 4 May 1769, Quitta, E. Quist. See also GK 166, 28 July 1769, Fredensborg, N. Scheven. For a more complete discussion of the war, see Greene, "The Anlo-Ewe," 145–46.

[29] The idea that by this time the Akwamu connection worked to the advantage of the Agave comes from late nineteenth- and early twentieth-century oral traditions collected by German missionaries. In 1877 C. Hornberger recorded traditions that described the Akwamu as the brothers of the Anlo, all of whom left their ancestral homeland, Notsie, together. The tradition goes on to state that the Akwamu split off from the Anlo at some point in their westward journey and settled in a different area, but that this could not erase the fact that they were still brothers. See Hornberger, "Etwas," 440. D. Westermann also noted that in the 1930s, the Tsiame—who made many efforts to recover the position of military leader or *awadada* as it was known after 1760—reinforced their rights to install their candidate in this office by identifying their clan ancestor, Akplomeda, as an Akwamu. See Westermann, "Die Glidyi-Ewe," 148. See also FN 39: Interview with Togbui Christian Yao Gbotoza Fiadzo, 16 October 1978, Anloga, on the more recent use of the term *awadada*.

[30] ADM 11/1661, 35; and FN 9: Interview with Mr. T. S. A. Togobo, 7 August 1978, Anloga.

and when he did return after the 1869 Agotime war, he refused to continue in the position as the Anlo military commander.[31]

Why then would the Tsiame and later the Agave accept the office of *awadada*? In the absence of evidence from eighteenth-century sources it is difficult to determine the answer in full. The desire for booty; the prestige associated with being acknowledged as possessing the spiritual support and technical knowledge to lead an army successfully in war; confidence in their own abilities—all of these might have been involved.[32] Perhaps the most critical, however, was their desire to establish themselves as integral members of Anlo society. For not only did these two clans accept the *awadada* position, they also amended their social practices and the symbolic meanings they attached to particular material objects so that they would conform with Anlo norms. By 1804, for example, both clans had probably relocated their *hlo* shrine houses to Anloga, in compliance with the requirement that all Anlo clans establish clan houses in the capital to which they should bring their newborns for ritual induction and their deceased for burial rites. The Tsiame clan house in the town of Tsiame had previously been the only site where such rituals took place. Prior to 1804 most Agaves returned their relatives' remains to their ancestral homes in the Agave area.

In addition to these adaptations, the Tsiame and Agave also conformed, over time, to a number of Anlo social practices. Both groups organized themselvs into clans with their own totems and taboos as means of protecting their own interests and ensuring unity within their ranks. Both also adopted Anlo marital preferences. Competition over land after 1730 when the Tsiame and sections of the Agave areas became part of Anlo generated a preference for clan endogamy on the part of those in Anlo associated with these districts. Competition over labor to produce additional commodities for trade developed as a result of the Anlos' greater involvement in the Atlantic slave trade. This, in turn, generated a preference for matrilateral cross-cousin marriages among the majority of Anlo residents, including the Tsiame and Agave.

The Agave also altered the meaning of one of the symbols with which they were associated. The Agave appear to have received from the Akwamu a three-pronged sword that the Akwamu and other Akan groups typically used as a symbol of their authority. The Agave use of this sword reinforced their association with the politically dominant Akwamu and became a symbol of their right to adjudicate disputes in Anlo.[33] Between 1730 and 1769, the Agave redefined their originally

---

[31] Anlo State Council Minute Books, 9 January 1935, Awunaga, Chiefs Kata, Adaku, Avege, and Agblevo . . . and others -v- Chiefs Zewu, Agbozo, Anakoo Attipoe, . . . and others, 378; FN 57: Interview with Mr. Robert G. Kofi Afetogbo, 22 December 1987, Anloga.

[32] In recognition of their role as well as the role played by the Tsiame in providing at one time the military leaders of the Anlo army, the polity also assigned both clans the responsibility of enstooling all the *awafiawo*, the military commanders, who served under the *awadada*. See ADM 11/1/1661, 4.

[33] According to a number of Agaves, this clan has more than one sword attached to the stool of office. They mention seven, a number often used by the Anlo to refer to a multiplicity of objects associated with spiritual forces. Multi-pointed swords are objects associated in this area with Akan material culture. For a discussion about these swords, see Doran H. Ross, "The Akan Double-Bladed Sword: A Case of Islamic Origins," in Dorah H. Ross and Timothy F. Garrard, eds., *Akan Transformations: Problems in Ghanaian Art History* (Los Angeles, 1983). See Anlo Traditional Council Minute Book, 1933–1935, 301, 371 for statements about the Agave swords and stool of office, as well as a discussion about the adjudication role played by the Agave in Anlo (372–73). Note that others outside the Agave clan associate this *hlo* with a three-prong sword. See FN 38: Interview with Togbui Ago Agbota and Togbui Kofi Ezu Agbota, 9 October 1978, Anloga.

secular symbol of office, the three-pronged sword, to make it conform to Anlo values, which placed considerable emphasis on a military leader having access to powerful spiritual forces. They accomplished this by referring to the sword as a *tro*, as indicated in the following account:

> The *tro* . . . [of the Agave clan] is embodied in a three-point sword. It was the *tro* used to know if they would win the battle. They bathe it and turn it upside down. If blood drips from the three prongs, then they will win; if not, they will lose. If you have committed a crime and you are taken to the *tro* to determine whether you are guilty or not, they have you kiss the *tro* and if you are guilty, you will vomit blood until you die.[34]

By redefining as a *tro* the symbol with which they were most associated, and by taking advantage of the change in relations between Akwamu and Anlo after 1730, the Agave clan attempted to position itself as an integral member of Anlo society. This same goal led the Agave and the Tsiame to adopt a number of cultural practices peculiar to the Anlo.

Inclusion of the Tsiame and Agave clans in the core administrative structure of the Anlo polity did not change the way in which the Anlo defined these two groups with respect to the other clans resident in the area, however. Late nineteenth- and early twentieth-century Anlo descriptions of their own society indicate that at that time the Agave and Tsiame were still described as clans whose patrilineal ancestors came from elsewhere:

> [T]he Agavewo . . . originate from the wedlock of a man from Agave, an Ewe town on the western side of the Volta, and an Anlo woman. . . . the Tsiameawo or Atsiameawo . . . reside north of the Keta Lagoon. Their forefather, Akplomeda, "the thrown spear," was an Akwamu who fled to Anlo during a war; he married the daughter of Adeladza, the first king of the Bate *hlo*.[35]

This attribution of foreign origins was not uniquely applied to the Agave and Tsiame. Late nineteenth- and early twentieth-century Anlo elders described the Dzevi in similar terms. Emphasis on the ethnic identity of these groups appears to have been the result, in part, of an effort by the political and religious authorities in Anlo to undermine those who might pose a threat to their positions. As discussed in Chapter 2, Anlo narratives indicate that at one point in time, the Dzevi priest and his god, Nyigbla, began to receive more acclaim than the *awoamefia* after the Anlo population credited Nyigbla with an important military victory. I dated this event to the mid-to late eighteenth century. These same narratives note that the *awoamefia* viewed this development as a threat to his prestige and that he responded by attempting to drive the priest and its god out of the area. These efforts were unsuccessful, however, and Anlo elders eventually reconciled the two. Thereafter, the Dzevi priest and the *awoamefia* are said to have "walked hand in hand," that is, they shared amicably the political and religious leadership of the polity. Many of the traditions recorded by German missionaries at the end of the nineteenth century and others still recited today belie the supposedly complete

---

[34] FN 38: Interview with Togbui Ago Agbota and Togbui Kofi Ezu Agbota, 9 October 1978, Anloga.

[35] Westermann, "Die Glidyi-Ewe," 147–48.

acceptance of the Nyigbla order into the Anlo leadership structure, however. Some traditions continue to emphasize the god's alleged foreign origins. Others claim that Nyigbla entered the area only after it was forced out of its own home area for committing a series of atrocities.[36] A number of these traditions one can associate with those who became disaffected from the Nyigbla order after it was discovered to have been selling some of its initiates into the Atlantic slave trade in the early 1800s. Others may have been generated during the late nineteenth century or after by local Christians who hoped to discredit the god. I would argue, however, that given the nature of the dispute, it is likely that the *awoamefia* and his advisors used their political and religious influence to emphasize the foreign origins of the Nyigbla priest and his god in the oral narratives.

The political and religious leadership in Anlo responded to the Agave and Tsiame in a similar fashion. Recognizing the potential threat that the Agave and Tsiame could pose to their authority, given the stature of their gods and the fact that by the mid-eighteenth century, they were an integral part of the society, the political and religious leaders in Anlo attempted to confine their prestige to the military sphere by continually reminding others of their non-Anlo ethnic origins. They emphasized the fact that they—unlike the "first five"—had no land in the early Anlo area. They differentiated the Tsiame and Agave from those who are said to have traveled together to the Anlo area and been among the first settlers by noting that they observed different naming and funeral customs. In this way, they were able to acknowledge the important role that the Tsiame and Agave clans were playing in the Anlo military—a position that few others were prepared to accept— while protecting their own position as the political and religious leaders of the polity.

What distinguished the Tsiame and the Agave from the Dzevi was the fact that when they found themselves unable to overcome opposition to their inclusion as integral members of Anlo society, they promoted the continued existence of traditions reinforcing their identification with their own home areas. This was not how the Dzevi handled their situation. If, for example, we examine the earliest recorded traditions about the Dzevi from the late nineteenth century, it is clear that either the Dzevi themselves and/or their supporters attempted to counter the efforts of the Anlo political and religious elite to keep alive knowledge of their foreign origins. They did so by stating that even though the god Nyigbla (the deity around which all Dzevi clan activities were organized) came from the Adangbe area of Gbugbla (Prampram), it had left that area never to return. In other words, the traditions propagated by the Dzevi and their supporters attempted to nullify the importance of the Dzevi's foreign origins by indicating that the Dzevi and their god were fully involved in Anlo affairs, and their former homeland no longer exercised any influence on them. They were fully committed to the Anlo polity.[37] The Tsiame and Agave took a very different approach. The Agave continued to claim land in the Agave area,[38] while the

---

[36] See, for example, FN 53: Interview with Togbui Afatsao Awadzi, 16 December 1987, Anloga and FN 78: Interview with Togbui Dzobi Adzinku, 20 January 1988, Woe.

[37] See Spieth, *Die Religion*, 145.

[38] FN No. 17: Interview with T. S. A. Togobo, 28 August 1978; and FN No. 39: Interview with Togbui Christian Yao Gbotoza Fiadzo, Anloga, 16 October 1978.

Tsiame continued to perform the rituals associated with the worship of Tsali and Tesi, not in Anloga at their new shrine house, but in the town of Tsiame.[39]

In responding in this way, these two clans reinforced existing ethnic and gender relations within Anlo society. Their continued attachment to their home areas reinforced the way in which the Anlo ethnically defined individuals and group. Direct attachment to Notsie rather than to another district within the region, and early residence in Anlo continued to constitute important factors in defining who was an ethnic insider and an ethnic outsider. This reinforced the prevailing norms that governed gender relations, for those who were so inclined could continue to point to the existence of an ethnicized "they" which could not be known and trusted completely to support the interests of Anlo. This also served as a basis for family elders to manage their affairs in the gendered ways of the past. The fact that clan endogamy continued to be a dominant preference in Anlo at the end of the nineteenth century indicates that this is precisely the way in which Anlo elders responded to the existence of an ethnicized "they" in their society.

Working the Margins:
Atitsogbi/Geraldo de Lima of Nineteenth-Century Anlo

A third factor that lent stability to gender and ethnic relations in eighteenth- and nineteenth-century Anlo involved the fact that some individuals accepted their positions because they saw their locations not as marginal, but rather as ones that placed them beneficially within the interstices that existed within Anlo society or between this polity and other communities. This is most apparent in the life of the nineteenth-century Anlo entrepreneur, Atitsogbi (also known as Geraldo de Lima).

Born during the late 1830s or early 1840s in Agoue,[40] Atitsogbi was considered an ethnic outsider in Anlo.[41] His residence in the area stemmed from his position as a household slave of the Portuguese trader, Cesar Cerquira de Lima, who had established a trading station in the Anlo town of Vodza, three miles east of Keta on the Atlantic coast, in the first half of the nineteenth century. It was from this town that Atitsogbi operated as an agent for Cerquira, buying from the local community the salt produced there in large quantities, combining this with European manufactures, and then conveying all to the towns along the Volta River where they were exchanged for slaves. The slaves were then marched to Vodza or to the other less well-patrolled ports to the east where they were sold to passing slave ships. By 1862, Atitsogbi's relationship with Cerquira appears to have evolved into that of trusted business partner and family member, for on Cerquira's death in that year,

---

[39] FN No. 40: Interview with Togbui Avege, II, 17 October 1978, Anloga.

[40] The estimated date of Atitsogbi's birth is based on an account by the chief of Kedzi, Acolatse I, who stated in 1912, that Geraldo was several years older than himself, he being born c.1850: ADM 11/1661, 34. Acolatse IV claimed that Acolatse I was born in 1840. FN 81: Interview with Togbui Joachim Acolatse IV, 26 January 1988, Keta. See also G. A. Sorkpor, "Geraldo de Lima and the Awunas, 1862–1904" (M.A. thesis, University of Ghana, 1966), 4, who obtained similar dates for Atitsogbi's birth from the grandson of Atitsogbi's wife; see Mamattah, *The Ewes*, 368, for a local version of Atitsogbi's genealogy.

[41] We have no information on when Atitsogbi joined Cesar Cerquira as a servant in Vodza, but according to the grandson of one of Atitsogbi's wives, he had been with Cerquira long enough to have been introduced into the Christian faith and to have adopted by 1855, the name Geraldo de Vasconcellos. See Sorkpor, "Geraldo de Lima," 4, and W. W. Claridge, *A History of the Gold Coast and Ashantee* (London, 1915), I, 548. Geraldo remained in the area until his death in 1904.

Atitsogbi inherited both the business and Cerquira's wives, as was the custom in nineteenth-century Agoue when a "brother" died.[42] He also inherited the latter's property and adopted his former master's name. In that year, Atitsogbi became known as Geraldo de Lima.

In assuming his "brother's" identity, Geraldo was apparently attempting to exploit the business and social advantages his master enjoyed as an Afro-European on the lower Gold Coast and in Europe and Brazil. Taking a master's name was at that time a fairly common tactic used by local Africans to enhance their economic and social status.[43] What is remarkable about Geraldo is that he achieved tremendous economic success. Geraldo did more than simply continue Cerquira's existing business; he modified it in response to changing economic conditions. As noted previously, the British, the Danes, and the French had expanded their efforts to extinguish the export slave trade on the upper Slave Coast during the late 1830s and 1840s. In the Anlo area this took the form of land-based military expeditions launched by the Danes in 1839, 1842, and 1844 to drive out the Spanish and Brazilian merchants operating in various towns on the Anlo littoral.[44] After their efforts were largely a failure, the Danes sold their possessions on the Guinea Coast, including the Anlo area, to the British in 1850, who further expanded the anti-slave trade campaign. A larger contingent of soldiers was assigned to the Keta fort, which then forced many of the local traders as well as the Brazilian and Spanish merchants to relocate their businesses. Most moved to the littoral villages of the Vodza and Kedzi on the eastern edge of Anlo territory and to the Agbosome coastal towns of Blekusu and Adina, all of which were outside the reach of the British soldiers stationed at Keta.[45] By the mid-1860s, the trade had come to an end. The few remaining Brazilian and Spanish traders had died or left the area completely. A number of local traders shifted their emphasis to the production and trade of local agricultural products using slave labor; others began to sell slaves on the domestic market, where there was growing demand for labor to be used in trade as carriers, and in the cultivation and processing of agricultural products in demand both in Europe and in the local economy.[46] Gbodzo of Woe, for example, abandoned the export trade in slaves and emphasized instead their use in the production and sale of animal and fish products.[47] Geraldo shifted to the export of rubber, cotton, and vegetable oils.[48]

His choice of the latter commodity was not an accident. Profits from the export of palm oil were particularly high in the Anlo area between 1861 and 1866 because at that time the Krobo (who were the principal producers) were boycotting a number of agents contracted by the English government to collect a fine im-

---

[42] Manoukian, "Ewe-Speaking People," 28.

[43] See for example, Kaplow, "Primitive Accumulation," 19–36; and Dumett, "African Merchants," 661–93.

[44] See Carstensen, *Indberetninger,* passim; Reindorf, *History of the Gold Coast,* Ch. XI; and Claridge, *A History of the Gold Coast,* 457–58.

[45] J. B. Yegbe, "The Anlo and their Neighbors, 1850–1890" (M.A. thesis, Institute of African Studies, University of Ghana, Legon, 1966), 19–38.

[46] See Sorkpor, "Geraldo de Lima," 2–21; D. E. K. Amenumey, "Geraldo de Lima: A Reappraisal," *THSG,* IX, 67; David Ross, "The Career of Domingo Martinez in the Bight of Benin, 1833–64," *JAH,* VI, I (1965), 88–89.

[47] FN 76: Interview with Togbui Anthonio Gbodzo II and his councilors, 20 January 1988, Woe.

[48] FN 97: Interview with Mr. J. G. Kodzo-Vordoagu, 24 February 1988, Tegbi.

posed on them. In an effort to market their oil through other agents, the Krobo began to sell to traders operating in the coastal towns east of the Volta River.[49] De Lima captured a significant amount of this trade by taking advantage of the fact that in 1855, Britain raised the ad valorem duties on exports from Britain to the Gold Coast from 1/2 to 2 percent. This policy forced the merchants operating on the British-controlled Gold Coast to increase the amount of money they demanded from customers in order to offset the higher duties.[50] Geraldo, who obtained his European goods from non-British ports, exploited this fact by offering these same commodities for lower prices, thereby increasing his own profits and attracting more customers, including those with palm oil to sell.

Geraldo also successfully exploited a second set of policies implemented by Britain on the Gold Coast. In 1862, Britain imposed a ban on the importation of firearms and ammunition, prompted by the deterioration in relations between Asante and the British over the question of jurisdiction over the southern provinces. In that year, the British refused to extradite from the coast to his home country Kwasi Gyani, an Asante citizen who had been accused of hoarding gold nuggets in violation of local Asante law. Anticipating that his actions would precipitate war, the governor of Cape Coast Castle, Richard Pine, ordered the immediate cessation of sales of firearms and ammunition to Asante from British sources.[51] In 1863, Asante invaded a number of the southern provinces, demonstrating their ability to overwhelm militarily British defenses on the coast, but the British still refused to relinquish Gyani and other refugees. Tensions continued through 1866, when British officer Conran noted the economic consequences of the conflict.

> [T]here can be no doubt as to the great sufferings the Ashantees have undergone during the last 2-1/2 years consequent on their being blockaded within their own territory, all communication without long line or sea coast have been shut out from them, depriving them therefore of the means of obtaining supplies such as arms, ammunition, cotton goods and salt being articles of trade, to them indispensable. . . . [52]
>
> There are but two modes through which the Ashantees . . . can receive supplies from the coast . . . the Assinee and Volta.[53]

References to a traffic in arms on the Volta could have only meant sales made by the Anlo. Anlo had traditionally provided such materials to Asante under similar circumstances throughout the later eighteenth century, and this relationship was strengthened during the first two decades of the nineteenth century. For example, when Britain refused to buy Asante's human exports and then imposed restrictions between 1807 and 1817 on the sale of firearms, Asante traders resorted to buying from Atoko and other towns on the Anlo littoral.[54] When Britain again restricted the flow of munitions in 1862, Asante resorted once more to sources in the Anlo area. Geraldo, whose operations were based in this district, was able to meet

---

[49] For a discussion of the Krobo oil boycott, see Wolfson, "A Price Agreement," 68–77.

[50] Reynolds, *Trade and Economic Change,* 131–32.

[51] Wilks, *Asante,* 220.

[52] Cited in Reynolds, *Trade and Economic Change,* 171–72.

[53] Cited in Wilks, *Asante,* 224.

[54] Reynolds, *Trade and Economic Change,* 59–60.

the Asante demand. His extensive contacts in Keta, Anexo, Agoue, and Grand Popo permitted him to obtain the war supplies in demand in Asante.[55] His residency in Vodza also gave him ready access to salt, which the Asante deemed necessary to stockpile in the event of war.

By taking advantage of the Krobo oil boycott and British trade policies, and by altering his identity to facilitate continuity in his relations with his European and Brazilian suppliers, Geraldo was able to become one of the most important traders in the area.

During this same period, Geraldo also began consciously to develop close ties to the Anlo political and religious elite. For example, foreign traders who operated in the Anlo area were expected to send to the *awoamefia* certain gifts in acknowledgement of his authority. Geraldo exceeded these expectations by not only providing such gifts, but also selling munitions to the Anlo army at particularly advantageous terms of trade.[56] He then used this relationship to recast his status as ethnic outsider into one in which he would be accepted as an Anlo citizen. He did so sometime between 1862 and 1865 by participating in an induction ritual that made him a member of the Adzovia clan (the *hlo* which supplied the Anlo *awoamefia*), and by becoming a major patron of one the most prestigious gods in Anlo, the Adzovia deity, Tomi.[57] Thereafter, he added to his European name the appellation Adzoviahlo, or Adzovia clan, to make explicit his affiliation with this politically and religiously influential social group.

Geraldo appears to have been motivated by the desire to protect his business interests. As noted above, Geraldo benefited tremendously from the Krobo oil boycott, but he did so at the expense of the firms and individuals who had been contracted by the British government to collect the fine imposed on the Krobo. The latter group, which included the firms of F. and A. Swanzy, Forster and Smith, and the independent merchant William Addo, pressured the British government to intervene. Britain responded in 1863 by posting government troops to interdict all trade with the Krobo area. These forces were withdrawn shortly thereafter, however, and the oil was again diverted to Geraldo and others operating in the Anlo littoral towns and at Kpong and Ada on the lower Volta River. F. and A. Swanzy and Forster and Smith then resorted to their own forces, which began to blockade the Krobo area in an effort to force the Krobo to bring the oil only to them. The use of such troops by both the government and the firms contracted to collect the Krobo oil must have impressed Geraldo with the need to have at his disposal similar military force. It was this, I would suggest, that prompted Geraldo to renegotiate his status as an ethnic outsider in Anlo by becoming a member of the Adzovia clan. Affiliation with this clan brought him not only the benefits that would have accrued to any member of such a social unit in Anlo (the ability to obtain support,

---

[55] See Duncan, *Travels*, 137–40, whose description of the traders in Whydah is representative of the individuals with whom Geraldo and others conducted their business. He mentions Spaniards, Portuguese, Sierra Leoneans, English descendants, and French merchants.

[56] FN 83: Interview with Mr. K. A. Mensah, 27 January 1988, Anloga.

[57] See Mamattah, *The Ewes*, 372–73, and Sorkpor, "Geraldo de Lima," 23–24, who collected traditions indicating that he had obtained membership in the Adzovia clan before the Anlos came to his assistance in the Funu war of 1865; these accounts contradict Amenumey, "Geraldo de Lima," 65, who states that Atitsogbi was given the name Adzoviahlo at birth.

both military and political, from fellow members), it also placed Geraldo in a position to gain such support from the clan that provided, in alternation with the Bate clan, the *awoamefia* of Anlo, and which had custody of the god Tomi, one of the most respected and feared gods in Anlo.

The year 1865 brought the first occasion on which Geraldo probably sought support from the Anlo. In March, a dispute erupted between Geraldo and a trader from Ada, whom Geraldo claimed had refused to settle a debt. After failing to get satisfaction, Geraldo forcibly took possession of eight canoes belonging to a second Ada trader. When the Ada leaders ordered Geraldo to return the canoes and their contents, he refused, and the dispute escalated into a much wider conflict that saw Geraldo and his Ada adversaries seizing each other's people, and killing and wounding a number of others. It was at this point that Geraldo requested protection from the Anlo, perhaps reminding them of his status as an Adzovia, and his close relations with many of the political and religious leaders. The Ada, along with the Gold Coast traders who operated in the area, requested the assistance of the British, citing their business rival, Geraldo, and the Anlo as threats to their own security and that of the Gold Coast. Both the British and the Anlo responded to the call to arms. In May 1865, the British sent first the *H.M.S. Lee* and then later, the *H.M.S. Dart* to negotiate the retrieval of Geraldo from the Anlo. The Anlo refused to comply; this was then followed by a series of battles known as the 1865 Funu or Atitetti war, and the 1866 Adidome and Datsutagba wars.[58]

Anlo support for Geraldo was lukewarm, perhaps because they recognized that he was operating principally in his own interests. In an account published in the NDMG's monthly publication, the German missionary Brutschin indicated that when the British arrived at the mouth of the Volta on 17 May 1865 following the appeals of the Adas and the merchants, they demanded that the Anlo hand Geraldo to them in three days. The Anlo promised to do so and then informed Geraldo of the British request, but they made no effort to apprehend him. They then contacted Asante and Akwamu, and requested their assistance in the event of war with the Accra and Ada. The Anlo sent only ten sheep, however, an offering Brutschin stated was considered quite paltry.[59] It is possible that the Anlo were simply stalling for time; and it is also possible that the rather small offering to the Asante and Akwamu was indicative of the fact that they did not take the threat of war and the need for allied assistance seriously. A different explanation, however, is offered in oral accounts delivered to a 1912 commission of enquiry by a number of Anlo military leaders and participants in the 1865 Funu war. These leaders indicate that it was, rather, indecision that prompted the Anlo's response to the British and the rather curious request sent to the Asante and Akwamu.

In previous years, the Anlo had had some rather nasty encounters with the various European powers on the coast. Keta was bombarded and completely destroyed by the Danes in 1847 after a dispute erupted between the Danish garrison in the Keta fort and the military leader, Dzokoto of Anyako. In 1850, when the British assumed control of the Keta fort, they posted a larger contingent of soldiers in the town than had the Danes, and these soldiers immediately began

---

[58] For descriptions of these battles see Africanus B. Horton, *Letters on the Political Condition of the Gold Coast* [1870] (London, 1970), 75–89; ADM 11/1/1661, 34–36, 93, 134–139; Yegbe, "The Anlo," 56–67.

[59] B. Brutschin, "Keta und Anyako," *Monatsblatt der Norddeutschen Missionsgesellschaft*, 16/184 (1866), 806.

PHOTO 3: The Keta Fort in 1893

to take a more active role against the slave trade by confiscating slaves destined for export. They also gave asylum to domestic slaves who fled to the fort for protection. In 1853, when the Anlo refused to pay the recently imposed British poll tax, they were eventually persuaded to do so by the British commandant in Accra, presumably under the threat of force. In 1855, German missionaries Brutschin and Plessing experienced just how much the Anlo had come to fear and dislike the British when they attempted to obtain permission to build a station in Keta. In their negotiations, they had to distinguish themselves clearly from the British in order to even enter into a dialogue with the Anlo leadership; and only after they had declared their peaceful intentions was a ban that forbade any citizen to sell foodstuffs or durable goods to them lifted and permission granted for them to establish a station in the town of Anyako.[60] Thus, when the British demanded that Anlo hand over Geraldo to them in March 1865, Togbui Acolatse, a military leader from the Anlo town of Kedzi, noted that of the *asafohenewo* or military leaders present, half were prepared to do so, presumably to avoid conflict with the British. The other half refused to honor the British request, and they convinced their more reluctant comrades to engage the British, the Adas, and the Accras in battle. According to Acolatse, the argument did not revolve around the issue of Geraldo's citizenship as an adopted member of the Adzovia clan; rather, it had to do with their chances of victory. As Acolatse noted, "Awuna [Anlo] had no money then . . . we are fond of war; kill some and catch some and sell and chop and marry their women; there was no work, we

---

[60] Plessing, "Briefe aus Keta," 244, and "Station Quitta," 176–77.

had to sell slaves." Accordingly, when the Anlo were defeated, having lost approximately one hundred men and capturing none of the enemy, they refused to continue to support Geraldo.[61] They saw no profit in such a venture, and they had much to lose. Instead, the majority of the Anlo leaders broke off the campaign and shifted their forces to the east where they had agreed to assist one Kuadzo Landzekpo of Agoue, who was engaged in a conflict with a business partner.[62] This conflict, known among the Anlo as the Second Agoue War, probably took place between mid- to late 1865 and the very first weeks of 1866.

While still in Agoue, the Anlo heard that Geraldo and his Anlo ally, Akroboto of Srogboe, had continued to harass the Adas by attacking the Volta River towns of Adidome, Amedika, and Kpong. By February 1866, the conflict had escalated to the point where the British were preparing to invade Anlo to open the trade routes closed by Geraldo's activities. Again, Anlo's participation in the subsequent conflict, known as the 1866 Datsutagba war, was less a result of their support of Geraldo, and more a response to the urgent need to defend their homes from their enemies. As Anlo military leader Acolatse noted, "we knew that if we stayed at Agoue, the Accras and the Adas would take all our properties." Descriptions of this battle exist elsewhere; of significance here is the fact that both sides claimed victory.[63] Thus, when Anlo negotiated with the British, they were unprepared to do anything that would suggest that they had been defeated or intimidated.[64] They refused to pay an indemnity to cover Britain's war expenses; they also refused to hand over Geraldo. The explanation given by the Anlo was that because Geraldo was a stranger, they had no right to capture him and give him to those whom he had wronged. This rationale was based on nineteenth-century Anlo customary law that required the lineage and/or clan to hand over to an offended party that person from among their ranks who had committed an offense.[65] By declaring Geraldo an outsider, the Anlo political and military leaders absolved themselves of the need to comply with the British request, according to their own laws.

---

[61] The Anlo forces suffered this defeat, despite their superior numbers, because the British used their gunboats to keep the Anlo at a distance, while inflicting heavy casualties. Geraldo continued to seek revenge for the Adas' actions, by attacking the Volta River towns of Adidome, Amedika, and Kpong, and forcing the cessation of all trade from the Krobo and Krepi district conducted along the Volta River. Only the Anlo military leader Akroboto of Srogboe was prepared to assist Geraldo. Geraldo supplemented his own forces and those of Akroboto by obtaining the assistance of the Malfi, located on the east bank of the Volta; he also travelled to the town of Adele, in the present Republic of Togo, to consult the priest of the war god, Nayo Friko, for assistance in battle; for information on this, see G. A. Sorkpor, "Notes on the Nayo Friko Shrine in Awuna," *Research Review* (Legon) 2, 3 (1966), 87–89.

[62] For a description of this conflict, see Kue Agbota Gaba, "The History of Anecho, Ancient and Modern" (Deposited at Balme Library, University of Ghana, Legon, 1965), 127–39. The first Agoue war of 1860 is also described in this account. See also Pierre Bouché, *La Côte des Esclaves* (Paris, 1885), 303; Anlo State Council Minute Book, 9 January 1935, Awunaga: Chiefs Kata, Adaku, and others on behalf of the Tsiame tribe -v- Chiefs Zewu, Agbozo, and others on behalf of Agave tribe, 378.

[63] The most detailed description of this conflict can be found in Horton, *Letters*, 78–89.

[64] According to the British, they were able to persuade the Anlo to agree to another treaty because they had frightened the Anlo by bombarding and destroying Geraldo's house in the coastal town of Vodza. See Claridge, *History of the Gold Coast*, 574–75; ADM 4/1/2: District Office Records, Keta, 250–51; ADM 11/1/1661, 93.

[65] Westermann, "Die Glidyi-Ewe," 142–45; Christian Aliwodsi, "Ein Sittenbild aus Anyako," *Monatsblatt der Norddeutschen Missionsgesellschaft*, 2/5 (1800), 28–29.

That this declaration of Geraldo's status as a stranger was more than a po-litical ploy on the part of the Anlo is indicated by the fact that while Geraldo continued to reside in Anlo, support for him among the Anlo, particularly from those most vulnerable to British bombardments from the sea, was quite weak.[66] In addition, while he is remembered among the Anlo as having become a mem-ber of the Adzovia clan and to have assumed the name Adzoviahlo as a marker of the same, he was always described in late nineteenth-century and early twen-tieth-century accounts by supporters and adversaries alike as a stranger from Agoue.[67] Thus, the Anlo statement to the British in 1866 about Geraldo's status as a stranger indicates that his induction into the Adzovia clan failed to alter the ethnic boundaries that defined him as an outsider. I would suggest that this was the case because Geraldo himself had sought not to alter his identity, but rather to supplement it for purely self-serving reasons. The Adzovia clan agreed to accept Geraldo because it stood to benefit economically by responding to the interests of reportedly one of the wealthiest individuals in Anlo. But very little, in fact, really changed. And Geraldo would not have had it otherwise. By oper-ating within the interstices that separated and connected Anlo society with the European and Brazilian trading world, Geraldo successfully manipulated both systems for his own interests while actively and intentionally remaining on the margins of both.

This strategy proved particularly effective for Geraldo in generating wealth, but it also served to reinforce existing notions about ethnic and gender relations within Anlo itself, for in pursuing his goal of establishing mutually beneficial rela-tions with the Anlo leadership, he opted to avoid associating with those who sought to challenge the existing order. For example, when he decided to establish an Anlo identity, he chose to align himself not with the politically and religiously powerful, but socially stigmatized Dzevi clan, but rather he opted to become a member of the equally powerful, but more prestigious Adzovia clan. After securing the support of his fellow clan members and the rest of Anlo in his 1866 conflict with the British, Geraldo chose to bolster their chances in battle not by appealing to the Anlo war god Nyigbla, which was still defined as a foreign god, but instead by appealing to the Nayo-Friko gods located in the Adele mountains in what is now north-central Togo. When Geraldo returned to Adele after the war to thank this deity for his military victory, he purchased the right to establish a Nayo-Friko daughter shrine in Vodza. But in so doing, he chose not to organize it on the same lines as Nyigbla or Yewe. It operated as did the other more traditional shrines in the area. Women could expect assistance from these gods if they were experiencing difficulties in conceiving a child, but not if they sought to challenge the ways their families were handling their marital affairs.[68] In this way, Geraldo contributed to a continuity in gender and ethnic relations in nineteenth-century Anlo society while he simulta-neously sought to manipulate this system for his own benefit.

---

[66] Another reason why the Anlo may have shied away from supporting Geraldo was that during the second Agoue war they suffered heavy casualties after Landzekpo's adversary sought the support of the British and the latter bombarded the Anlo from the ocean.

[67] ADM 11/1/1107: Awuna Native Affairs (1878–1901),.Letter of Evidence—8/5/89: Chief Tete Mamimey to Tamaklo, 5 July 1888; ADM 11/1/1661, 34–35.

[68] For information on the Nayo Friko shrine, see Sorkpor, "Notes.

Conclusion

From 1679 to the end of the nineteenth century, much had changed in the character of gender and ethnic relations in Anlo. But much had also stayed the same. Particular groups and individuals continued to be defined as ethnic outsiders; the majority of women still saw their ability to influence their marital affairs limited by their elders and their husbands. Many reasons account for this situation. Some were unwilling to take advantage of the opportunities to alter their social status because they feared the consequences. Others might have seized the opportunities that were available to them, but did not have the chance to do so. Still others simply had no interest. One of the consequences of this situation was that not only did there exist continuity in the ways in which men and women, and individuals and groups interacted with one another throughout the eighteenth and nineteenth centuries, but gender relations and ethnic relations continued to influence one another even as these relations shifted, changed, and stayed the same after 1679.

5

Ethnicity in Colonial Anlo: The Gender Connection

Britain extended colonial control over Anlo in 1874. This event precipitated massive changes in the political, economic, social, and religious culture of this polity. Of concern here is the effect these changes had on the way in which this community socially defined the individuals and groups that together constituted its resident population. During the nineteenth century, those who were defined patrilineally as ethnic outsiders could achieve prominent positions within the Anlo political and military hierarchy, but in order to do so they—like Togbui Gbodzo of Woe—had to make an unconditional commitment to the Anlo polity, and were more likely to have been successful if they were also financially prominent, well-connected, and supported by their families. Others, like the Tsiame and Agave, and Geraldo de Lima—who opted to maintain their linkages to their home districts or to the Europeans with whom they had been associated—the Anlo continued to position on the margins of their society. The British imposition of colonial rule began to change this by the early twentieth century. During the mid-nineteenth century, one well-known individual, John Tay, pursued the same approach taken by De Lima. He established close relations with the Anlo political and military elite, but he also maintained close ties with the Europeans who operated in the area. In 1847, for example, when the Anlo military retaliated against the Danes (who had murdered an Anlo citizen) by blockading and besieging the fort at Keta, John Tay "secretly provided [his European trade partners] with corn and some fowls" in order to sustain them while they attempted to extricate themselves from their predicament.[1] In 1865, Tay reinforced his ties with the political elite of Anlo by serving as translator for the Anlo army when they were negotiating with British forces and the Adas immediately before the outbreak of the Attiteti or Funu War.[2] In 1885, Awoamefia Amedor Kpegla recognized the right of John Tay's son and successor to serve as the leader of the section of Dzelukofe in which he and his descendants lived, but that was the extent to which Tay as the descendant of a stranger was allowed to exercise au-

---

[1] Reindorf, *History of the Gold Coast*, 159.

[2] ADM 11/1/1661, 134–36; S. C. 14/1, 22–25.

thority over others.[3] After the British began to administer the Anlo area as a colonial possession, they sought in 1909 to recognize one person as the head chief of each town and village. One of the communities affected by this was the town of Dzelukofe, which had numerous chiefs (*fiawo*), none of whom were considered the political or religious head of the town. That position was held by Togbui Dzelu II, the descendant of Togbui Dzelu I, the founder of Dzelukofe. Recognizing, however, that the person who held this government-recognized office of *dufia* (town chief) had to work effectively within the British colonial administrative system, the *awoamefia*, the leaders of the Anlo military, and Togbui Dzelu II opted to ignore the fact that Tay and his descendants were technically strangers, having established residence in the town only in the early nineteenth century as immigrants from Accra. They appointed C. T. Agbozo, a descendant of John Tay, to assume the chiefship of Dzelukofe on behalf of Dzelu II. They made this choice because Agbozo was literate and therefore presumably better able to deal with the British on behalf of the town.[4] The same circumstances prompted similar appointments in the towns of Keta and Kedzi.[5] Thus, in attempting to meet the challenge presented by British colonial rule, the Anlo expanded even further the boundaries within which ethnically distinct individuals could operate as insiders within the Anlo political system. Literacy in English was thus added to the late nineteenth-century criteria of the geographical origins of one's ancestors, their time of arrival in Anlo, their religious power, and wealth.

Expansion of this boundary also involved a redefinition of the origins of groups previously defined as ethnic outsiders. I have already indicated, for example, that the Anlo clearly defined several clans in the late nineteenth century as foreign *hlowo*, because they had different naming and funeral customs and because their ancestors were associated with non-Anlo areas. This categorization system has continued to inform the way in which the Anlo view those described as ethnically distinct, but since the mid-twentieth century, another set of traditions has begun to counter this emphasis on difference. In these traditions, a common origin is emphasized and the differences still noted in the funerary and naming systems are explained away as the result of historical accidents. For example, the Anlo note that while the Dzevi and Wifeme clans have names that are identical with those found in the Ga and Adangbe areas of Ghana, they nevertheless can trace their origins to Notsie, from which the ancestors of all those who claim to be Anlo and Ewe are said to have come. The fact that their clan names are not ones associated with the Ewe or the Anlo is explained by the notion that the ancestors of the Dzevi and Wifeme simply lost their way on their westward journey from Notsie. Instead of settling on the coast with the Anlo ancestors, they crossed the Volta and lived among the Ga and Adangbe peoples

---

[3] See ADM 11/1/1113, Chief C. Agbozo, Keta, to C. Napier Curling, Commissioner of the Eastern Province, Keta, 14 July 1902; and Anlo Traditional Council Minute Book, No. 3 (14/4/60–23/7/87), 18.

[4] Anlo Traditional Council Minute Book, No. 3 (14/4/60–23/7/87), 19, 37.

[5] See Anlo Traditional Council Minute Book, No. 3 (14/4/60–23/7/87), 123, on the appointment of Acolatse as the head chief of Kedzi by the descendants of Abofrakuma; See FN 87: Interview with Togbui James Ocloo IV, Keta, 3 February 1988, on the appointment of Chief James Ocloo to be head chief of Keta by Amegashi Afeku and the Anlo *awoamefia*, Amedor Kpegla. In both cases, the individuals appointed were not strangers, but they were chosen, in part, because of their long association with the Europeans.

where they adopted a number of Adangbe customs before they returned to their relatives in the Anlo area.[6]

I argue here that the Anlo embraced this redefinition process because of the way in which the British and the Germans before 1918, and then the British and the French thereafter, imposed colonial rule in the area. These difficulties led to the development of a new identity based on one's status as a native speaker of the Ewe language. The educated elite in Anlo encouraged the adoption of this new identity as a means to urge the Anlo citizenry to emphasize that which they shared in common with other Ewes and more importantly with those in their midst who had previously been described as ethnic "others." The Anlo population accepted this new identity construct because of their own experiences as fisherfolk and traders operating in the Akan-speaking areas of the Gold Coast, but acceptance was not their only response. They also used this new identity to generate a new understanding of local social relations that was firmly grounded within their own cultural system, which gave priority to a sense of shared identity based on fictive or real kinship and marital ties.

Equally important is the fact that this change in we/they relations within Anlo had a significant impact on gender relations. Ethnic outsiders no longer needed to establish and/or maintain alliances with others within the society who also felt marginalized. Many, because of the changed political climate, were able to take advantage of the emergent orientation among the Anlo to give priority to an Ewe identity and they successfully redefined themselves socially as insiders without having to solicit the support of others in Anlo. At the same time, colonialism and the spread of Christianity undermined Anlo respect for traditional religious beliefs, the very system that some outsiders had used to forge a mutually beneficial relationship between themselves and those young women who had also wanted to defy their marginalization. I argue that one of the consequences of these two developments—the decline in the need for ethnic outsiders to establish and/or maintain ties with those disadvantaged by the Anlo because of their gender, and the decline in the power of traditional religious beliefs to influence behavior—was that twentieth-century women who sought to defy the social norms governing their lives found themselves with fewer means of support. They could still seek assistance from their mothers and their mothers' families to counterbalance the power of their patrilineages, but such religious orders as Nyigbla and Yewe no longer provided alternate sources of support. Weakened by the growth of Christianity and the expansion of colonial rule, traditional religion in general and the Yewe and Nyigbla orders in particular diminished over time in both popularity and power. This, in turn, reduced the number of alternatives available to young women.

This chapter examines the way in which colonialism facilitated the invention of an Ewe identity, a development that had a major impact on twentieth-century gender relations. I begin with a discussion of the colonial policies implemented by the British, German, and French administrators and their impact on Anlo efforts to

---

[6] See FN 8: Interview with Mr. T. S. A. Togobo, 3 August 1978, Anloga; FN 9: Interview with Mr. T. S. A. Togobo, 7 August 1978, Anloga; FN 21: Interview with Mr. T. S. A. Togobo, 31 August 1978, Anloga; and FN 15: Interview with Togbui Le II, 15 August 1978, Anloga. See also Amenyah Archives, 31 June 1956, Letter from J. D. Amenyah to Ivor G. Wilks, Tamale; Nukunya, *Kinship and Marriage*, 198.

maintain relations with their neighbors in Togoland. I argue that in their efforts to offset the difficulties created by the debilitating mix of German and English, and then French and English colonial policies, a number of educated Anlo began to emphasize the need for Ewe unification under one colonial power. This was accompanied by increased support within Anlo political circles for efforts to promote Ewe culture and unity. These actions impacted not only the political scene in the Gold Coast and in British and French Togoland, but also the social categorization of the Anlo clans. Traditions about the origins of those clans that had been previously identified as ethnically distinct were amended—with the support of the clans in question—to emphasize the idea that all originally came from the Ewe homeland in Notsie (with the principle exception of the Blu). I then discuss how this social realignment affected the ability of young women to alter their own social positions in Anlo society.

Anlo and the Eastern Ewe Under European Colonial Rule

Prior to the establishment of European colonialism, Anlo maintained extensive religious, social, and economic ties with a number of the polities to their east that were later to come under German rule. After the death of an Anlo *awoamefia* and the enstoolment of his successor, for example, it had become customary by at least the early nineteenth century for the Anlo to send a delegation to the town of Notsie to inform the chief priest of their change in leadership. The Anlo performed this ritual to recognize their age-old association with one of the religious orders in Notsie from which they had obtained the *tsikpe*, the symbol of authority on which the *awoamefia* based his right to rule. Notsie priests were also regularly consulted by the Anlo when the polity faced such natural disasters as floods, droughts, or epidemics.[7] Religious connections also existed between Anlo and the coastal towns situated between Anexo and Whydah. We know, for example, that the Yewe religious order in Anlo came from this particular district, as did a number of other deities and cultural practices.[8] Many within the Anlo population who were defined as strangers or latecomers in the eighteenth and nineteenth centuries originated from the coastal towns east of Anlo. Some became assimilated into the existing clans in the area or joined the Amlade *hlo* and in time severed their connections with their home areas. Others maintained their connections to their communities of origin, however, and thus established the foundation for what became significant ties of kinship between Anlo and the areas to the east that were later occupied by the Germans. Affinal ties existed as well: marriages between Anlo families and those who lived in Gbagida, Anexo, and Agoue had been common from at least the mid-seventeenth century.[9] Business relations between these two areas—also in

---

[7] FN 62: Interview with Mr. K. A. Mensah, 5 January 1988, Anloga; S.C. 14/3, 311–12.

[8] See Chapter 3 above for the origins and history of the Yewe order; see also David Locke with Godwin Agbeli, "Drum Language in Adzogbo," *Black Perspective in Music*, 9, 1 (1981), on the origins of the Dzogbo drum language in Anlo.

[9] In the mid-seventeenth century, one of the major trade routes in the area existed along the Atlantic littoral and within the extensive lagoon systems, connecting the Anexo, Agoue, and Whydah areas to the lower and middle Gold Coast through Anlo. See Law, *The Slave Coast* , 46–47.

existence since at least the seventeenth century—intensified in the early nineteenth century as slave traders who were attempting to evade European anti-slave trade efforts moved continually between their businesses in Anlo on the upper Slave Coast and offshoots of those businesses they established in the middle Slave Coast communities of Whydah and Anexo.

Efforts by the Ewes in Anlo and the coastal polities to the east to maintain this network of social, cultural, and economic ties in the late nineteenth and twentieth centuries faced serious difficulties with the imposition of colonial rule. Britain first extended its control over the Anlo area in 1850 after it purchased Danish claims to the area. Although the British subsequently withdrew from the area in 1859, they re-extended their authority over the Anlo littoral in 1874. From that point in time to the mid-twentieth century, Anlo became part of the Gold Coast Colony, administered by Britain and subject to its laws and administrative policies. In 1884, Germany—prompted by the desire to establish its place in international politics through the acquisition of colonies—made claims to and subsequently colonized those areas east of Anlo. The imposition of two distinct administrative policies on an area that was so intimately interconnected by familial, religious, and business ties presented a number of difficulties for the residents of the area. After Britain claimed control of the Anlo area in 1874, they began to extend to the area the same customs duties that they had imposed on the Gold Coast Colony, the revenue from which was to be used in financing the colonial administration of the colony. In 1856, this customs duty stood at 2 percent of the value of the imported goods, with higher rates for alcohol, tobacco, firearms, and gunpowder. In 1877, three years after the colonization of Anlo, the British raised the general rate to 4 percent; in 1888, they raised the rate on a number of items to 10 percent. The British imposition of these duties after their 1874 colonization prompted many within the polity to relocate at least a portion of their business activities to the towns and villages to the east, just outside the British customs zone, in an area not yet claimed by any European power. Because these merchants continued to market many of their imports in areas that were controlled by Britain, however, they faced harassment by the British who attempted to stop them from evading the customs duties and selling their goods in the Gold Coast at prices that gave their fellow Gold Coast merchants—who were unable to evade the duties—particularly stiff competition. The Hausa troops posted to Keta by the British to enforce the customs regulations seized goods they suspected had been brought into the territory illegally; they shot and killed a number of individuals believed to be smugglers, and burnt to the ground two villages they suspected of harboring merchants who were evading the customs duties.[10]

---

[10] See Francis Agbodeka, *African Politics and British Policy in the Gold Coast, 1868–1890: A Study in the Forms and Forces of Protest* (Evanston, 1971), 73–76, for a general summary of these events. See also ADM 11/1/1107: Assistant Inspector H. Graham, Commander, Awunah Northern Expeditionary Force, Christiansborg, Accra, to the Inspector General, Gold Coast Constabulary, 15 June 1889; ADM 11/1/1113: Chr. Rottman, G. B. Williams, E. H. Ditchfield, agent for F. and A. Swanzy, Quitta to His Excellency Sanford Freeling, of the Gold Coast Settlement; A. B. Ellis, District Commissioner, Quitta, to the Colonial Secretary, Christiansborg, 22 July 1878; G. B. Williams, Brigars Factors, Quittah, to E. M. Bannerman, Accra, 9 April 1878; A. B. Ellis, District Commissioner, Quittah, to the Colonial Secretary, Christiansborg, 5 August 1878; Francis A. Lamb, District Commissioner, Kwitta, to the Honorable Colonial Sec-

As British efforts to curb smuggling became increasingly effective, many of the Anlo traders opened businesses in the towns and villages even further to the east in German colonial territory (Lome and Gbagida, for example) and therefore outside British jurisdiction, from which they could conduct import and export activities free of British colonial policies.[11] However, the benefits of this move eventually proved illusory as the Germans imposed their own regulations. As D. E. K. Amenumey noted:

> The [German colonial] regime . . . withheld from the indigenous people equality of commercial opportunity with Europeans. The former could only engage in retail trading; to the Europeans was reserved the exclusive right of importing goods. Similarly, no African could export his own produce, being compelled, if he wanted to dispose of it at all, to sell to Europeans, a restriction which pressed particularly hard on the indigenous commercial community of Lome and Anecho.[12]

In addition, by 1894 the Germans in Togo, the French in Dahomey, and the British in the Gold Coast had established a unified customs zone which eliminated what few advantages those who purchased imports from the European traders had had in Togo in relation to those who operated solely on the Gold Coast.

Additional problems arose after the turn of the century when the Germans discovered that they were still unable to collect enough customs duties to cover their administrative costs. In 1904, the Germans increased their import duties to 10 percent, 6 percentage points above those imposed by the British in Anlo and other parts of the Gold Coast colony. They also began to require all Africans— with the exception of chiefs, advanced mission students, and the residents of Lome and Anexo after 1907—to perform twelve days of forced labor or to "discharge this obligation through the payment of six marks." In 1908, they established an income tax for Lome and Anexo which they imposed to supplement the pre-existing taxes already levied on rubber tappers, dog owners, and those firms that sold liquor and/or maintained a liquor stand.[13] This plethora of regulations and the financial burdens that the Germans imposed on the peoples of

---

retary, Christiansborg, 24 September 1889; ADM 41/4/20: Samuel Dunkan -v- Aboushie, 14 March 1883, Quitta, 425; See also "Die Unruhen im Anglo-Gebiet," *Norddeutsche Missionsgesellschaft*, 3 and 4/10 (1855) 42, 46–58, which provides an eyewitness account of how the actions of the Hausa troops eventually escalated into a major confrontation between the British, Geraldo de Lima, and the residents on the north side of the lagoon. The villages of Anyako and Konu burned to the ground. This same account notes that better relations developed at this time between the Anlo and the Agotime because of their shared hostility to the Hausa troops.

[11] ADM 11/1/1113: Charles A. Fraser, District Commissioner, Quitta, to the Honorable Colonial Secretary, Christiansborg, 21 February 1884; J. H. Cramer, Captain, Commander Expeditionary Force, Cantonments, Accra, to the Acting Inspector General, Accra, 4 September 1899; ADM 12/3/1: Samuel Rowe, Governor, Government House, Lagos, to the Right Honorable Earl of Derby, 21 April 1883; ADM 12/3/3: W. Brantford Griffith, Christiansborg Castle, Accra, to the Lord Knutsford, GCMG, 21 May 1889.

[12] Amenumey, *The Ewe Unification Movement*, 4. Many Togolese transported their goods to Keta rather than to the German-controlled port of Lome and then took their money and purchased their manufactured goods in Lome. This was made possible by the fact that no restrictions existed on the use of British pounds and German marks in either the Anlo area or in German Togoland. See Arthur J. Knoll, "Taxation in the Gold Coast Colony and in Togo: A Study in Early Administration," in Prosser Gifford, William Roger Lewis, and Alison Smith, eds., *Britain and Germany in Africa* (New Haven, 1967), 418–53.

[13] Knoll, "Taxation," 443–47.

Togo did not go unnoticed by the Anlo. Many Togolese from the Atlantic lit-
toral—some of whom had relatives, business partners, and co-religionists in
Anlo—fled to the Anlo area in order to avoid the hardships associated with
German colonial rule, and were thus in a position to make ordinary as well as
more prominent citizens aware of their plight.[14] Concern about the conditions in
German Togo was first expressed officially in 1914 with the outbreak of World
War I, when Togbui Sri II, the *awoamefia* of Anlo, offered ten thousand men to
the British government to help defeat the Germans in Togo. He did so—while
refusing to allow Anlo citizens to participate in the war in East Africa—because
of his specific desire to eliminate the hardships suffered by those with whom the
Anlo were so closely affiliated.[15] The defeat of the Germans brought only a temporary change in conditions for their Togolese colonial subjects.

After the Germans in Togo surrendered in 1914,[16] the British Gold Coast
governor, Hugh Clifford, and the French lieutenant governor of Dahomey, M.
Mouflard, divided the administration of the former German colony between their
respective governments. The Gold Coast assumed responsibility for the eastern
sections of Togo: the districts of Lome, Misahohe, Keta Krachi, and part of
Mangu-Yendi (Sansanne Mangu); Dahomey administered the eastern districts of
Anexo, Atakpame, Sokode-Bassari, and the other section of Mangu-Yendi. This
brought large sections of the German-controlled Ewe-speaking areas under British colonial administration, which meant that at least temporarily, many found
their situation as colonial subjects much improved. The British ended the use of
forced labor, declined to continue the direct taxation system employed by the
Germans, and allowed Africans to engage in the formerly restricted import-ex-
port business.[17] In those areas administered by the French, however, little
changed. The French continued to demand forced labor and the payment of taxes
in order to defray the cost of occupation. In 1919, a second division of the colony
occurred in which France—with the acquiescence of Britain and the endorse-
ment of the League of Nations—received control over the port of Lome and
additional areas in the southwest.[18] One of the principal consequences of this re-

---

[14] I emphasize here the relations that existed between the Anlo and those in the coastal towns under
German colonial rule because of the long-standing business and familial ties that connected the two
areas. Some animosity existed between the Anlo and those in the interior because of Anlo's alliance
with the Asante in wars directed against the Ewes in the interior; these relations were normalized only
after British intervention. See "Die Unruhen," 38–39, 42–49. Relations were also strained because up to
the 1890s the Anlo continued to attack those from the interior in order to maintain their monopoly over
the trade on the coast. See Buhler, "The Volta Region," 93–112; ADM 11/1/1113: C.A.O. Therin, District
Commissioner, Kwitta, to the Honorable Colonial Secretary, 22 September 1899; Ghana National Archives, Ho [hereafter Ho Archives], Item No. 77: Anyako Native Affairs (Case 21/31): 2/8/29–7/11/40,
Keta.

[15] Amenumey, *The Ewe Unification Movement*, 10.

[16] For a discussion of the actual military activities in Togo, see Michael Crowder, "The 1914–1918 European War and West Africa," in J. F. A. Ajayi and Michael Crowder, eds., *History of West Africa*, II (New
York, 1974), 486–90.

[17] Amenumey, *The Ewe Unification Movement*, 10–12; Claude E. Welch, *Dream of Unity: Pan-Africanism and
Political Unification in West Africa* (Ithaca, 1966), 53–56, 69.

[18] For a succinct discussion of the political maneuverings that lead to this particular re-division, see
Welch, *Dream of Unity*, 53–56. See Amenumey, *The Ewe Unification Movement*, 11–20, for a discussion of the
role of the League of Nations.

division was that those in Anlo found themselves again separated from the people with whom they had their closest ties.

French administration of Togo after the First World War departed somewhat from the expedient measures taken by the French during the war. They continued their use of forced labor and direct taxes, but maintained far fewer customs posts throughout the territory, which allowed greater movement of goods between the two colonies. During the German administration of Togo, British currency was the most frequently used exchange unit in both the Anlo area and in Togo, a situation that supported continued economic relations between the two areas; the French left in place this particular monetary situation through the second decade of the 1900s. By the 1930s, however, in response to the Depression, they altered their policies. They introduced the French franc as an alternate currency in the colony and then banned the use of British West African currency, forcing the Togolese to exchange their pounds for francs at an artificially low rate; they also increased the direct taxation rates. Togolese response to these measures was immediate: the educated elite called for the return of German rule, the termination of French administration, and/or the unification of the Ewes in Togo with the Ewes in the Gold Coast. Riots erupted in Lome in 1933, and individual Togolese continued to move to the Gold Coast to avoid the systems of forced labor and taxation, and to seek higher paying jobs. Equally significant is the fact that this period also saw "a gradual increase in the feelings of Ewe ethnic unity."[19]

The Invention of an Ewe Identity and Its Reception among the Anlo

Protests about the colonial imposition of a boundary separating the Anlo from the Ewe-speaking peoples to the east began as early as 1918 when several educated Togolese approached Lieutenant Colonel Rowe, the commander of the British forces in Togo, and discussed the desirability of transferring control of all Togo to the British. Petitions and appeals advocating the same arrangement followed in 1919 and 1920. As a number of authors have noted, this early protest movement primarily involved a very limited sector of the population in Togo and the Ewe-speaking Gold Coast. The majority were merchants and educated chiefs who were closely affiliated with the business community in Anlo, Lome, and Anexo.[20] All had benefited financially during the years between 1914 and 1919, when British rule over much of the former German Togo united these areas with the Gold Coast Colony;

---

[19] These developments are cited by many as the beginning of the post–World War II Ewe unification movement. See Welch, *Dream of Unity*, 58–61, 64; Amenumey, *The Ewe Unification Movement*, 20–28.

[20] The signatories to the various petitions included Augustino de Souza, R. D. Baeta, S. L. Van Lare. T. A. Anthony, and T. W. Tamaklo, all men from prominent trading families. See Amenumey, *The Ewe Unification Movement*, 12–13. Fia Sri II of Anlo was also closely affiliated with the merchant community. Prior to his enstoolment he had been a storekeeper in Sierra Leone with the Williams, a particularly prominent business family based in Keta, Denu, and Gbagida. In 1892, he served as an agent for Messrs. Blackstock and Co.; he subsequently traveled to Victoria in Cameroon and established a store there. See Napoleon Agboada, "The Reign and Times of Togbui Sri II of Anlo, 1906–1956 (History Department long essay, University of Ghana, Legon, 1984), 2.

all feared the detrimental impact that French administrative rule might have on their economic interests.[21] Evidence of this comes from the petition sent by Octaviano Olympio, president of "The Committee on Behalf of Togoland Natives" and supported by the Bremen missionary-educated Anlo *awoamefia*, Togbui Sri II. This petition stated that:

> The absorption of Togoland into France's colonial possessions will sever members of the Ewe speaking tribe in Togoland from those in the southeastern portion of the Gold Coast Colony and seriously interfere with their economic progress. Any linguistic changes [that is, the imposition of French] will materially and adversely affect employment thereby encouraging emigration and depopulation.[22]

Involvement by the Anlo educated elites in the protests declined during the remainder of the 1920s as the anticipated detrimental effects of French rule on commerce failed to materialize. Interest in and concern about the way in which the French governed the eastern Ewe continued, nevertheless, and by the 1930s, Fia Sri and others began to emphasize not just the desirability of having the British rule their Togolese relatives and business partners, they also began to advocate the idea that the Anlo must begin to see themselves as one with the Ewes in British Togoland, and that all Ewes, wherever they resided, had to look to themselves if they were to develop the capability of managing their own affairs within the modern world system.

This expansion in the way in which some Anlo began to view themselves—as a people who shared important bonds with all other Ewe-speaking peoples, rather than just with the specific Ewe and Akan peoples with whom they had religious, economic, military, and family ties—developed in the mid-1930s. In 1934, for example, Reverend F. K. Fiawoo and Reverend Osabute Aguedze of Anlo noted that the Gold Coast colonial government had failed to make available to them the kinds of educational opportunities they would need to advance. At that time, no secondary schools existed in Anlo or in the Ewe-speaking area of the Gold Coast known as the Volta Triangle; and the number of positions open to Ewe-speaking students from that area in secondary schools elsewhere was extremely limited. With strong support from Fia Sri II and the educated Anlo community in Keta and Anloga, the Anlo State Council agreed to support the development of a secondary school in Anloga by providing financial support.[23] In 1938, Fia Sri also proposed to the State Council that they cease using Akan terms for the names of their military officers and the divisions of the army, and use Ewe terms instead.[24] Between the mid-1930s and mid-1940s, he supported the imposition of an annual state tax that would be used not only to

---

[21] This interpretation can be found in Welch, *Dream of Unity*, 58.

[22] Cited in Amenumey, *The Ewe Unification Movement*, 14.

[23] The school opened in 1937 and was known at that time as the New Africa University College. Today, it is called Zion Secondary School. The financial support pledged by the State Council was not forthcoming throughout the 1940s because of the members' unwillingness to impose a highly unpopular tax on each Anlo male. See Anlo State Council Minute Book: June 1934–November 1946: 13, 460, 481–84, 583, 585, 866; ADM 39/1/120: Memorandum from the Chiefs, Linguists, and *Hanua* of Anlo to Governor Burns, Accra, 13 November 1944, Section 19 on Education; Agboada, "Reign and Times of Togbui Sri II," 17.

[24] Anlo State Council Minute Book, from January 1935: Minutes of the Anlo State Council, June 1938, 302.

support local educational institutions and public works, but would also be used to assist their Ewe neighbors in both British and French Togoland.[25] By 1945, these local initiatives had become part of a larger effort spearheaded by educated Anlos in Accra to foster a greater sense of cultural unity between their fellow Anlos and all other Ewes. In 1947 Daniel Chapman, a senior tutor at Achimota College outside Accra, launched a publication entitled *The Ewe Newsletter*, which saw wide distribution in Anlo and in other Ewe-speaking areas of the Volta Triangle, British and French Togoland. The publication promoted consciousness of an Ewe cultural unity and the need for united action to support their common interests. These same themes were noted in several petitions to the British secretary of state for the colonies, Colonel Oliver Stanley, in 1943. The petitioners—including a number of educated Anlos—stated that "the [colonial] frontiers had operated detrimentally against the original unity and the aspirations of the Ewes," and that the latter "regarded [their] common ancestral background . . . with almost the sacredness of a fetish, as reflected in the persistent linguistic affinity and similarity of outlook on life." They also emphasized the idea that all Ewes needed "to march forward together to [achieve] fuller development."[26]

Scholars who have studied the rise of an Ewe identity offer a number of explanations as to why the Anlo and other Ewes in the Volta Triangle began to focus their efforts on the creation of this wider identity after the 1920s. D. E. K. Amenumey and Claude Welch suggest that the Anlo educated elite and others began "to subordinate the [politically independent] divisions or dukowo and dialects to the goal of Ewe unity" because of the difficulties created for the Ewe residents of the Gold Coast when the French in Togoland declared their allegiance in 1940 to the Vichy government in France and then closed the border with the British Gold Coast. They note that:

> The thriving commercial network of "Eweland" was sundered. As a result, residents of French Togoland could not obtain many commodities, notably salt, which had been imported from Keta. Funeral processions were stopped at the boundary, a highly unpopular action. A rigorous system of compulsory labor was instituted, and despite the frontier restrictions, many thousands fled. Those who remained in French Togoland were subjected to numerous deprivations, leading to widespread social and political malaise. Even after the Free French government took over, workers were required to supply the government with palm oil and grain.[27]

This explanation provides insight into why the Ewe unification movement became an important political force after World War II, but it does not explain why the *awoamefia* of Anlo, Togbui Sri II, began to make efforts to establish greater connections between his people and other Ewes well before 1940. I. E. Aligwekwe provides a more appropriate explanation. He associates the development of an Ewe

---

[25] Anlo State Council Minute Book, June 1934–November 1946, 864.

[26] Cited in I. E. Aligwekwe, "The Ewe and Togoland Problem: A Case Study in the Paradoxes and Problems of Political Transition in West Africa" (Ph.D. dissertation, Ohio State University, 1960), 145–46.

[27] This quote is from Welch, *Dream of Unity*, 65; Amenumey, *The Ewe Unification Movement*, 36–37 expresses similar views.

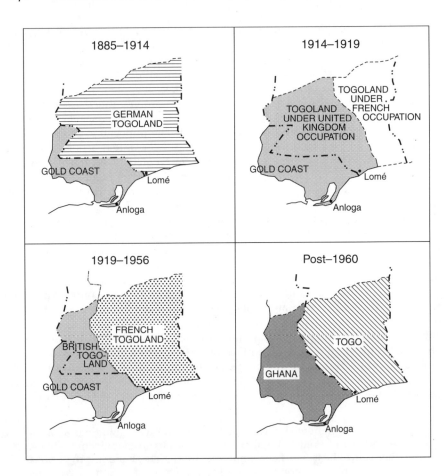

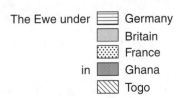

Map 6: The Partitioning of the Ewe (based on Coleman, "Togoland," 8–9)

identity with the increasing concern among the Gold Coast Ewes that their minority position within the colony would substantially limit their ability to have the government meet their needs. He notes that:

> The Ewes of the Gold Coast were sensitive of being a minority, or one of the small and inconsequential tribes in the Gold Coast. They were fully

aware of the fact that Great Britain, as the sovereign power over the Gold Coast, would not countenance the interference of any international agency in the affairs of the Gold Coast which she regarded as domestic; that she would not permit the detachment from the Gold Coast in satisfaction of tribalistic demands. If the whole of Eweland could be unified and placed under British control as part of the Gold Coast, this would increase the importance of the Ewes in the Gold Coast and give them great bargaining power in its affairs. As the two Togolands were not colonies of France and Great Britain, but mandates or trust territories [placed under these two powers by the League of Nations], it was possible, they felt, to secure international action to permit the Ewes of the Togolands to join those of the Gold Coast.[28]

Statements by F. K. Fiawoo and Togbui Sri II cited above about the lack of government support for education in the Volta Triangle, and the need for the Ewes to look to themselves to obtain the funds needed to develop, provide additional support for Aligwekwe's claims that educated Anlo felt their minority status within the Gold Coast limited their ability to benefit from government support.

Of greater significance for this study is the fact that the people of Anlo responded positively to the call to see all Ewes as one. According to Claude Welch in his study of the Ewe unification movement, the idea was "supported by all ,"[29] because of the difficulties the Anlo experienced during World War II in maintaining contacts with their relatives in French Togoland. Again, I would argue that there must be other reasons for the Anlos' apparent willingness to establish a much greater identification with their northern Ewe neighbors with whom they historically had had fairly poor relations. Anlo identification with the Ewes of British Togoland appears, instead, to have developed because the general population shared with the educated elite the fear that they could suffer as a result of their significant minority status in the Gold Coast. Educational opportunities became the focal point for these fears because the Anlo found that their children's economic opportunities were quite limited without this kind of training. The lagoon fishing industry was under great pressure from over-fishing by the turn of the century, the copra industry collapsed in the mid-1930s with the onset of Cape St. Paul's Wilt, and the limited land resources in the area provided only a few opportunities for commercial farming. Obtaining an education in the government-supported school system or participating in migrant fishing were among the only alternatives available to many. Accordingly, the Anlo population reacted with greater interest in Ewe unity as proposed by educated Anlos when some suggested that the British government was not doing all that it should to support the educational system in Anlo.[30]

---

[28] Aligwekwe, "The Ewe and Togoland Problem," 149–50.

[29] Welch, *Dream of Unity*, 72. None of the scholars cited here discuss the role that missionaries or government officials played in generating an Ewe identity. Only Debrunner, *A Church*, 122–23, discusses this point, anticipating the work of Vail. While I recognize this aspect of Anlo ethnic history, the focus here is on the reasons the Anlo accepted this new identity.

[30] See Anlo State Council Minute Book, June 1934–November 1946, 585 and 866. Considerable opposition did exist among the Anlo not to schooling but to the way their school taxes were used. See Sophia Amable, "The 1953 Riot in Anloga and Its Aftermath" (B.A. long essay, History Department, University of Ghana, Legon, 1977), for a full discussion of this issue.

Increased Anlo identification with their northern Ewe-speaking neighbors may have also been enhanced by the experiences many had while participating in migrant fishing. After World War I, numerous groups of Anlo men and women traveled to other coastal areas, including the Fante area of the Gold Coast, in order to pursue their commercial fishing activities. For many, this was probably the first time they had traveled outside their home area, and/or to a district where they were a distinct linguistic minority. In these new locations, they conducted themselves as they had in their own home villages, but those among whom they came to live—often temporarily, just for the fishing season—came to view the Anlos' prosperity with jealousy and suspicion. Stories circulated that associated the Anlo with "blood-curdling" crimes. R. W. Wyllie indicates, for example, that from at least the 1930s "Fanti [children] learned to view the Anlos as thieves, kidnappers, sorcerers and ritual murderers."[31] The social tensions that accompanied these beliefs—and the very fact that these beliefs were held by a non-Ewe speaking people— must have heightened the Anlo's awareness of their linguistic and cultural background and generated some sense of identification with other Ewe-speaking peoples whom they would have encountered in the Gold Coast. As the Anlo developed a heightened interest in emphasizing the commonalties that existed between themselves and other Ewe-speaking peoples in British and French Togoland, so they also began to alter the way in which they viewed the constituent members of their own society.

Shifting Ethnic Boundaries in Twentieth-Century Anlo

Late nineteenth- and early twentieth-century oral traditions recorded by German missionaries indicate that the Anlo identified a number of clans, in part, by the non-Anlo origins of their ancestors. The Tsiame and Agave were described as the descendants of individuals who came from Akwamu and the Volta River Tongu towns, respectively; members of the Dzevi clan are said to have come from the Adangbe area; the Wifeme clan was described as the "descendants of [Amega] Le who had immigrated from a Volta island and found shelter with an Anlo woman called Wi." In 1978 and 1987 when I interviewed a number of Anlo elders about the histories of the various clans in Anlo, I discovered that the traditions that had defined the Tsiame, Agave, Dzevi, and Wifeme clans as ethnically distinct clans were still in place, but the emphasis on difference that figured so prominently in these earlier traditions no longer existed as one of the principal ways of discussing the social position of these clans. Emphasized instead were the commonalties that bound all the clans to one another. This was accomplished by altering the older traditions somewhat, and placing them within a larger framework that emphasized the notion that the ancestors of all of the Anlo *hlowo* (with the exception of the Blu clan) came from Notsie and that what differences existed among them had to do with accidents of history. One sees this in contemporary geneaological charts of the Anlo clans as shown in Figure 7.[32] One also sees it in the new tradi-

---

[31] Robert B. Wyllie, "Tribalism, Politics and Eviction: A Study of an Abortive Resettlement Project in Ghana," *Africa Quarterly* (New Delhi), IX, 2 (1969), 132–33.

[32] This chart is based on information received in interviews with Anlo clan elders. See Greene, *Field Notes, passim.*

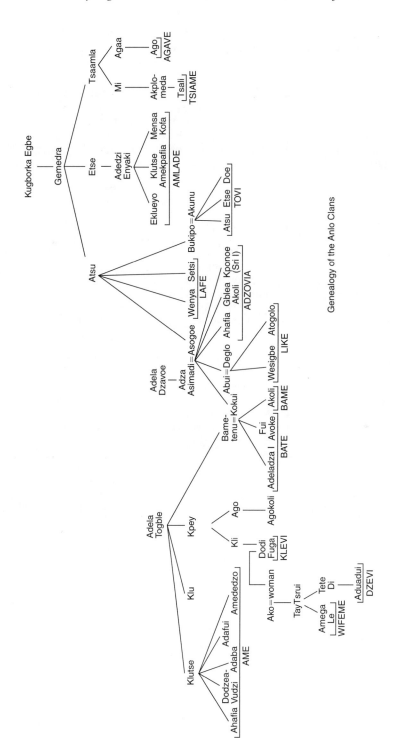

FIGURE 7: Genealogy of the Anlo Clans

tions about those clans previously described as ethnic outsiders. For example, the early twentieth-century tradition that the ancestor of the Tsiame clan, Akplomeda, was an Akwamu has disappeared; in the more recent clan genealogies, he is said to be the direct patrilineal descendant of Togbui Egbe, one of the most revered ancestors of the Anlo. The Agave are no longer described primarily as the descendants of non-Anlos, but as the patrilateral relatives of the Tsiame, Amlade, and Lafe clan, all of whom descended from Togbui Egbe. The fact that the Dzevi and Wifeme clans have among their traditional clan names several that are of Adangbe origin is no longer cited by Anlo elders as proof of their non-Anlo origins. Instead, other explanations are offered. The one most commonly cited for the Wifeme states that:

> [Togbui Le, founder of the Wifeme clan] moved from Amedzofe [the place where mankind originated] to Notsie. He was originally an Ewe man. The Anlos settled [on the littoral] before Le. Le [on his journey from Notsie] lost his way. He roamed about, went across the River Volta, stayed in Labode, then left and founded Legon. . . . He was troublesome and couldn't stay among the people. He left and went to Kpong . . . where a servant of his killed a cat that belonged to the chief of Kpong. The chief demanded that Le give one man from his followers for every piece of fur on the cat. He hated Le anyway. Le tried to save his people and he proposed to make canoes to take them and sell things in order to make the payment instead of giving up his men. After digging out a tree for a canoe, he packed his people in and escaped at night when the river was high and after packing his belongings. He went to Dofo and lived there with his descendants. One day, he met a hunter from Ada called Kplitikplibi, who told him he knew a man at Ada who looked just like him. Le told him how he had lost his uncle. The hunter went back to Ada and another came. He saw Le's bracelet which was made of bone, and he said he knew of a man who had the same in Anlo, at the estuary. When the hunter went back, he went to [Dodi Fuga,] founder of the Klevi clan. The hunter also said this man in Dofo had a bracelet just like [Dodi Fuga's], so the founder of the Klevi clan took off his bracelet and gave it to the hunter because this was made by his people. The hunter took the bracelet back [to Dofo]. Le recognized it and asked the hunter to lead him to where he got it. They made a canoe, went to Anloga and reunited with the Klevi clan. . . .
>
> Being away so long, he was considered a stranger . . . they were speaking Krobo. He settled with a woman who was his [maternal] uncle's daughter, who was called Awi. . . . His descendants formed a clan, [the Wifeme clan].[33]

By placing emphasis on the Wifeme clan's ancestor's residence in Notsie, his genealogical connection to the more socially centered ancestor of the Klevi clan, and by identifying one of his followers with the still common Ewe cultural practice of consuming domesticated cats, this tradition supports the idea that the Wifeme were Ewes if not ethnic Anlos; it also explains their Adangbe naming customs by point-

---

[33] FN 8: Interview with Mr. T. S. A. Togobo, 3 August 1978, Anloga; FN 9: Interview with Mr. T. S. A. Togobo, 7 August 1978, Anloga; FN 15: Interview with Togbui Le II, 15 August 1978, Anloga.

ing to their long residence in Krobo. Contemporary traditions about the Dzevi accomplish the same for this clan.[34]

This shift in the way in which the Anlo defined those who were previously described as ethnic "others" appears to have taken place by the mid-twentieth century. When I conducted oral interviews with Anlo elders about the histories of the various clans, I was told quite explicitly that changes, particularly in the ethnic identity of the Wifeme clan, had occurred only since the 1959 enstoolment of the present *awoamefia*, Togbui Adeladza II. The Blu clan—which had previously consisted of those families that later separated into the Blu and Wifeme clans—split in the late 1950s and began to elect their own representatives to Togbui Adeladza's council. It was also at this same point that Anlo elders began to accept and propagate the notion that Amega Le, founder of the Wifeme clan—unlike the ancestors of the Blu—was an Ewe who had ancestral kinship relations with the Anlo.[35] I attribute this shift in emphasis to the rise of an Ewe identity and the attendant desire by some to increase the sense of unity that the Anlo felt not only with other Ewe-speaking peoples in the Togolands but also with the various groups that together constituted the Anlo polity. To accomplish the latter task, traditions were altered to generate an awareness among all Anlos that they as a group shared a common heritage and were therefore one, whether their ancestors were among the first to arrive or the last. Of central importance were their ties to one another through reinvented kinship and marital relations and their common connection to the town of Notsie.

Evidence to support this connection between the more recent changes in the ethnic identity of certain groups and the invention of an Ewe identity comes from the fact that not only did this shift in the Wifeme's identity occur at the height of the Ewe unification movement, immediately after World War II, but also those who were in a position to influence others within Anlo society were strong advocates of both Ewe unity and a change in the Anlos' perception of themselves. One such individual was T. S. A. Togobo. Although mission-educated, Togobo had been deeply involved in the affairs of the Adzovia clan and in the activities of the advisory council of the *awoamefia* since the 1930s. He served as a close personal advisor to the *awoamefia*, Togbui Sri II (1907–1959), and actively encouraged the acceptance of an Ewe identity and a more inclusive definition of Anlo society through his support of efforts to establish the first secondary school in the Ewe-speaking area to serve both local and regional interests. In the late 1970s, he emphasized the idea that the founder of the Wifeme clan, Amega Le, was an Ewe, and that historical linkages bound the Anlo not only to the eastern Ewe, but also to those who lived

---

[34] Contemporary Anlo traditions state that the founder of the Dzevi clan was Aduadui. He is said to have joined the Dzevi (the clan of his maternal relatives) only after his own paternal relatives (members of the Tsiame clan) refused to support his involvement with the god Nyigbla. By defining Aduadui as the founder of the Dzevi clan as well as a Tsiame clan member, these traditions obliterate his maternal relations who probably did come from the Adangbe area. They focus on Aduadui and emphasize those genealogical connections that link the Dzevi to other Ewe speakers and to Notsie, in particular. See FN 32, Interview with Togbui Sefoga, 30 September 1978, Anloga; and FN 53: Interview with Togbui Alex Afatsao Awadzi, 16 December 1987, Anloga.

[35] FN 65: Interview with Togbui Dzobi Adinku, 6 January 1988, Anloga; and FN 8: Mr. T.S. A. Togobo, 3 August 1978, Anloga.

in what had formerly been British Togoland.[36] Another influential person was Togbui Dzobi Adzinku, an elder of the Bate clan—the *hlo* that, with the Adzovia, provides the *awoamefia* of Anlo—and the brother and close advisor to the present *awoamefia*, Togbui Adeladza II. In interviews he, too, supported the notion that the Wifeme clan's founder had genealogical connections to the Anlo despite their Adangbe cultural veneer, and that the northern Ewe were "siblings" and that they should not have fought one another as they did long ago.[37] This support by such prominent elders for a redefinition of the the way in which the Anlo hierarchically categorized their population, along with the expressions of support for Ewe unification that came from the educated elite, contributed significantly to the social changes that have occurred in Anlo during the mid-twentieth century.

Members of the affected clans themselves had also worked to effect such changes in their image. In 1877, German missionary C. Hornberger recorded Wifeme oral traditions which at that time emphasized that their ancestor, Amega Le, had lived in Notsie with the other Ewe clan ancestors, participated in the westward migration from that town, became separated from the main body, and then rejoined them some time later.[38] Only in the mid-twentieth century, however, did the efforts of the Wifeme and others to become more accepted as ethnic insiders within Anlo society yield results, as the political elite and the Anlo population in general supported (for their own reasons) an expansion in the way in which "we" and "they" were defined.

The Gender Dimension of Ethnic Change

Twentieth-century shifts in Anlo ethnic relations that saw numerous clans (as well as individual families) previously defined as outsiders redefined as insiders had great significance for gender relations. Previously one of the ways in which outsiders sought to reposition themselves within the Anlo social hierarchy was to attract the support of others who also felt disadvantaged by the prevailing social norms. In the eighteenth century, the Dzevi organized its Nyigbla religious order to attract women by giving its female initiates the right to exercise greater authority in their marital households. In the nineteenth century, the ethnic outsider Elias Quist reorganized the Yewe religious order and attracted large numbers of women by allowing them to have more influence in both their natal and their husbands' households. Both efforts proved highly effective in altering both gender and ethnic relations. By the early twentieth century, however, the alliances that had developed between those ethnic outsiders and Anlo women who sought to defy their social marginalization were no longer necessary. The criteria used to define "we" and "they" in Anlo had begun to shift. The increased movement of Anlo fisherfolk into non-Ewe speaking areas, the political incorporation of the Anlo polity into the Gold Coast Colony, and concerns about relatives and friends resident in German- and later French-controlled Togoland prompted the Anlo to develop and accept a

---

[36] FN 8: Mr. T.S. A. Togobo, 3 August 1978, Anloga.

[37] FN 52: Interview with Togbui Dzobi Adzinku, 15 December 1987, Anloga and FN 65: Interview with Togbui Dzobi Adinku, 6 January 1988, Anloga.

[38] Hornberger, "Etwas," 437–40.

new, more expansive definition of themselves as Ewe. This development, in turn, led the people of Anlo to redefine the Anlo "we" so as to include many who had previously been defined as "they."

In seizing the opportunity to become fully accepted members of Anlo society, however, many ethnic outsiders also abandoned the institutions that had provided Anlo women with the support they needed to challenge the prevailing pattern of gender relations in nineteenth-century Anlo. This is perhaps most apparent if we briefly review the history of the Yewe order organized by the ethnic outsider, Elias Quist. Formed by Quist in the mid-nineteenth century as a means to gain both economic and social prestige within Anlo, this order not only made Quist one of the best-known figures in Anlo, it also successfully challenged the character of gender relations in Anlo by giving women the opportunity to escape abusive husbands and unwanted betrothals. Support for this order by Quist's descendants changed considerably, however, with the expansion of Christianity and Western education.

In 1907, the most influential members of the Adzovia clan (whose turn it was to install the new *awoamefia*) elected Cornelius Kwawukume (Fia Sri II) because they believed his formal education in Keta at the Bremen Mission would help the Anlo polity better adjust to and take advantage of whatever benefits might be available from British colonialism. Even before his installation, he made it clear that, as a Christian, he would not follow many of the practices that were influenced by the traditional belief system. He shortened the time during which he as the candidate to be installed as *awoamefia* had to undergo ritual induction into the office. He discontinued the practice of keeping the *awoamefia* secluded from public view. He fully supported efforts by the British colonial government to ban the customary practice of burying the dead under the floors of their former homes by establishing public cemeteries. He eliminated the ban on sewn clothing that had been enforced by the Nyigbla order. He gave his full support to the construction of a Bremen Mission church in Anlo, in defiance of many of the traditional priests and their followers.[39] Others in Anlo followed his lead. In 1913, Togbui Nyaho Tamaklo—the wealthiest and most powerful chief in Anlo—distanced himself from his own Yewe order by becoming a Christian.[40] During this same period, as noted in the introduction to this chapter, the chief of Dzelukofe handed over his office to C. T. Agbozo, a descendant of John Tay, despite his technical status as a stranger, because Agbozo was literate.

These examples illustrate the fact that by the early twentieth century, the Anlo had begun to use a very different set of criteria to define the bases of social prestige. Association with Christianity became an important foundation for political as well as social prestige, along with connections to Notsie, wealth, time of settlement, and literacy. In response, many ethnic outsiders began to distance themselves from the traditional religious orders that had once provided them with greater status within the Anlo social hierarchy. The Quists were no exception.

In the early 1920s, a number of Quist's children broke with their father's Yewe order and with those relatives who continued to worship the Yewe gods by at-

---

[39] ADM 11/1/910: Awuna Native Affairs, Resolution of the Anlo State Mass Meeting held at Keta on 17, 18, and 19 August 1927 on the New Native Administrative Ordinance, 1927; ADM 39/1/602: Togbi Sri II, Awoame Fia–40th Anniversary Celebration of . . . A. M. Frank, Assistant District Commissioner, Keta, 1/23; Agboada, "Reign and Times of Togbi Sri II."

[40] FN 74: Interview with A. W. Kuetade-Tamaklo, 19 January 1988, Tegbi.

tempting to wrest control of the lands occupied by the latter.[41] Their actions obviously involved a dispute over the control of valuable resources, but they also had profound implications for gender relations. The fact that Quist's Yewe descendants lost this case meant that women who wished to defy the ways in which their families handled their affairs could no longer gain the support of a powerful force in Anlo society. Yewe no longer wielded that kind of economic, political, or religious influence.

Yewe-backed challenges to the character of gender relations within Anlo society were also undermined by the traditional political elite. During the mid-1930s, the chiefs of Anlo—led by the *awoamefia*, Togbui Sri II, and supported by Christian missionaries and colonial officials—made a major effort to limit the activities of Yewe, specifically to hamper the ability of women to join this order and thereby defy their parents and/or husbands. In 1934, for example, the Anlo State Council issued the following statement:

> It is ruled . . . that . . . a woman below the age of 21 years could not be admitted to the fetish. Any woman from the age of 21 year upwards should not be admitted to the fetish without the knowledge and consent of her parents and husband if any.[42]

Under this kind of pressure, Yewe declined significantly in popularity.[43] Nyigbla—which had provided an alternative form of support for women seeking to challenge Anlo norms about gender relations—had already lost influence at the end of the nineteenth century because the god, as a war deity, had been unable to stem the expansion of British colonial rule, and the wars in which it claimed to lead the Anlo army were no more.[44]

Thus, by the middle of the twentieth century, as ethnic relations shifted to be more inclusive under the pressures of colonialism, these same influences generated changes in gender relations, resulting in a decline of support available to women who wished to challenge the prevailing norms that disadvantaged them because of their gender.[45]

Conclusion

In this chapter, I have focused on the history of ethnic change in twentieth-century Anlo, and the impact this change had on gender relations in the polity. I noted that

---

[41] Judicial Court Record Book, 1921: In the Native Tribunal at Awuna, . . .held at Awunaga, 14 March 1921 before the Honorable Fia Sri II, Awame Fia of Awuna," 273–336.

[42] Anlo State Council Minute Book, 29 June 1934–5/7 November 1946: Minutes of the Awuna Dua State Council of the Eastern Province of the Gold Coast Colony and Protectorate held at Awunaga on the 17th day of April 1935, 73.

[43] Torgby, "Origin and Organisation," 29; Fiawoo, "Influence of Contemporary Social Changes."

[44] Fiawoo, "Influence of Contemporary Social Changes," 225.

[45] This was the case not only because Nyigbla and Yewe no longer exercised the same influence in Anlo as they had in the past, but also because the new institutions introduced and/or supported by colonialism—cash crop agriculture, European schools, and wage labor—all had their own patriarchal biases that reinforced the marginalization of women. See Mamattah, *The Ewes*, 282–307 on the specific curriculum supported by the Christian missionaries in Anlo, and Chapter 6 below on the history of gender relations within the Anlo cash crop economy.

when the Western-educated elite of Anlo found their interests detrimentally affected by the division of the region into districts administered separately and differently by the British and the Germans, and then by the British and the French, they responded by promoting the development of an Ewe identity. Other Anlo embraced this new identity because their experiences as migrants had heightened their awareness of the differences separating their own culture from those of their non-Anlo neighbors, and also encouraged them to emphasize the similarities that linked them to other Ewe-speaking peoples. More significant for this study is the fact that the acceptance of this new Ewe identity encouraged changes in ethnic relations within Anlo, which in turn generated changes in gender relations. All those defined as ethnic outsiders found it increasingly unnecessary and (with the expanding influence of Christianity) even undesirable to support the traditional religious orders that had once provided women with the opportunity to challenge gender relations within Anlo. This development altered gender relations by diminishing the number of options available to women who sought to defy the norms that governed male-female relations.

6

Gender in Colonial and Post-Colonial Anlo: The Ethnic Connection

During the first half of the twentieth century when changes in ethnic relations undermined women's ability to use the Nyigbla and Yewe religious orders to challenge certain aspects of Anlo gender relations, the very cultural practices that many women found oppressive also began to change. We know, for example, that by the 1890s some young women initiated their own marriage arrangements, often without seeking the approval of their elders. Such actions, termed *dze hia* (concubinage), were increasing in frequency throughout the second half of the nineteenth century, as German missionary accounts indicate. But we also know that parental control over marital arrangements was still the norm.[1] By the 1960s and 1970s, however, this pattern had changed considerably. Nukunya noted in 1962, for example, that "today, young people are more and more claiming the right to choose their own spouses." He recorded the fact that 50 percent of the marriages in Woe and Alakple were established by mutual choice.[2] J. Dickson conducted a similar though smaller study in Anloga in 1979–1980 and noted that 65 percent of marriages in that town were by mutual choice.[3]

Changes also appear to have taken place in the extent to which marriages end in divorce. Late nineteenth-century accounts of Anlo marital practices are largely silent on this issue, and thus it is difficult to determine the divorce rate during this period. Anlo elders claim that divorce (*atsugbegbe*) was rather rare, as opposed to the more common practice of separation. German missionary records suggest that nineteenth-century families would have strongly discouraged divorce, particularly the wife's family, since both her paternal and maternal lineages could suffer financial losses and social isolation. The divorce would damage relations between the families involved

---

[1] See Binetsch, "Beantwortung mehrerer," 44; Nukunya, *Kinship and Marriage*, 77–78; Ellis, *Ewe-Speaking Peoples*, 199.

[2] Nukunya, *Kinship and Marriage*, 179.

156

and require the woman's family to return the bridewealth, which could be quite substantial given the fact that infant betrothal was fairly common, and payments and gifts associated with such marriages were frequent and occurred over a long period of time.[4] By 1962, however, divorce was no longer unusual. Nukunya recorded in that year that the marriages of 39.4 percent of the men and 22.7 percent of the women resident in the Anlo towns of Woe and Alakple ended in divorce; and the percentage cited for women is said to have been much lower than the actual rate because many women were reluctant to discuss their marital histories.[5]

These twentieth-century trends are not unusual; researchers have documented parallel developments in other Ewe-speaking communities and throughout Africa.[6] Most offer similar explanations for these phenomena, focusing primarily on the impact of European colonial rule on the African family. Scholars associate the rise of individual choice in marriage, for example, with the following:

1) the labor migration of unmarried young people (e.g., school leavers) away from their natal homes and parental control;

2) economic independence, where young people earned their own money by participating in the colonial and independent African economy, which also freed them from dependence on their parents to arrange marriages of social and economic benefit;

3) colonial intervention, where laws prohibited infant betrothals;

4) the spread of Western ideology through the educational system and the popular media, emphasizing the value individual choice in marriage, and "love" as the basis of such unions; and

5) the related decline in the ritual prestige of elders, which could otherwise have deterred the young from arranging their own marital affairs.[7]

---

[3] Dickson, "Marital Selection," 161; this same trend has been noted among other Ewe-speaking groups. M. Verdon stated in his 1983 study of the Abutia-Ewe, for example, that "parents have . . . lost the power to arrange marriages and exact services and prestations from future sons-in-law." Verdon, *The Abutia Ewe*, 166. Parents in the Peki town of Tsito, according to J. Bukh in her 1973 and 1976–1977 studies, also do not have "much say in their children's choice of [a] marriage partner." Bukh, *The Village Woman*, 45. For examples of changing marital forms in other African communities, see Mair, *African Marriage and Social Change*, 35–36, 68, 149–50, 152–53.

[4] See Binetsch, "Beantwortung mehrerer," 47, one of the very few early discussions about divorce among the Anlo; he gives no indication as to its frequency, although his description implies that it was not very common.

[5] Nukunya, *Kinship and Marriage*, 104–107.

[6] See Jette Bukh, for example, who indicates in her study of Tsito households that of the thirty-one women (aged twenty-nine to seventy) from whom she collected life histories, twenty had been divorced once, and seven more than once. M. Verdon recorded the divorce rate among the living population of Abutia as 46.5 percent for men and 44.9 percent for women. Verdon, *The Abutia Ewe*, 193 and "Divorce in Abutia," 56; Bukh, *The Village Woman*, 44–47. Note that Verdon suggests that very high rates existed as early as 1890. I find this difficult to believe. It appears that Verdon came to this conclusion because Abutia women could always return to their natal homes and the refunding of the bridewealth or service caused little difficulty for a woman's family because it amounted to so little. Verdon fails to discuss the alliance-value or friendship-reinforcing value of marriage; emphasis is placed instead on the contractual, legal, ritual, and ceremonial character of marriage. See Verdon, "Divorce," 56–58.

[7] For a discussion of these various factors, see Mair, *African Marriage and Social Change*, passim, and Lucy Mair, *Marriage* (Baltimore, 1971), Ch. 12; Kenneth Little and Ann Price, "Some Trends in Modern Marriage Among West Africans," *Africa* XXXVII, 4 (1967); and Dickson, "Marital Selection," Chapter Nine.

Increased divorce rates are associated with a similar set of factors. Under colonial rule, many Africans left their homes to work in those areas most integrated into the European economy. This development is said to have increased the stress on marriages, as many migrants—mostly men in the initial years—found their wages insufficient to cover both their own expenses and their obligations at home. Many also developed relations with women at their new locations to whom they gave a certain amount of their income that might otherwise have been sent home. Wives responded to this loss of support by establishing liaisons with local men who could assist them.[8] Migrant men, who then returned home and accused their wives of adultery, faced a rebuttal in which they themselves were accused of lack of financial support. Divorce is said to have often followed, especially if women had the right to retain custody of their young children, could return to their natal residence, had the opportunity to establish an independent source of income, and if their parents and lineage elders were unwilling to work vigorously to salvage the marriage because they had become much less involved in their children's marital affairs. All of these conditions were present in Anlo by the 1960s and are said to have contributed to greater individual choice in marriage, a higher divorce rate, and a major change in the way in which family members interacted with one another.[9]

Of interest here is the fact that while changes in twentieth-century gender relations brought an expansion in the ability of Anlo women to influence their own marital affairs, this same period saw women lose enormous ground in terms of their economic status. Prior to the late nineteenth century, Anlo women inherited land from their maternal and paternal relations. They also received land from their husbands. As usufruct owners of all these properties, women used this land to grow crops and sell them in order to achieve a certain degree of economic independence. This began to change by the late nineteenth century, however, as shifts in the Anlo economy wrought by the demise of the slave trade encouraged many Anlos to engage in commercial agriculture. Faced with growing demands from family members for access to a limited amount of land, lineage elders eliminated nephews as inheritors of land acquired by their maternal uncles. They then excluded women from inheriting lineage land altogether and encouraged the latter, instead, to derive their independent source of income—previously obtained by selling surplus agricultural produce from their farms—from trade. At the same time, women also began to face increasing uncertainty about the support they could expect to receive from their husbands because of unpredictable developments in the commercial agriculture and fishing industries from which most men resident in Anlo obtained their incomes. This was the case, in part, because many men succumbed to social pressures to marry additional wives and/or demonstrate in some other form their social and economic status. This placed increasing burdens on wives to

---

[8] See Nukunya, *Kinship and Marriage*, 109; Verdon, "Divorce," 49; George Panyin Hagan, "Marriage, Divorce and Polygyny in Winneba," in Christine Oppong, ed., *Male and Female in West Africa* (Boston, 1983).

[9] See Nukunya, *Kinship and Marriage*, 109–20, 181–83, who discusses these developments among the Anlo, but associates an increased divorce rate with the spread of Christianity. See also David M. Schneider, "A Note on Bridewealth and the Stability of Marriage," *Man* LIII, 74, 75 (1953); Esther N. Goody, "Conjugal Separation and Divorce Among the Gonja," in Meyer Fortes, ed., *Marriage in Tribal Societies* (London, 1962); Betty Potash, "Some Aspects of Marital Stability in a Rural Luo Community," *Africa* 48, 4 (1978); Verdon, "Divorce," 49, and *The Abutia Ewe*, 191, 213; Bukh, *The Village Woman*, 45–46.

sustain the household on their own, a burden that undercut wives' abilities to protect what little economic independence they were able to derive from trade. In response to these challenges, women began to see that they had to be economically responsible for themselves. This understanding prompted many to establish and/or participate in women's economic cooperatives. This development in turn encouraged women both inside and outside these organizations to challenge the prevailing pattern of gender relations. Their success has meant that the boundaries defining normative gender roles and relations among the Anlo have expanded further than ever before.

These twentieth-century changes in gender relations have done more than alter the way in which men and women interact with one another, however. They have also impacted Anlo ethnic relations. I argue here that when Anlo women began organizing themselves into cooperatives and work-based associations so as to counter their economic marginalization, they also reinforced the growing tendency to focus less on the identity of an individual based on his or her clan affiliation and more on their identity as an Ewe. This argument stands in direct opposition to the notion offered by Leroy Vail, that women either had no ethnic identity or that they tended to retard rather than support the development of the larger ethnic identities that emerged during the colonial period. I argue instead that gender relations as impacted by the activities of women had a critical influence on ethnic identities and relations. The purpose of this chapter is to document the impact that developments in the Anlo economy had on Anlo gender relations and the way in which changes in gender relations affected ethnic relations and identities in twentieth-century Anlo. I begin this chapter with an analysis of the gendered character of Anlo economic relations within the family before the imposition of colonial rule, for only by discussing this aspect of Anlo history can one fully appreciate the impact that the shift to commercial agricultural production had on the gendered way in which Anlo families managed their economic affairs during the colonial and postcolonial periods.

Men, Women, and the Family in Nineteenth-Century Anlo

European documentary sources and oral accounts about the Anlo economy during the first half of the nineteenth century indicate that, except for the occasional involvement in a war that generated prisoners and thus potential slaves, the majority of residents were engaged in subsistence agriculture and fishing. Production took place on the household level, whose members—most often a man and his wife or wives, their children, perhaps slaves, and, on occasion nieces and nephews—all participated largely according to their age and gender.[10] Men, for example, took responsibility for clearing (or organizing the labor to clear) new fields and those that had been left fallow. Both men and women then planted, weeded, and harvested the crops, while women took principal responsibility for marketing the surplus. Men held the exclusive right to fish in the Keta Lagoon and the Atlantic Ocean; their wives, sisters, and daughters smoked, salted, and dried the catch, and

---

[10] Divisions of labor were also influenced by age and status as slave or free, but there is limited information about this aspect of the late nineteenth-century family economy.

sold the surplus in local markets. Profits from the sale of agricultural produce and fish appear to have been rather limited for most. The exceptions to this included those families who had the labor and the capital to engage in the large-scale production or purchasing and resale of fish that was transported into the interior to be exchanged for slaves, ivory, and agricultural produce such as palm oil produced elsewhere in the region. Profits for the majority of Anlo males came from the sale of the produce cultivated on their lands and their fish catches. Wives received money or gifts from their husbands in recognition of their contribution to the household, but they also obtained income from the sale of the produce they cultivated on their own fields and on those fields they received from their husbands and lineage elders.[11]

By the middle of the nineteenth century, however, significant changes began to occur in this system. The European demand for tropical oils had begun to replace the demand for slaves. Many Anlo men—motivated by the seemingly quick profits and the minimal capital and labor needed to enter the tropical oils business—made efforts to meet this new demand. During the 1850s and 1860s, the agricultural commodity on which they focused most of their attention was palm oil. Many initially experimented with the cultivation of oil palm, the tree crop from which palm oil was obtained, but as the agricultural environment in the area was unsuitable for the cultivation of healthy trees, the production of palm oil from local sources remained quite small.[12] Most focused their energies on transporting locally produced salt and fish to the Krobo district and to the forested areas north of Anlo where they exchanged their goods for palm oil. Others offered for pay their headloading and canoe services that many needed to move the palm oil from the interior to the coast.[13] Thus, even though the Anlo area produced very little palm oil of its own, Keta—the commercial center of the area—became one of the largest exporters of palm oil in the 1850s and 1860s.[14]

By the late nineteenth century, however, profits from the sale and transport of palm oil plummeted with the extension of British colonial rule over the Anlo area.

[11] This is the pattern found among the Ewe of Tsito and Abutia; in the absence of data from Anlo, we can assume that this was also the pattern among the Anlo during the eighteenth and nineteenth centuries. See Bukh, *The Village Woman*, 51, 53. Verdon, *The Abutia Ewe*, 146–51. Women had the right to inherit one-half the amount of lineage land inherited by their brothers. Access to this land was made possible by the fact that most women spent considerable amounts of time visiting the households of their fathers and/or their brothers. See Nukunya, *Kinship and Marriage*, 44, and Westermann, "Die Glidyi-Ewe," 142. Women also obtained additional sources of income from poultry production, and from the sale of cooked food to strangers. See Reindorf, *History*, 157; Charles W. Thomas, *Adventures and Observations on the West Coast of Africa and Its Islands* (New York, 1860), 243–44; G. Kwaku Nukunya, "Some Historical and Geographical Influences on Economic Development in Anlo: An Overview" (paper presented at the Seminar on Coastal Societies in the Nineteenth Century, Institute of African Studies, University of Ghana, Legon, 1981), 14–15; Grove and Johansen, "Historical Geography," 1407.

[12] On the effort to grow oil palms in Anlo see FN 53: Interview with Togbui Afatsao Awadzi, 16 December 1987, Anloga; Missionar Merz, "Die Oelpalme," *Monatsblatt der Norddeutschen Missionsgesellschaft*, 11/3 (1878), 168; and E. Salkowski, "Eine Hochburg des Heidentums," *Bremer Missions-Schriften*, No. 20 (1907), 10.

[13] FN 53: Interview with Togbui Afatsao Awadzi, 16 December 1987, Anloga; FN 61: Interview with Mr. Xovi Banini, 5 January 1988, Anloga; FN 97: Interview with Mr. J. G. Kodzo-Vordoagu, 24 February 1988, Tegbi; Aliwodsi, "Ein Sittenbild aus Anyako," 28–29; S. C. 14/2, p. 127.

[14] The significant quantity of palm oil exported from Keta during this period was due in part to the Krobo oil boycott. See Wolfson, "A Price Agreement." See also Thomas, *Adventures and Observations*, 246.

In 1874, the British defeated the Anlo in battle, and then began the process of bringing the polity under imperial control. In their efforts to govern the district, the British posted Hausa troops in the commercial town of Keta. There they were to enforce the laws, regulations, and initiatives that the British had already imposed on their Gold Coast Colony, immediately west of the Anlo area. The Anlo engaged in a number of individual and collective efforts to circumvent British colonial rule, but by the 1890s the colonialists had succeeded in both suppressing all military opposition and imposing an administrative structure.[15] The British actions of greatest significance for those Anlo men active in the palm oil trade involved the imposition of import duties. Payment of these fees—which the British imposed on liquor, firearms, and ammunition, the very goods most in demand by palm oil producers for their oil—meant that Anlo traders could no longer outbid their competitors on the Gold Coast by offering the mentioned goods to the palm oil producers at lower prices. The British also opened the trade routes that linked the Anlo coast to the interior. These had been closed for several years by a number of Anlo traders who profited handsomely from forcing palm oil producers to sell their goods to them in the interior. By opening these roads, the British further undermined Anlo profits from the palm oil trade, since inland producers now had the opportunity to bypass Anlo middlemen and sell their oil directly to buyers on the coast. Many Anlos abandoned involvement in the palm oil trade thereafter.[16]

Anlo men did not return to subsistence agriculture, however. Instead, they shifted to the commercial production of copra, shallots, and sugar cane to meet the growing demand for these commodities on the Gold Coast and in Europe. One consequence of this shift to commercial agriculture was that land became much more valuable. This is evident from the fact that during the 1880s and 1890s some of the most prominent chiefs in the area began to invest financially in the acquisition of major tracts of land both on the littoral and in the areas bordering the Keta Lagoon. Many of these lands were purchased as the European practice of private property took hold within the area; in other cases, these chiefs were able to obtain land by taking advantage of the massive indebtedness that had begun to emerge during the 1850s because of changes within the economy and social culture of the Anlo. For example, when an individual became indebted to one of these chiefs, the latter would no longer accept pawns in lieu of immediate payment. Instead, they acquired the debtor's land.[17]

A second consequence of the increasing emphasis on commercial agriculture involved a change in the areas where Anlo men had traditionally concentrated their agricultural activities. European documentary sources and oral accounts about Anlo agriculture during the eighteenth and early nineteenth centuries indicate that the cultivation of crops on the Anlo littoral took place in the coastal depressions that extend from the Volta River up to the town of Tegbi. Land in this particular agri-

[15] For a discussion of the British colonial conquest of Anlo and its early administration, see Agbodeka, *African Politics*, 62–75.

[16] See "Die Unruhen," 42–50; S.C. 14/1: p. 211; ADM 11/1/1107; Buhler, "The Volta Region of Ghana," Ch. IV; G. Müller, *Geschichte der Ewe Mission* (Bremen, 1904), 109–110.

[17] See FN 65: Togbui Dzobi Adzinku, 6 January 1988, Anloga; FN 74: Mr. A. W. Kuetuade-Tamaklo, 19 January 1988, Tegbi; FN 91: Togbui Joachim Acolatse IV, 5 February 1988, Tema; FN 97: Mr. J. G. Kodzo-Vordoagu, 24 February 1988, Tegbi; Judicial Council Minute Book, 1913, p. 383–487.

cultural area, only sixteen to seventeen-and-one-half square miles, was by no means plentiful, as the Anlo practiced within this limited area a system of shifting cultivation that required large tracts of land to be left fallow for several years in order for them to recover their fertility. Nevertheless, it was sufficient to provide both strangers and the resident population with enough land to grow food crops for their own consumption, which they then supplemented during periods of drought with the purchase of food from communities to the north of the lagoon.[18] Other areas on the Anlo littoral, specifically those located on the lagoon margins which had the same kinds of clayey soils found in the coastal depressions, had been deemed unsuitable for cultivation because they were infused with salt from the Keta Lagoon. These were left for strangers, women, and the wealthy. Immigrants who later formed the Dzevi clan established their shrine house in this area; women collected wickers for use in making baskets, and the wealthy used the grasses that grew on that section of the littoral as feed for their cattle.[19]

By the mid- to late nineteenth century, however, the population increase on the coastal sandbar had forced most cattle owners to relocate their herds to areas north and west of the Keta Lagoon. Women continued to claim certain areas for themselves to support their basket-making activities, and many had also begun to cultivate sugar cane in this same area, a crop that could withstand the periodic flooding of the Keta Lagoon and which the women used for smoking fish.[20] The sale of their surplus cane and baskets provided many women with additional income to which they added their profits from marketing their surplus crops.[21] Because these areas had limited value to most men, women were able not only to claim these areas for themselves, but also to bequeath them to their daughters.[22]

The emergence of sugar cane as a commercial crop changed this gendered pattern of land use. Oral traditions collected by Nukunya indicate that as the

---

[18] Sandra E. Greene, "Land, Lineage and Clan in Early Anlo," *Africa*, 51, 1 (1981); J. M. Dotse, *Shallot Farming in Anloga, Ghana: A Case Study in Agricultural Geography* (University of Cape Coast, Ghana, 1980), 52.

[19] See FN 30: Interview with Mr. T. S. A Togobo, 26 September 1978, Anloga; FN 32: Interview with Togbui Sefoga, 30 September 1989, Anloga; FN 42: Boko Seke Axovi, 1 November 1978, Anloga; FN 44: Interview with Togbui Dzobi Adzinku, 6 November 1978, Anloga; FN 45: Interview with Togbui Dzobi Adzinku, Anloga; FN 50: Interview with Boko Seke Axovi, 12 March 1979, Anloga; Van Dantzig, *The Dutch*, 200; WIC 124: Minutes of Council Meeting, Elmina, 17 February 1718; Rawlinson Manuscript, Bodleian Library, Oxford (c. 747) 24 August 1694, Edward Barbar, Alampo, to Cape Coast. See also Barbot, *A Description*, 194; H. M. Daendels, *Journal and Correspondence of H. M. Daendels*, Pt. 1, November 1815–January 1817. Translated by E. Collins (Legon, 1964), Vol. 2, 226, R. Roelossen to Gov-General Daendels, Accra, 13 November 1816; Monrad, *Bidrag*, 228; Nukunya, "Land Tenure," 70.

[20] Travelers' accounts from the 1850s note the existence of cattle on the Anlo littoral; by the 1870s, however, most herds appear to have been relocated. See Plessing, "Station Quitta," 177; Plessing, "Briefe aus Keta," 248; Schiek and Tolch, "Keta," *Monatsblatt der Norddeutschen Missionsgesellschaft*, 22/263 (1872), 1193; George MacDonald, *The Gold Coast, Past and Present: A Description of the Country and its People* (London, 1898), 247. These same sources comment on the extensiveness of the sugar cane fields. See Härtter, "Der Fishfang im Ewelande," 52, on the use of sugar cane to smoke fish. See Arthur Rosenfeld, *Sugar Cane Around the World* (New York, 1955), 95–96, 105–106, on the soils appropriate for the cultivation of sugar cane.

[21] Women also made additional income from sale of poultry, most of which was sold to passing steamers, and then conveyed to the lower and central Gold Coast. See Thomas, *Adventures and Observations*, 244.

[22] Nukunya, "Land Tenure," 70.

Photo 4: The Sugar Cane Market in Anloga at the Turn of the Century

commercial value of sugar cane increased (presumably fueled in part by the development of a local industry in which cane juice was distilled into liquor), Anlo men, particularly those in Woe, became more involved in its cultivation. As a result, by the late nineteenth century the lands on which the cane was grown gradually passed from women into the hands of their male descendants.[23] Given the ways in which property was transmitted in late nineteenth-century Anlo, this development could have occurred as a result of male elders, as the principal lineage leaders, taking control of these areas upon the death of the female land-holder, and giving preference to her male rather than female descendants. It is also possible that the female landholders themselves began to bequeath these areas to their sons rather than their daughters.[24] In both instances the likely rationale for these decisions had to do with the fact that men had greater access to labor than women, and were thus in a position to make the most profitable use of the land, for their own benefit and that of their lineages, through the labor-intensive commercial cultivation of sugar cane. Males were in such a position because they had the right to marry more than one woman, and they had access

[23] Ibid. The connection suggested between the increased demand for sugar cane and a local liquor industry is based on the fact that liquor was in high demand in the areas where the sugar-producing Anlo purchased their palm oil. In addition, sugar was one of the popular products used in the distillation of *akpeteshie* (home-brewed gin).

[24] Bequeathing property to designated descendants in one's lifetime is particularly significant because such an act prevented lineage elders from allocating that property to anyone else. Such property was called *fiaboe*. See Anlo Traditional Council Minute Book, 1931–1932 and 1933–1935: Awleshi Kwashikpui and others -v- R. J. Acolatse and others, pp. 877–927 and 25–99, respectively. See also Nukunya, "Land Tenure," 75.

to the labor of their wives and their own children, as well as to the labor of younger members of either their own or their wives' families who were living with them at the time.[25] Women had no automatic rights to any of these sources of labor. Accordingly, women in Woe found their ability to continue using these areas as a source of income severely curtailed by the end of the nineteenth century.

The same situation occurred in the Anloga area, where men obtained rights to plots on the margins of the Keta Lagoon not for use in the cultivation of sugar cane, but rather for use in the cultivation of shallots. This crop, like sugar cane, had been grown in the area for domestic consumption since at least the mid-eighteenth century. With the introduction of steamships in the 1850s on the West African coast, traffic between various ports in the area increased, as did the demand for local provisions. The Anlo area became well known for its supplies of poultry, which the ships' crews purchased not only for their own consumption but also for sale on the Gold Coast. Accounts from the mid- to late nineteenth century indicate that the Anlo also experimented to see whether a demand existed for a number of other locally produced goods. Among these were beeswax, honey,[26] and, it would appear, shallots, which the Anlo began to produce on a commercial basis by the late nineteenth century, as indicated in the following 1907 account by E. Salkowski, a German missionary.

> If one travels from our station in Woe across the countryside to Anloga, one is surprised by how lush the vegetation is here . . . on the lagoon side, the eye sweeps over well cultivated fields. The Anloga negro is better off than any of his other fellow negroes far across the sand dune that stretches miles wide. He harvests peanuts and tiger nuts, beans and fetri [okra]; he eats his own yams and pepper from his own field, and after meals, he chews sugar cane from his own plantation. Even corn fields sway when the wind blows over the lagoon. But the onion takes first place among the products of this area. As Erfurt in our country [Germany] is the flower city, and as the Lubbener area of Brandenburg is pickle country, the surrounding area of Anloga is onion country. . . . Anloga onions not only make their way into [Keta] town on the heads of the carriers and traders, they are also bought up by speculators in large quantities and transported in sacks or containers by steamships to comparable places along the coast. Now we understand how important the onion culture is for Anloga, and why the Anlos dedicate so much time, energy and care to this work.[27]

This transformation of the shallot from a subsistence crop to a commercially produced product was, no doubt, a boon for lineages in Anloga, but it gradually caused the women of this community to lose access to the increasingly valuable land on the margins of the Keta Lagoon that had previously provided them with an independent source of income.

---

[25] Many were also in a position to use their profits from the sale of sugar cane and palm oil to purchase slaves (primarily women and children) during this period. See H. Seidel, "Der Sklavenhandel in Togo," *Deutsche Kolonialzeitung* 12 (1899), M. Seeger, "Die Sklaverei im Togolande und der englischen Goldküsten Kolonie," *Deutsche Kolonialzeitung* 5 (1892); Marian Johnson, "The Slaves of Salaga," *JAH* 27 (1986).

[26] Thomas, *Adventures and Observations*, 245.

[27] Salkowski, "Eine Hochburg," 10.

Between the late nineteenth century and the 1960s, the ability of Anlo women to profit from the sale of the surplus agricultural produce they cultivated on their remaining lands was also threatened as changes in the fishing and copra industries increased competition within Anlo families for access to land.

Contractions in the Fishing and Copra Industries and the Problem of Land Shortages

Before the nineteenth century, the production and sale of fish had constituted a major sources of income for Anlo men and women. Most fish were obtained from the Keta Lagoon. By the late nineteenth century, however, the majority of the fish caught by Anlo men and sold by Anlo women came from the ocean. One cause of this transition was the overfishing of the Keta Lagoon. In 1784, the Danish physician and traveler P. E. Isert noted that "the lagoon is full of delicious fish, crawfish as well as thin oysters about one foot long."[28] By 1872, however, the German missionaries Schiek and Tolch noted that while "an enormous number of fish reside in [the lagoon], they, for the most part, do not get big . . . perhaps because they are caught too early." By 1907, lagoon fish were no longer the dominant source of this commodity sold locally and in more distant markets. Instead, as German missionary G. Härtter noted, "the largest quantity of fish are caught in the ocean."[29] At that time, this transition had little impact on women's economic independence, but subsequent changes in the fishing industry were not so benign.

Some time between 1850 and 1874, a prominent merchant couple by the name of John Tay and Afedima (the sister of Togbui Gbodzo of Woe) introduced into the Anlo area a beach seine used in Europe that became known locally as the *yevudo*.[30] Prior to the introduction of this new net, the most common type of fishing device used by the Anlo in the Atlantic Ocean was the *agli*, a purse seine, that was cast and retrieved from canoes operating off the Anlo coast. Catches were limited in size and the surf, which could be particularly rough on many sections of the Anlo littoral, encouraged most fishermen to concentrate their efforts in the shallow, calm waters of the Keta Lagoon.[31] The adoption of the new type of net allowed Anlo fishermen to catch large quantities of fish from the ocean. G. Härtter, a German missionary who observed the use of this net in the first decade of the twentieth century, provides a description of the *yevudo* as it was constructed and deployed at that time.

---

[28] Cited in Grove and Johansen, "Historical Geography," 1394.

[29] Schiek and Tolch, "Keta," 1193–4; Härtter, "Der Fishfang im Ewelande," 52.

[30] FN 86: Interview with Togbui Tay-Agbozo IV, 3 February 1988, Dzelukofe; FN 88: Interview with Togbui Tay-Agbozo IV, 4 February 1988, Dzelukofe; and FN 93: Interview with Togbui Amegashi Afeku IV, 19 February 1988, Accra-Nima. The dating of the introduction of the *yevudo* is based on the fact that Tay first appears as a locally prominent figure in European documentary sources in the 1860s. He died in 1874. See ADM 11/1/1113: Chief C. Agbozo, Keta, to C. Napier Curling, Keta, 14 July 1902.

[31] See Robin Law, "Trade and Politics Behind the Slave Coast: The Lagoon Traffic and the Rise of Lagos, 1500–1800," *JAH* 24 (1983), 321n.4, and Robert W. Wyllie, "Migrant Anlo Fishing Companies and Socio-Political Change: A Comparative Study," *Africa* XXXIX, 4 (1969), 397, who both mention of the difficult surf in the Anlo area.

PHOTO 5: Fishermen using the *Yevudo* in the mid-1960s

[T]he *yevudo* . . . is 60–100 meters long, 3–4 feet wide and the middle has a sack (*voku*) that catches large and small fish. The net is held with two strong pieces of rope. On one side of the net are attached little weights (50 centimeters from one another) and on the other side are two stakes, *kpotiwo*. On the stakes are attached 300–400 meters of rope. The net itself is reinforced with cotton anywhere from 2–4 times.

The day of fishing, the boat is prepared and 3–4 men get on board, giving to one man on shore the end of the rope to hold. As soon as the cable is unrolled the net is thrown into the sea and the boat is paddled transversely. Once all of the net is in the water, the boat is turned around and heads for shore, with men on shore pulling the net in with the two rope ends. As soon as the two stakes are seen, more men rush into the water to hold them under water. Slowly more of the net begins to appear and the concern moves to the sack in the middle of the net. The *voku* is sewn tightly with strong rope. As soon as the *voku* lands on shore, it is emptied. Sometimes there are no fish, but never are there more than a hundred caught. The process is repeated until enough fish are caught or the fishermen are tired.[32]

After the introduction and adoption of this net, the Anlo made a number of modifications in its design, enlarging both the net as a whole, as well as the *voku*, in order to increase its capacity to encircle large quantities of fish. As the size of the fish caught in the Keta Lagoon grew smaller and both the size and the quantity of fish from the ocean increased with the adoption and modification of the *yevudo* net, ocean fishing came to dominate the Anlo fishing industry. Few Anlo fishermen, however, had the financial and labor resources needed to operate the *yevudo* in the limited number of areas on the Anlo littoral where the surf permitted ocean fishing.[33] Accordingly, many

---

[32] Härtter, "Der Fishfang im Ewelande," 56–58.
[33] Wyllie, "Migrant Anlo Fishing Companies," 397.

found that the only way they could continue to participate in the fishing industry was to work for the wealthier *yevudo* owners.[34] Many men who chose not to pursue this particular avenue focused their energies instead on commercial agriculture. This, in turn, placed greater pressure on families to allocate less land to women and more land to men.

Changes in the copra industry also placed pressure on women's ability to maintain access to land from which they could obtain profits for their own use. Between 1875 and the late 1930s and early 1940s, the Keta District became one of the largest producers of copra in the British colony of the Gold Coast.[35] The most extensive stands of palms in this area were located in the eastern section of the district, within the Agbosome Traditional Area, but many Anlos both owned farms and worked in this area. In addition, a major coconut plantation existed in the town of Attiteti, on the westernmost edge of the Anlo traditional area, while numerous smaller stands of trees thrived within virtually every Anlo town on the littoral. The sale of the copra produced from the fruit of the coconut tree provided an important source of income to the Anlo, supplementing the profits they obtained from their involvement in the shallot, sugar cane, and fishing industries. In 1932, however, the coconut palms on the ocean side of the Anlo town of Woe became infected with a disease known as Cape St. Paul's Wilt. The disease spread rapidly throughout the area, and by 1942, ten years after the outbreak, copra was no longer exported from the area, as the number of trees that survived the disease were only sufficient to supply the local market.[36]

The contraction in the fishing industry and the collapse of the copra industry had an impact on men as well as women, since both were deeply involved in the two industries.[37] After the onset of Cape St. Paul's Wilt in the early 1930s, for example, growing numbers of men and some women began to participate in migrant

---

[34] Surgy, *La Pêche Traditionelle,* Chapter Three, Section Two.

[35] For a history of the coconut industry in Anlo, see K. B. Dickson, "Development of the Copra Industry in Ghana," *The Journal of Tropical Geography,* 19 (1964); see also C. L. Skidmore and J. S. Martinson, "A Survey of the Coconut Area in the Keta–Ada District," *Gold Coast Department of Agriculture Bulletin,* 23 (1930), "The Coconut Industry," 101-102, and "Cattle Manure on Coconuts in the Keta District," 108, both in *Gold Coast Farmer,* 2 (1933); C. N. Coombes, "Some Notes on the Development of the Ghana Coconut Industry," *Ghana Farmer,* 2 (1958); J. T. H. Stein, "Agriculture in the Keta–Ada District," Gold Coast Department of Agriculture Bulletin, No. 22, 1929.

[36] See sources in note 35 above, as well as B. L. Chona and P. G. Addoh, "Cape St. Paul Wilt," *Bulletin of Ghana Crop Research Institute,* 3 (1970).

[37] Men monopolized those activities associated with catching the fish: the weaving, mending, and drying of nets, and participation in the catch itself, while women focused on moving the fish away from the shore as quickly as possible, sorting that portion belonging to their male relatives or husband by size, then smoking or salting it, selling it, and then paying a portion of the profits to the male fishermen who caught them. See Härtter, "Der Fishfang im Ewelande," 55; and Walthier Manshard, "Die Küsten und Flussfischereien aus Ghana," *Die Erde: Zeitschrift der Gesellschaft für Erdkunde zu Berlin* 89 (1958), 21. These two accounts are the earliest recorded discussions of ocean fishing in the Anlo area. See also Polly Hill, "Ewe Seine Fishermen." in Polly Hill, ed., *Studies in Rural Capitalism in West Africa* (Cambridge, 1970) and Surgy, *La Pêche Traditionelle.* In the copra industry, both men and women were involved in the planting and care of the seedlings, although women and hired men tended to focus on weeding while men managed the cattle that were tethered to the palms so that the liquid and solid waste produced by the cows could be applied as fertilizer directly to the palms. Men harvested the nuts, while women managed the manufacturing of the copra and coconut oil, as well as selling raw coconuts and coconut oil on the local market. See FN 49: Interview with Togbui Afatsao Awadzi, 5 February 1979, Anloga.

PHOTO 6: Coconut groves on the Keta Lagoon in the Early 1900s

fishing as a major source of income, moving along the West African coast in search of fishing grounds less congested than those that had begun to characterize the Anlo area. Others left to work in cocoa-producing areas; and still others used the financial resources at their disposal or took advantage of the education they had received in the area missionary schools to establish businesses in other parts of the Gold Coast.[38] The remaining men and women involved in these two industries— particularly those on the Anlo littoral who had not received a European educa- tion—focused their attention on other income-producing activities within the dis- trict, the most lucrative of which were the commercial production of shallots and sugar cane. (Sugar cane continued to be cultivated on the littoral through the 1930s after which farmers shifted to the even more profitable crop of shallots.) But as more and more people sought to engage more fully in commercial agriculture, in part to offset the loss in income that had resulted from overfishing and the de- struction of the copra industry, the Anlo also began to face serious problems of land shortage.[39]

---

[38] Dotse, "Agricultural Geography," 65, 102; FN 70: Interview with Mr. Kwami Kpodo, 12 January 1988, Woe; G. Kwaku Nukunya, "The Effects of Cash Crops on an Ewe Community," in J. Goody, ed., *Changing Social Structure in Ghana* (London, 1975), 61.

[39] Boserup, Gleave and White, and Gyasi argue that farmers who face the problem of land shortage tend to respond to such difficulties by making specific changes in the way in which they handle their lands. Among these changes are the adoption of more intensive cultivation methods, such as manuring, in order

Of concern here is the impact these developments had on the gendered way in which families managed the allocation of their resources. It appears that as more and more people sought to engage in commercial agriculture, husbands and elders responded to the increased demands for land by establishing new criteria for the allocation of both lineage and personally acquired lands.

Women and the Burden of Economic Change

During the late 1800s and early 1900s, the Anlo practiced bilateral inheritance, in which both sons and daughters inherited land from their mothers and fathers. Land inherited by a daughter was not reclaimed by her brothers on her death; rather her land would be inherited by her own sons and daughters. At the time, this passage of land from a father to his daughter's children was not seen as a loss for the male members of the family, as relations between the two families were reinforced through two additional practices: the much-preferred marriage between mother's son and brother's daughter (matrilateral cross-cousin marriage), and the avunculate, which saw a mother's son living with and working for his mother's brother for extensive periods of time, and then inheriting those assets acquired during the uncle's life-time.[40]

By the mid-twentieth century, however, family elders who followed the traditional bilateral system of inheritance of inherited property and the avuncular inheritance of acquired property found that the demand for land from family members far outstripped the available plots. Conflicts between lineage members escalated as family members involved in the commercial fishing and copra industries sought to move more completely into the agricultural sector of the economy, while continued subdivision often left plots too small for profitable agriculture. These developments affected the family management of land in three ways. First, nephews were gradually eliminated as automatic members of the inheritance pool unless they had contributed a significant amount of labor to the development of the lands in question. This solution was given official sanction during the 1940s when the *awoamefia* of Anlo issued a decree in which he urged that the practice of giving

---

to increase yields and frequency of cropping. An examination of the agricultural history of the Anlo area indicates that the problem of land shortage and the adoption of more intensive methods had begun to characterize the agricultural practices of the Anlo situated on the littoral by at least the period between 1900 and 1930. See Ester Boserup, *The Conditions of Agricultural Growth: The Economics of Agrarian Change under Population Pressure* (Chicago, 1965), 56–64; M. B. Gleave and H. P. White, "Population Density and Agricultural Systems in West Africa," in M. F. Thomas and G. W. Whittington, eds., *Environment and Land Use in Africa* (London, 1969); E. A. Gyasi, "Population Pressure and Changes in Traditional Agriculture: Case Study of Farming in Sekesua–Agbelitson, Ghana," *Bulletin of the Ghana Geographical Association* 18 (1976); Dotse, *Shallot Farming*, 15; G. Benneh, "Land Tenure and Sabala Farming in the Anlo Area of Ghana," *Research Review* (Legon) 7, 2 (1971) 74; G. Kwaku Nukunya, "The Anlo-Ewe and Full-Time Maritime Fishing: Another View," *MAST* 2,2 (1989) 171n.2.

[40] FN 61: Interview with Mr. Xovi Banini, 5 January 1988, Anloga, and FN 70: Interview with Mr. Kwami Kpodo, 12 January 1988, Woe. Anlo Traditional Council Minute Book No. 3 (14/4/60–23/7/87), Chief Tsagli -v- Joachim Acolatse III, 122–23; Anlo Traditional Council Minute Book, 1931–1932, 877–927; Anlo Traditional Council Minute Book, 1933–1935, p. 25–26, 86–87; S. C. 14/3, 337; Härtter, "Sitten und Gebräuche," 43; Westermann, "Die Glidyi-Ewe," 141–42, 145, 264, 266, 133–34; see also Ward, "An Example," Dickson, "Marital Selection," and Nukunya, *Kinship and Marriage*, on the prevalence of matrilateral cross-cousin marriage. See also Patten, "Avuncular Family," 140, 210n.2.

land to nephews be dropped.[41] Second, women (who had already begun to lose access to lands traditionally passed from mother to daughter because of their enhanced value for commercial agriculture) also lost their automatic rights of inheritance to family land by the 1960s. Twenty years later S. Patten observed that it had become rare for daughters to inherit any land at all.[42] Third, husbands no longer allocated specific portions of their agricultural plots to their wives to do with as they pleased. There simply was not enough land to continue this practice. Instead, women could only work on their husbands' plots, helping to cultivate both subsistence and commercial crops using an intercropping and rotation system.

During this same period, from the 1930s to the 1960s, it appears that increasing numbers of women also began to face unpredictable support from their husbands. We know, for example, that after World War I, many Anlo males began to participate in migrant fishing on a large scale.[43] Some ten to fifteen years later, in the 1930s, the destruction of the copra industry prompted another group of men to leave the area to work in the cocoa industry.[44] If the Anlo migrants were like so many others who left their home areas to work elsewhere, their departure was often accompanied by more limited support for their spouses. The cost of living away from their homes and families, the desire for local companionship (which would have required men to spend a certain amount of their discretionary income on local women), and fluctuations in their wages caused by poor agricultural yields or fish catches all contributed to the decreased support many migrant men gave their wives still resident in their home areas. [45] Inadequate support was not limited to migrant men, however. Others who remained in the area, no doubt, also found it difficult at times to provide the kind of support expected and needed by their wives. If floods damaged one's sugar cane and shallot fields, as happened for many in 1917, 1929, 1931–1932, 1934, 1943, and 1963, these commercial farmers would have found it difficult to meet all their financial obligations.[46] By the 1940s, these obligations would have included the on-going expenses associated with then-current farming practices: the purchasing of seeds, fertilizer, and labor, and the education of one's children, an expenditure more and more Anlo families were prepared to make as opportunities to make money in government, the skilled trades, and other service sectors expanded. Men also felt pressured to devote a certain amount of income to projects and practices that demonstrated their social standing within the community. These included polygyny and the construction of homes using more prestigious building materials such as cement and metal roofing sheets. The extent to which Anlo men valued these practices as markers of their status in the 1960s was noted by G. K. Nukunya:

---

[41] Patten, "Avuncular Family," 123.

[42] Nukunya, *Kinship and Marriage*, 44n.1; Nukunya, "Land Tenure," 73; Patten, "Avuncular Family," 123.

[43] FN 70: Interview with Mr. Kwami Kpodo, 12 January 1988, Woe. G. Kwaku Nukunya, *The History of the Woe Evangelical Presbyterian Church, 1887–1987* (Woe, Ghana, 1987), 20.

[44] Dotse, "Agricultural Geography," 65.

[45] Numerous scholarly studies have been conducted on the effects of male labor migration on the household. See Mair, *African Marriage and Social Change*, 20–25; Verdon, *The Abutia Ewe*, 144; Christine Obbo, *African Women: Their Struggle for Economic Independence* (London, 1980), 84; Hagan, "Marriage." See Nukunya, "The Anlo-Ewe and Full-Time Maritime Fishing," 160, 163–64, on the financial ups and downs of the fishing industry.

[46] ADM 39/1/173; Dotse, "Agricultural Geography," 9–25.

Polygyny earns prestige and respect. According to the Anlo themselves, if you have only one wife she will not respect you. . . . The incidence of polygyny is comparatively high in Woe and Alakple. Although only 42.4 percent representing 94 out of 222 men, had more than one wife at the time of our census, 64.4 percent had experienced polygyny at least once in their lives.

My informants were [also] unanimous in their view that what differentiated an adult [male] from a child both in the past and in the present was the former's establishment of an independent house and ipso facto his independence from his father. An adult son as a rule does not live in his parents' house. . . . Within the last three decades, story buildings and bungalows, the goal of every ambitious Anlo youth, have replaced the old traditional mud huts.[47]

In their efforts to meet these new social standards, men increasingly expected their wives to contribute more and more to the upkeep of the household.[48]

These two developments—the loss of access to lineage land and plots from their husbands with which they could do as they wished, and a decrease in regular support from husbands—had particularly serious consequences for women, since the only way a wife could supplement her *asigbe* (the market-day money that a husband was required to give to his wife to purchase food and other necessities for the household) was to use her own independent income.[49] Yet the ability of most women to supplement substantially their household budgets was severely limited by decisions taken by their natal families and their husbands. As indicated, lineage elders limited women's access to lineage land on which they could grow their own crops for sale; husbands no longer gave wives exclusive use rights to portions of their own land. Furthermore, few opportunities existed for women in the colonial and independent Ghanaian economy. Most parents limited their investments in their daughters' education. Positions open to those who did receive Western education were quite limited because of the emphasis on schooling women to perform those tasks deemed appropriate for their gender.[50] Most parents and elders chose, instead, to encourage their daughters to engage in some form of trade, an occupation in which so many women came to participate that it was difficult to obtain significant profits unless one had considerable skill and a source of financial support.[51] In response to these developments, Anlo women began to seek alternative ways to maintain their economic independence.

Anlo Women Respond

Oral traditions and European documentary sources indicate that during the nineteenth century men and women tended to work cooperatively to produce and

---

[47] Nukunya, *Kinship and Marriage*, 132, 142; Nukunya, "Effects of Cash Crops," 67.

[48] Nukunya, *Kinship and Marriage*, 109.

[49] Ibid.

[50] See Claire C. Robertson, *Sharing the Same Bowl: A Socio-Economic History of Women and Class in Africa* (Bloomington, 1984), 136–37 and 141–45, for a general discussion about the education of women in southern Ghana.

sell their agricultural crops and fish. By the middle of the twentieth century, however, Anlo women had significantly limited their participation in the cultivation
of crops, particularly cash-crops. For example, in his discussion of the labor activities associated with shallot farming, Nukunya noted in 1962 that the sowing,
weeding, harvesting, and preparation of the onions for sale, once activities in
which both women and men participated, was now a "predominantly male af-
fair . . . only a few [wives] help their husbands [when] many hands are needed;
a polygynous farmer may . . . have assistance from his wives [but only] if they
are free."[52] This lack of participation by women in the cultivation of cash crops
exists elsewhere in Africa. Many explain this phenomenon by discussing the factors that either "pushed" and/or "pulled" women out of this kind of activity.
Ester Boserup, for example, emphasized the extent to which colonial policies
pushed women out of cash crop agriculture by giving preference to male farmers when they introduced more productive methods of cultivation and technical
assistance into these communities. This, in turn, is said to have led to women's
inability to produce at the same level as men. The result, according to Boserup,
"is that women [were] discouraged from participating in agriculture and [were]
glad to abandon cultivation whenever the increase in their husband's income
[made] it possible."[53] C. Ember, on the other hand, argues that intensive agriculture "pulled" women away from working on the land by generating changes in
their household duties. She states, "women in intensive agricultural societies have
significantly more . . . domestic work because they have more food processing
and preparation, more other household chores, and perhaps, most important, more
children."[54]

While Anlo women experienced both "push" and "pull" effects, the specific
characteristics of these factors were quite different from those described by
Boserup and Ember. European interest in the Anlo shallot industry dates only to
the 1940s; the colonial government did little to promote the crop prior to that
period because they did not include it as a priority for export.[55] Shallots were
grown for domestic consumption, and many of the innovations introduced into
the industry by the 1940s, such as the use of cow manure from Tongu for fertilizer, and the use of sanding to make the lagoon-side soils agriculturally useful

---

[51] See FN 69: Interview with Togbui Dzobi Adzinku, 7 January 1988, Anloga. See Robertson, *Sharing the
Same Bowl*, Chs. 4–5, for a detailed discussion of these issues as they affected the Ga women of Accra.
Sonia Gustavson Patten and Godwin K. Nukunya, "Organizational Responses to Agricultural Intensifica-
tion in Anloga, Ghana," *African Studies Review* 75, 2/3 (1982), 72–74. See also Christine Oppong, *Marriage
Among a Matrilineal Elite: A Family Study of Ghanaian Senior Civil Servants* (Cambridge, 1974), 92–94, who
discusses this phenomenon as it existed among the matrilineal elite of Ghana at mid-century.

[52] Nukunya, *Kinship and Marriage*, 158–59; see also Patten, "Avuncular Family," 181.

[53] Ester Boserup, *Woman's Role in Economic Development* (New York, 1970), 56.

[54] Carol R. Ember, "The Relative Decline in Women's Contribution to Agriculture with Intensification,"
American Anthropologist 85, 2 (1983), 299.

[55] See for example Stein, "Agriculture," 160, who fails to even mention the cultivation of shallots among
the food crops grown in the area. Cited in Hill, "Notes," 1. In 1941, the colonial government began to
keep records of the quantities of shallots exported from Anlo via the Anyanui and Tefle ferries and at
customs posts at Aflao and Ave-Aferingba. See S. T. Quansah, "The Shallot Industry, Incorporating a
Recent Survey of the Anloga Growing Area," *New Gold Coast Farmer*, 1, 2 (1956), 45. More government
interest and support developed in the early 1950s when the Department of Agriculture established an
experimental plot testing the effects of mineral nutrients on shallot growing.

were by local initiative.[56] Colonial intervention had little to do with pushing women out of cash crop agriculture in Anlo. The second argument—that women were "pulled" into additional domestic work—rests on the notion that intensive agriculture is associated with higher fertility rates (which makes it necessary for women to spend more time on childcare) and a shift from root crop production to grains (which require more preparation for cooking). There is no evidence that Anlo fertility rates have increased at a rate higher than those found among other groups in Ghana that do not practice intensive agriculture,[57] and the Anlo have always relied on grain cultivation as the basis of their diet.[58] I would argue instead that Anlo women "exited" the cash crop agricultural system when the opportunity presented itself, as the second part of Boserup's explanation suggests. Lack of access to land on which they could obtain profits for themselves pushed women out of serious involvement in this type of cultivation. The opportunity to spend more time engaged in activities that gave them a source of independent income pulled them away. Evidence to support this thesis comes from the history of the shallot and fishing industries.

In the 1930s, when many Anlos on the littoral abandoned sugar cane and copra as cash crops and became involved in the intensive cultivation of shallots as a means to maintain or enhance their income, they found that household members (wives, children, and possibly nieces and nephews) could no longer perform all the tasks associated with the cultivation and harvesting of a crop that was sown throughout the year.[59] It therefore became necessary, certainly by the 1950s, for many to hire labor to perform some of the more arduous and time-consuming tasks. These included the carting of beach sand from the Atlantic littoral to the agricultural fields where it would be used to raise the beds above the water table, the cutting of a variety of grasses which were then dried and inserted into the sides of the beds to prevent erosion, and the grading of the harvested shallots by size. Farmers also hired labor to supplement the work of household members in the planting, weeding, watering, sowing, and bundling of shallots to be sold. It appears, however, that this use of hired labor by males provided many wives with the opportunity to avoid heavy involvement or any involvement at all in this kind of work. When Nukunya interviewed shallot farmers in the town of Woe in 1962, he found that many women did not assist their male relatives or their husbands in the cultivation of their cash crops. In 1978, Patten observed the same in Anloga.[60] Instead, with the support and encourage-

---

[56] These practices were well in place by the time the independent government of Ghana began to make the services of the Department of Agriculture available to local shallot farmers. See Quansah, "Shallot Industry," G. Kwaku Nukunya, "Onion Farming by the Keta Lagoon," *Bulletin of the Ghana Geographical Association*, II, 2 (1957), and Lamar E. Fort, "The Shallot Industry in South Anlo District, Ghana," *Ghana Farmer* IV, 3 (1960).

[57] See Samuel Gaisie, "Fertility Trends and Differentials," in John Caldwell, ed., *Population Growth and Socio-economic Change in West Africa* (New York, 1975), who discusses fertility rates throughout Ghana and finds the major variables affecting the rates have more to do with education, socio-economic status, contraceptive knowledge, degree of urbanization, malnutrition, disease, age at marriage, and physical mobility rather than the kind of agriculture practiced.

[58] FN 50: Interview with Boko Seke Axovi, 12 March 1979, Anloga.

[59] Dotse, *Shallot Farming*, 15.

[60] Patten, "Avuncular Family," 181.

ment of their natal families, women focused their energies on trade, which would provide their own source of income.

Similar developments appear to have occurred in the fishing industry. When lagoon fishing had declined in importance in the late nineteenth and early twentieth centuries, most Anlos interested in continued involvement in this activity as a profit-making business did so by associating themselves with wealthy *yevudo* owners. A number of the fishermen who pursued this course may have attached themselves to net owners to whom they were related, but most often they worked for whomever needed their labor, and all worked as employees, receiving quite specific benefits and compensation for their services.[61] The commercialization of this industry appears to have also transformed the relationship that existed between the fishermen and the women who took responsibility for processing and marketing the fish—most often the wives, sisters, and/or daughters of the fishermen. These women no longer assisted the male fishermen as part of their spousal or kinship responsibility; instead they worked with the fishermen in order to generate profits for their own use.[62] They purchased fish on credit from the company with which their male fisherman was associated; they then preserved and sold the fish at a price that allowed them to repay the loan and keep some of the profits for themselves.[63]

Women also established a number of gender-based networks or unions to increase the profits they could obtain from marketing. S. Patten, who has discussed these networks in detail as they operated in 1978, indicates that they operated on both a formal and an informal level. For example, women appear to have had an informal relationship with the wholesalers to whom they sold their male relative's shallots. According to Patten, at the end of each market day, male farmers expected their female relatives who were selling their produce in the market on their behalf to give an account of the day's business and to hand over whatever sales receipts they had received, less the costs they had incurred for transportation and food. Many women, however, retained more than the latter amount so as to gain compensation for the time spent in the market. They were able to do so, despite the objections of their husbands or male relatives, because the head of the wholesalers refused to divulge the selling price for that market day when approached by the farmers. As many noted, "wives are not well-rewarded for their marketing efforts; most take a small amount out [of the profits] for themselves. . . . [The husbands have] no need to know about this."[64]

Women who operate as wholesalers, and those who work for the male farmers, headloading sand and manure to the fields, and/or conveying the crops from the fields to the farmers' house where they prepare them for the market, all have

---

[61] See Manshard, "Die Küsten"; Rowena M. Lawson, "The Structure, Migration and Re-settlement of Ewe Fishing Units," *African Studies* 17, 1 (1958); Hill, "Ewe Seine Fishermen"; Surgy, *La Pêche Traditionelle*; G. Kwaku Nukunya, "Letter—Pan African Fishermen," *West Africa* 2433 (1964) and "The Anlo-Ewe and Full-Time Maritime Fishing"; Paul Jorion, "Going Out and Staying Home: Seasonal Movements and Migration Strategies among Xwla and Anlo-Ewe Fishermen," *MAST* 1, 2 (1988).

[62] See Lawson, "Structure, Migration, and Re-settlement" 22, who gives the earliest accounts of this relationship; note that Robertson, *Sharing the Same Bowl*, 194–95, reports similar developments in the fishing culture of the Ga peoples of Accra.

[63] See Hill, "Ewe Seine Fishermen," and Surgy, *La Pêche Traditionelle*, for detailed descriptions of this relationship.

[64] Patten, "Avuncular Family," 194.

PHOTO 7: The Shallot Market in Keta in the mid-1960s

more formal organizations, which they have used to support and/or improve their economic position within the local agricultural system. In 1976, for example, the women in the town of Anloga who worked for farmers headloading sand and manure to the fields and who were organized into a number of separate organizations agreed to cooperate with one another in an effort to demand an increase in the rate they received for each hour of work. At that time, they received 1.50 cedis for four hours' work; they demanded that they receive the same rate as the men whom the farmers also hired to assist with the agricultural work. That rate was 4 cedis for four hours. The farmers complied.

The Anlo Shallot Marketing Union and the Tomato Sellers Union, both wholesale organizations composed almost exclusively of women, have engaged in similar action. For the sake of brevity, however, I include here only a description of how the shallot wholesalers have operated to protect each others' interests.

> The market in Anloga, as in the entire [Anlo] area, is held every fifth day. Unionized shallot sellers, most of them also Ewe women, arrive from Accra and Kumasi on alternate market days. . . . [L]ong-standing relationships [have sprung] up between individual [women from Anloga and their counterparts in Kumasi and Accra]. The partners refer to one another as *asisi* or market spouse. It is a relationship that is characterized by congeniality, hospitality (food, or a place to sleep may be offered), economic benefits (the Anlo union members extend credit to their *asisiwo* from outside, who in turn purchase preferentially from their partners in the relationship), and sometimes long-lasting friendship.
>
> It is also a relationship that has been poorly understood by male farmers in the area. In 1975, a group of farmers decided to bypass the local women in the marketing process and truck the shallots to Kumasi for sale to Kumasi market women. The men were not prepared to sell on credit; they were not aware of the marketing arrangements the women worked out. The men lowered their asking price to induce the Kumasi women to buy, but they refused to take advantage of the situation because it would have eliminated their Anloga "market spouses" involvement in the very lucrative trade and because they had no alternative source of credit. So the shallots rotted. . . .[65]

By pursuing these cooperative strategies, and by taking advantage of the use of hired labor in commercial agriculture and the commercialization of relations between net owners and male fishermen, Anlo women have managed to maintain some measure of their economic independence despite the challenges created by their husbands, parents, and lineage elders, who opted to sacrifice the interests of their female relatives and wives as a means of responding to their own problems and opportunities.

These efforts, in combination with the impact of European colonial rule, have generated signficant changes in Anlo gender relations. Divorce has become an accepted option available to individuals experiencing marital difficulties, along with separation and membership in Yewe;[66] individuals, both men and women, can opt to marry or remain single.[67] Selection of a spouse can take many forms: families

---

[65] Ibid., 192, 193–94.

[66] See FN 111: Interview with Mr. Richard Tetteh, 28 March 1992, Ithaca, New York; and Torgby, "Origin and Organisation," on the character of Yewe and its appeal to women from the 1970s to the 1990s.

[67] See Lynne Brydon, "Women at Work: Some Changes in Family Structure in Amedzofe—Avatime, Ghana," *Africa*, 42, 2 (1979), and "Avatime Women and Men, 1900–1980," in Christine Oppong, ed., *Female and Male in West Africa* (Boston, 1983), who discusses the development of non-marriage among the women of Avatime. It is likely that the same is true for Anlo women.

can arrange the marriage, individuals may opt to marry someone suggested by their parents; or the young can choose their spouse free of either lineage control or influence.[68] A few women continue to inherit a limited number of agricultural plots, and daughters have successfully challenged lineage efforts to exclude them from inheritance of land,[69] but they can also purchase land outright if they have the capital to do so.[70] Women can assist their husbands in the cultivation of their cash crops or they can legitimately refuse to do so and concentrate their energies on activities that generate income for themselves such as marketing. Household heads, a group that previously consisted almost exclusively of men and older women who were widowed, now include younger women who are divorced and who have chosen not to remarry, the wives of migrant husbands, and women who are still married to their husbands but who have the income to build their own homes, and do so in anticipation of possible divorce or separation.[71] This expansion in the boundaries that had previously defined normative gender roles and relations among the Anlo has occurred not only because of the dramatic changes introduced by colonial rule and European culture, but also because Anlo women have continued to challenge into the twentieth century those aspects of Anlo gender relations that disadvantage them.

The Ethnic Dimension of Gendered Change

Changes in gender relations in twentieth-century Anlo have also facilitated changes in ethnic relations and identities as Anlo women responded to their economic marginalization. This is most apparent if we briefly re-examine the history of gender relations in Anlo. In Chapters 1 and 2, I noted that in the late nineteenth century, Anlo women took principal responsibility for educating their offspring about their clan identity. They taught them the specific rules and ritual prohibitions of their clans. They encouraged their children to view marriage to a fellow *hlo* member as particularly refined. This socialization, in turn, contributed to a relatively high rate of clan endogamy as well as the reinforcement of ethnic divisions within the society which defined certain clans as ethnic insiders and others as outsiders. During this same period, Anlo women gained a degree of social and ritual protection and were able to maintain their economic independence by using, in part, their status as clan members to demand support from their particular *hlo*, since this body's raison d'être was to use the control it had over powerful gods and/or specific tracts of land for the benefit of its members.

By the mid-twentieth century, however, much had changed. Many whom the Anlo had previously defined as ethnic "others" had been redefined by the educated and political elite in Anlo as integral and central members of Anlo society. The commercialization of agriculture created intense demands for the very limited

---

[68] See Dickson, "Marital Selection," for a detailed discussion of these options and the frequency with which they occur.

[69] See Nukunya, "Land Tenure," 74.

[70] See Patten and Nukunya, "Organizational Responses," 75.

[71] See Nukunya, *Kinship and Marriage*, 127–36, and Nukunya, "Effects of Cash Crops," as well as Patten, "Avuncular Family," 160–61.

agricultural lands in the area. At the same time, clan elders gradually lost authority over the landed property of the *hlo*, and clan affiliation as a source of identity and protection lost much of its significance. Family elders no longer automatically bequeathed land to daughters and sisters. Husbands no longer gave a portion of their land to their wives on which to grow their own crops. These facts raise a number of questions about the nature of the social identities that Anlo women imparted to their children as they prepared them for their future roles in Anlo society. Did twentieth-century Anlo women continue to encourage their children to view themselves first as members of particular clans? Or did their experiences as women encourage them to alter the way in which they socialized their children? Answers to these questions can only be tentative at this stage, but the evidence that does exist suggests that many Anlo women actively participated in supporting the identity changes that the Anlo embraced during the colonial period and after because of the impact that the twentieth-century changes in gender relations had had on their lives. This is perhaps most apparent from analyses of contemporary marital patterns. We know, for example, that intra-clan marriage has declined significantly since the late nineteenth century. Yet we also know that parents—both mothers and fathers—continue to exert considerable influence (although not control) over the marital choices of their children. In 1969, Nukunya reported that 71 percent of all marriages in Anlo were *fomesro* unions (marriages between patrilateral or matrilateral relations) because such marriages were preferred by all. In 1983, Dickson reported that 69 percent of all Anlo marriages were *fomesro* unions. In his words, "parental *influence* as opposed to *control* is still a major factor in marital selection in Anlo as reflected in . . . the continuing frequency of *fomesro* marriage . . . [even] as mutual choice marriage is on the rise and parental arrangement on the decline."[72] The fact that so few women marry within their own clan even while parents continue to influence their choices suggests that many parents—mothers included—de-emphasize the value of clan endogamy. It is less relevant for their own social or economic well-being or for that of their children because of the commercialization of agriculture, the intense competition for an insufficient supply of land, and the decline in the power of traditional religious beliefs. A person's clan identity no longer influences how individuals and groups will interact with him. It no longer determines the economic assets to which one has access. In response to this change Anlo women—as mothers and aunts—no longer give priority to those boundaries that once defined certain clans as ethnic insiders and others as outsiders. Such identities are also no longer socially or economically relevant to themselves or to their children.

This change in the way Anlo women socialize their children may have been a consequence, in part, of their exposure to and acceptance of some aspects of European culture. But I believe that their own experiences as women have contributed much more to this development. When their own clan elders lost the ability to use their religious and economic assets to help women maintain their social and economic status, and when their own lineages began to deprive them of the right to inherit land, many women responded by establishing non-kin-based unions and cooperatives to protect their economic interests in ways that the clan system was no longer capable of doing. It was this experience, I would suggest, that most in-

---

[72] Dickson, "Marital Selection," 165.

fluenced Anlo women to de-emphasize the significance of clan identity. Their actions, in turn, contributed significantly to a more general acceptance among the Anlo of the notion that the identity of one's clan as ethnic insider or outsider is largely irrelevant.

Changes in gender relations not only encouraged a reduced emphasis on ethnic divisions based on the social identity of one's clan. It also promoted acceptance of the recently developed Ewe ethnic identity. Perhaps the best illustration of this fact comes from an analysis of the Anlo Shallot Marketing Union. I indicated above that when Anlo women found themselves increasingly deprived of their rights to gain access to land, they established a number of gender-based cooperatives and unions as a means to maintain some level of control over their lives as workers and traders. Those involved in the marketing of shallots formed the Anlo Shallot Marketing Union in the 1950s. They then began using kinship terminology (*asisiwo*, market spouses) when referring to their business partners in Accra and Kumase to reinforce the economic interests that brought them together. More important for this study is the fact that the vast majority of these *asisiwo* are Ewe (and not necessarily Anlo). According to Gracia Clark, this is most unusual. In her study of the ethnic and gendered character of the Kumasi central market, most coastal women (of whom the Anlo would be included) concentrate their retailing and wholesaling efforts in their own home areas. They leave the long-distance wholesale trade in locally produced goods to the Kumasi market to Asante women. The only exception are those involved in wholesale distribution of shallots. This activity has been dominated by Ewe women since the 1930s. Significantly, the way in which these women have maintained that dominance entails the use of their Ewe identity to limit competition. As Clark notes,

> Ewe women traders from [the] Volta Region admitted no outsiders on their route, bringing truckloads of shallots to Kumasi from irrigated farms near Keta and Anloga to supplement seasonal supplies from Asante villages. . . .[73]

The success of their efforts are noticeable to anyone who ventures into the Anloga market on market day. They can be found sitting under a well-constructed shelter rather than in the open or under trees. Market women coming from outside Anlo to buy shallots can be found consulting these women whenever they need credit, since any member of the Anlo Shallot Union is in a position to offer credit to others. Their success has also contributed significantly to ethnic change in Anlo. By using to their great advantage the new identity construct of being "Ewe," members of the Anlo Shallots Union, by example, have encouraged others to embrace this new identity.

Conclusion

This chapter has illustrated the fact that major changes were occurring in gender relations between the late nineteenth century and the late twentieth century. Many

---

[73] Gracia Clark, *Onions Are My Husband: Survival and Accumulation by West African Market Women* (Chicago, 1994), 321.

more women began to exercise greater influence over their own marital affairs by selecting their spouse and initiating divorce with or without their parents' consent. Woman also began to lose their economic independence. Lineage elders, over time, diminished the quantity of land they were prepared to allocate to the women in their families. By the late twentieth century, women found it all but impossible to inherit any land at all. They also lost access to the agricultural plots previously allocated to them by their husbands. These developments, in turn, meant that women found it increasingly difficult to profit from the commercialization of agriculture. The response by women introduced yet another set of changes in Anlo gender relations. Women organized themselves into gender-based cooperatives and unions, and through these, retained some measure of their economic independence, an independence which—in combination with the impact of Western education, migration, and the decline of traditional religious beliefs—saw women expand the norms that governed gender relations in late twentieth-century Anlo. Divorce has now become an acceptable option. Women may select their own spouse, have their parents arrange marriages for them, or remain single. They may live with their husbands, brothers, or fathers. They can also establish themselves as head of their own household if they have the resources.

This chapter has also emphasized the fact that the changes occurring in twentieth-century gender relations have continued to affect ethnic relations. With the loss of their ability to participate as farmers in commercial agriculture because of the actions taken by their families and husbands, Anlo women began to alter the way in which they socialized their children. They de-emphasized the significance of clan identity as an important factor influencing how one should interact with others. They also used the recently developed Ewe identity within their unions and cooperatives as a means to protect their economic interests. These, in turn, reinforced the changes that were occurring in Anlo ethnic relations, changes that involved the development of a more inclusive definition of the "we" within Anlo, and acceptance of a new broader identification with other Ewe-speaking peoples in the region.

Conclusion

Much has been written separately about gender and ethnicity in precolonial Africa, but rarely are these two phenomena considered together within the same study. This social history of precolonial Anlo has broken with this tradition in order to emphasize the fact that gender and ethnic relations significantly influenced one another from the seventeenth through the twentieth centuries. We cannot fully understand the history of either one in isolation; the two were intimately and inextricably connected. Changes in one had a direct impact on the other.

This study has also expanded the analytical tools used to study male/female relations in precolonial Africa as a separate area of study. It has emphasized the importance of situating changes in gender relations within the larger context of the demographic, political, social, economic, and religious changes that were occurring within precolonial Africa. It has demonstrated the extent to which both the patrilineage and the marital household were major locations for the oppression of women. Evidence in support of these points is given throughout this study, with particular prominence in the first two chapters. There, I discussed the political events on the upper Slave Coast that brought numerous refugees into the Anlo area in the late seventeenth century and the way in which most refugees were continually defined by the earlier residents as "other" throughout the eighteenth and nineteenth centuries. I then linked these developments directly to changes in gender relations which saw both ethnic insider and outsider family elders significantly limit the extent to which they took young women's voices into consideration when making decisions about their lives. As a result, young women found themselves increasingly marginalized within their own patrilineages in comparison with young men. Many who found themselves negatively affected by these developments accepted their situation, while others opted to resist. It was the actions of this latter group which brought about even greater changes in gender relations in Anlo by the end of the nineteenth century. These findings in themselves are not unique. Other scholars have documented similar developments during the colonial period. What distinguishes this study from others is that it avoids demonizing the individuals and groups who marginalized members of their own families on the basis of gender. It also refrains from using the notion of "false consciousness" to explain why some young women participated in their own marginalization. I document the fact, for example, that most Anlo family elders did indeed disadvantage their

181

young women. I note, however, these elders (a group that included both men and women) did so in the context of competing with other patrilineages for social prestige and for the control of the arable land resources. I also document the fact that many of the young women who were being disadvantaged supported their family's decisions. They did so not because they were unaware of alternatives. Rather, they frequently found the alternatives unattractive or unattainable because of ritual injunctions. Others were simply prepared to sacrifice their own personal interests for the sake of their families because they saw no distinction between the two. Focusing on this complex interplay of gender relations, kinship obligations, and external forces does not deny the fact that women were being disadvantaged and that many young women within Anlo recognized their situation and fought against it. Rather, by highlighting the fact that men and women made a variety of choices as to how they would respond to changing demographic, social, political, economic, and religious conditions, this study has emphasized the importance of moving the discussion of gender relations beyond the simplistic, analytical categories of oppression and agency. We must also determine why African women and men as individuals and as members of social groups made particular choices, consciously or unconsciously, when they did. Only then can we begin to understand why gender relations in any given society changed in particular ways.

This study has examined the history of ethnic relations in precolonial Anlo using the same analytical tools noted above. It has examined the context in which changes in Anlo ethnic definitions of "we" and "they" occurred. It has documented the fact that many ethnic outsiders worked to defy their social marginalization. It has explained why some achieved success, why others did not, and why still others were uninterested in altering their social identity and status as outsiders. This study has also challenged some of the prevailing definitions of ethnicity. Vail and Ranger have defined ethnicity as a contemporary concept created by colonizers, missionaries, and educated Africans, in which the sense of "we" and "they" was based on invented cultural, linguistic, and/or regional groupings. I have extended this definition of ethnicity to include fictive and real kinship constructions and notions about the relative time at which one's ancestors settled in a particular area. This expansion allows one to emphasize the fact that ethnic identities, as redefined, did exist in precolonial Africa, and that those who were marginalized in Anlo because of their ethnicity were very much involved in the reshaping of their own identities well before the advent of colonialism or missionary influence. Those who sought to alter their identities as "ethnic outsiders" de-emphasized their kinship ties to non-Anlos and the latecomer aspects of their ethnic identity. They argued instead that their ancestors were intimately connected to the ancestors of other Anlos because all were related and had lived together in the ancestral town of Notsie before their immigration to Anlo. At the same time, they utilized *within* their groups the notion that the members therein were the descendants of a common ancestor and therefore they should support the effort of the entire group to recast its identity. By extending the definition of ethnicity to include kinship and relative time of settlement, it becomes obvious that not only were many who had been socially defined as ethnic outsiders able to redefine themselves as insiders, but that they did so by redeploying for their own benefit the same local concepts that had been used to marginalize them socially. Their success challenged and eventually altered the prevailing character of Anlo ethnic relations during the eighteenth and nineteenth centuries. It also encouraged the Anlo to continue to use these local definitions during the twentieth century as they modified their conceptions of "we" and "they" under the influence of colonial rule.

A final concern addressed in this study involves the age-old issue of continuity and change. This study has emphasized the fact that signficant changes have occurred in gender and ethnic relations in Anlo since the late nineteenth century. Women have gained much greater control over their marital affairs. They can choose their own spouses and divorce them if they so desire; they can remain single. They have begun to purchase land for themselves when they find that they have been excluded by their families from the landed inheritance system. They are also beginning to establish themselves as heads of their own households. Similarly, many groups in Anlo previously disadvantaged because of ethnic identity have been successful since the advent of colonialism in reformulating their traditions, their rituals, and their identities so that they are no longer considered as ethnic outsiders. Yet, in both areas of social life, continuities with the past remain. Women continue to be the ones most often disadvantaged within their families when conditions require that such choices be made. There still exist in Anlo groups that are socially marginalized because they are defined as ethnically distinct from others within the society.

I have indicated, for example, that the Blu clan still feels the stigma of being defined as "other." In interviews with two of the clan's elders in 1978, they asked rhetorically with a mixture of anger and exasperation, "Can we be strangers after 100 years?" Two other groups, the Ame and Getsofe, face the same situation. Both *hlowo* are still remembered principally as having come to Anlo as captives, despite their invented ties of kinship and marriage to the other Anlo clans. Their association with Notsie is downplayed or non-existent. Late nineteenth- and early twentieth-century traditions as well as more contemporary narratives about both indicate that no one knows from where they came. The Ame, for example, are portrayed as constituting a group having no genealogical connection with the Notsie polity and culture with which the Anlo favorably associate themselves. The Getsofe are said to have come from the sun (*Ve* = sun, *tso* = come from, *fe* = home, that is, those that come from the sun). Both groups are assigned images that emphasize significant differences that separate them from the Anlo because of their supposed inhuman characteristics. The Abolo ancestors of the Ame, for example, are recalled as having committed a particularly heinous crime, one which forced the Anlo to drive all except those whom they captured out of the area. A similar tale is recited with regard to the Getsofe's ancestors, who are portrayed as wild and unmanageable in behavior, as well as not quite human in physical appearance. These narratives—still recited today although more often than not in private—indicate the continued existence of ethnic boundaries stigmatizing certain groups within Anlo society.[1]

---

[1] See FN 9: Interview with Mr. T. S. A. Togobo, 7 August 1978, Anloga; FN 18: Interview with Boko Seke Axovi, 29 August 1978, Anloga; FN 21: Interview with Mr. T. S. A. Togobo, 31 August 1978, Anloga; FN 59: Interview with Togbui Amawota, 23 December 1987, Anloga; FN 60: Interview with Togbui Tete Za Agbemako, 5 January 1988, Anloga; FN 61: Interview with Mr. Xovi Banini, 5 January 1988, Anloga; FN 65: Interview with Togbui Dzobi Adzinku, 6 January 1988, Anloga; ADM 11/1/1661, 97–98; Westermann, "Die Glidyi-Ewe," 148. See also Anlo State Council Minute Book, 9 January 1935, Chiefs Kata, Adaku, Avege, and Agblevo per Samuel Nutsuga for themselves and on behalf of the Tsiame tribe -v- Chiefs Zewu, Agbozo, Anakoo, Attipoe, and Zioklui, Davodji Banini et al. for themselves and on behalf of Agave Tribe, 374–75; and Patten, "Avuncular Family," 83–84.

Kinship relations and notions about relative time of settlement continue to be reinvented and used by all to reinforce specific ethnic definitions of "we" and "they." Gender and ethnic relations continue to influence one another. The existence of these specific areas of continuity and change within twentieth-century Anlo gender and ethnic relations reveals that while the particular nature of these relations has changed over time, Anlo men and women, ethnic insiders and outsiders, continue to employ the strategies used by their ancestors in the eighteenth and nineteenth centuries in their attempts to manage the forces affecting their lives.

Sources

Archival and Oral Sources

Denmark

Rigsarkiv, Copenhagen
GK: Guineiske Kompagnie
12–21: Kyst dokumenter, 1769–1778
144–150: Sekret protokoller, 1769–1778
152–159: Palaberbøger, 1767–1770, 1773–1777
162–172: Brevebøger, ført på Christiansborg, 1766–1775
173: Fiskalens, kopibog på Christiansborg, 1766: 18/10–1768: 17/3
183–191: Gaeldbøger, 1766–1773
196: Fortet Fredensborg Omkostningsbøger, 1774: 30/6–1776: 31/12
203: Orlogsomkostningsbøger, 1777 1/1–30/6
Gtk: Generaltoldkammerts Archiv, 1760–1848
Schimmelmanske Papier vedk. Kommissionerne betraeffende Guinea og Negerhandelen samt Forskellige Vestindiske Papier, 1778–1809
Guineiske Sager og Akstykker, 1765–1802 (ujournaliserede)
VgK: Vestindiske–guineiske Kompagnie
120–126: Breve og Dokumenter fra Guinea, 1683–1684, 1697–1754
188: Guvenør og andre betjente i Guinea, 1732–1754
800–883: Sekret protokoller ført på Christiansborg i Guinea, 1723–1754
884: Dag-journalen, ført på Christiansborg, 1679–1705
886–889: Brevebøger, ført på Christiansborg i Guinea, 1703–1705, 1709, 1723–1754

England

Public Records Office, Kew
T70/–: Treasury Papers, African Companies
30: Inward Letter Books, 1751–1818
54: Letters sent to Cape Coast Castle, 1764–1793
1565: Detached Papers, Parts I and II, 1792
Chancery Masters Exhibit
James Phipps Papers (C113/126–295), c. 100–1723
BT/6–: Board of Trade
6: Correspondence from the Committee, 1771–1788.

Bodleian Library, Oxford
Rawlinson Manuscripts, c. 745–747: Correspondence between Cape Coast Castle and Outforts, including Dixcove.

France

Archives National, Paris
Archives des Colonies: the full citation is contained in the footnotes.

Germany

Bremen Stadt Archives
Letters: 23 January 1857: B. Schlegel, Keta to Norddeutsche Missionsgesellschaft, Bremen

Ghana

Anlo Traditional Council Archives, Anloga
Anlo Traditional Council Minute Book, 1931–1932
Anlo Traditional Council Minute Book, 1933–1935
Anlo State Council Minute Book, June 1934–November 1946
Anlo State Council Minute Book, 9 January 1935
Anlo Traditional Council Minute Book, No. 3: 14/4/60–23/7/87
Tosu, L. P. (n.d.) Anlo Traditional Council Documents: A Short Account of the Awada-da Stool of Anlo.
Anlo Traditional Council Questionnaire: Kwashie Misewo Akorli, Stool Name: Dufia Akamu Adela Akpa, III. 3 April 1950.

Balme Library, University of Ghana, Legon
Furley Collection: Extracts from the Dutch, Danish and English Archives
    N37–N38: 1710–1715
    N40–N48: 1715–1757
    N– [sic]: D–1761
    N52–N54: 1765–1769
    N106—Miscellaneous 18th Century: B–WIC, Correspondence, 1716–1718

District Court Grade II Library, Anloga
Judicial Council Minute Books: 1913, 1919, 1921

Institute of African Studies, University of Ghana, Legon
Aduamah, E. Y. (n.d.) Ewe Traditions, 1–19.

National Archives of Ghana, Accra
ADM 4/1: Minute Books, 1896
ADM 11/: Administrative Papers of the Secretary of Native Affairs
    1091: Petition from Fia Adama II
    1/1107: Awuna Native Affairs (1978–1901)
    1/1113: Keta Native Affairs (1886–1910)
    1/1661: Notes of Evidence. Commission of Enquiry, 1912: Awuna, Addah, and Akwamu
    1/1246: Keta Native Affairs
ADM 12/3/1–3: Confidential Prints
ADM 39/1/173: Ho District

ADM 41/4/20–22: District Office Records, Keta
S.C. 14/1–14/3: The Old Diary—Remarkable Occurrences of the Gold Coast and Ashanti . . .

Ghana National Archives, Ho
Item No. 77: Anyako Native Affairs (Case No. 21/31): 2/8/29–17/11/40, Keta:Hector Atakpa, Acting Chief Anyako to the Honorable Awoame Fia, Togbui Sri II of Anlo, Anloga, 21 August 1930.

Netherlands

Algemeen Rijksarchief, The Hague
ANBKG: Het Archief van de Nedelandsche Bezittingen ter Kuste van Guinea; the additional aspects of this citation are contained in the footnotes.

United States

Center for Research Libraries, Chicago, Illinois
Amenyah Archives: Correspondence between I. Wilks and J. D. Amenyah

Greene Field Notes: on deposit with the author
FN 1: Mr. T. S. A. Togobo, 12 June 1978, Anloga
FN 2: Mama Ketor, 12 June 1978, Anloga
FN 4: Mama Dzagba, 12 June 1978, Anloga
FN 5: Mr. T. S. A. Togobo, 20 June 1978, Anloga
FN 6: Boko Seke Axovi, 1 August 1978, Anloga
FN 8: Mr. T. S. A. Togobo, 3 August 1978, Anloga
FN 9: Mr. T. S. A. Togobo, 7 August 1978, Anloga
FN 10: Boko Seke Axovi, 6 August 1978, Anloga
FN 11: Mr. T. S. A. Togobo, 7 August 1978, Anloga
FN 14: Togbui Trygod Yao Zodanu, 11 August 1978, Anloga
FN 15: Togbui Le II, 15 August 1978, Anloga
FN 16: Togbui Le II, 16 August 1978, Anloga
FN 17: Mr. T. S. A. Togobo, 28 August 1978, Anloga
FN 18: Boko Seke Axovi, 29 August 1978, Anloga
FN 20: Togbui Alex Afatsao Awadzi, 30 August 1978, Anloga
FN 21: Mr. T. S. A. Togobo, 31 August 1978, Anloga
FN 22: Togbui Yao Trygod Zodanu, 1 September 1978, Anloga
FN 24: Boko Seke Axovi, 5 September 1978, Anloga
FN 27: Togbui Dzobi Adzinku, 15 September 1978, Anloga
FN 30: Mr. T. S. A. Togobo, 26 September 1978, Anloga
FN 32: Togbui Sefoga, 30 September 1989, Anloga
FN 33: Boko Seke Axovi, 3 October 1978, Anloga
FN 34: Togbui Alex Afatsao Awadzi, 3 October 1978, Anloga
FN 35: Boko Seke Axovi, 4 October 1978, Anloga
FN 36: Togbui Ago Agbota and Togbui Kofi Ezu Agbota, 9 October 1978, Anloga
FN 37: Boko Seke Axovi, 9 October 1978, Anloga
FN 38: Boko Seke Axovi, 16 October 1978, Anloga
FN 39: Togbui Christian Yao Gbotoza Fiadzo, 16 October 1978, Anloga
FN 40: Togbui Atsu Klogo and Togbui Avege II, 17 October 1978, Anloga
FN 41: Boko Seke Axovi, 31 October 1978, Anloga
FN 42: Boko Seke Axovi, 1 November 1978, Anloga
FN 43: Mr. T. S. A. Togobo, 31 October 1978, Anloga

FN 44: Togbui Dzobi Adzinku, 6 November 1978, Anloga
FN 45: Togbui Dzobi Adzinku, 8 November 1978, Anloga
FN 47: Mr. T. S. A. Togobo, 8 November 1978, Anloga
FN 49: Togbui Afatsao Awadzi, 5 February 1979, Anloga
FN 50: Boko Seke Axovi, 12 March 1979, Anloga
FN 52: Togbui Dzobi Adzinku, 15 December 1987, Anloga
FN 53: Togbui Afatsao Awadzi, 16 December 1987, Anloga
FN 54: Togbui Tse Gbeku, 16 December 1987, Anloga
FN 55: Togbui Kosi Axovi, 17 December 1987, Anloga
FN 57: Mr. Robert G. Kofi Afetogbo, 22 December 1987, Anloga
FN 58: Mr. William Tiodo Anum Adzololo, 23 December 1987, Anloga
FN 59: Togbui Amawota, 23 December 1987, Anloga
FN 60: Togbui Tete Za Agbemako, 5 January 1988, Anloga
FN 61: Mr. Xovi Banini, 5 January 1988, Anloga
FN 62: Mr. K. A. Mensah, 5 January 1988, Anloga
FN 63: Mr. L. A. Banini, 5 January 1988, Anloga
FN 64: Mr. J. N. K. Dogbatse, 5 January, Anloga
FN 65: Togbui Dzobi Adzinku, 6 January 1988, Anloga
FN 69: Togbui Dzobi Adzinku, 7 January 1988, Anloga
FN 70: Mr. Kwami Kpodo, 12 January 1988, Woe
FN 72: Mr. Christian Nani Tamaklo and Mr. Stephen Kodzo Quist, 13 January 1988, Keta
FN 73: Mr. Johnnie Victor Kwame Adzololo, 14 January 1988, Keta
FN 74: Mr. A. W. Kuetuade-Tamaklo, 19 January 1988, Tegbi
FN 75: Mr. Kwami Kpodo, 19 January 1988, Woe
FN 76: Togbui Anthonio Gbodzo II and his councilors, 20 January 1988, Woe
FN 77: Mr. Kwami Kpodo, 20 January 1988, Woe
FN 78: Togbui Dzobi Adzinku, 20 January 1988, Anloga
FN 81: Togbui Joachim Acolatse IV, 26 January 1988, Keta
FN 82: Mama Dzagba, 27 January 1988, Anloga
FN 83: Mr. K. A. Mensah, 27 January 1988, Anloga
FN 86: Togbui Tay-Agbozo IV, 3 February 1988, Dzelukofe
FN 88: Togbui Tay-Agbozo IV, 4 February 1988, Dzelukofe
FN 91: Togbui Joachim Acolatse IV, 5 February 1988, Tema
FN 92: Togbui Amegashi Afeku IV, 18 February 1988, Accra-Nima
FN 93: Togbui Amegashi Afeku IV, 19 February 1988, Accra-Nima
FN 94: Mr. Klevor Abo, 20 February 1988, Accra-Legon
FN 96: Togbui Anthonio Gbodzo II and his councilors, 24 February 1988, Woe
FN 97: Mr. J. G. Kodzo-Vordoagu, 24 February 1988, Tegbi
FN 100:Togbui Awusu II, 29 March 1988, Atoko
FN 102:Togbui Midawo Alowu Attipoe, 6 April 1988, Anyako
FN 105:Mr. Kwami Kpodo, 20 April 1988, Woe
FN 108:Togbui Dzobi Adzinku, ? June 1988, Anloga
FN 111:Mr. Richard Tetteh, 28 March 1992, Ithaca, New York

Books and Articles

Afelevo, Stefano H. Kwadzo. "Ein Bericht über den Yehwekultus der Ewe. Herausgegeben mit deutscher Übersetzung und Anmerkungen von D. Westermann." *Mitteilungen des Seminars für Orientalische Sprachen*, 33/3 (1930), 1–55. Originally published in 1894.
Afonja, Simi. "Changing Modes of Production and the Sexual Division of Labor among the Yoruba." *Signs*, 7, 2 (1981), 299–313.

————"Land Control: A Critical Factor in Yoruba Gender Stratification." In Claire Robertson and Iris Berger, eds., *Women and Class in Africa*, 78–91. New York: Africana Publishing Company, 1986.

————"Changing Patterns of Gender Stratification." In Irene Tinker, ed., *Persistent Inequalities: Women and World Development*, 198–209. New York: Oxford University Press, 1990.

Agbodeka, Francis. *African Politics and British Policy in the Gold Coast, 1868–1890: A Study in the Forms and Forces of Protest*. Evanston: Longman/ Northwestern University Press, 1971.

Akinjogbin, I. A. *Dahomey and Its Neighbors, 1708–1818*. London: Cambridge University Press, 1967.

Aliwodsi, Christian. "Der Schlangendienst." *Monatsblatt der Norddeutschen Missionsgesellschaft*, 2/5 (1800), 27–28.

————"Ein Sittenbild aus Anyako." *Monatsblatt der Norddeutschen Missionsgesellschaft*, 2/5 (1800), 28–29.

Alpers, Edward A. "State, Merchant Capital and Gender Relations in Southern Mozambique to the End of the 19th Century: Some Tentative Hypotheses." *African Economic History*, 13 (1984), 23–55.

————"Ordinary Household Chores: Ritual and Power in a 19th Century Swahili Women's Spirit Possession Cult." *International Journal of African Historical Studies*, 17, 4 (1984), 677–702.

Amadiume, Ifi. *Male Daughters, Female Husbands: Gender and Sex in an African Society*. London: Zed Books, 1987.

Amenumey, D. E. K. "Geraldo de Lima: A Reappraisal." *Transactions of the Historical Society of Ghana*, IX (1968), 65–78.

————"New Myths in the History of Ghana: Anlo and the Asante Empire." *Universitas*, 4, 2 (1975), 181–86.

————*The Ewe Unification Movement*. Accra: Ghana Universities Press, 1989.

Anderson, Benedict. *Imagined Communities: Reflections on the Origin and Spread of Nationalism*. London: Verso Press, 1983.

"Anyako." *Monatsblatt der Norddeutschen Missionsgesellschaft*, 18/215 (1868), 291.

Arhin, Kwame. "Strangers and Hosts: A Study in the Political Organisation and History of Atebubu Town." *Transactions of the Historical Society of Ghana*, XII (1971), 63–81.

Barbot, J. *A Description of the Coasts of North and South Guinea*. London: Churchill, 1732.

Barnes, Sandra T. "Ritual, Power and Outside Knowledge." *Journal of Religion in Africa*, XX, 3 (1990), 248–68.

Barth, Fredrik. *Ethnic Groups and Boundaries: The Social Organization of Culture Difference*. London: George Allen and Unwin, 1969.

Bates, D. A. "Geology." In J. B. Wills, ed., *Agriculture and Land Use in Ghana*, 51–61. London: Oxford University Press, 1962.

Bay, Edna. "Introduction." In Edna Bay, ed., *Women and Work in Africa*, 1–17. Boulder: Westview Press, 1982.

Benneh, G. "Land Tenure and Sabala Farming in the Anlo Area of Ghana." *Research Review* (Legon), 7, 2 (1971), 74–94.

Berger, Iris. "Rebels or Status–Seekers? Women as Spirit Mediums in East Africa." In Nancy J. Hafkin and Edna G. Bay, eds., *Women in Africa: Studies in Social and Economic Change*, 157–181. Stanford: Stanford University Press, 1976.

————"Deities, Dynasties and Oral Tradition: The History and Legend of the Abachwezi." In Joseph Miller, ed., *The African Past Speaks*, 61–81. Folkstone, England: Dawson, 1980.

Binetsch, Gottlob. "Beantwortung mehrerer Fragen über unser Ewe–volk und seine Anchauungen." *Zeitschrift für Ethnologie* (Braunschweig) 38 (1906), 34–51.

Biørn, A. R. "Biørn's Beretning 1788 om de Danske Forter og Negrier." *Nogle Bidrag til Kundskab om den Danske Straekning paa Guinea Kysten* (Thaarups Archiv for Politik, Statistik og Huusholdingsvideskaber, 1797–1798, III). Copenhagen (1788), 193–230.

Bledsoe, Caroline. "The Political Use of Sande Ideology and Symbolism." *American Anthropologist*, 11 (1984), 455–73.

Boserup, Ester. *The Conditions of Agricultural Growth: The Economics of Agrarian Change under Population Pressure*. Chicago: Aldine, Atherton, 1965.

———*Woman's Role in Economic Development*. New York: St. Martin's Press, 1970.

Bosman, W. *A New and Accurate Description of the Guinea Coast*. London: J. Knapton, 1705.

Bouché, Pierre. *La Côte des Esclaves*. Paris: E. Plon, 1885.

Bourret, F. M. *Ghana: The Road to Independence, 1919–1957*. Stanford: Stanford University Press, 1960.

Bowdich, T. E. *Mission from Cape Coast to Ashantee*. London: J. Murray, 1819.

Brooks, George E. "The Signares of Saint–Louis and Gorée: Women Entrepreneurs in 18th Century Senegal." In Nancy Hafkin and Edna Bay, eds., *Women in Africa*, 19–44. Stanford: Stanford University Press, 1976.

Brutschin, B. "Keta und Anyako." *Monatsblatt der Norddeutschen Missionsgesellschaft*, 16/184 (1866), 806–807.

Brydon, Lynne. "Women at Work: Some Changes in Family Structure in Amedzofe–Avatime, Ghana." *Africa* 42, 2 (1979), 97–111.

———"Avatime Women and Men, 1900–1980." In Christine Oppong, ed., *Female and Male in West Africa*, 320–29. Boston: Allen and Unwin, 1983.

Bukh, Jette. *The Village Woman in Ghana*. Uppsala: Scandinavian Institute of African Studies, 1979.

Carney, Judith, and Michael Watts. "Disciplining Women? Rice, Mechanization and the Evolution of Mandinka Gender Relations in Senegambia." *Signs* 16, 4 (1991), 651–81.

Carstensen, Edward. *Guvenør Carstensen's Indberetninger fra Guinea, 1842–50*. Edited by Georg Nørregård.Copehagen: I. Kommission hos G. E. C. Gad, 1964.

"Cattle Manure on Coconuts in the Keta District." *Gold Coast Farmer*, 2 (1933), 108.

Chona, B. L., and P. G. Addoh. "Cape St. Paul Wilt." *Bulletin of Ghana Crop Research Institute*, 3 (1970), 3–8.

Christensen, James Boyd. "The Adaptive Functions of Fanti Priesthood." In W. R. Bascom and M. J. Herskovits, eds., *Continuity and Change in African Cultures*, 257–78. Chicago: University of Chicago Press, 1959.

Claridge, W. W. *A History of the Gold Coast and Ashanti*, 2 volumes. London: Cass, 1915.

Clark, Gracia. *Onions are My Husband: Survival and Accumulation by West African Market Women*. Chicago: University of Chicago Press, 1994.

"The Coconut Industry." *Gold Coast Farmer*, 2 (1933), 101–102.

Cohen, Ronald. "Ethnicity: Problem and Focus in Anthropology." *Annual Review of Anthropology*, 7 (1978), 379–403.

Coleman, J. S. "Togoland." *International Conciliation*, No. 509. New York: Carnegie Endowment for International Peace, 1956, 3–91.

Collier, Jane Fishbourne. *Marriage and Inequality in Classless Societies*. Stanford: Stanford University Press, 1988.

Colson, Elizabeth. "The Assimilation of Aliens among Zambian Tonga." In Ronald Cohen and John Middleton, eds., *From Tribe to Nation in Africa*, 35–54. Scranton: Chandler Press, 1970.

Committee of Enquiry (Volta Region), Seventy-eighth Sitting, Thursday, 17 October 1974.

Coombes, C. N. "Some Notes on the Development of the Ghana Coconut Industry." *Ghana Farmer*, 2 (1958), 16–20.

Crenshaw, Kimberlè Williams. "Beyond Racism and Misogyny: Black Feminism and 2 Live Crew." In Robert W. Gordon and Margaret Jane Radin, eds., *Words that Wound*, 111–32. Boulder: Westview Press, 1993.

Crowder, Michael. "The 1914–1918 European War and West Africa." In J. F. A. Ajayi and Michael Crowder, eds., *History of West Africa*, Volume 2, 484–513. New York: Columbia University Press, 1974.

Dakubu, M. E. Kropp. "Linguistic Pre-History and Historical Reconstruction: The Ga–Adangbe Migration." *Transactions of the Historical Society of Ghana* XIII (1972), 87–111.

———"A Survey of Borrowed Words in Dangme." *Research Review* (Legon) 4, supp. (1973), 81–128.

Debrunner, H. W. *A Church Between Colonial Powers: A Study of the Church in Togo.* London: Lutterworth Press, 1965.

Dickson, K. B. "Development of the Copra Industry in Ghana." *The Journal of Tropical Geography*, 19 (1964), 27–34.

———*A Historical Geography of Ghana.* London: Cambridge University Press, 1969.

"Die Unruhen im Anglo-Gebiet." *Norddeutsche Missionsgesellschaft*, 3 and 4/10 (1855), 36–58.

Dumett, Raymond E. "Pressure Groups, Bureaucracy and the Decision-Making Process: The Case of Slavery Abolition and Colonial Expansion in the Gold Coast, 1874." *Journal of Imperial and Commonwealth History*, IX (1981), 193–215.

———"African Merchants of the Gold Coast, 1860–1905: Dynamics of Indigenous Entrepreneurship." *Comparative Studies in Society and History*, 25, 4 (1983), 661–93.

Dumett, Raymond, and Marion Johnson. "Britain and the Suppression of Slavery in the Gold Coast Colony, Ashanti and the Northern Territories." In Suzanne Miers and Richard Roberts, eds., *The End of Slavery in Africa*, 71–116. Madison: University of Wisconsin Press, 1988.

Duncan, John. *Travels in Western Africa in 1845 and 1846.* London: Richard Bentley, 1847.

Edholm, Felicity, Olivia Harris, and Kate Young. "Conceptualising Women." *Critique of Anthropology* 3, 9, and 10 (1977), 101–30.

Ekholm, Kajsa. "External Exchange and the Transformation of Central Africa Social Systems." In J. Friedman and M. J. Rowlands, eds., *The Evolution of Social Systems*, 115–36. Pittsburgh: University of Pittsburgh Press, 1977.

Eldredge, Elizabeth. "Women in Production: The Economic Role of Women in Nineteenth Century Lesotho." *Signs*, 16, 4 (1991), 707–31.

Ellis, A. B. *The Ewe-Speaking Peoples of the Slave Coast of West Africa.* Chicago: Benin Press, 1890.

Ember, Carol R. "The Relative Decline in Women's Contribution to Agriculture with Intensification." *American Anthropologist*, 85, 2 (1983), 285–304.

Fage, J. D. "A New Check List of the Forts and Castles of Ghana, edited with information contributed by Douglas Coombs, J. R. Lander, A. W. Lawrence, G. E. Metcalfe, Margaret Priestly and Ivor Wilks." *Transactions of the Historical Society of Ghana*, 1, Pt. 1 (1959), 57–67.

Falola, Toyin. "From Hospitality to Hostility: Ibaden and Strangers, 1830–1904." *Journal of African History*, 26 (1985), 51–68.

Fiawoo, Dzigbodi Kodzo. "Ewe Lineage and Kinship Sub-Ethnic Group Variation." In Christine Oppong, ed., *Legon Family Research Papers, No.1: Domestic Rights and Duties in Southern Ghana*, 163–66. Legon: Institute of African Studies, University of Ghana, 1974.

———"Clan Endogamy and Patrilateral Parallel Cousin Marriage in Tongu, Ghana." In Christine Oppong, ed., *Legon Family Research Papers, No. 1: Domestic Rights and Duties in Southern Ghana*, 167–85. Legon: Institute of African Studies, Unversity of Ghana, 1974.

Fort, Dr. Lamar E. "The Shallot Industry in South Anlo District, Ghana." *Ghana Farmer*, IV, 3 (1960), 108–10.

Fynn, J. K. *Asante and Its Neighbors, 1700–1807.* London: Longman, 1971.

Gaba, C. R. "Sacrifice in Anlo Religion, Part 1." *Ghana Bulletin of Theology*, 3, 5 (1968), 13–19.

Gaisie, Samuel. "Fertility Trends and Differentials." In John Caldwell, ed., *Population Growth and Socio-economic Change in West Africa*, 339–45. New York: Columbia University Press, 1975.

Gleave, M. B., and H. P. White. "Population Density and Agricultural Systems in West Africa." In M. F. Thomas and G. W. Whittington, eds., *Environment and Land Use in Africa*, 273–300. London: Methuen, 1969.

Goody, Esther N. "Conjugal Separation and Divorce among the Gonja." In Meyer Fortes, ed., *Marriage in Tribal Societies*, 14–54. London: Methuen, 1962.

Goody, Esther N., with Jack Goody. "The Circulation of Women and Children in Northern Ghana." In. Esther N. Goody, ed., *Parenthood and Social Reproduction: Fostering and Occupational Roles in West Africa*, 91–109. London: Cambridge University Press, 1982.

Goody, J. *Technology, Tradition and the State*. London: Oxford University Press, 1971.

Greene, Sandra E. "Land, Lineage and Clan in Early Anlo." *Africa*, 51, 1 (1981), 451–64.

———"Conflict and Crisis: A Note on the Workings of the Political Economy and Ideology of the Anlo-Ewe in the Precolonial Period." *Rural Africana*, 17 (1983), 83–96.

———"The Past and Present of an Anlo-Ewe Oral Tradition." *History in Africa*, 12 (1985), 73–87.

———"Social Change in 18th Century Anlo: The Role of Technology, Markets and Military Conflict." *Africa: The Journal of the International African Institute*, 58, 1 (1988), 70–86.

Green-Pederson, Sv. E. "The Scope and Structure of the Danish Negro Slave Trade." *Scandinavian Economic History Review* 19, 2 (1971), 149–97.

Grier, Beverly. "Pawns, Porters and Petty Traders: Women in the Transition to Cash Crop Agriculture in Colonial Ghana." *Signs* 17, 2 (1992), 304–28.

Gros, Jules. *Voyages, Aventures et Captivité de J. Bonnat Chez les Ashantis*. Paris: E. Plon, 1884.

Grove, Jean M., and A. M. Johansen. "The Historical Geography of the Volta Delta, Ghana, During the Period of Danish Influence." *Bulletin de l'I.F.A.N*, XXX, 4 (1968), 1374–421.

Guy, Jeff. "Gender Oppression in Southern Africa's Precapitalist Societies." In Cherryl Walker, ed., *Women and Gender in Southern Africa to 1945*, 33–47. London: James Currey, 1990.

Guyer, Jane. "Household and Community in African Studies." *African Studies Review* XXIV, 2/3 (1981), 87–137.

———"Beti Widow Inheritance and Marriage Law: A Social History." In Betty Potash, ed., *Widows in African Societies: Choices and Constraints*, 193–219. Stanford: Stanford University Press, 1986.

Gyasi, E. A. "Population Pressure and Changes in Traditional Agriculture: Case Study of Farming in Sekesua-Agbelitson, Ghana." *Bulletin of the Ghana Geographical Association*, 18 (1976), 68–87.

Hafkin, Nancy J., and Edna G. Bay, eds. *Women in Africa: Studies in Social and Economic Change*. Stanford: Stanford University Press, 1976.

Hagan, George Panyin. "Marriage, Divorce and Polygyny in Winneba." In Christine Oppong, ed., *Male and Female in West Africa*, 192–203. Boston: Allen and Unwin, 1983.

Härtter, Gottlob. "Sitten und Gebräuche der Anloer." *Zeitschrift für Ethnologie* (Braunschweig) 38/1–2 (1906), 40–51.

———"Der Fishfang im Ewelande." *Zeitschrift für Ethnologie* (Braunschweig) 38/1–2 (1906), 51–63.

Hay, Margaret Jean. "Queens, Prostitutes and Peasants: Historical Perspectives on African Women, 1971–1986." *Canadian Journal of African Studies*, 22, 3 (1988), 431–47.

Herring, R. S., D. W. Cohen and B. A. Ogot. "The Construction of Dominance: the Strategies of Selected Luo groups in Uganda and Kenya." In Ahmed Idah Salim, ed. *State Formation in Eastern Africa*, 126–61, New York: St. Martin's Press, 1985.

Herskovits, Melville J. *Dahomey: An Ancient West African Kingdom*, Volume 2. Evanston: Northwestern University Press, 1967.

Hicks, George L., and Philip E. Leis, eds. *Ethnic Encounters: Identities and Contexts*. North Scituate, Mass.: Duxbury Press, 1977.

Hill, Polly. "Ewe Seine Fishermen." In Polly Hill, ed., *Studies in Rural Capitalism in West Africa*, 30–52. Cambridge: Cambridge University Press, 1970.

Hilton, Ann. "Family and Kinship among the Kongo, South of the Zaire River from the 16th to the 19th Centuries." *Journal of African History*, 24 (1983), 189–206.

Hogbeza, 1978. Accra: Anlo Traditional Council, 1978.

Hopkins, A. G. *An Economic History of West Africa*. London: Longman, 1973.

Hornberger, Christian. "Etwas aus der Geschichte der Anloer." *Quartalblatt der Norddeutschen Missionsgesellschaft*, 82: 436, 442; 83: 445–50; 84: 452–58; 85: 460–66, (1877).

Horton, Africanus B. *Letters on the Political Condition of The Gold Coast.* London: Frank Cass, 1970. Originally published in 1870.

Horton, Robin. "From Fishing Village to City-State: A Social History of New Calabar." In Mary Douglass and Phyllis Kaberry, eds., *Man in Africa*, 37–58. London: Tavistock, 1969.

Isert, Paul Erdmann. *Voyages en Guinée et dans les îles Caraïbes en Amerique. Tirés de sa correspondence avec ses amis. Traduits de l'allemand.* Paris: Maradan, 1793.

Jennings, Lawrence C. "French Policy Toward Trading with African and Brazilian Slave Merchants, 1840–1853." *Journal of African History*, XVII, 4 (1976), 515–28.

Jewsiewicki, Bogumil. "The Formation of the Political Culture of Ethnicity in the Belgian Congo." In Leroy Vail, ed., *The Creation of Tribalism in Southern Africa*, 324–49. London: James Currey, 1991.

Johnson, Marian. "Ashanti East of the Volta." *Transactions of the Historical Society of Ghana*, VIII (1965), 33–59.

———"The Slaves of Salaga." *Journal of African History*, 27 (1986), 341–62.

Jorion, Paul. "Going Out and Staying Home: Seasonal Movements and Migration Strategies among Xwla and Anlo-Ewe Fishermen." *MAST* 1, 2 (1988), 129–55.

Kaplow, Susan B. "The Mudfish and the Crocodile: Underdevelopment of a West African Bourgeoisie." *Science and Society*, XLI, 3 (1977), 317–33.

———"Primitive Accumulation and Traditional Social Relations on the Nineteenth Century Gold Coast." *Canadian Journal of African Studies*, XII, 1 (1978), 19–36.

Kea, R. A. "Akwamu–Anlo Relations, c. 1750–1813." *Transactions of the Historical Society of Ghana*, X (1969), 29–63.

———*Settlements, Trade and Polities in the Seventeenth Century Gold Coast.* Baltimore: Johns Hopkins University Press, 1982.

Kettel, Bonnie. "The Commoditization of Women in Tugen (Kenya) Social Organization." In Claire Robertson and Iris Berger, eds., *Women and Class in Africa*, 47–61. New York: Africana Publishing Company, 1986.

Keyes, Charles F., ed.. *Ethnic Change.* Seattle: University of Washington Press, 1981.

Klein, Herbert S. "African Women in the Atlantic Slave Trade." In Claire C. Robertson and Martin A. Klein, eds., *Women and Slavery in Africa*, 29–38. Madison: University of Wisconsin Press, 1983.

Kludze, A. K. P. "Family Property and Inheritance among the Northern Ewe." In Christine Oppong, ed., *Legon Family Research Papers, No. 1: Domestic Rights and Duties in Southern Ghana*, 199–211. Legon: Institute of African Studies, 1974.

Knoll, Arthur J. "Taxation in the Gold Coast Colony and in Togo: A Study in Early Administration." In Prosser Gifford, William Roger Lewis, and Alison Smith, eds., *Britain and Germany in Africa*, 418–53. New Haven: Yale University Press, 1967.

Kopytoff, Igor, ed.. *The African Frontier: The Reproduction of Traditional African Societies.* Bloomington: Indiana University Press, 1987.

Krige, Eileen Jensen. "Women-Marriage, with Special Reference to the Lovedu: Its Significance for the Definition of Marriage." *Africa* 44 (1974), 11–37.

Kumekpor, Maxine. "Some Sociological Aspects of Beads with Special Reference to Selected Beads Found in Eweland." *Ghana Journal of Sociology* 6, 2/ 7, 1 (1970/1971), 100–108.

Kumekpor, T. "The Position of Maternal Relatives in the Kinship System of the Ewe." In Christine Oppong, ed., *Legon Family Research Papers No. 1: Domestic Rights and Duties in Southern Ghana*, 212–33. Legon: Institute of African Studies, 1974.

Launay, Robert. *Traders without Trade.* Cambridge: Cambridge University Press, 1982.

Laurentin, Anne. "Nzakara Women." In Denise Paulme, ed., *Women in Tropical Africa*, 121–78, Berkeley: University of California Press, 1960.

Law, Robin. *The Horse in West African History.* New York: Oxford University Press, 1980.

———"Trade and Politics Behind the Slave Coast: The Lagoon Traffic and the Rise of Lagos, 1500–1800." *Journal of African History* 24 (1983), 321–48.

———*The Slave Coast of West Africa, 1550–1750.* New York: Oxford University Press, 1991.

Lawson, Rowena M. "The Structure, Migration and Re-settlement of Ewe Fishing Units." *African Studies* 17, 1 (1958), 21–27.

Little, Kenneth, and Anne Price. "Some Trends in Modern Marriage among West Africans." *Africa* XXXVII, 4 (1967), 407–24.

Locke, David, with Godwin Agbeli. "Drum Language in Adzogbo." *Black Perspective in Music* 9, 1 (1981), 25–50.

Lonsdale, John. "When Did the Gusii (or Any Other Group) Become a 'Tribe.'" *Kenya Historical Review* 5, 1 (1977), 123–33.

———"African Pasts in Africa's Future." *Canadian Journal of African Studies*, 23 (1989), 126–46.

MacCormack, Carol. "Slaves, Slave Owners, and Slave Dealers: Sherbro Coast and Hinterland." In Claire C. Roberston and Martin A. Klein, eds. *Women and Slavery in Africa*, 271–94. Madison: University of Wisconsin Press, 1983.

MacDonald, George. *The Gold Coast, Past and Present: A Description of the Country and its People.* London: Longman, 1898.

Mair, Lucy. *African Marriage and Social Change.* London: Frank Cass, 1969.

———*Marriage.* Baltimore: Penguin Books, 1971.

Mamattah, Charles M. K. *The Ewes of West Africa.* Accra: Advent Press, 1979.

Mann, Kristin. "Women, Landed Property and the Accumulation of Wealth in Early Colonial Lagos." *Signs*, 6, 4 (1991), 682–705.

Manoukian, Madeline. "The Ewe-Speaking People of Togoland and the Gold Coast." In. Daryll Forde, ed., *Ethnographic Survey of Africa*, 9–63. London: International African Institute, 1952.

Manshard, Walthier. "Die Küsten und Flussfischerien aus Ghana." *Die Erde: Zeitschrift der Gesellschaft für Erdkunde zu Berlin*, 89 (1958), 21–33.

Marks, Shula. "Patriotism, Patriarchy and Purity: Natal and the Politics of Zulu Ethnic Consciousness," in Leroy Vail, ed., *The Creation of Tribalism in Southern Africa*, 215–40. London: James Currey, 1991.

McCaskie, T. C. "State and Society, Marriage and Adultery: Some Considerations Towards a Social History of Pre-colonial Asante." *Journal of African History*, 22 (1981), 477–94.

McSheffrey, Gerald M. "Slavery, Indentured Servitude, Legitimate Trade and the Impact of Abolition in the Gold Coast, 1874–1901: A Reappraisal." *Journal of African History*, 24 (1981), 349–68.

Meillassoux, Claude. *Maidens, Meal and Money.* New York: Cambridge University Press, 1981.

Merz, Missionar. "Die Oelpalme." *Monatsblatt der Norddeutschen Missionsgesellschaft*, 11/3 (1878), 168–73.

Miller, Joseph C. *Way of Death.* Madison: University of Wisconsin Press, 1988.

Molyneux, Maxine. "Androcentrism in Marxist Anthropology." *Critique of Anthropology* 3, 9, and 10 (1977), 55–81.

Monrad, H. C. *Bidrag til en Skildring af Guinea-kysten og dens Indbyggere og til en Beskrivelse over de Danske Colonier paa denne Kyst.* Copenhagen: A. Seidelin, 1822.

Mousser, Bruce L. "Accommodation and Assimilation in the Landlord–Stranger Relationship." In B. K. Swartz, Jr., and Raymond E. Dumett, eds. *West African Cultural Dynamics: Archaeological and Historical Perspectives*, 495–514. The Hague: Mouton, 1980.

Müller, G. *Geschichte der Ewe Mission.* Bremen: Norddeutsche Missionsgesellschaft, 1904.

Mullings, Leith. "Women and Economic Change in Africa." In Nancy J. Hafkin and Edna G. Bay, eds., *Women in Africa: Studies in Social and Economic Change*, 239–64. Stanford: Stanford University Press, 1976.

Musisi, Nakanyike B. "Women, 'Elite Polygyny' and Buganda State Formation." *Signs* 16, 4 (1991), 757–86.

Newbury, David. *Kings and Clans: Ijwi Island and the Lake Kivu Rift, 1780–1840.* Madison: University of Wisconsin Press, 1991.

Nørregård, Georg. *Danish Settlements in West Africa, 1658–1850.* Boston: Boston University Press, 1966.

Nukunya, G. Kwaku. "Onion Farming by the Keta Lagoon." *Bulletin of the Ghana Geographical Association*, II, 2 (1957), 12–13.

———"Letter—Pan African Fishermen." *West Africa*, 2433 (1964), 73.

———*Kinship and Marriage among the Anlo-Ewe*. London: Athlone Press, 1969.

———"Land Tenure, Inheritance and Social Structure among the Anlo." *Universitas*, 3, 1 (1973), 64–81.

———"The Effects of Cash Crops on an Ewe Community." In J. Goody, ed., *Changing Social Structure in Ghana*, 59–71. London: International African Institute, 1975.

———*The History of the Woe Evangelical Presbyterian Church, 1887–1987*. Woe, Ghana: Woe Evangelical Presbyterian Church, 1987.

———"The Anlo-Ewe and Full-Time Maritime Fishing: Another View." *MAST* 2, 2 (1989), 154–73.

Obbo, Christine. *African Women: Their Struggle for Economic Independence*. London: Zed Press, 1980.

Oppong, Christine. *Marriage among a Matrilineal Elite: A Family Study of Ghanaian Senior Civil Servants*. London: Cambridge University Press, 1974.

Osswald, Carl. *Fifty Years' Mission Work at Keta*. Bremen: Bremer Missionsschriften, 1903.

Owusu-Ansah, David. "Power of Prestige? Muslims in 19th Century Kumase." *Anthropological Papers of the American Museum of Natural History: The Gold Stool—Studies of the Asante Center and Periphery*, 65 (1987), 80–92.

Packard, Randall M. "Debating a Common Idiom: Variant Traditions of Genesis among the BaShu of Eastern Zaire." In Igor Kopytoff, ed., *The African Frontier: The Reproduction of Traditional African Societies*, 149–61. Bloomington: Indiana University Press, 1987.

Patten, Sonia G., and Godwin K. Nukunya. "Organizational Responses to Agricultural Intensification in Anloga, Ghana." *African Studies Review*, 75, 2/3 (1982), 67–77.

Plessing, Fredrich. "Station Quitta in West-Afrika." *Monatsblatt der Norddeutschen Missionsgesellschaft*, 4/42 (1854), 176–78.

———"Briefe aus Keta." *Monatsblatt der Norddeutschen Missionsgesellschaft*, 5/57 (1855), 244–48.

Postma, Johannes Menne. *The Dutch in the Atlantic Slave Trade, 1600–1815*. London: Cambridge University Press, 1990.

Potash, Betty. "Some Aspects of Marital Stability in a Rural Luo Community." *Africa* 48, 4 (1978), 380–97.

———"Gender Relations in Sub-Saharan Africa." In Sandra Morgan, ed., *Gender and Anthropology: Critical Reviews for Research and Teaching*, 189–227. Washington, D.C.: American Anthropological Association, 1989.

Quansah, S. T. "The Shallot Industry, Incorporating a Recent Survey of the Anloga Growing Area." *New Gold Coast Farmer*, 1, 2 (1956), 45–49.

Radcliffe-Brown, A. R., and Daryll Forde, eds. *African Systems of Kinship and Marriage*. London: Oxford University Press, 1950.

Ranger, Terence. *The Invention of Tribalism in Zimbabwe*. Gweru, Zimbabwe: Mambo Press, 1985.

Rattray, R. S. "History of the Ewe People." *Etudes Togolais* 11, 1 (1967), 92–98.

Reindorf, Carl. *History of the Gold Coast and Asante*. Basel: Missionsbuchhandlung, 1895.

Reiminick, Ronald A. *Theory of Ethnicity: An Anthropologist's Perspective*. New York: University Press of America, 1983.

Reynolds, Edward. *Trade and Economic Change on the Gold Coast, 1807–1874*. Essex: Longman, 1974.

Robertson, Claire. "Ga Women and Socio-economic Change in Accra, Ghana." In Nancy J. Hafkin and Edna G. Bay, eds., *Women in Africa: Studies in Social and Economic Change*, 111–33. Stanford: Stanford University Press, 1976.

———*Sharing the Same Bowl: A Socio-economic History of Women and Class in Africa*. Bloomington: Indiana University Press, 1984.

Robertson, Claire, and Martin A. Klein, eds., *Women and Slavery in Africa*. Madison: University of Wisconsin Press, 1983.

———"Introduction: Women's Importance in African Slave Systems." In Claire Robertson and Martin A. Klein, eds., *Women and Slavery in Africa*, 3–25. (Madison: University of Wisconsin Press, 1983).

Robertson, Claire, and Iris Berger. "Introduction: Analyzing Class and Gender—African Perspectives." In Claire Robertson and Iris Berger, eds., *Women and Class in Africa*, 3–24. New York: Africana Publishing Company, 1986.

Rømer, L. F. *Tilforladelig Efterretning om Kysten Guinea*. Copenhagen: L. H. Lillie, 1760.

Rosenfeld, Arthur. *Sugar Cane Around the World*. New York: University of Chicago Press, 1955.

Ross, David. "The Career of Domingo Martinez in the Bight of Benin, 1833–64." *Journal of African History*, VI, I (1965), 79–90.

Ross, Doran H. "The Akan Double-Bladed Sword: A Case of Islamic Origins." In Doran H. Ross and Timothy F. Garrard, eds., *Akan Transformations: Problems in Ghanaian Art History*, Monograph Series No. 21, 60–69. Los Angeles: Museum of Cultural History, University of California, Los Angeles, 1983.

Royce, Anya Peterson. *Ethnic Identity: Strategies of Diversity*. Bloomington: Indiana University Press, 1982.

Sacks, Karen. *Sisters and Wives: The Past and Future of Sexual Equality*. Urbana: University of Illinois Press, 1982.

Salkowski, E. "Eine Hochburg des Heidentums." *Bremer Missions-Schriften*, No. 20 (1907), 1–28.

Samarin, William J. "Bondjo Ethnicity and Colonial Imagination." *Canadian Journal of African Studies*, 18, 12 (1984), 345–65.

Schiek and Tolch. "Keta." *Monatsblatt der Norddeutschen Missionsgesellschaft*, 22/263 (1872), 1193–94.

Schlegel, J. Bernhard. "Beitrag zur Geschichte, Welt- und Religionsanchauung des Westafrikaners, namentlich des Eweer." *Monatsblatt der Norddeutschen Missionsgesellschaft*, 7/93, 397–400, 7/94, 406–8 (1858).

Schmidt, Elizabeth. *Peasants, Traders and Wives: Shona Women in the History of Zimbabwe, 1870–1939*. Portsmouth, NH: Heinemann, 1992.

Schneider, David M. "A Note on Bridewealth and the Stability of Marriage." *Man*, LIII, 74, 75 (1953), 55–57.

Scott, Joan Wallach. *Gender and the Politics of History*. New York: Columbia University Press, 1988.

Seeger, M. "Die Sklaverei im Togolande und der englischen Goldküsten Kolonie." *Deutsche Kolonialzeitung* (Berlin) 5 (1892), 54–56.

Seidel, H. "Der Yew'e Dienst im Togolande." *Zeitschrift für afrikanische und oceanische sprachen*, 3 (1897), 157–85.

———"Der Sklavenhandel in Togo." *Deutsche Kolonialzeitung* (Berlin) 12 (1899), 123.

Skidmore, C. L., and J. S. Martinson. "A Survey of the Coconut Area in the Keta–Ada District." *Gold Coast Department of Agriculture Bulletin*, 23 (1930), 157–65.

Smith, M. G. "Pluralism in Precolonial African Societies." In Leo Kuper and M. G. Smith, eds., *Pluralism in Africa*, 91–151. Berkeley: University of California Press, 1969.

Sobania, Neal. "Fishermen Herders: Subsistence, Survival and Cultural Change in Northern Kenya." *Journal of African History*, 29 (1988), 41–56.

Sorkpor, G. A. "Notes on the Nayo Friko Shrine in Awuna." *Research Review* (Legon) 2, 3 (1966), 87–98.

"Special Report on Localities by Local Authorities." *Population Census of Ghana—1984*. Accra: Eddy Williams, 1989.

Spiess, Carl. "Könige der Anloer." In H. F. Helmot, ed., *Weltgeschichte 3: Westasien und Afrika*, 574. Leipzig and Vienna, Bibliographisches Institut, 1901.

———"Ein Erinnerungsblatt an die Tage des Sklavenhandels in West Afrika." *Globus*, (Braunschweig) 92 (1907), 205–8.

Spieth, J. "Von den Evhefrauen." *Quartalblatt der Norddeutschen Missionsgesellschaft*, VI (1889), 1–8.

———*Die Religion der Eweer in Süd Togo.* Leipzig: Gottingen, 1911.

Sprigge, R. G. S. "Eweland's Adangbe: An Enquiry into an Oral Tradition." *Transactions of the Historical Society of Ghana*, X (1969), 87–128.

Stein, J. T. H. "Agriculture in the Keta–Ada District." Gold Coast Department of Agriculture Bulletin, No. 22, 1929.

Stearns, Peter N. "Toward a Wider Vision: Trends in Social History." In Michael Kammer, ed., *The Past Before Us: Contemporary Writings in the United States*, 205–30. Ithaca: Cornell University Press, 1980.

Surgy, Albert de. *La Pêche Traditionelle sur le Littoral Evhé et Mina (De l'embouchure de la Volta au Dahomey).* Paris: Groupe de Chercheurs Africanistes, 1966.

———*Contribution a l'Étude des Cultes en Pays Keta.* Paris: Groupe de Chercheurs Africanistes, 196–.

Tamrat, Tadesse. "Processes of Ethnic Interaction and Integration in Ethiopian History: The Case of the Agaw." *Journal of African History*, 29 (1988), 5–18.

Taylor, William B. "Between Global Process and Local Knowledge: An Inquiry into Early Latin American Social History, 1500–1900." In Olivier Zunz, ed., *Reliving the Past: The Worlds of Social History*, 115–190. Chapel Hill: University of North Carolina Press, 1985.

Tenkorang, S. "The Importance of Firearms in the Struggle Between Ashanti and the Coastal States, 1708–1807." *Transactions of the Historical Society of Ghana* IX (1968), 1–16.

Thomas, Charles W. *Adventures and Observations on the West Coast of Africa and Its Islands.* New York: Negro Universities Press, 1860.

Thompson, Richard H. *Theories of Ethnicity: A Critical Appraisal.* New York: Greenwood Press, 1989.

Thornton, John. "Sexual Demography: The Impact of the Slave Trade on Family Structure." In Claire Robertson and Martin A. Klein, eds., *Women and Slavery in Africa*, 39–48. Madison: University of Wisconsin Press, 1983.

Tilly, Charles. "Retrieving European Lives." In Olivier Zunz, ed., *Reliving the Past: The Worlds of Social History*, 11–52. Chapel Hill: University of North Carolina Press, 1985.

Vail, Leroy, editor. *The Creation of Tribalism in Southern Africa.* London: James Currey, 1991.

Vail, Leroy, and Landeg White. "Tribalism in the Political History of Malawi." In Leroy Vail, ed. *The Creation of Tribalism in Southern Africa*, 151–92. London: James Currey, 1991.

Van Allen, Judith. "'Aba Riots' and Igbo 'Women's War'? Ideology, Stratification and the Invisibility of Women." In Nancy J. Hafkin and Edna G. Bay, eds. *Women in Africa: Studies in Social and Economic Change*, 59–85. Stanford: Stanford University Press, 1976.

Van Dantzig, A. *The Dutch and the Guinea Coast.* Accra: Ghana Academy of Arts and Sciences, 1978.

Van Landewijk, J. E. J. M. "What was the Original Aggrey Bead?" *Ghana Journal of Sociology*, 6, 2/ 7, 1 (1970/1971), 89–99.

Verdon, Michel. "Divorce in Abutia." *Africa* 52, 4 (1982), 48–65.

———*The Abutia Ewe of West Africa: A Chiefdom that Never Was.* Berlin: Mouton, 1983.

Ward, B. "An Example of 'Mixed' Systems of Descent and Inheritance." *Man* 55, 2 (1955), 3–5.

Ward, W. E. F. *The Royal Navy and the Slavers.* New York: Pantheon Books, 1969.

Webster, J. B. "Political Activity in British West Africa, 1900–1940." In J. F. A. Ajayi and Michael Crowder, eds. *History of West Africa*, Vol. 2, 568–95. New York: Columbia University Press, 1974.

Welch, Claude E. *Dream of Unity: Pan-Africanism and Political Unification in West Africa.* Ithaca: Cornell University Press, 1966.

198 SOURCES

Welman, C. W. *The Native States of the Gold Coast, History and Constitution, Pt. 1, Peki.* London: Dawson, 1969.
Westermann, D. *The Study of the Ewe Language.* London: Oxford University Press, 1930.
———"Ein Bericht über den Yehwekultus der Ewe." *Mitteilungen des Seminars für Orientalische Sprachen* (Berlin) 33/3 (1930), 1–55.
———"Die Glidyi-Ewe in Togo." *Mitteilungen des Seminars für Orientalische Sprachen*, XXXVIII (1935), v–332.
Wilks, I. "The Rise of the Akwamu Empire, 1650–1710." *Transactions of the Historical Society of Ghana*, III, Pt. 2 (1957), 99–136.
———*Asante in the Nineteenth Century.* Cambridge: Cambridge University Press, 1975.
———"Land, Labour, Capital and the Forest Kingdom of Asante: A Model of Early Change." In J. Friedman and M. J. Rowlands, eds., *The Evolution of Social Systems*, 487–534. Pittsburgh: University of Pittsburgh Press, 1977.
———*Wa and the Wala.* Cambridge: Cambridge University Press, 1989.
Wilson, Monica. "Strangers in Africa: Reflections on Nyakyusa, Nguni and Sotho Evidence." In William A Shack and Elliott P. Skinner, eds., *Strangers in African Societies*, 51–66. Berkeley: University of California Press, 1979.
Wolfson, Freda. "A Price Agreement on the Gold Coast—The Krobo Oil Boycott, 1858–1866." *Economic History Bulletin*, VI, 1 (Series 2) (1953), 68–77.
Wyllie, Robert W. "Migrant Anlo Fishing Companies and Socio-Political Change: A Comparative Study." *Africa*, XXXIX, 4 (1969), 396–410.
———"Tribalism, Politics and Eviction: A Study of an Abortive Resettlement Project in Ghana." *Africa Quarterly: A Journal of African Affairs* (New Delhi), IX, 2 (1969), 131–40.
Young, M. Crawford. "Nationalism, Ethnicity and Class in Africa: A Retrospective." *Cahiers d'Etudes Africaines*, XXVI (1986), 103, 421–95.
Zunz, Olivier. *Reliving the Past: The Worlds of Social History.* Chapel Hill: University of North Carolina Press, 1985.
———"Introduction." In Olivier Zunz , ed., *Reliving the Past: The Worlds of Social History.* 3–10. Chapel Hill: University of North Carolina Press, 1985.
———"The Synthesis of Social Change: Reflections on American Social History." In Olivier Zunz, ed., *Reliving the Past: The Worlds of Social History*, 53–114. Chapel Hill: University of North Carolina Press, 1985.

Dissertations and Unpublished Papers

Agboada, Napoleon. "The Reign and Times of Togbui Sri II of Anlo, 1906–1956." B.A. long essay, History Department, University of Ghana, Legon, 1984.
Aligwekwe, I. E. "The Ewe and Togoland Problem: A Case Study in the Paradoxes and Problems of Political Transition in West Africa." Ph.D. dissertation, Ohio State University, 1960.
Amable, Sophia. "The 1953 Riot in Anloga and Its Aftermath." B.A. long essay, History Department, University of Ghana, Legon, 1977.
Amenumey, D. E. K. "The Ewe People and the Coming of European Rule: 1850–1914." M.A. thesis, University of London, 1964.
Buhler, Peter. "The Volta Region of Ghana: Economic Change in Togoland, 1850–1914." Ph.D. dissertation, University of California, San Diego, 1975.
Daendels, H. M. Journal and Correspondence of H. M. Daendels, Pt. 1, November 1815–January 1817. Translated by E. Collins. Legon: Institute of African Studies, University of Ghana, 1964.
Dickson, J. "Marital Selection Among the Anlo Ewe of Ghana: From Parental to Individual Choice." Ph.D. dissertation, Duke University, 1982.

Dotse, J. M. "Agricultural Geography of the Keta District." M.A. thesis, University of Ghana, Legon, 1969.

——Shallot Farming in Anloga, Ghana: A Case Study in Agricultural Geography. Curriculum and Teaching Department, University of Cape Coast, Ghana, 1980.

Fiawoo, Dzigbodi Kodzo. "The Influence of Contemporary Social Changes on the Magico-Religious Concepts and Organization of the Southern Ewe-speaking Peoples of Ghana." Ph.D. dissertation, Edinburgh University, 1959.

Gaba, Kue Agbota. "The History of Anecho, Ancient and Modern." Deposited at Balme Library, University of Ghana, Legon, 1965.

Gaba, C. R. "Anlo Traditional Religion: A Study of the Anlo Traditional Believer's Conception of and Communion with the 'HOLY.'" Ph.D. dissertation, University of London, 1965.

Governor Carstensen's Diary, 1842–1850: Selected Translations (196?).

Greene, Sandra E. "The Anlo-Ewe: Their Economy, Society and External Relations in the Eighteenth Century." Ph.D. dissertation, Northwestern University, 1981.

Hill, Polly. "Notes on the Socio-economic Organisation of the Anloga Shallot Growing Industry," Draft paper, Institute of African Studies, University of Ghana, Legon, 1965.

Kea, R. A. "The Salt Industries of the Gold Coast, 1650–1800." Unpublished paper, Institute of African Studies, University of Ghana, Legon, 1966.

——"Ashanti–Danish Relations, 1780–1831." M.A. thesis, University of Ghana, Legon, 1967.

——"Trade, State Formation and Warfare on the Gold Coast, 1600–1826." Ph.D. dissertation, University of London, 1974.

Nicholson, Sharon Elaine. "A Climatic Chronology for Africa: Synthesis of Geological, Historical and Meteorological Information and Data." Ph.D. dissertation, University of Wisconsin, Madison, 1976.

Nukunya, G. Kwaku. "Some Historical and Geographical Influences on Economic Development in Anlo: An Overview." Paper presented at the Seminar on Coastal Societies in the 19th Century, Institute of African Studies, University of Ghana, Legon, 1981.

Patten, Sonia Gustavson. "The Avuncular Family, Gender Asymmetry, and Patriline: The Anlo Ewe of Southeastern Ghana." Ph.D. dissertation, University of Minnesota, 1990.

Quarcoopome, Nii Otokunor. "Rituals and Regalia of Power: Art and Politics among the Dangme and Ewe, 1800 to Present." Ph.D. dissertation, University of California, Los Angeles, 1993.

Quaye, I. "The Ga and their Neighbors, 1600–1742." Ph.D. dissertation, University of Ghana, Legon, 1972.

Sorkpor, G. A. "Geraldo de Lima and the Awunas, 1862–1904." M.A. thesis, Institute of African Studies, University of Ghana, 1966.

Tay-Agbozo, C. "The Background History of the Anlos (Including Origins, Immigration and Settlement) and the Origin and Development of the Chieftancy Dispute Between the Adjovia and Bate Clans." B.A. honors thesis, Department of History, University of Ghana, Legon, 1971.

Torgby, Richard Tetteh. "The Origin and Organisation of the Yewe Cult." B.A. long essay, Department for the Study of Religion, University of Ghana, Legon, 1977.

Turner, Jerry Michael. "Les Brésiliens: The Impact of Former Brazilian Slaves Upon Dahomey." Ph.D. dissertation, Boston University, 1975.

Wilks, I. "Akwamu, 1650–1750: A Study of the Rise and Fall of West African Empire." M.A. thesis, University of Wales, 1958.

Yarak, L. "Political Consolidation and Fragmentation in a Southern Akan Polity: Wassa and the Origin of Wassa Amenfi and Fiase, 1700–1840." Unpublished paper, 1976.

Yegbe, J. B. "The Anlo and their Neighbors, 1850–1890." M.A. thesis, Institute of African Studies, University of Ghana, Legon, 1966.

INDEX

Abalenu war, 120
Ablera, 86
Aboadzi, 86
Abolo, 120, 183
Abolo war, 120 n.17
Abuakwa, 121
Accra, 18, 24-25, 35, 59, 72, 74-74, 93, 96, 118, 121, 132
    market women from, 176, 179
Achimota College, 145
Acolatse, 132
Ada, 57-59, 63, 72, 76, 82, 83, 120, 122, 132, 133
    Danish fort at, 74
    defeat by Anlo, 57-59, 63
Adagla, 120, 121, 123
Adangbe, 35, 49, 62, 71, 73, 82, 126, 137-38, 148, 150, 152
Addo, William, 130
Adedzi Enyaki, 65
Adedzi Gbekle, 75, 123
Adeladza (founder of Bate clan), 53-54
Adeladza II, 151-52
Adidome, 133
Adidome war, 131
Adina, 113, 128
Aduadui (founder of Dzevi clan), 25, 55
Adultery, 111
Adulthood, markers of, 171
Adza, 65
Adzovia clan, 49 n.2, 52-53, 66, 80, 110, 130-31, 134, 151, 153
    acquisition of gods, 86-87
    and *awoamefia*, 49 n.2, 53, 64, 76, 86
    shrines of, 88
Afedima (maternal cousin of Gbodzo), 74, 165

Afelevo, Stefano Kwadzo, 97-98, 101, 113-16
Aflao, 37, 57, 58, 85
Afonja, S., 9
Afro-Europeans, 69-71, 74, 94, 112, 128
Afu, 87
Agave clan, 25-26, 57-58, 61, 109, 120, 150
    association with Akwamu, 118, 121, 124-25
    as ethnic "outsiders," 109-110, 124-26, 136, 148
    and land, 124-26
    and military leadership, 49 n.2, 121, 123-25
    origins of, 117, 118, 126
    shrines of, 124
    sword as a god, 124
Agavedzi, 117
Agbedzeme, 87
Agbosome, 128
Agbosome Traditional Area, 167
Agbozo, C.T. (descendant of John Tay), 137, 153
Agbui (Avleketi), 95
Agokoli, 53
Agonas, 25
Agotime, 37, 75, 83, 141 n.10
Agotime war, 124
Agoue, 127-28, 130, 133, 134, 139
Agoue war (second), 133
Agowowomu, 118
Agriculture
    cash-cropping, 128, 158, 161, 164, 167-68, 170, 172-74, 176, 178, 180
    division of labor, 4-5, 1598
    expenses of, 170
    intensification, 172-173

for subsistence, 159, 162, 170
Agu, 75
Agudza, 58, 83, 88
Ako war, 26
Akplomeda (father of Tsali), 119, 123 n. 29, 150
  as descended from Egbe, 150
Akpotsui, 109, 120
Akroboto, 133
Akuapem, 57, 82, 83, 121, 122
Akwamu, 16, Ch. 1 *passim*, 56-57, 59, 62, 75, 83, 109, 118, 122-23, 125, 132
  alliance with Anlo, 57, 59
  collapse of, 56, 59
  conquest of Anlo, 20, 23, 56, 87
  and matrilineality, 24, 33-35, 39, 42
Akyem, 36, 37, 57, 82, 83, 85, 121
Alagbati, 29
Alakple, 66, 156, 157
Aligwekwe, L.E., 145
Allada, 33
Alovi, 37
Alpers, E., 9
Ame clan, 2, 27, 49 n.2, 61, 63, 72, 76, 183
  special status of, 3
  stereotypes of, 183
Amedika, 133
Amedor Kpegla, 136
Amedzofe, 150
Amega Le (founder of Wifeme clan), 26, 148, 151, 152
Amegashi Akofi (grandfather of Gbodzo), 72, 76
Amenumey, D.E.K., 141, 145
Amenyah (chief of Atoko), 30
Amenyah, J.D., 25
Amesimeku (nephew of Sri), 53
Amlade clan, 50, 59, 61-63, 68, 78, 117, 150
  and ancestors, 67-68
  and enstoolment, 61, 64-65
  ethnic redefinition of, 50-52, 65-68, 78, 80, 108, 109, 139
  "first five" and, 61, 63, 65-68, 78, 108
  and gods, 64, 67
  and land, 61, 63, 65
  origins of, 50, 61, 64-67

relationship to Lafe clan, 61, 64-66
  socialization of children, 68
Ammunitions, *See* Firearms
Ampam, 86
Ampofo, 85
Ancestors
  as autochthonous gods (*dzokple-anyiwo*), 2, 4, 27-28, 47, 108
  as immigrant gods, 2, 4, 27-28, 47, 65, 108
  of slaves, 67
  time of settlement, 2, 4-6, 14, 26, 47, 48-49, 66, 102, 106, 108, 137, 153, 182
  See also "First five," Gods
Anexo, 38, 57, 59, 61, 65-67, 69, 71-72, 76, 82, 83, 85, 95, 96, 121, 123, 130, 139-43
  defeat of Anlo, 56, 59, 62-64
Anlo
  alliance with Keta, 82-83
  conquest by Akwamu state, 20, 25, 56
  defeat by Ada, 57-58, 122-23
  defeat by Anexo, 56-57, 62
  defeat by British, 133-34
  effect of Sagbadre war on, 82
  origins of, 2, 8, 14, 48-49
  other Ewe groups and, 8-9, 21-23, 136-140, 143, 151, 153
  population of, 1
  production in, 4-5, 15
  relations between villages, 88
  State Council, 144-45, 154
  stereotypes of, 148
  and Togo, 137, 142-43
  and World War I, 142-43, 148, 170
  and World War II, 147, 151
Anlo Shallot Marketing Union, 176, 179
Anloga, 18, 20, 25-26, 37, 54, 58, 62, 66, 67, 86, 88-89, 96, 103, 118, 127, 144, 147, 156, 164, 167, 173, 175, 176, 179
Anum, 75
Anyage (Kofi Fiayidziehe), 62, 76
Anyako, 80, 116, 132, 141, n.10
Aowin, 36, 121
Arhin, K., 12
Asante, 36, 121, 123, 129-30, 132
Assin, 36
Atakpame, 142
Atikpoe, 75

Atitetti war, *See* Funu war
Atitsogbi, *See* Geraldo de Lima
Atogolo, 116
Atoko, 80, 129
Atsu, 65
Avenor, 57, 87, 115
Avleketi, *See* Agbui
Awadatsi, 64, 87
Awoamefia, See Political authority
Axolu (military leader of Anexo wars), 123
Aya (Adangbe god), 62 n.29
Bame clan, 63
Barbot, 92
Barnes, S., 12
Basket production, 162
Bate clan, 49 n.2, 52-54, 66, 80, 131
   and *awoamefia*, 49 n.2, 53-54, 64, 76, 131, 152
   relations with gods, 54, 131
   shrines of, 88
Beeswax, 164
Besa, David (brother of Stefano Afelevo, 115
Betrothal, *See* Marriage
Binetsch, G., 35, 40, 44, 79, 102, 104, 105, 111
Biørn, A. (governor of Keta fort), 85
Birth ceremonies, 40, 124
Blekusu, 128
Blu clan,
   arrival of ancestors, 4
   as ethnic "outsiders," 2, 4, 18, 66, 71, 77, origins, 2, 66, 81, 95, 108, 148, 151, 183
   relation to homeland, 66
Boe (wife of Honi), 95, 96
Boserup, E., 172
Botsi, 86
Bridewealth, *See* Marriage
Britain
   abolishment of slave trade by, 68-69, 93, 97, 128, 132
   and colonial administration, 136-38, 140, 142-44, 147-48, 152-55, 161
   defeat of Anlo by, 80, 133-34, 161
   defeat of Germans, 142
   and Geraldo de Lima, 131-34, 141 n.10

   role in Keta war, 89
   taxation by, 132, 140
   and trade, 37, 69, 133, 161
   trade restrictions by, 128-40, 161
Brutschin, B., 132
Burial, *See* Funeral customs
Cape Appollonia, 36
Cape St. Paul's Wilt, 147, 167
Carstensen, E., 70
Cerquira de Lima, Cesar, 127
Chapman, Daniel, 145
Children, 5, 9, 20, 23, 25, 30, 38-39, 41, 44-45, 68, 88-89, 91, 110, 147, 172, 177, 179-180
   affiliation to maternal kin, 20, 28, 30-31, 32, 34, 41, 44-45
   custody of, 158
   induction into clan, 88
   See also , Socialization
Christianity, 5, 8, 80, 97, 113-15, 126, 137, 153-54; *See also*, Missionaries
Clans (*hlwo*), 1, 22, 31, 45, 47, 48, 88, 108
   classification of, 1-2, 4, 48, 138, (fig.) 149, 154
   endogamy, 17, Ch.1 *passim*, 51, 68, 79, 100, 106, 109, 111, 112, 124, 177, 178
   identity and, 8-9, 14, 31, 48, 51, 67, 145, 159, 177, 179
   induction ceremonies, 88, 124
   names of, (fig.) 2-3, 137
   nkeke-kpui-towo group, 2
   nkeke-legbe-towo group, 2
   origins of, 2, 8, 14, 20, 23, 26, 48, 66, 102, 106, 108, 137-39, 148, 153
   sub-clans (*hlo dome hlo*), 48
   warfare between, 32, 45-46
   See also, Ancestors, "First five," and names of individual clans (Ame, Blu, etc.)
Clark, G., 179
Clifford, Hugh, 142
Clothing, bans on, 94, 112, 153
Cocoa, 168, 170
Commomore (chief of Twifo), 36
Concubinage, 7, 79, 81, 102, 105-106, 108, 112, 156, 178
Cooperatives, 9, 159, 174, 179, 180
Copra industry, 99, 147, 161, 165, 167-69

decline of, 167, 170, 173
division of labor in, 167
effect of Cape St. Paul's Wilt, 147, 167
Cross-cousin marriage, *See* Marriage
Crowther Commission, 53
Customary law, 111
Da (Voduda), 62, 95
Dacon, 86
Dahomey, 92, 141, 142
Datsutagba, 131, 133
Debt, 81, 99, 102-106, 161
Dede (wife of Atogolo), 116, 117
and ban on Nyigbla, 117
Degeni, 85
Denmark
Abalenu war and, 123
abolishment of the slave trade by, 68, 74, 93, 97, 128, 132
Keta war and, 85-86, 95, 132
Sagbadre war and, 82-83
and trade, 37-38, 56, 57, 82, 95, 136
Deti, 29
Dickson, J., 42, 156, 178
Divorce, 8, 90, 156, 158, 162, 176, 180, 182
Dodi Fuga (founder of Klevi clan), 150
Dofo, 150
Dogbo, *See* Adzovia clan
Drought, 54, 139
Dusifiaga, See Military organization
Dutch, and trade, 36
Dze hia, See Concubinage
Dzelu I, 137
Dzelu II, 137
Dzelukofe, 80, 99, 114, 136-37, 153
Dzevi clan, 18, 25, 27, 49, 50-52, 57, 59, 62, Ch. 3 *passim*, 108, 109, 126, 134, 137, 150, 152, 162
as "ethnic outsiders," 59, 63, 78, 80, 81, 93, 117, 125, 137, 148
and land, 63
names of, 150
origins of, 25, 59, 62, 148
political ascendancy of, 49-51, 55, 59, 64, 78, Ch. 3 *passim*
See also, Nyigbla
Dzeziziawo branch (of Like clan), 116
Dzobi Adzinku, 152
Dzokoto, 132

Dzokpleanyiwo, See Ancestors, Gods
Dzotsiafe, 87
Education, *See* Socialization, Schools
Egbe, 61, 64-65, 67, 150
shrine of, 67
Elders, control over young women, 42-47, 51-52, 77-78, 79-81, 89-90, 100, 105-106, 108-109, 111-13, 117, 127, 134-35, 156, 171, 178, 182
Eldredge, E., 9, 10
Ellis, A.B., 22, 92
Elmina, 35
Ember, C., 172
English, *See* British
Enstooling, 61, 64, 88, 139
and Amlade clan, 61, 64
and Lafe clan, 61, 64
Ethnicity
colonialism and, 8
definitions of, 12, 182
historiography and, 12-15, 181
independence and, 8
prior to colonialism, 13, 15, 20, 23
Ethnic "insiders," 2, 14, 23-24, 32, 47, Ch. 2 *passim*, 79, 80, 101, 106, 110, 127, 137, 152, 181
decline of importance of, 177-79
Ethnic "outsiders," 2, 5-6, 8, 14, 23-24, 28, 32, 47, Ch. 2 *passim*, 79, 80, 81, 101, 102, 108-110, 127, 135-37, 150-53, 177-79, 181-82
Ewe
The Ewe Newsletter, 145
ethnic redefinition of, 138-39, 144
and identity, 138, 143-45, 148, 150-52, 155, 159, 179, 180
language, 138, 144, 151, 155
minority status of, 146-47
unification of, 143-45, 147
F. & A. Swanzy, 130
Facial Marking, 88
Falola, T., 12
Fante, 35, 36, 121, 148
and economic embargo, 121
Fiasidi , See Religious Orders
Fiawoo, F.K., 144, 147
Fictive kinship, 8
Firearms, 36, 121-22, 129-30, 161

"First five," 2, 49-52, 61, 63, 65-68, 108, 125

Fishing industry, 4-5, 15, 36-37, 59, 102, 118, 147, 158, 160, 162, 165-67, 172-74
  division of labor, 4-5, 159, 167, 174
  migrancy and, 148, 152, 168, 170
  ocean fishing, 166
  over-fishing, 165, 168

Fishing nets
  beach seines (*yevudo*), 165-67
  ownership of, 167, 176
  purse seine (*agli*), 165

Flynn, J.K., 36

Foasi ritual, 87-91, 112, 116

Fofie Order, 67

Foli (servant of Le), 53

Fon, 92

Forster and Smith, 130

French, 37, 69
  colonial administration, 138-39, 141, 143-44, 148, 152, 155
  forced labor, 142-43
  monetary policy of, 143
  taxation by, 142-43
  and Vichy government, 145

Funeral customs, 2-3, 31, 40-41, 88, 124, 137, 153
  and debt, 6, 31, 104
  of "first five," 2, 49, 126
  length of ceremony, 3
  time of burial, 3-4
  waiting custom, 4

Funu war (Atitetti war), 131-32, 136

Ga, 82, 137

Gbagida, 139, 141

Gbodzo (chief of Woe), 50-52, 71-78, 95, 165
  descendants of, 76-78
  as *dusifiaga*, 52, 76, 93, 106, 108
  as "ethnic outsider," 71, 76-78, 106, 108, 117, 136
  ethnic redefinition of, 52, 76-78, 93, 106, 108, 136
  and maternal kin, 73-74
  and slave trade, 73, 128
  wealth stool of, 73

Gbugbla (homeland of Nyigbla), 59, 126

Gemedra (ancestor of Lafe and Amlade clans), 65

Gender and historiography, 9-12, 181

Gender relations, 4-7
  continuity of, 112
  effect of religious orders on, 80, 90-93, 100-102, 106, 113
  ethnic identity and, 7, 14, 68, 71, 81, 106-107, 109-110, 112, 127, 134-35, 137, 153, 156, 159, 178-80
  See also, Marriage, Women

Geraldo de Lima (Atitsogbi), 110, 127-34, 141 n.10
  Adzovia clan and, 130-31, 134
  as ethnic "outsider," 127, 130-31, 133-34, 136
  and firearms trade, 130
  and palm oil trade, 128-30
  relations with gods, 134
  and salt trade, 130
  and slave trade, 128

German colonial administration, 138-41, 152, 155
  defeat by British, 142
  forced labor policies, 141-142
  taxation and, 141-42
  trade restrictions by, 141

Getsofe clan, 61, 63, 183
  stereotypes of, 183

Gli, 55

Gods, 2, 4, 27-28, 47, 54, 62-63, 64, 80, 82, 91, 95, 101, 118, 134, 177
  dzokpleanyi, 2, 4, 27-28, 47, 54
  hierarchy of, 87-89
  immigrant gods, 2, 4, 27-28, 47, 76
  and snakes, 62
  See also Ancestors and names of individual gods (Egbe, Nyigbla, etc.)

Green-Pederson, Sv. E., 38

Guy, J., 10

Guyer, J., 9

Gyani, Kwasi, 129

Hanya, 87

Härtter, G., 77, 165

Hausa, 140, 161

Hebieso (So), 95

Hlowo , *See* Clans

Honey, 164
Honi, 62 n.29, 95, 96
Hopkins, A.G., 102
Hornberger, C., 152
Hozikpui (wealth stools), *See* Stools
Immigration, 5, 14, Ch. 1 *passim*, 78, 94, 162
  of Afro-Europeans, 94
  economic effect of, 5-6
  and land, 5-6, 28, 47, 78
  origins of, 2, 3, 14, 20, 47
  time of settlement, 2, 4, 14, 23-24
  See also, Clans, Ancestors
Income, from trade, 157-58, 162, 167-68, 171, 173, 174
Inheritance, 4, 8, 28, 34, 41, 46, 73
  of baskets, 4
  changes in, 169
  of land, 4-5, 8, 28-29, 33, 46, 61, 68, 162-64, 168, 170, 171, 176, 178
Initiation ceremonies, 92, 97
Isert, P., 83, 165
Ivory trade, 160
Jacobson, C., 30
Jewsiewicki, B., 30
Kedzi, 128, 132, 137
Keta, 57-58, 80, 82, 85, 88, 95-97, 103, 114, 117, 123, 127, 130, 132, 137, 140, 144, 145, 153, 160, 161, 167
  alliance with Anlo, 82-83
  Danish fort at, 74, 85, 95, 136
Keta Krachi, 142
Keta Lagoon, 4, 15, 27, 32, 35, 36, 54, 57-59, 61, 83, 118, 120, 162, 165-66
Keta war, 85, 88, 123, 128
Keteku (cabuseer of Agotime), 37
Kinship, 11, 20-21, 47, 183-84
  affinal ties, 139
  differences between Anlo and other Ewe, 22-23, 34, 46
  ties between Anlo and other Ewe, 139, 151
  See also, Matrilateral relations
Kioge, J., 83
Kisseku, 86
Klevi clan, 27, 63, 150
Kliko, 85
Kofi Fiayidziehe, *See* Anyage

Kome, See Wards
Konu, 141
Koranten (Ada cabuseer), 57
Kotoku, 121
Kouto-Ewe, 30
Kovenor war, 120 n.17
Kuwo Nunya (mother's brother of Gbodzo), 72
Koy Nantri, 86
Kpetsimine
  and Nyigbla order, 72
  as mother of Gbodzo, 72
  as a trader, 72-73
Kpoduwa, 83, 85, 88
Kpong, 133, 153
Krepi, 37, 75, 102, 121
Krobo, 57, 122, 128-29, 153, 160
  and oil boycott, 130
Kuadzo Landzekpo, 133
Kumase, 122
  market women in, 176, 179
Kumekpor, T., 30
Kwawu, 83, 102, 122
Kwawuga (military commander of Keta war), 85-86, 123
Kwawukume Cornelius, *See* Sri II
Kwesi (Ada cabuseer), 57
Labor
  hiring of, 173, 174, 176
  rights to, 38, 39, 42, 44-45, 47, 99, 108, 124, 159, 163-64
Ladoku, 24-27, 29, 32
Lafe clan, 49, 61, 63, 150
  an enstoolment, 61, 64-65
  gods of, 63-64, 66
  and land, 64
  relationship with Amlade clan, 61, 64-66
Lagbo (grandfather of Elias Quist), 96
Land, 4-5, 8, 28-29, 33, 46-47, 59, 61, 68, 78, 115, Ch. 6 *passim*
  clans and, 27, 31-32, 46, 49, 61, 63-64, 78, 86, 108, 124
  commercialization of, 161
  effect of flooding on, 26-27, 162, 170
  shortage of, 158, 162, 165, 167, 168, 169, 170, 182

women's right to, 4-5, 8, 17, 28-29, 46,
  6 8
Larte, 57
Lashibi, 29
Latebi, 24
Launay, R., 12
Le (founder of Wifeme clan), 53
Letsa Gbagba, 103
Levi-Strauss, C., 42
Like clan, 50, 109, 116
Literacy, and ethnic boundaries, 137, 153
Livestock industry, 35-36, 69, 162
Lome, 141-143
Lonsdale, J., 13-14
Madzezilawo branch (of Like clan), 109
  ban on religious orders, 116-117
  origins of, 116
  status of ethnic "outsiders," 109
  women in, 116-117
Malfi, 57-58, 122
Mama Bate, 54
Mama We (mother of Elias Quist), 96
Mangu-Yendi, 142
Marks, S., 14
Marriage
  arrangements for, 6, Ch. 1 *passim*, 51,
    68, 78, 80, 100, 105-106, 108-109, 134-
    35, 153, 156, 158, 176-77, 180
  ceremonies, 104
  challenges to, 79, 90-93, 101, 105-106,
    134, 154, 171
  cross-cousin, 12, 19, (fig.) 22, (fig.) 43,
    Ch. 1 *passim*, 79, 90, 100, 112, 124, 169
  and demographic pressure, 10
  diffeences between Anlo and other
    Ewe groups, 22-23
  to *fiasidi*, 89
  fomerso, 42, 178
  historiography of, 11
  to initiates (*zizidzelawo*), 92
  payments, 81, 104-105, 157
  polygyny, 22, 39, 163, 170
  and slave trade, 10, 38-39, 90
  Western influence on, 79-80
Matrilateral relations, 11 n.12, Ch. 1
  passim, 73, 90, 169
  laws pertaining to, 158

and residence, 20, 30-31, 34, 39, 41
McCaskie, T.C., 9
Mepe, 57
Migrancy, 148, 157-158, 168, 170, 180
Military organization, 118
  Dusifiaga (right-wing commander),
    52, 75, 76, 85
  Miafiage (left-wing commander), 85
Misahohe, 142
Missionaries, 13, 16, 154
  German, 13, 59, 76, 79, 82, 94, 98, 103,
    106, 111, 113, 125, 132, 148, 152, 156,
    164, 165, 182
  and schools, 80, 144, 151, 153, 161, 168
  and trade, 132
Mora, Don Jose, 74-75
Mouflard, M., 142
Mouser, B., 12
Musisi, N., 9
Naming, 40, 99, 126, 137, 150
Nayo-Friko, 134
  shrines of, 134
New Africa University College, 147
Ningo, Danish fort at, 74, 122
Nkeke-kpui-towo group, *See* Clans
Nkeke-legbe-towo group, *See* Clans
Nonobe war, 57, 120 n.19
Norddeutsch Missionsgesellschaft, 79
Notsie, 2, 8, 28, 49, 50, 51, 53, 59, 65-68,
  81, 92, 108, 127, 137-39, 148, 150-53,
  182-83
Notsiesi (wife of Atogolo), 116
Nukpekpe ritual, 97-98
Nukunya, G.K., 2, 21, 30, 31, 42, 44, 68,
  77, 156, 157, 162, 170, 172, 173, 178
Nyaho Tamaklo, 153
Nyaxoenu, 29, 53
Nyigbla 27, 49, 51, 56-57, 59, 63-64, 76,
  78, Ch. 3 *passim*, 108-109, 111, 113, 116,
  125-26, 134, 137
  centralization of gods under, 87
  decline of, 116, 126, 154
  initiates of (*zizidzelawo*), 87-88, 90-92,
    112, 116, 152
  origins of, 59
  priests and, 55, 59, 63-64, 78, 82, 85-
    92, 96, 112-13, 125

religious order, 55, 61, 63, 72, Ch. 3 *passim*, 112, 126, 152-53
role of women in, 72, Ch. 3 *passim*, 109, 112, 116, 156
slave trade and, 112-13, 116, 126
and snakes, 62 n.2
See also, Religious orders
Oath-taking rituals, *See Nukpekpe* ritual
Ocloo, James, 53
Oklu, 86
Olympio, Octaviano, 144
Palm oil industry, 102-103, 128-30, 160-61
Patrilineages (*to-fome*), 1, 10, 30, 47, 72, 87, 108, 181-82
demographic pressure and, 11
and exogamy, 21, 29
and land, 171, 178, 180
and non-Anlo Ewe groups, 22
slave trade and, 11
women's role in, 5, 11, 20, 23, 31-32, 41-42, 46, 51-55, 68, 109, 111-12, 156, 158, 163, 176, 180-81
Patten, S., 170, 173, 174
Pawns (*Woba*), 103, 161
Peki, 75, 103
Peki war, 75, 75, 123
Pine, Richard (governor of Cape Coast Castle), 129
Plessing, F., 41, 103, 132
Political authority, 8, 10, 49, 49 n.2, 52-53, 65, 76, 78, 80, 136-37, 154
of *awoamefia*, Ch. 2 *passim*, 82, 94, 103, 112-13, 119, 125, 130, 137, 139, 153
and education, 143-45, 151, 155
exclusion of women from, 77, 80
and religious orders, 59, 63, 80, 88, 95, 125-26
Portugal, and slave trade, 69, 74
Possession, 91, 101, 114
Priests, 55, 59, 63-64, 78, 82, 85-90, 92, 112, 119, 125, 139
acquistion of *fiasidiwo*, 64, 87, 89-90
women as, 91-92
Quist, Elias, 58, 81, 95-96, 101, 108, 152
descendants of, 153-154
as ethnic "outsider," 95, 101, 106
and shrine ownership, 96-98

slave trade and, 98, 112
Quist, Issac (father of Elias Quist), 95
Rain-making, 53-54
Ranger, T., 13-14, 182
Refugees, 1, 20, 24, *See also*, Immigration
Reindorf, C.C., 69, 74
Religious orders, 6-8, 10, 11, 61
Ch. 3 *passim*, 153
decline of, 138
dispute settlement through, 87
fiasidiwo and, 64, 87, 89-91
and religious authority, 10, 52, 55, 59, 63-65, 85-88, 125, 154
slave trade and, 72, 98, 112-113, 126
women's participation in, 6-8, 10, 11, 72, 80-81, 87, 108-109, 113, 155
See also, Nyigbla, Yewe
Rowe, Lt. Col., 143
Sagbadre war, 82-83, 120 n.19
Salkowski, E., 164
Salt trade, 35-37, 58, 102, 122, 127, 130, 145, 160
Samarin, W., 13-14
Sape Agbo, 85
Schiek and Tolch, 165
Schlegel, J. Bernhard, 71, 94, 98, 102
Schmidt, E., 10
Schools, 170
and girls, 171
mission-run, 80, 144, 151, 153, 161, 168
secondary, 144, 151
state-sponsored, 147
and Western influence, 153, 180
Shallot industry, 161, 164, 167-68, 170, 172-73, 179
division of labor, 172
Shia, 75
Shrines
economic aspects of, 95
of Nayo-Friko, 134
ownership of, 96-99
relocation of, 67, 86, 88-89, 124, 162
and slave trade, 98
of Yewe, 95-98
Slave trade, 10-11, 16, 18, 20, 23, 36-39, 56-57, 68, 71-74, 93, 96-98, 112-13, 116, 124-28, 133, 139, 160

abolishment of, 68-69, 74, 93, 102, 128, 139, 158
child slaves, 38-42
and Fofie Order, 67
status of female slaves, 23, 38-39, 41, 72, 90
and wealth in people, 41-42
Smuggling, 140-41
Snakes, as symbols, 62
So (Hebieso), 95
Social change, 183 and *passim*
Social history, 15-16, 181 and *passim*
Socialization, 8-9, 44, 51, 67-68, 77, 109-111, 112, 177-78, 180
and European culture, 178
Sokode-Bassari, 142
Songaw lagoon, 58
Spieth, J., 22, 44, 67, 77
Sri, 53, 55
Sri II (Cornelius Kwawukume), 142, 143 n.20, 144, 151, 154
and cultural tax, 145
Stanley, Col. Oliver, 145
Stools, 53, 55, 66-67, 86, 139
role in rain-making (*tsikpe*), 53, 86
as symbol of office, 53, 139
wealth stools (*hozikpui*), 72-73, 104
See also, Enstooling
Sugar cane industry, 161-62, 164, 167-68, 170, 173
Sui, 64
Tado, 67
Tay, John, 136-37, 153, 165
descendants of, 136
ethnic redefinition of, 137
and trade with Europeans, 136
Tay-Agbozo, C., 53
Tefle, 120, 122
Tefle-Agave war, 120 n.17
Tegbi, 114, 116, 161
Tema, 18
Tesi, 118-20, 127
Tettega (father of Gbodzo), 71-73
Todzi River, 35
To-fome, See Patrilineages
Togbloku, 58
Togo, 139-43

"The Committee on Behalf of Togoland Natives," 144
division by British and French, 142, 143
under British, 142-45, 147-48, 152
under French, 143-45, 147-48, 152
under Germans, 140-43, 152
Togobo, T.S.A., 151
Tomato Sellers Union, 176
Tomi, 55, 130-131
Tongu, 119
Tove, 75
Tovi clan, 63
Trade, Ch. 1 *passim*, 59, 66, 99, 102-103, 122, 124, 128-30, 140-41
Afro-Europeans and, 69-71, 74, 95-96, 112, 128
in beads, 71-72
with Europeans, 24, 35-38, 41, 69-71, 74-76, 99, 102, 132, 135, 140-41, 143-44, 160, 172
with missionaries, 132
in poultry, 164
restrictions on, 128-30, 140-41
and wholesalers, 174, 176, 179
See also names of specific goods (Palm oil, Salt, etc.)
Trowo, See Gods
Tsali, 118-20, 127
Tsiame (town), 127
Tsiame clan, 58, 61, 109-110, 118-20, 150
alliance with Akwamu, 120
as ethnic "outsiders," 110, 124-26, 136, 148
gods of, 118-20, 126
homelands of, 110, 127
and land, 124-25
and military leadership, 110, 120, 123 n. 29, 124
origins of, 118, 126
shrines of, 124
Tsikpe, See Stools
Twifo, 36
Unions, 174-76, 179, 180
Vail, L., 13-14, 159, 182
Vodu, 114
Voduda (Da), 95

Vodza, 110, 114, 127, 128, 130
War, 56-58, 63-64, 82-85, 88, 118, 120, 123, 131-32
Ward, B., 33
Wards, 21, (fig.) 29
  and marriage practices, 21, 22, 29, 42, 100, 111
Wassa, 36-37, 121
Wealth
  and access to capital, 39-40, 47
  social displays of, 24, 40, 47, 73, 112
  social status and, 81, 102, 106, 108, 134, 137, 153
  and stools, 72-73, 104
Welch, C., 145, 147
Wenya (Lafe clan ancestor), 61, 64-65
Westermann, D., 21, 31-34, 44, 46, 67, 111
Weta, 57, 85
Whuti, 116
Whydah, 33, 69, 71-72, 92, 112, 139-40
Wife-beating, 91, 101, 153
Wifeme clan, 18, 26-27, 53, 62, 63, 137, 151-52
  as ethnic "outsiders," 148
  and Ewe identity, 150
  and land, 63
  names of, 150
  origins of, 148
Wilks, I., 12
Woe, 50-52, 58, 70-72, 74-77, 80, 95, 98, 113-14, 117, 156-57, 164-65, 167, 173

Women
  decisions about marriage and, 4-6, 11, 20-21, 42-44, 47, 80-81, 100, 105-106, 108-109, 134-35, 151-54, 156, 158, 176-77, 180
  as heads of households, 177, 179, 180, 183
  older women, 5, 43-47, 90
  participation in trade, 159, 171, 174, 179-80
  and property, 4-5, 8, 28-29, 46-47, Ch. 6 *passim*, 183
  as slave owners, 38-39, 72
  taboos relating to, 77
  visits to natal kin, 39, 90, 158
Wute, 115
Wyllie, R.W., 148
Xoda, 95
Yewe order, 62, 81, 93, 95-102, 105-106, 108-109, 112-17, 137, 139, 152-53
  decline of, 154
  and dispute settlement, 99
  initiates of, 97, 102
  and naming, 99
  priests, 99, 101
  role of women, 81, 100, 105, 109, 113, 117, 156
  shrines of, 96-99
  and slavery, 98
Zewu, 75
Zizidzelawo, See Nyigbla